CW00338457

ROBIN BUTLER

ROBIN BUTLER

AT THE HEART OF POWER FROM HEATH TO BLAIR

MICHAEL JAGO

First published in Great Britain in 2017 by
Biteback Publishing Ltd
Westminster Tower
3 Albert Embankment
London SE1 7SP
Copyright © Michael Jago 2017

Michael Jago has asserted his right under the Copyright, Designs and Patents Act 1988 to be identified as the author of this work.

All rights reserved. No part of this publication may be reproduced, stored in a retrieval system or transmitted, in any form or by any means, without the publisher's prior permission in writing.

This book is sold subject to the condition that it shall not, by way of trade or otherwise, be lent, resold, hired out or otherwise circulated without the publisher's prior consent in any form of binding or cover other than that in which it is published and without a similar condition, including this condition, being imposed on the subsequent purchaser.

Every reasonable effort has been made to trace copyright holders of material reproduced in this book, but if any have been inadvertently overlooked the publishers would be glad to hear from them.

ISBN 978-1-78590-079-2

10 9 8 7 6 5 4 3 2 1

A CIP catalogue record for this book is available from the British Library.

Set in Adobe Garamond Pro

Printed and bound in Great Britain by
CPI Group (UK) Ltd, Croydon CR0 4YY

CONTENTS

Preface		vii
Introduction		xi
Chapter 1	Childhood and School, 1938–1956	1
Chapter 2	St Dunstan's and Oxford, 1956–1961	17
Chapter 3	The Treasury and the Labour Government, 1961–1970	33
Chapter 4	The Quiet Revolution and the Think Tank, 1970–1972	49
Chapter 5	10 Downing Street: First Tour, 1972–1974	67
Chapter 6	Intermezzo: Between Tory Governments, 1974–1979	85
Chapter 7	Midpoint, 1979	105
Chapter 8	Four Busy Years, 1979–1983	113
Chapter 9	Visibility, 1984–1985	137
Chapter 10	Consolidation, 1985–1987	155
Chapter 11	Cabinet Secretary: The First Years, 1987–1990	169
Chapter 12	Civis Britannicus Sum, 1990–1991	193
Chapter 13	Annus Horribilis, 1992	211
Chapter 14	Ireland: Tentative Steps, 1993	231
Chapter 15	The Most Difficult Moments, 1994–1995	245
Chapter 16	New Labour, 1997–1998	261
Chapter 17	Passing the Torch, 1997	283
Chapter 18	Master of University College, 1998–2008	297
Chapter 19	The Butler Report, 2004	323
Chapter 20	Baron Butler of Brockwell, Cross-Bencher	345
Chapter 21	Out of the Limelight	359
Appendix	Lord Butler's Civil Service Career	373
Bibliography		375
Endnotes		383
Index		405

PREFACE

SIR ROBIN BUTLER BECAME Cabinet Secretary in January 1988 and served for ten years. In accordance with the thirty-year rule, therefore, the bulk of papers relevant to his tenure will not be released before 2018; many will not be available until 2027. At the time of writing, many primary sources for his decade as Cabinet Secretary and head of the Home Civil Service are not available.

This biography will, therefore, not be the definitive and final account of the life and career of Lord Butler of Brockwell. It is based on accounts of contemporaries, colleagues, family and friends. And, of course, on the recollections of Lord Butler himself. However, as he said on *Desert Island Discs*, even on a desert island the secrets would remain inside; he has a well-deserved reputation for absolute discretion. The objective of this book is not to ferret out well-buried secrets, but to trace the life of Robin Butler against the changing background of British politics in the last decades of the twentieth century and the first decade of the twenty-first. At the dinner to celebrate his retirement from the Civil Service in 1997, his guests included Lady Wilson of Rievaulx, widow of Harold Wilson, Prime Minister for the first time in 1964, and members of the New Labour Cabinet that came to power in 1997. Such a guest list represents an enormous span.

During the thirty-six years that Butler worked in the Civil Service, the nature of Cabinet government was altered – some would say streamlined – dramatically. In the decade that he served as Cabinet Secretary, he worked with Prime Ministers as different as Margaret Thatcher, John Major and Tony Blair. Each of them found him exceptionally able, efficient and professional.

But, as his predecessor Lord Armstrong points out, in Blair, Butler confronted a Prime Minister who wanted to bypass the system.[1] By the time he retired, he was sanguine in his acceptance of the fact that Tony Blair, Jonathan Powell and Alastair Campbell did not share his respect for traditional methods. He sees himself as the last traditionalist before the modernising of the Cabinet Secretary's role under Richard Wilson, Andrew Turnbull and Gus O'Donnell.

Butler laboured successfully to preserve the traditions of the Civil Service – above all, political impartiality – while implementing far-reaching changes and greater mobility between the service and the outside world. He occupies a pivotal role in the list of Cabinet Secretaries, preserving time-honoured values and ushering in change. It is that role, examined while the paint is still fresh, that is the subject of this biography.

As Lord Butler's biographer, I should declare a personal interest. I followed Robin Butler, eight years after him, both at secondary school and at University College, Oxford. We did not meet until he was already Master of our Alma Mater, but our early lives were similar in several ways, and that made for the basis of a friendship between us.

I am greatly indebted to Lord Butler for sparing large swathes of time to discuss his career and for allowing me to see his personal papers and the memoir *Dear Descendants*, written for his family. As in previous books, I owe a huge debt to Professor Patricia Owens and Dr Raymond Davis, another Univ alumnus, for their generous help in reading the manuscript and making valuable corrections of fact, style and emphasis.

My understanding of the Civil Service and the role of Cabinet Secretary has been enhanced immeasurably by the wisdom and experience of Lord Armstrong of Ilminster, Lord Donoughue of Ashton, Lord Hennessy of Nympsfield, Baroness Hogg and The Rt Hon. the Lord O'Donnell, all of whom knew Lord Butler during his career in Whitehall. Others, who knew him at other points in his career and who have contributed greatly to the narrative, include Liv Anderman, the late Maurice Balme, George Cawkwell, Dr Robin Darwall-Smith, Marion Hawtree, Jeremy Lemmon, Robin Martin, Professor Christopher Pelling, Bethany Sagar-Fenton, David Sykes, Mark Vandevelde and Can Yeginsu.

Assistance, witting or unwitting, in things great and small, ranging from the quality of undergraduate essays on Plato to literary style and to the purchase of uranium, has been provided by Professor Jonathan and Sarah Dancy, Iain Harris, Juliet Jamieson, Seth Johnston, Chris and Frances Pye, Richard Savage, Jeremy and Jane Scott, Robin and Amanda Shield and Mick Smith. For his inimitable contribution as researcher par excellence, I am once more in the debt of Simon Fowler.

I am grateful to Mick Smith too, for his encouragement as commissioning editor of Biteback Publishing, where the contribution of Olivia Beattie and Namkwan Cho to bringing this book to print has also been invaluable. As ever, my agent Andrew Lownie has combined encouragement with a critical eye to structure and content.

As before, I have enjoyed the constant encouragement and support of my family – Carol, James and Elizabeth Jago.

INTRODUCTION

ON 2 FEBRUARY 2004, almost a year after the invasion of Iraq, Lord and Lady Butler, Robin and Jill, were in Teotihuacán. Butler, a non-executive director of HSBC, had been attending a board meeting in Mexico City and the couple had originally planned to go to Texas to see the George Bush Museum.* Butler was involved in the planning for the Churchill War Rooms in London and wanted to see the most modern American presidential library as a touchstone for the project. Unfortunately, the Super Bowl, the championship match of the American Football season, was being played in Houston that Sunday and all hotels were full.

As they returned from Teotihuacán – 'the place where the gods were created' – to Mexico City, their guide's mobile phone rang and she, somewhat bemused, passed the phone to Butler, saying that 10 Downing Street was apparently on the line. He was put through to Jonathan Powell,† who said portentously: 'Robin, your country needs you again.' At that moment, the car passed between two mountains and the connection was lost.[2]

Butler had no difficulty in surmising what Powell wanted. The Robb-Silberman Commission had just been set up in the USA and, despite Tony Blair's insistence that there would be no more enquiries into the Iraq War, he clearly felt that he would have to follow the American example. Jill urged her husband to have nothing to do with so patently political a project, as

---

* The George H. W. Bush Presidential Library and Museum is a most impressive structure. It was opened in 1997 and occupies a ninety-acre site on the campus of Texas A&M University in College Station, ninety-five miles northwest of Houston.

† Chief of Staff to Prime Minister Tony Blair.

this could only be a poisoned chalice. Butler, however, found the challenge 'irresistible'.[3] Of the intelligence fiascos of all time, the matter of the absence of weapons of mass destruction (WMD) in Iraq was the greatest. American, British, Israeli and French intelligence had all claimed that Saddam Hussein possessed WMD; the French later denied having made such a claim and the intelligence itself turned out to be false. How, he mused, had so monstrous a mistake – if mistake it was – been made?

This assignment propelled the former Cabinet Secretary, already a familiar figure around Whitehall, onto a wider public stage. With the publication of the Butler Report, his became a household name, and was accordingly both praised and reviled. It is the Butler Report that will keep his name in front of historians for many years to come.

Butler had been in the public eye on occasion during his thirty-six years in the Civil Service, not from any lust for publicity, but as a result of events. He had been in the room with Margaret Thatcher when an IRA bomb destroyed the Grand Hotel in Brighton in October 1984; sanctimonious tongues had wagged when his testimony to the Scott Inquiry in 1992 was reported as suggesting that a moderate amount of deceit was necessary and acceptable in government. These occasions had been the stuff of short-term interest. Now, Butler was held up for public scrutiny as a symbol of the establishment – 'urbane, unflappable and understanding … a prize example of our ruling classes' in the words of Robin Cook.[4] What sort of man was he, this former mandarin, clearly out of step with New Labour? Opinion divided, not entirely according to views of Butler himself, but according to the more emotive question of whether or not the Prime Minister should be tried as a war criminal. All opinions flowed from that judgement, two levels up in the political hierarchy. There had already been the Hutton Report, widely condemned as a whitewash. Was the Butler Report to be another? Who was this man anyway?

No one who knew Robin Butler can have doubted that he would accept the responsibility. John Major described Butler sympathetically, but bluntly, as 'easy-going, helpful and efficient – and one of the most competitive men I have ever met'.[5] He had risen to the top of the Civil Service, overtaking senior men, and been appointed Secretary to the Cabinet at the age of just forty-nine. He would not shirk such an assignment; he came to the task from a conventional background; an Oxford graduate with a double first in 'Greats' – classical literature, ancient history and philosophy. Two of his three immediate predecessors, Sir Robert Armstrong and Sir Burke Trend, had also read 'Greats' at Oxford. Sir Robin Butler, subsequently ennobled as Baron Butler of Brockwell, almost certainly has the distinction of being the last Cabinet Secretary and head of the British Civil Service to have undergone the classical training that was once the preferred discipline for an ambitious civil servant. The four-year degree course, previously almost *de rigueur* as a qualification for a Permanent Under-Secretary or an ambassador, no longer has the cachet of excellence that distinguished it for two centuries.* The course itself has changed fundamentally and, while still demanding, is less exacting than it was half a century ago when the young Robin Butler was admitted to read 'Greats'.[6]

In 2004, Butler already seemed to represent a bygone era, a less frantic and less media-driven age, when the Prime Minister, *primus inter pares*, governed through collective Cabinet responsibility. Born just before the Second World War, coming to maturity as Britain's diminished post-war role became apparent, Frederick Edward Robin Butler was himself a symbol of an era of vanished imperial ambitions. He joined the Civil Service in 1961, as Harold Macmillan's tired Tory government began to stumble; he worked at the very centre of the Thatcher revolution from 1983 to 1990, and retired from Whitehall soon after New Labour came to power in 1997.

The story of Butler's relentless rise, of his absolute, if compartmentalised, morality, belongs to a century of radical change. His achievement – in human terms, at least – lies in a remarkable combination of confidence and humility, of principle and realism, ever backed by a broader and uncompromising loyalty to a code that New Labour decried as outdated, elitist, risible. In an interview on BBC's *The World at One*, Peter Hennessy (later Lord Hennessy of Nympsfield) captured that quality in a somewhat macabre way, describing it as 'the reincarnation of the flower of England's youth that died on the

* There are plentiful stories of senior officials in the Foreign Office and Home Civil Service who spoke Latin to each other. Sir Percy Sillitoe, Director-General of the Security Service, complained bitterly that senior officers routinely told jokes in Latin to exclude him.

Somme. And, if that had befallen [Butler], heaven forbid, he's the kind of person they would have written little biographical vignettes about for the next 30 years and mourned his passing.'[7]

For this reason, Hennessy said, 'people are never entirely sure about Robin'. Without doubt, there were false steps – in political terms, indefensible blunders – that threatened to destroy his laboriously built reputation. His credulity over the matter of Jonathan Aitken's weekend stay at the Ritz in Paris; his conclusion that a grotesque intelligence error had been made in Iraq, but that no blame could reasonably be attached to any individual – these might easily be seen as whitewash and resolute defence of the system that had spawned his own success. Yet they also bear effective testimony to the evolution of Butler's philosophical pragmatism. There had been a mellowing, even a softening of brittle absolutes. There had been no ethical compromise.

There was never any doubt that he would be successful, no doubt of his ability or ambition. The young Butler was perhaps too certain of himself, incurring from his preparatory school headmaster the comment in a report that 'Robin is too fond of Robin'.[8] During his last year at Harrow, his housemaster commented on his over-assertive manner of getting things done, warning that he needed to develop more tactful methods.[9]

If observers treat Robin Butler with a measure of caution, it is probably because he is patently 'head-boy material'. He is the natural leader of the team, encouraging, reproving where necessary, making time for proper briefings, ever positive, calm under fire. He reflects long before acting, but acts with certainty and decisiveness. His Harrow-and-Oxford-ness is neither a pose nor a carapace. It is a part of him that he makes no attempt to hide. It is easy to see why Robin Cook and New Labour may have been tempted to see him as a natural target.

What is less easy is to fit him neatly into the succession of Cabinet Secretaries and heads of the Civil Service. He was the natural product of the culture that produced Burke Trend and Robert Armstrong; he also represented a reassuring standard of morality and decency that was invaluable to the Blair government in 2004. There is something of Cincinnatus about him: recalled for an important task, he performs it and retires to his farm. Even if his farm is a short bicycle ride from Whitehall, beside Westminster Cathedral, the non-political implication is accurate. He was succeeded by more politically responsive men. Not more or less powerful, but more obviously modern; economists like Gus O'Donnell and Jeremy Heywood, from the University of Warwick and the London School of Economics, rather than other Oxford classicists.

A natural traditionalist – he deplores the term 'conservative' – Butler now sits as a cross-bencher in the Lords. He remains idealistic and open-minded in the manner of a far younger man. He is eagerly receptive to the views of his grandchildren, alive to 21st-century literature and theatre, quick to read political trends. Some time before the 2015 general election, he identified the importance of the Scottish National Party and was excited by an invitation to speak to the assembled boys of Harrow School about this political phenomenon.

Any biography of Lord Butler of Brockwell is unlikely to be a pot-boiler. Although he has been described as 'one of the two or three men who actually run the country', he has a well-earned reputation for absolute discretion. Few beans will be spilled in the pages that follow. If there are revelations, they will most likely concern the rare combination of moral certainty and tactical flexibility that endowed Butler with the qualities necessary for him to uphold the values of his revered Civil Service during periods when successive governments were accused of sleaze or dishonesty, and, at the same time, to introduce far-reaching reform both in the admission process and in the mission statement of the service. In his embracing of change within the service and his absolute certainty of the need for non-political appointments in Downing Street, he is at once the product of a half-century of rapid change, a reassuring symbol of old-fashioned ethics, and an open-minded reformer when reform is needed.

From a distance, it is easy to miss many of those qualities. In Britain, judgements are too often based on the subtle shades of accent, of vocabulary, the myriad indicators that enable Britons to determine to their satisfaction where anyone stands on the social scale. Butler is so patently a product of the establishment that observers have become fixated by the obvious and have failed to grasp his complexity. Owen Jones makes that mistake in his book

The Establishment: And How They Got Away with It, describing Butler as 'born to rule'; the son of the director of a paint company is scarcely 'born to rule' by virtue of going to a private school. Tom Bower, in *Broken Vows*, trots out the old cliché, referring to 'the star schoolboy who led Harrow's Bible Society'.[10] The implication is clear, tedious and wide of the mark: that Butler was head boy at Harrow does not entail that he was a pious altar-boy in an increasingly secular society.

When Harold Wilson and his close entourage returned to 10 Downing Street in 1974, two members of his Policy Unit, Joe Haines and Bernard Donoughue, were most pessimistic about the prospect of working closely with Butler, whose background, they felt, guaranteed that he would be an obstructive Tory in their midst. Within a very short time, Donoughue realised that he was working with 'the most outstanding civil servant with whom I ever had to deal, at any level'.[11] When the time came for Butler to return to the Treasury, Donoughue and Haines did their best to retain him at Downing Street.[12]

In the 1960s and the 1970s, Butler was a high-flyer, a civil servant who was likely to become at least a Permanent Secretary and who was being groomed for that responsibility. After two spells of working closely with Margaret Thatcher, first as Principal Private Secretary, later as Cabinet Secretary, he found himself, in 1990, for the first time in his career, adviser to a Prime Minister younger than himself. No longer a promising tyro, he was suddenly a benign elder statesman. As Sarah Hogg recalls:

> He did have a paternalistic manner and he was positively helpful to his juniors. For my part, when I was at No. 10 I was grateful to him for his kindness. He didn't have to be nice to me. I knew Permanent Secretaries who wanted me to fail. Robin was not like that.[13]

His last seven years in the Civil Service were not easy. Many different political climates would have provided a more fitting end to his career.

From the Cabinet Office, Butler returned to University College, Oxford, his Alma Mater, where he already held an honorary fellowship. Many public figures who accept a position as Head of House in Oxford or Cambridge are content to sit back and reflect on the kudos that their presence brings to the college. Butler did not belong to that group; indeed, it is possible that the college got a great deal more than the Fellows had bargained for. They found themselves with a Master and wife – as Robin and Jill had long looked forward to a job that they could do together – committed to taking 'Univ' to the top of every Oxford table possible: to the top of the academic results-based Norrington table; to the top of the financial development table; and, naturally, to the Head of the River in the Summer Eights, for, equally naturally, the young Butler had been an athlete and had won a rugby Blue as well as a double first.

Mixed into Butler's Oxford days were other assignments: membership of the Royal Commission on reform of the House of Lords; chairmanship of the Butler Inquiry. After Oxford, other appointments followed: chairmanship of Kings Health Partners, the South London Academic Health Science Centre; member of the Board of Governors of the Better Government Initiative; member of the Parliamentary Security and Intelligence Committee. Along the way, in 2003, he was invested as a Knight of the Garter.

By any standards, Butler's has been a most successful career. Its success is unusual in that it has flourished in quite different environments; yet Butler is no Vicar of Bray. The issues that occupy him as a cross-bencher in the House of Lords are the same issues that have engaged him since the 1970s, which caused friction with Margaret Thatcher in the 1980s, and which provoked confrontation with Alastair Campbell and Jonathan Powell in the 1990s – relations between the executive, special advisers, the Civil Service and Cabinet – the very *modus operandi* of democracy. If he is judged to be out of date or antediluvian in his views of government, that judgement springs from a superficial knowledge of his curriculum vitae. Values trump media-driven fashion; substance wins over style.

It is no surprise that his Oxford degree included philosophy, in which he was tutored by the remarkable Peter Strawson. Political talk with Butler is not unlike philosophy-talk with Strawson. One thought that one had a grasp of the issues until Strawson would interject a previously unseen variable, a simple factor that altered the entire calculus. When Butler performs a similar trick, suggesting for example that relations between media and politicians entered a new phase when newspapers began to refer to the Prime Minister only by his last name, one realises that he reads and thinks deeply and extensively on every aspect of a subject. Things do not just happen; he works extremely hard on every task he undertakes.

Jill once hosted a tea party at which Mary Wilson, a resident in the same block of flats as the Butlers, and Cherie Blair were guests. Butler persuaded his granddaughter Elizabeth to ask first Lady Wilson, then Mrs Blair whether they would advise her to marry a future Prime Minister. 'No', replied Lady Wilson, 'your life is not your own.' Mrs Blair said 'Yes!' and then later commented, 'but even better to be PM yourself'.[14] The exchange delighted Butler – nothing is ruled out, there is always the unexpected twist that keeps all possibilities alive.

The combination of traditionalism – he is right; it is more accurate than 'conservatism' – with the acceptance of innovation is vital to understanding Butler. There are things that he holds sacred and does not feel it necessary to justify. Set against that is a mind constantly straining to improve the quality of everything retained. This often involves logical leaps and, as Haines and Donoughue discovered, the assumptions one makes about the probable outcome of those leaps are not always correct.

Now safely retired, he is still committed to ensuring that Cabinet ministers are able to use the resources of the Civil Service to reach their own, informed, policy decisions. It is possible that he is fighting a battle that he cannot win, seemingly attempting to put the clock back to the world of Trollope and the Pallisers. There are many practical explanations for the accretion of power by the centre. When government policy is announced through the media and the media are fed their measured ration of 'exclusives' from Downing Street, how realistic is it to crusade for a return to traditional Cabinet government? What 21st-century Prime Minister will voluntarily surrender the increasingly 'presidential' power of the office in the interests of greater collective responsibility?

CHAPTER 1

CHILDHOOD AND SCHOOL, 1938–1956

FREDERICK EDWARD ROBIN BUTLER, always called 'Robin' by his family, was born on 3 January 1938 at the Cornelia Hospital, Poole, Dorset, the first child of Bernard and Nora (née Jones). Bernard Daft Butler, Robin's father, was the son of Frederick Butler, born in 1876, who had married Ann Daft, the daughter of the leading batsman in English cricket. Richard Daft topped the English batting averages in 1867 but was soon eclipsed by the rise of a younger man, the remarkable William Gilbert ('W. G.') Grace. For the rest of his career, Richard Daft generally finished second to W. G. in the batting averages.

When Robin, a cricket-mad small boy, asked his father what his middle initial stood for, Bernard told his son the one untruth that Robin ever caught him in, replying 'Douglas'. Presumably, his embarrassment at having 'Daft' as a middle name overcame his pride in his famous grandfather. Had Robin trawled the archives of the local paper, he would have discovered his father's full name and learned that

> in support of a summons against Bernard Daft Butler, of Oxford Road, Bournemouth, of having driven a car in such a position as to not have proper control over it, P. C. Witt of the mobile constabulary said he saw defendant driving through Canford with an arm round a young woman sitting beside him.[1]

In the event, the case was dismissed; the identity of the woman in the car, presumably Bernard's fiancée Nora Jones, was not mentioned, and Robin's father evaded the full majesty of the law. It was not until his teenage years that Robin discovered the intoxicating truth that his great-grandfather was a famous cricketer. Equally intoxicated, half a century later, was John Major, another passionate cricket lover with an encyclopaedic knowledge of cricket history and statistics.[2]

Richard Daft was born in Nottingham on 2 November 1835. He was apprenticed in the wool trade, but his life changed in 1854 when his uncle died, leaving his fortune to be distributed equally among his nieces and nephews. Daft received an annual income the equivalent of about £10,000 today and moved, albeit precariously, into the middle class. He was a remarkable all-round athlete who played football for Notts County and most sports competently. During the 1850s, Daft played increasingly serious cricket. When he began to play first-class cricket, in 1858, he began his career as a 'Gentleman', rather than as a 'Player'.* By the end of the following year, he was a regular in the All-England XI. In 1862, he married Mary, the only daughter of Butler Parr, the owner of a brewery in Radcliffe-on-Trent. In 1870, he took over as captain of the Nottinghamshire team and scored 565 runs at an average of 51.36 – second only to the great W. G. himself. Competitiveness grew between the two greatest batsmen of the era. In 1879, Daft captained a team that toured the eastern states of the USA, but his career was coming to an end; after a disappointing season in 1880, he retired in January 1881 at the age of forty-five, having enjoyed ten years as county captain.

After stepping down, he devoted his time to the sports warehouse that he had built up in Nottingham and to the brewery left by his father-in-law, which he purchased from the estate for £4,050. He continued to play occasionally for Nottinghamshire and, as late as 1883, in his fifty-eighth year, scored eighty in a match for South Notts. He also wrote his reminiscences, published as *Kings of Cricket* in 1892. In 1898, having seriously over-extended

* Gentlemen received no pay for playing and were treated like officers, staying in hotels rather than cheaper boarding houses when the team toured.

himself with the acquisition of the Trent Bridge Inn, Richard Daft was forced into bankruptcy. This took a severe toll on him and he died on 18 July 1900.

His son-in-law, Frederick Butler, Ann Daft's husband and Robin's grandfather, was also an accomplished athlete. A scholar of New College, reading natural science, he won an Oxford Blue for football in 1897–98 and, by some bizarre twist, won an international cap for Switzerland in 1899. His son Bernard, Robin's father, inherited his sporting ability and played wing three-quarter in the England rugby trials of 1929. He performed well and would probably have been selected for the British team's tour of New Zealand in 1930 if he had been able to take time off work. By then engaged to Nora Jones, however, and working in the Jones family business, Leyland Paints, Bernard asked his future father-in-law for leave to join the tour. With the blunt response that Bernard needed to choose between his business career and rugby, Fred Jones brought Bernard's rugby career to a premature end.

Fred Jones was, it seems, accustomed to getting his own way. Originally from North Wales, he held a variety of jobs – including spells as a veterinary assistant and a measurer for plate glass windows – before working for Walpamur, the paint and wallpaper makers. In 1922, he left Walpamur to found his own business, Leyland Paint and Varnish. A handsome man with a cultivated Edwardian elegance, he took great care of his appearance and, in his late fifties, began to indulge himself with regular pedicures. This last attention to detail, his daughters believed, was in preparation for leaving his wife for a younger woman, a *sortie* that Fred performed at the age of sixty. Leyland Paint and Varnish established the Jones family in the prosperous merchant class and grew into a thriving family business. Robin met his grandfather Jones only a few times; very possibly relatives felt that he should be shielded from the 'black sheep' of the family. For his grandson, he was always a presence, however, an important figure in the background, the founder of the family firm that employed Bernard; the source of the family fortunes.

Two of Fred's sons joined him in the company, and his eldest son, Fred Junior, succeeded him as chairman. It was this family concern that Bernard Butler joined when he became engaged to Nora Jones, his close friend since schooldays. In 1930, after taking his future father-in-law's advice, Bernard was posted to Bournemouth to take charge of the company's sales office. He and Nora were married in April 1933. They were an attractive pair. Bernard, 'a man's man', retained a trim, athletic build, while Nora was a wistful-looking beauty with clear blue eyes and auburn hair. In Lytham St Annes, where they both lived before their marriage, they were a familiar couple on the tennis court, winning enough mixed doubles tournaments to provide ornaments and furniture for their home when they married.

After their honeymoon, they returned to Bournemouth, where they had bought their first house at a cost of £950, the price, Robin later remarked, of a doll's house that he saw for sale in Harrods in the 1960s. Their first child, Timothy, died in childbirth, so joy and sheer relief accompanied Robin's successful entry into the world in 1938. Although the boy was always to be called 'Robin', Bernard and Nora paid their respects to Nora's elder brothers with his first two names, Frederick and Edward.

Nora was devoted to her son, the more so, perhaps, because of the loss of Timothy. She remained a powerful influence on Robin's life, resenting his departure for boarding school and invariably picking a quarrel as that departure approached. Her life was to bring her many disappointments, but her pride in her son was constant, and he was always a source of joy.

Soon after Robin was born, Bernard, after eight years with Leyland, was given the responsibility of opening the company's London office in the West End. The family promptly moved from the south coast to the London suburbs, taking a flat in Herga Court, a new development close to Harrow School. The move had important consequences for their infant son, as Harrow School was to feature large in Robin's youth and adult life.

When war broke out in 1939, Bernard was thirty-two years old, over the age of call-up to the Armed Forces. Accordingly, he joined the ranks of ARP (Air Raid Precaution) wardens, who patrolled the streets to enforce the blackout and assess the need for emergency services during an air raid. On one occasion, Bernard removed an incendiary bomb from the roof of Harrow's 'Old Schools', a Jacobean building dating from 1615. One of Robin's earliest memories is of the glow of burning buildings during the Blitz. As the air raids intensified, Bernard and Nora decided that mother and son should leave the dangerous environs of London and return to Lytham St Annes, where they stayed, first with Nora's sister Hilda, later renting the ground floor of a house in Derbe Road.

In 1941, Nora, pregnant with her second child, developed German measles. The implications of contracting rubella during pregnancy were not known at the time and, as a result of that short illness, Diana was born with weak eyesight, seriously impaired hearing and, most significantly, a hole in the heart that was not diagnosed until she was seventeen. Had it been diagnosed at birth and repaired within five days, the disability might have been only minor, but undetected, it had the most serious consequences. From earliest childhood, she was considered 'delicate' but it was not until Robin was six years old that he learned of a specific, substantive condition. He remembers to this day the moment he was told that Diana might be deaf.

In 1942, Bernard was called up and joined the RAF. In the years of his father's absence, Robin's picture of the war was painted by listening to a 78 rpm recording of 'Lili Marlene' on his wind-up gramophone. Many years later, he explained that he was fascinated by the song, as it showed him the human side of the war from a German point of view.[3]

After postings in Britain, in early 1945, Bernard sailed to India where he served for the remainder of the war. In common with many combatants, he never spoke of his experience as a Flight Lieutenant in Bombay, never maintained contact with fellow officers. His war came to an end in 1946 in Singapore, where he was involved in the repatriation of British troops. He returned to Herga Court, thin and jaundiced, to rebuild his family life and resume work in the West End office of Leyland Paints.

The rebuilding of family life was literal as well as figurative, for Bernard immediately undertook the massive project of clearing and levelling a large plot of land on Harrow Hill and building High View, a small, square two-storey house. Working for Leyland five and a half days a week, Bernard had only short weekends to devote to the project, and for over two years he devoted his spare time to reclaiming the overgrown land and, with the help of two local labourers, to building a modest three-bedroom house from scratch. Small but functional, with enough land for a chicken coop, a pigsty, a concrete strip for a matting cricket pitch, and a tennis court, High View became the family home.

Robin, eight years old in 1946, was sent to Orley Farm preparatory school, a brisk ten-minute walk from Herga Court. At the time, it was a small school with about ninety boys, a training ground for the better public schools, particularly Harrow, its close neighbour. In spite of living within easy walking distance, Bernard and Nora decided that Robin should attend Orley Farm as a boarder in his last two years in preparation for life away from home at Marlborough, their public school of choice.

When he was aged nine, Robin had his first taste of the stage, a hobby that grew to occupy much of his time in his teens and twenties. He made his stage debut, having been brought in at the last moment to play the part of Polly Hoppit, the hero's cousin in Erich Kästner's *Emil and the Detectives*. Three years later, he played the lead in *Richard of Bordeaux*, a controversial work with a sympathetic treatment of Richard II, that had had its premiere, directed by John Gielgud, in 1933. The part of King Richard is a challenging role, portraying a sensitive young man, not at all the petulant autocrat of Shakespeare's play. Unfortunately, no reviews of his performance survive.

During his time at Orley Farm, Robin demonstrated considerable academic ability as well as passion and skill on the playing field. Somewhat precocious in the classroom, he tackled calculus as a thirteen-year-old; equally precocious in his general conduct, he was judged 'rather too boisterous' by the headmaster.

Before he sat the entrance scholarship at Marlborough, Robin took the Harrow scholarship exam for practice. When he won the Shepherd Churchill award,* coming second in the examination, his headmaster urged Bernard and Nora to accept the scholarship, the bird in the hand, with a value of £120 a year. Fees at Harrow in the 1950s typically ran to about £900 a year, including full board, so the scholarship made a significant contribution to costs.

If Robin was, as his headmaster suggested, too fond of Robin at the age of thirteen, there were few cures more effective than a spell as a junior in a typical public school of that era. For their first two years at Harrow, boys were subjected to persistent ritual humiliation by older boys. In a system of

* The Shepherd Churchill scholarship was awarded to the boy who, in the opinion of the examiners, intellectually, athletically and spiritually was most likely to develop into 'the whole man'.

military discipline designed to teach unquestioning obedience of any order from a senior boy, there was little scope for a thirteen-year-old to give vent to individuality. One survived largely by reflecting that in due course one would have the right to inflict on future juniors the indignities that one suffered. By the age of seventeen or eighteen, a boy had earned the opportunity for payback.

The nabobs of the system were the members of the Philathletic Club, athletes who represented the school in one or more of the three major sports – cricket, rugby football and Harrow football.* Members of 'the Phil' wore bow ties, sported grey waistcoats on Sundays, were empowered to fine boys for real or imagined offences, and were generally treated as deities on Harrow Hill. Scholars, by contrast, were identified by the label '*Sch*' permanently attached to their name in school lists, but received vastly less adulation than members of 'the Phil'. Academic work was sneered at, and the ambitious Harrovian of the time affected to spend no time working but to achieve success effortlessly.

Robin quickly adopted the school ethic, seeking academic success, but ostensibly giving his greatest attention to athletic pursuits. At the end of the Easter term in 1952, his housemaster Kenneth Snell was concerned that the Shepherd Churchill scholar was too focused on sport to the exclusion of more intellectual pursuits, writing in his report:

> He did well to get into the Torpid XI [junior house team] as well as to play fives for the house. Games clearly occupy a good part in his interests, and he has all-round ability. As he grows up he must also take full advantage of the many intellectual activities here; and I am glad to see him taking part in the play for next term.

By the summer term of that year, he had won two school prizes for English Literature and was playing cricket for the Junior Colts XI, showing early signs of dogged determination: 'Butler watched the ball well and batted right through the innings – though his scoring strokes are limited.'[4]

---

* Harrow, in common with Eton and Winchester, has a sport unique to the school.

That 1952 summer term offered the first evidence of the breadth of the young Butler's ability. He excelled in the classroom, winning the Fred Watkins Prize for Latin Prose; on the school's Shakespearean stage (a remarkable replica of the sixteenth-century Globe Theatre stage built in the school's Speech Room), he performed the role of Flute in *A Midsummer Night's Dream* with 'gormless simplicity'; he scored twenty-eight not out in a Junior Colts match against Eton, and earned himself a double-edged compliment in a summary of the team's season: 'Butler was very hard to dislodge and showed signs of developing a few scoring strokes as the term progressed.'[5] This comment must have given Bernard considerable pleasure since he had used the matting cricket pitch at High View to help his son to develop an impregnable defence as a batsman. An aggressive fast bowler (taking 5 for 18 in an inter-house match), he had learned to be equally determined in defence when occasion demanded.

By the summer of 1953, as his housemaster had hoped, he was taking more advantage of the school's 'intellectual activities'. At the early age of fifteen, he joined the editorial staff of *The Harrovian*, the school magazine. On the Shakespearean stage, again, he played the Bastard in *King John*. Through athletic prowess, he was able to impress his peers and work his way up the system, playing for Junior Colts, then Colts and ultimately the school's first teams in all three major sports. As a classics scholar, he impressed the masters who taught him; as a member of various extra-curricular clubs, particularly as an actor in the annual Shakespeare plays, he was part of the school's intellectual elite. One contemporary recalled that the only thing that he could not do was sing.

Those who taught him remembered both his ability and his lust for winning academic prizes. Maurice Balme, a classics master, recalled that he was the most exceptional boy whom he taught at Harrow – not necessarily the most brilliant or original thinker, but the boy who applied a considerable intelligence most effectively.[6] In his penultimate year, on Speech Day in June, Robin collected nine prizes for subjects ranging from the composition of Greek elegiacs to the study of Shakespeare. This while playing wing forward in the school's first XV and opening the bowling for the cricket XI.

During the course of 1955, he established his position as one of the school's leaders. His housemaster commented both on his tendency to take on numerous tasks and on his tendency to impulsiveness and 'lack of tact'. Reading between the lines, one receives the impression that the young Butler did not suffer fools gladly and that he was being urged to show more patience. It seems that he took the advice to heart for, to no one's surprise, the headmaster, Dr R. L. ('Jimmy') James, decided to appoint him head of the school in his last term.

This decision came close to being reversed. Robin's house, Druries, had an unimpressive athletic record, consistently losing inter-house matches to other houses. Butler recalls that during his five years at the school, Druries failed to win a single inter-house match in any of the major sports. In the spring of 1955, however, under his captaincy, they managed to score first in a Harrow football match. Harrow football is a bizarre sport, part rugby and part soccer, designed for the thick, deep mud of the playing fields at the foot of Harrow Hill. One defensive technique of the sport is for a player to fall on the ball, grasping it between his knees and to remain on the ground while his team mates gather to start their own offensive. In this particular match, Butler, having noted that there is no stated limit in the sport's rules as to how long a player can remain with the ball between his knees, fell onto the ball and remained there. For the balance of the second half he knelt on the ground, maintaining possession while his teammates pushed the opposition back. As a result, the final scoreline was 1–0 for Druries.

Predictably, this imaginative method of winning was frowned upon by Charles Laborde, the master in charge of Harrow football. Furious at Robin's opportunism and at his reasoned defence of his actions, he urged Dr James to reconsider his decision to appoint as head of the school a boy who could brazenly defy the spirit of sportsmanship by such a rank desire to win. Protest as he might, Laborde was unable to influence James's decision. Robin – or 'Freddie', as he was known throughout his schooldays* – became head of the school, a fitting end to a highly successful public school career. Even sixty years on, Butler maintains, with a semi-convincing innocence, that he

* Although he was always known as 'Robin' by his family, a master at his prep school coined the nickname 'Freddie' from his first name, and it stuck to him throughout his school years. Butler did not thank the master for that.

was surprised that Laborde reacted as he did. Inevitably, when Butler became a public figure, the story of the house match was bandied about Whitehall. Peter Hennessy, Whitehall's principal commentator, asked Butler about the incident and received a written reply: 'The point is that kneeling on the ball was within the rules. The convention was that you then stood up and struggled forward. My innovation was to notice that the rules didn't require you to do so. When I next see you I will demonstrate.'[7]

Perhaps his most ambitious performance came at the annual Governors' Speech Day in June 1956. One traditional duty of the head of the school was to read a speech in Latin, known as *Contio Latina*, to the school governors, in front of the assembled school, parents and guests. Robin, who had already won a scholarship to University College, Oxford, was hungry for a fresh academic challenge. When E. V. C. ('Plum') Plumptre, the head of Classics, proposed that he write and deliver his own *Contio*, he leapt at the idea. This was the first occasion since 1907 on which a boy had written his own speech; then, it had been written and delivered by J. R. M. ('Jim') Butler, no relation of the Butlers of Herga Court, but rather the uncle of Richard Austen ('Rab') Butler.* Curiously, one Harrow contemporary, speaking of Robin Butler in 2015, mentioned, before any other memory, that he had written his own *Contio*.

Jeremy Lemmon, two years older than Robin at Harrow, who was later, as a teacher, the school's head of English, remembers the young Butler with clarity. Unsurprised by his later success, he recalled that 'he was always interested in politics and government and was one of the very ablest people in the school'. Musing on what might have been, he continued: 'He was never likely to be a captain of industry. He might have entered politics, or the diplomatic service, or become a university don. Even as a boy, piety and goodness were his manifest qualities.'[8]

From his early teens, Butler was serious and disciplined. He combined a practical side with what Lemmon described as 'a serious academic mind', and it was that which separated him from his athletic colleagues. The captain

* Professor J. R. M. Butler later achieved fame as the editor of the *Official History of the Second World War* and as a distinguished fellow of Trinity College, Cambridge.

of cricket, Lemmon recalled, 'was great fun and no more. With Robin there was always much more.' Indeed, Butler found so much more to occupy him that sometimes his interests clashed. Sporting commitments forced him to withdraw from a Harrow Players production of *Twelfth Night* that was going on tour. From early days, he set himself an exhausting schedule. He was always busy.

The theatre, Lemmon remembered with a chuckle, was his milieu. 'We used to mock him quite a lot because he always wanted the best part in the Harrow plays and we did rather tease him when he didn't land the part he wanted. He was definitely ambitious and he didn't like it when that ambition was not fulfilled.' That ambition was, moreover, a decidedly individual ambition. 'He would like to think that he was a team player', Lemmon commented with a smile. 'But I don't think he was really. He did like being the star.'

The annual Shakespeare play continued to be an important part of Butler's school life. His performance as Philip the Bastard in *King John* was well reviewed, with the comment that he had captured Shakespeare's perception of the character growing in complexity as the play proceeded. The following summer saw an excellent production of *Much Ado about Nothing*, well reviewed by *The Times*, with the comment that he exhibited 'just the right variation of gender' as Benedick.[9] This was the role that he most enjoyed playing. His crowning achievement for the critics, however, came in his last year when he played the Earl of Kent in *King Lear*. The school magazine's review referred to 'a first-class Kent: whether suggesting natural honesty or affecting a saucy roughness, he carried complete conviction'.[10]

In his last two years at Harrow, Butler soared above his contemporaries. If he erred at all, it was in the breadth of activities that he embraced, as his housemaster doubted that he could do them all justice. Yet he somehow managed success in almost everything that he attempted, even challenges outside the classics, his prescribed course of study. His tutors Plumptre and Mark Warman saw him as a potential academic, although Jeremy Lemmon believes that his intelligence always had a more practical bent, that he was not an 'intellectual' in the generally accepted sense. He was always a participator, but if he was part of a team he was always there to lead it, to be an example, a restraining influence. 'He was never raffish', Lemmon recalled: 'There was a fun-loving side to his character that one saw in post-rugby match sessions, but he maintained a serious public demeanour.'

Despite this image of a rather too-perfect adolescent, both Lemmon and Robin Martin, a younger Harrovian who later worked with Butler in the Civil Service, recalled that he had a greater compassion for others less privileged than is typical among competitive alpha males. Both observers attributed this to the concern that he felt for his sister Diana. Once her deafness was diagnosed at the age of three, Bernard and Nora were advised to send her away to a specialist school, as she would not learn to lip-read and speak if she continued to live at home.

At the age of five, then, Diana was sent from home to Reading, to a boarding school for the hearing-impaired. Butler recalls that it was 'a heart-wrenching decision' for his parents, 'especially as [his] mother suffered a miscarriage – one of several – at about the same time'. The differences between the schools that brother and sister attended could hardly have been greater. Butler conscientiously kept in touch with his sister, writing regular letters, sending a card on St Valentine's Day. For her part, Diana adored her brother and kept a scrapbook of his achievements at school and at Oxford.

Alongside that compassion, there is ample evidence of a certainty that he would succeed. Perhaps most remarkable is the extent to which the young Butler hoarded trophies and memorabilia of his schoolboy achievements. From his autograph book, in which he proudly affixed signatures of famous cricketers (including that of the legendary Don Bradman) to school reports, to reviews of his performances in school plays and, later, with the Old Harrovian Players, a mass of *juvenilia* remain in the archive. While most schoolboys hasten to 'put away childish things', the young Butler meticulously retained them, as if guessing that one day an historian would trawl through them to write his biography. It smacks less of arrogance than of assured certainty – and a justified pride in his schoolboy achievements. The other side of that coin is that the mature Butler has retained a schoolboyish *joie de vivre* into his eighth decade. For all the gravitas of a former Cabinet Secretary, he still retains the enthusiasm of an ambitious and competitive adolescent.

In 1956, when he left Harrow, he could postpone decisions about his long-term career, as that seemed to lie six years in the future. The next two years were to be devoted to National Service, after which he was to go up to University College, Oxford for a four-year course. Beyond that, he had little idea of what the future held. Bernard was certain that he did not want his son to follow him into the family business of Leyland Paints, believing that, as illustrated by *The Forsyte Saga*, the first generation starts a business, the second develops it, and by the third generation there are too many family members to accommodate. Instead, hoping that his son would opt for a career in law, he had taken him to the Royal Courts of Justice in 1954. Butler recalled the experience:

> We asked the clerk if there was anything interesting to watch and he directed us to Court Number One. Here there was a contested divorce case, where the plaintiff was being taken to bits by counsel. It was a completely clinical job for the barrister, but for the lady it was her life that was being destroyed. I had visions of myself cross-examining and this leading to an execution. That experience put me off the Law.[11]

During the Easter holidays from 1952 to 1956, he went to stay with a schoolfriend, Patrick Conolly-Carew* at their magnificent house Castletown, about twelve miles west of Dublin, where Butler was introduced to riding, as both Patrick and his sister Diana rode competitively.† In 1956, the two boys had a mild adventure involving Patrick's father's car after a bibulous dinner in Dun Laoghaire. They were fortunately able to return the car intact, a happy outcome since, four years later, Lord Carew was able to help Butler and influence his choice of career. He arranged for him, as he was about to come down from Oxford, to meet Sir Edmund Compton, Comptroller and Auditor General at the Treasury. Sir Edmund advised Butler to take the Civil Service exam and, if he did well, to go to the Treasury, advice that he followed in all particulars.

Butler recalls, however, that at the age of eighteen, he was not conventionally ambitious, but 'lived from rugby match to rugby match', and it was not

---

* Now the 7th Baron Carew.

† Patrick rode in the Munich Olympics of 1972; Diana competed at the Mexico City Olympics in 1968.

until he neared the end of his university years that he thought seriously about what he wanted to do. Bernard had instilled the concept of public service and sent him off to VPS (Varsities and Public School*) camp in the summers. As Harrow Hill was both where he attended school and where he lived, his father thought it important that he should go somewhere else during the holidays. The camps were 'Low Church evangelical places', Butler recalled:

> Slightly naughtily they encouraged kids to commit their lives to Christ. I was put under pressure by the logical syllogism that if the Bible is true, then Christianity must be the most important thing in everyone's life. By the time I went to Oxford the religion evaporated but the commitment to public service remained. So I wasn't attracted by banking or the City, and working for the media was beneath contempt.[12]

The principal reason for the 'evaporation' of religion from Butler's life was what he considered the narrow and joyless view of life propagated by the evangelicals. For all that life was a serious business, and for all that Christianity entailed public service, life was to be enjoyed, and he was able to enjoy it as strenuously as anyone else.

An important feature for Butler, perhaps, of the VPS camps was that there he met three famous cricketers: David Sheppard, John Dewes and John Bridger. Sheppard had made his England debut in 1950 while an undergraduate at Trinity Hall, Cambridge. Converted to evangelical Christianity in his Cambridge years, he was ordained in 1955. The following year, he was prominent in Butler's pantheon as he was recalled to the England side and scored 113 against Australia in the fourth test at Old Trafford. Dewes, also a Cambridge Blue, played for Middlesex and opened the England batting with Len Hutton against Don Bradman's all-conquering 1948 team. Bridger, nine years older than Sheppard, had read theology at Cambridge before taking holy orders. He played for – and eventually captained – Hampshire between

* These camps, founded by Eric Nash (1898–1982, known by his nickname 'Bash') were also known as 'Bash camps'. Nash was a powerful evangelist who converted many of his acquaintances to Christianity, including David Sheppard (later Bishop of Liverpool).

1946 and 1954. It is probable that the Revd David Sheppard's cover drive was every bit as important to the young Butler as his theology.*

Bernard's pride in his son knew no bounds. Throughout his teens, Butler had been at boarding school, but never far from home. As a result, his relations with his parents were closer and less formal than those of a boy whose principal contact with parents was by the Sunday letter. In a touching gesture, Bernard wanted to record his son's achievements when he left Harrow, and he wrote a formal but loving letter, brimming with pride, as though it were an official record of Butler's success. 'It may surprise you', he wrote, 'to get a letter from me.' It was, he said, 'really being written for you to keep as a measure of our love and esteem and in the hope that it may in due course inspire your children to emulate their famous father'.[13]

The young man who left Harrow in the summer of 1956 was a textbook example of the successful product of a public school education in the 1950s. Trained in the classics, able to write Greek lyrics and Roman elegiac couplets with the same deft skill, highly competitive on and off the playing field, serious about his confirmation into the Church of England and possessed of Christian charity towards the less fortunate, Butler duly turned up for his medical examination in preparation for serving his two years of National Service in Her Majesty's Armed Forces.

---

* The Old Trafford test match immortalised not only the name of the Revd David Sheppard, but also that of Jim Laker, the Surrey bowler who took nineteen wickets in England's victory by an innings. Sheppard was the first Church of England minister to play first-class cricket. From 1975 to 1997, he was Bishop of Liverpool. On his retirement, he was awarded a peerage and sat on the Labour benches in the House of Lords until his death in 2005.

CHAPTER 2

ST DUNSTAN'S AND OXFORD, 1956–1961

A 'TRIPLE BLOOD' AT Harrow, standing at 6ft 3in. in his stockinged feet, broad-shouldered and well-muscled, Butler was astounded and embarrassed when the medical staff at the Acton army recruiting centre turned him down flat. He had suffered from asthma and had a weakness in his left eye. Those two deficiencies were enough to disqualify him; a vision of two pleasant years in Hong Kong with the Royal Fusiliers was abruptly dispelled.

In addition to the blow to his ego, there were practical considerations. University College was able to advance his admission date by one year but, clearly, could not give him a place at three months' notice. With the assistance of Dr James, the Harrow headmaster, he was able to fall back on that 'old faithful' solution for the year between public school and university – a spell of teaching in a prep school. James spoke to his friend Rupert Martin, formerly headmaster of King's School, Bruton, who had become joint headmaster at St Dunstan's Preparatory School in Burnham-on-Sea in Somerset, where the mud in the estuary was considered beneficial for his health.

As the low man on the ladder in a school already replete with teachers of the classics, Butler drew the job of teaching history, geography and Scripture, subjects that he felt spectacularly unqualified to teach. During his year at St Dunstan's he read Evelyn Waugh's *Decline and Fall* and later felt able to vouch for the authenticity of the hero Paul Pennyfeather's feelings when he taught at a Welsh prep school. From the start, the auguries at St Dunstan's were poor. Asked to escort the London party of boarders on the train to

Somerset, he was at first impressed by their neat grey suits. Very soon, however, bedlam broke out and by the time they arrived at Burnham-on-Sea, 'all were dishevelled, I more than most'.[1]

Early in his time at St Dunstan's, two crises of global strategic importance flared up. During the autumn of 1956, the crisis over the Suez Canal and the ruthless crushing of the Hungarian Revolution stand out as events that might easily have led to wider war, possibly involving the United States and the Soviet Union. Looking back on the tense months of October and November, Butler is objective and surprisingly dispassionate. He had grown up during the Second World War and in its immediate aftermath; he had lived in a world where dramatic political and military shifts altered the strategic balance day by day. To the young man of eighteen, the events of autumn 1956 were no more dramatic than the measured advance of General Montgomery's Army Group after D-Day.

Much more pressing on a daily basis was how the apprentice schoolmaster could assert his authority over a group of mischievous twelve-year-old boys. Closer in age to his pupils than to most of his colleagues, he strove to make learning interesting for the boys and, inevitably, was repaid by creative 'ragging'. On Guy Fawkes's night, 5 November 1956, he came upon boys lighting a firework in the school gymnasium. The adult in him saw that this was dangerous in a wooden structure; the adolescent in him felt that the boys should not be deprived of their fun. So he took the firework into the open and lit it. When it exploded 'with a very satisfactory flash and bang', the boys had vanished, leaving the junior master to explain the explosion to the headmaster, who had unexpectedly appeared.

On another occasion, in his second term at the school, at evening roll call he was handed a pen that had apparently been dropped by a boy. When no one claimed it, he opened it to see if it was a fountain pen or a ball-point. The pen promptly exploded dramatically, causing Butler to recoil 'about six feet'. Seeing this as a supreme test of his authority, he established that the boy who 'found' the pen knew it was explosive and marched him to the headmaster's study to be beaten. He subsequently discovered that Robin Martin, the headmaster's eleven-year-old son (who years later worked with him at the Treasury), had supplied the explosive caps.

Only once did his youthful exuberance lead to serious consequences, as he wrote to Bernard:

> Yesterday was my unlucky day, I'm afraid, for when I got back to school I had an accident which will stop me playing rugger until after Christmas. I was ragging with some of the boys and, while I was being chased, I slipped on some polished lino and put my hand through a glass door. I couldn't feel anything at all and ran on, thinking how lucky I was not to have hurt myself when I felt something dripping and saw that I had gashed my thumb ... my forearm was also bleeding very heavily ... The Doctor says I haven't a chance of playing rugger again before Christmas.[2]

The enforced absence from the rugby field was a great disappointment, as Bridgwater and Albion RFC provided a welcome dose of contact with the outside world. Butler enjoyed the rugby itself, the team companionship, the kind of adult apprenticeship, he believed, that he would have gained from his National Service. Somehow Bridgwater had gained the impression that he had played for the Richmond England Schoolboys XV and accordingly placed him in their first squad, which involved a forceful introduction to the senior game. Butler earned his spurs with a try in the club's win over local rivals Taunton.

Before going up to Oxford in October 1957, he returned to play for Bridgwater and, at the end of September, was invited to play for Somerset against Monmouthshire. A leg injury prevented him from playing, but when he arrived for the Oxford freshman trials he was able to say, stretching the truth only slightly, that he was a county player. For their part, the club and the town adopted him as one of their own and, in future years, the local *Burham and Highbridge Gazette* proudly reported when he won his Oxford Blue, when he was knighted and when he was appointed Cabinet Secretary. Indeed, on the latter occasion, under the headline 'Cabinet Post for Burnham Teacher', it managed to convey the impression that Butler was plucked from the classroom at St Dunstan's to sort out the Cabinet Office.[3]

During the cricket season, he turned out for the local team, Burnham-on-Sea. The team members initially resented the arrival of the golden boy from Harrow, and he found their attitude 'condescending'. Grudgingly, they placed him in the club's second XI, reluctantly promoting him when he scored some runs. As the season wound on, however, he became one of the team and was accepted as a worthy addition to the squad.

All in all, the academic year of 1956/57 was a time in which he learned something of the application of authority and of the world beyond Harrow Hill. An innocent summer dalliance brought his first experience of sexual attraction, an experience that he found alarming in its intensity. Of teaching as a profession, the most lasting impression that he gained was a negative one.

It was inevitable that, after attending the VPS camps, he would at least consider teaching as a career. It was equally inevitable that he would reject it. He was mature enough to recognise that his principal asset as a teacher was youthful enthusiasm and that, after a few years, that asset would have either depreciated or been ground away by conflict. Even so, at the age of eighteen, he doubted his suitability. There was already something of an architect in him and he leaned towards a career that could be built and extended; the repetitive nature of teaching would not satisfy that.

Nonetheless, he wanted to discharge his responsibilities well during his year at St Dunstan's, and suffered a blow to his pride when one boy, whom he considered brilliant, told him that another boy had said that he could teach nothing except physical training. The criticism struck home and Butler wrote to his parents that 'I stepped up my teaching for the rest of the week'. Looking about him in the staff common room, while accepting that all his colleagues were pleasant, amusing, thoroughly decent people, he found the prospect of becoming like them less than attractive. They were not, he later wrote, 'reassuring role models'.[4]

The year of teaching, transition from a teenage world to a form of salaried employment, together with a different brand of rugby from the public school version, had been a maturing process and at Oxford he gravitated to the company of friends who had done their National Service. Two of his close friends at University College ('Univ') had seen action during their two years in the forces: Robin Fox in the Royal Navy at Suez, and David Miers in the Cameron Highlanders at Aden.

From the day he arrived in Oxford, Butler was active on every front.

Taking stock of his assets and their market value, he rapidly identified the arenas in which he would compete. As an open scholar, he would be expected to do well academically, and he was confident that he could handle the first part of his course with relative ease. Classics, also known as 'Greats' or *Literae Humaniores*, was divided into two unequal parts: five terms of Greek and Latin literature and language, followed by seven terms of ancient history and philosophy from the pre-Socratics, through Plato and Aristotle, to the present day.

The second part of the course would be more challenging, as he was not a natural academic historian and, in common with most of his contemporaries, had no experience of philosophy. Reasonably enough, he deferred the challenge of philosophy for the time being and aimed for a first in Honour Moderations in the spring of 1959, a Blue in the University Rugby XV and to be president of the Univ Junior Common Room. From those achievements other honours would flow. Somewhat surprisingly, he did not include the Oxford Union in his ambitions; this was a decision that he later regretted.[5]

For the first part of the classics course he was taught by one of University College's most remarkable Fellows. A. F. ('Freddie') Wells, the legend went, had been asked by the Professor of Latin after his Honour Moderations if he would be prepared to devote his life to the Latin language. With a shy smile, Wells had replied simply: 'It never occurred to me to do anything else.' The story, although almost certainly apocryphal, does capture the man's certainty of purpose, combined with humility and a passionate desire to teach. One of the most dedicated of teachers, he was, in the words of his obituary in *The Times*, 'not a prolific scholar'. Beyond some truly beautiful pieces of Latin and Greek prose and verse, little of the written work of Freddie Wells has survived.[6]

Instead, Wells devoted himself to teaching. If a tutorial, scheduled to last for an hour, strayed into interesting waters and needed more time, he would simply rearrange his schedule to accommodate the extra time needed. Undergraduates recall tutorials that lasted two or even three hours, sessions of incalculable benefit to those concerned. Since Wells's personal inclination was to Virgil and Horace, two of Butler's favourite Roman poets, the association augured well from the outset.

In addition to his responsibilities as a classics tutor, Freddie Wells was also dean of the college, responsible for its discipline and smooth running. When Butler was given *The Rules and Customs of University College*, he read it assiduously, and noticed a sentence stipulating that 'all electrical appliances must be approved by the Dean'. By nature an obeyer of rules, he duly took his electric shaver to the Dean for inspection, whereupon he was treated to Wells's delicately mocking humour. No undergraduate had ever showed him his razor before, Wells told Butler deadpan. It really was a very nice razor; he was glad to have been shown it. Would there be anything else? Despite the minor triumph when he pointed out the relevant sentence in 'Rules and Customs' to the dean, Butler was left with the disturbing feeling that he had been gently mocked – and the certainty that university was to prove very different from school.

The prospect of winning a rugby Blue, on the other hand, initially appeared remote. The two wing-forwards in the Blues XV were internationals: Peter Robbins of England and Robin Davies of Wales. The 1957 season, therefore, saw Butler playing with the Greyhounds, the university's second XV, an occupation that he described as 'great fun', but far from the challenge of playing in the senior team. That would have to wait for another year.

The last years of the 1950s were also, in retrospect, the last years of Oxford as it had been between the wars. The Oxford generation in which Butler found himself still wore sports jackets and ties as their daily dress, still dined formally gowned in hall most evenings. Dons still addressed him as 'Mr Butler' rather than by his first name. First names, for that matter, were still referred to as 'Christian names'. Overall, there was a great preponderance of men from public school, although Univ, by tradition and design a more egalitarian college than most, had a broader cross-section of British youth than the more conservative, socially exclusive colleges such as Christ Church or Trinity.

Butler, who had at first been attracted by the unique academic reputation of Balliol, was delighted with his ultimate choice of University College and quickly settled in. Univ possessed the oldest of the college dining clubs, the Shakespeare Club, to which he was elected in his second year. As an athlete, he was also elected to Vincent's Club and, as an old boy of one of 'the better' schools, to the Bullingdon Club, today a lampooned symbol of the privileged upbringing of David Cameron, Boris Johnson and other Old Etonians. The university was still very much a man's world, with more than thirty men's colleges and just five for women. In the 1950s, there were not even female Fellows of Univ, let alone female undergraduates.

For his first two Oxford years, Butler was perfectly comfortable in a way of life that was a natural sequel to public school. Academic work, serious rugby, sherry parties with male contemporaries and occasional females, dinner strictly among males, all dressed in sports jackets, ties and academic gowns, essay clubs and dining clubs at which young men affected the pretensions of their age and class – all this was the stuff of 'fitting in' in 1950s Oxford. In these activities, Butler was a team player, a natural participant.

The academic work was, for the first two years, a continuation of the classics course at Harrow. More scholarship, more strenuous and wide-ranging literary analysis was required, but the fundamentals – translating to and from Greek and Latin – remained essentially the same. Butler had an easy familiarity with both languages and, with serious application, could be fairly certain of success in Honour Moderations, thirteen three-hour papers at the end of his fifth term. As to rugby, he accepted that, for one year at least, he would not win his Blue. In his second year, he was more confident but, possibly because Honour Moderations were approaching, he began to suffer from insomnia and found himself in a permanent state of exhaustion. As a result, he was dropped from the Blues XV and was compelled to shelve his ambition for another year.

In the spring of 1959 came Honour Moderations, in which, predictably, Butler earned a First. The marks he received, however, are curious and, as Wells wrote to him, 'there are some surprises here'. There were alpha marks distributed liberally among many subjects, but his General Paper was marked as beta-alpha, a disappointment, and there were other surprising beta marks. None of which, it should be said, took away from the achievement of a very good first-class degree. Freddie Wells, writing to congratulate him, regretted that 'I shall miss one of the pleasantest year of pupils I've ever had'.[7]

In the summer, he made his first trip to Greece with Andrew Primrose and Hugo Morriss. The three undergraduates set off by car to drive through

France, Switzerland and Italy to Brindisi and thence by ferry to Piraeus. The trip had all the elements of an undergraduate vacation – a petrol pump that repeatedly failed; the loss of Butler's camera to pickpockets; sleeping *al fresco* to enable each to live on £1 per day – but it induced a love of Greece that has stayed with him ever since. From Athens, they toured Attica before heading out to Delphi and the Peloponnese. The magic of Mycenae, Olympus, Corinth and Epidaurus is beautifully captured in his letters home. The 'rugged but breathtaking scenery' and 'an ancient city in every valley' added a mystical quality to his factual knowledge of classical Greek cities.

As a young man who judged himself harshly, demanding constant re-affirmation of his own worth through different symbols of success, he was well on track after his Moderations. His third year posed new challenges in the second section of the 'Greats' course and the renewed battle to win a rugby Blue. Predictably, Butler added more challenges to his catalogue of ambitions. Less predictable was the particular challenge that his third year brought in the Trinity (summer) term.

From classical literature and language, 'Greats' students embarked on two years of ancient history and philosophy. Ancient history, like Honour Moderations, involved a deeper, more academic approach to a subject already familiar; philosophy, however, was completely new. Once again, Butler was fortunate, since Univ offered exceptional tutors in both subjects: the remarkable George Cawkwell as his ancient history tutor and the legendary Peter Strawson in philosophy.

Of the two, Cawkwell was the more accessible. Not only was ancient history relatively well-known territory, Cawkwell was a familiar 'type' to the young scholar-athlete. A New Zealander, an athlete and international rugby player (by some charismatic chance of ancestry, he had represented Scotland on the rugby field), a devout Christian and an equally devoted college man, he and the young Butler formed an immediate bond that developed into close friendship in later years. Peter Strawson captivated Butler, as he captivated the majority of his students, with the versatility of his mind and his ability to address the most complex philosophical issues and present them in comprehensible terms.

Butler concluded fairly early in his study of philosophy that the 'Greats' syllabus fell into three broad sections: Greek philosophy – Plato and Aristotle – where part of the challenge lay in the translation of Greek abstracts into tangible English philosophical concepts; moral and political philosophy, which required a similar, applied analytical approach; and all that fell under the broad heading of 'logic', including the philosophy of perception, of knowledge and of language. He very soon recognised that he was not the sort of thinker who would make much of an impact in these last areas – and, perhaps more importantly, that remote abstract thought of this kind was not a discipline that appealed to him. Yet, since he was to be examined in the subject, he would need to provide clear and original answers to such questions. In typical fashion, therefore, he developed a practical approach to philosophy – to prepare forty-minute essays on a number of topics likely to appear in final examination papers. On moral and political issues, he was secure and articulate in his personal beliefs, which may or may not have helped. In the third category, where personal opinions were simply irrelevant, he hit upon a technique that he hoped would satisfy the examiners, treating philosophical puzzles as soluble brainteasers rather than as serious intellectual issues.

The essays that Butler wrote early in his study of philosophy in 1959 are happily preserved among his papers.* The first of these discusses the sun, divided line and cave similes of Plato's *Republic*.[8] These are about gaining knowledge, also laying the foundations of Plato's contention that only philosophers are equipped to rule. The essay reads as if Butler, not quite at home with the metaphysical similes used to illustrate the acquisition of knowledge, treats the whole question as a challenge, not unlike the solution of a detective story. The result is a thoroughly worthy essay that has signally failed to engage the writer's intellect. It opens with a clear statement of limited intent:

> My purpose in this essay is to establish a general relation between the three illustrations which Plato uses in the latter part of Book VI and the earlier part of Book VII. I shall not deal with difficulties, which certainly exist,

* The collection also includes a miscellany of papers read to university and college societies, rugby programmes and press cuttings.

> in the interpretation of the individual illustrations. For example, there are clearly real difficulties about the divided line in the distinction between dialectical and mathematical methods, and also in the comparison between mathematics and the use of *eikones* of visual things.

By contrast, his essay on political liberty, naturally enough expressed in Cold War terms, is the work of a young man forming his own opinions on the traditional issues of moral and political philosophy. His enthusiasm for the subject leads him into broad, youthful generalisations and occasional platitudes about the relative value of liberty and life. But the overarching mood is one of a practical idealist seeking a fairer society. Unafraid to deal with hypotheses, he shuffles imagined situations where liberty is threatened or extinguished. A tentative conclusion involves accepting Isaiah Berlin's two concepts of liberty – positive freedom and negative freedom. The differences between these two early essays in philosophy are marked.

Two years later, when he sat his final exams, his intellectual preference for substantive moral issues was clear from the results. On the Logic paper, he scored a predictably solid beta triple plus. On the Moral and Political Philosophy paper, he achieved his best mark overall, an alpha double minus.

The year of 1959 was *annus mirabilis* for Butler. There was his first trip to Greece, cementing his love of the classics and laying the foundation for a lifelong romance with Athens and the Peloponnese. He ran for president of the Junior Common Room and was elected, in no small part thanks to his excellent memory. He studied the photographs of college freshmen until he felt able to greet younger men in the quadrangle by their first names. And, most gratifying in that long lacuna before the next examination, despite breaking his nose in an early trial, he won his rugby Blue after two excellent matches in the month before the Varsity Match at Twickenham. On 7 November, the university XV had a thrilling 22–0 win over Cardiff. 'Tousle-haired wing-forward Robin Butler threatened to beat Cardiff single-handed on a couple of occasions', was the report in one newspaper.[9] Two weeks later, on 21 November, after a match against Harlequins at Twickenham, he was awarded his coveted place in the Blues XV.

The Varsity Match of 8 December 1959 was the high point of his rugby career. The Light Blues of Cambridge were the pre-match favourites, their team built around the talented midfield combination of Steve Smith* (scrum half for England) and Gordon Waddell (fly half for Scotland). Waddell, however, was injured and unable to play; without that understanding at half-back, many Cambridge movements were stillborn. Solid defence characterised both sides' tactics, and at the final whistle Oxford had won by three penalty goals to one.

Butler's playing career almost ended the following term when he tore a cruciate ligament in an inter-college match and then worsened the injury by playing again too soon. As a result, he later recorded, he never played rugby again with the same uninhibited enthusiasm. He retained his place in the Oxford XV for the 1960 Varsity Match, but Oxford were unable to repeat their win of the previous year, losing 0–13 in a match in which 'Oxford were outplayed almost everywhere'.[10]

The third year of the 'Greats' course is relatively undemanding, and Butler took advantage of this respite to present two papers to the Canning Club, the conservative essay society, and to the Univ literary society on very different subjects. The first of these, presented to the Canning in May 1960 to commemorate the fiftieth anniversary of a paper given by Rupert Brooke to the Fabian Society at Cambridge, examined the obligations of a socialist state as provider of education and patron of the arts. It is very unlikely that Butler's conclusions were shared by the club's generally conservative membership.

After an assault on the notion of 'culture for the rich', there followed a detailed analysis of the state's expenditure, through the Arts Council and other channels, in support of the arts, demonstrating that the Arts Council had paltry, insignificant sums with which to assist living painters, sculptors, poets and writers. In 1960, this amounted to £55,000, less than 1 per cent of the total government expenditure on the arts. The well-argued, challenging paper ended with the assertion that the government had an obligation not only to make enjoyment of the arts available to the people, but also to allocate funds to those artists who most needed patronage. Otherwise, 'it is in

* Steve Smith taught geography and economics and coached rugby at Harrow School between 1960 and 1965, before going to Caterham School as headmaster.

danger of neglecting the artist himself, who most needs patronage, and of devoting its support not to the struggling but to the established, not to the living but to the dead'.*

The second paper, given to the college literary society run by the history don Tony Firth, reveals a more unconventional side of the young Butler. On journeys between Oxford and London, he had observed the 'spectacular rise of West Wycombe Hill and the gold ball which crowns it'. This monument marks the domain of Sir Francis Dashwood and the caves he quarried, the Hell Fire Caves, the home of Sir Francis's creation, the Hell Fire Club. Fascinated by the intersection of this eighteenth-century phenomenon and equally intrigued by an ostensibly respectable man who followed the motto *Fay ce que voudras*,† Butler asked his audience at the end of his paper:

> What is the solution? The only solution that I can suggest is to ask you to think yourselves back over two hundred years, to a time when everything was partly a joke – sex, politics, even the Church – and not the grim duty as which we tend to represent them. The Victorians rigidly separated duty and pleasure. Only if we can for a moment forget the distinction can we see how a man could be at once rake, religious and politically responsible.[11]

It was a well-researched paper, challenging in its objectivity and in its avoidance of conventional moral judgements. It was certainly not what his audience might have expected from a former head boy of Harrow. Or, for that matter, from a future Cabinet Secretary, Whitehall's head prefect.

All Butler's activities and triumphs, even being elected president of Vincent's Club, faded into relative insignificance against a chance meeting in that Trinity term. Every men's college had a boat club and every boat club had a 'rugger boat', filled with beefy athletes, many like himself, rowing for the first time. Finding that he liked the sport, Butler attended the college

---

* This paper, entitled 'The State and the Arts', was presented in the second week of May 1960. In the previous week, Princess Margaret had married Anthony Armstrong Jones (later Earl of Snowdon) and the state expenditure on the wedding of the Queen's sister had aroused a good deal of controversy. The essay is among Lord Butler's personal papers.

† In Old French, 'do whatever you will'.

regatta, where Gillian ('Jill') Galley, a second-year undergraduate reading mathematics at St Hugh's College, had volunteered to sell programmes. He invested three shillings (fifteen pence) in buying strawberries for her as a pretext to initiate *pourparlers*, before inviting her to cox his pair in the coxed pairs race. After a momentary confusion between right and left, Jill steered their boat firmly into the bank while their opponents swept past. Butler's crewmate Robert Fox 'swore lustily' at Jill, who promptly 'climbed onto the bank and strode off with her nose in the air'.

Undeterred, Butler pursued her and, by the autumn of 1960, the pair were inseparable – to the point of climbing into the ground at Twickenham in evening dress after the Blues Match ball in December, where Butler re-enacted Twickenham's most famous tries. Not, on the surface, the most romantic approach, but quite in character.

So began their last year at Oxford, a year that Butler remembers as 'idyllic'. Varsity rugby came to an end after Twickenham, as the Blues team now turned to developing their team for the next season's match. This brought home to him that his time as an undergraduate was limited, that final exams were only a few months away. He and Jill developed a routine, spending the days apart in different libraries, and their evenings together immersed in academic work.

The spectre of 'Schools', the final exams held in late May and early June, is fearsome for all undergraduates, no matter how well they have prepared themselves. Butler was convinced that his revision had been inadequate and that he was ill equipped for the exams. Indeed, he confesses to this day that he still has dreams in which his knowledge of Roman history is too sparse. After sitting his finals, his conviction that he had not won a First was strengthened when he was not required for a 'viva', the oral exam often used to decide the class in which a borderline student should be placed.

In common with many undergraduates who are reasonably confident of gaining a first-class degree, he was uncertain just where that would place him in the academic landscape. The competitive Butler, always aiming high, would have been very happy to win Oxford's ultimate academic honour – a prize fellowship at All Souls College. At the same time, however, he doubted that he would be one of the two scholars in his year to whom All Souls offered that distinction. The idea of a graduate degree, working towards a normal research fellowship and an academic career, had less appeal. Still divided, he took Sir Edmund Compton's advice and sat the exam for the administrative class of the Civil Service, persuading himself that 'it was a second string'.

Forty years later, Butler remembered how Lord Carew and Sir Edward Compton had influenced him.[12] He also expressed gratitude to his Oxford friend Peter Jay, who had gone down from Oxford and joined the Treasury a year ahead of him.* Butler recalled

> [his] encounter with him in the Gridiron Club when he returned to Oxford, already a figure of legendary brilliance, and now a demigod who had passed with legendary brilliance into the Treasury. He encouraged me to opt for the Treasury in the Civil Service exam. He subsequently helped me even more by leaving the Treasury. If he had chosen to stay, I have no doubt that it would have been he rather than I who would have been Head of the Civil Service over these last ten years.[13]

This encouragement from a near contemporary may have tipped the balance. Butler prepared for the written papers, which were followed by two days of tests. Candidates were required to chair a committee; to study a file on a hypothesised problem and offer a solution; to write a letter in the name of a Minister; and to write a profile of oneself, both from the point of view of an admirer and from that of a critic. When he came first, with 280 points from a maximum of 300, he was provisionally admitted to the Civil Service, with admission conditional on his receiving at least a second-class honours degree. Whether or not he truly still saw it as a second string at this point, he could at least be certain that, barring disastrous mistakes in his final exams, he had a job to go to in the autumn.

With Schools behind them, he and Jill set off on a tour of Greece with

---

* Peter Jay, a friend of Butler, was considered the brightest man in his generation at Oxford. He was the son of Douglas and Peggy Jay and son-in-law of James Callaghan. He worked briefly in the Treasury before a successful career as a journalist and television presenter. He also worked as Chief of Staff to Robert Maxwell.

David Miers* and his girlfriend Annabella Loudon. The holiday was a welcome month of relaxation after the pressure of exams – so much so that Butler, enchanted by Aegina, Delos and Crete, claims almost to have forgotten that he was awaiting results. In the event, these were delivered in the form of a telegram awaiting him at the poste restante in Athens. The four words 'MAGNIFICENT FIRST LOVE DAD' had been arranged with a gap between the third and fourth words, rather than between the second and third. In fact, the ambiguity perfectly fitted the facts, as he had proposed to Jill on the Acropolis on a night of a full moon and they returned from Greece officially engaged.

* David Miers, later Sir David Miers, was ambassador to Greece from 1989 to 1993. While Butler's proposal to Jill on the Acropolis in 1961 was marred by the presence of crowds of tourists, Sir David, as ambassador, was well placed to arrange for a calmer replay of the proposal thirty years later. The two men remained friends throughout their careers. In 1998, Butler wrote a poem made up of five limerick-style stanzas to commemorate Miers's seventieth birthday.

CHAPTER 3

THE TREASURY AND THE LABOUR GOVERNMENT, 1961–1970

THE CIVIL SERVICE INITIALLY appealed to Butler because of its competitive entry process; as ever, he responded well to the challenge of a set piece, coming first in the examination and electing to go to the Treasury as it was 'at the centre of things'. He had also been advised by Sir Edmund Compton that the Treasury was the gateway to early preferment. In the entrance examination, he had edged out David Walker, a Cambridge economist, by ten points. From the outset, he saw Walker as one who would be a likely competitor when they both attained the higher reaches of the service. He was relieved when Walker moved from the Treasury to the Bank of England, where he ultimately rose to be Deputy Governor.

Jill began her first job, teaching at St Paul's Girls' School, and moved into a flat between King's Road and Chelsea Bridge. Her fiancé found less fashionable accommodation in Gledstanes Road, Barons Court – seedy but handy for Queen's Club – and began work as assistant principal in the Commonwealth and Foreign Division of the Treasury for an annual salary of £800.* His responsibility was the control of non-staff expenditure of the Foreign, Commonwealth and Colonial Offices. The word 'control' was used loosely and was effectively a euphemism for the policy of denying any and

* The nomenclature of rank in the Civil Service is, at first sight, bizarre. Permanent Secretaries are at the top of the ladder, followed by Second Secretaries, Deputy Secretaries, Under-Secretaries and Assistant Secretaries. Way down the ladder come the principal clerks, whose title is confusingly shortened to 'principal'. Thus the grandiose sounding 'principal' is quite junior, while assistant principals are the lowest administrative officers on the food chain.

all requests for 'supplementary estimates' in excess of the annual estimates voted by Parliament.

In the socially stratified ethic of the era, administrative officers started work later than clerical workers, and Butler was told that he should not arrive for work before 9.30 or 10.00 a.m. or he would be considered a security risk. He wrote to his parents that he was expected to work until some time between 5.30 and 7.00 p.m. – and, by the way, he added, he could use several white shirts if his father could spare them.[1]

On moving into his office, Butler found a large pile of letters seeking approval for supplementary estimates. Uncertain of how to proceed, he approached his immediate superior and asked for advice on procedure. 'You refuse them all', came the reply. His role was to refuse every such request on the principle that those with a reasonable case would appeal to his superior. With a good degree from Oxford, he would be able, it was assumed, to find plausible reasons for refusing the requests.[2] His performance, he learned, would be judged by how few such refusals were challenged by appeal. This and other instances of micro-managed parsimony made an impression on the young assistant principal, and more particularly demonstrated that success would flow from a policy of obstruction, of denying as many requests as possible. Years later, when he was in a position to make changes within the service, it was such negativism that he sought to banish.

In typically pragmatic fashion, he recognised that, to seem efficient, he should write as many letters of refusal as possible and that he ran the risk of being slowed by logjams of work in the typing pool. He therefore took the decision, most unusual for a young man in 1961, to type his own letters; he wrote to Diana:

> I think it's rather important for my job that I should learn to type as I sometimes have to send off letters so quickly that I can't wait for them to be done in the typing pool. Is there any chance that I could some time borrow your type writer [*sic*] for a short time to see if I could learn?[3]

The months of late 1961 and early 1962 were a frantic period in the life of a young unmarried man living London life to the maximum: five long days of work each week, rugby at weekends, acting in amateur dramatics, keeping up with contacts from Harrow days. In January, Butler damaged his knee, playing for the Civil Service against the Navy, but was playing again by March, when he 'made some splendid breaks' for Richmond.[4] Meanwhile, as he pointed out to his parents, 'all our young married friends are doing their own decoration most successfully'.[5] It was time to take the next logical step in his life with Jill.

At first, in common with most of their friends, Robin and Jill did not much stray outside a fairly small geographical area bounded by St Paul's Cathedral, the River Thames, Putney Bridge and Hampstead. They intended to marry in the summer of 1962 but, as Bernard pointed out to them at Christmas, they had nowhere to live. Moreover, buying even a modest flat within their West London habitat was out of the question with the £5,000 that they had budgeted for the purchase. When their estate agent proposed a flat in Dulwich, they scoffed at the idea of living 'in the suburbs of Kent'* until the agent pointed out that there was an excellent train service from Victoria, convenient for both Robin's and Jill's work. For £5,850, a gift from Bernard and Nora, they bought a two-bedroomed flat off College Road in West Dulwich. Butler moved in with a Univ friend at Easter, and he and Jill spent weekends redecorating. On 25 August, they were married at St Thomas's Church in Southborough, outside Tunbridge Wells.

For their honeymoon, they drove through France into Spain and down the Mediterranean coast to Valencia. One of the highlights was a visit to the Roman ruins of Sagunto, a town that had played a crucial part in the Second Punic War.† The most worrying moment came at a bullfight in Girona. One bull jumped out of the arena and Jill was quite reasonably 'very nervous thereafter as [they] were sitting in the second row and the man on the other side of her was wearing a red shirt'.[6]

When Butler joined the Treasury, a Conservative government had been in power for ten years. By 1961, after the election of John F. Kennedy as

---

* The idea that Dulwich was in Kent illustrates how little Robin and Jill strayed from central London. In fact, Dulwich was in Surrey until the creation of the County of London in 1889.

† The siege and capture of the Roman fortified town of Saguntum by Hannibal in 219 BCE set in train the Second Punic War, which lasted until 202 BCE.

President of the USA, the Macmillan Cabinet had a distinctly outdated look. The rhetoric and the sentiments expressed on the 'New Frontier' were vibrant symbols of a new decade, while the United Kingdom seemed to offer outmoded platitudes. The Tory government had the air of a group of tired old men; clever younger men began to question the self-satisfied assurance of the pre-war generation. The age of satire accompanied the decline of public respect for government. The media assumed the right to intrude into all corners of politics. The debuts of *Beyond the Fringe* (1960), *Private Eye* (1961) and *That Was the Week that Was* (1962), all roughly contemporary with Butler's arrival in Whitehall, were robustly critical of the status quo. A movement that began with satirical but good-humoured portrayal of Harold Macmillan as an Edwardian relic became increasingly aggressive and contemptuous. Government became less remote, far less sacrosanct, more vulnerable to intrusive enquiry.

When Hugh Gaitskell died suddenly in 1963 and Harold Wilson became leader of the Labour Party, there was a widespread excitement at the prospect of a younger generation coming to power in Britain. Then, as Macmillan's government stumbled from scandal to scandal and Macmillan himself was forced by ill health to retire, that excitement intensified. The Tory Party responded by choosing the 14th Earl of Home as its leader and thus committing electoral suicide. Renouncing his peerage, he became Prime Minister as Sir Alec Douglas-Home.

It was not necessary to be far to the left to be à la mode; one could be an old Harrovian, like Andrew Osmond* of *Private Eye*, or an old Salopian, like Richard Ingrams, the magazine's editor, provided one was adequately sceptical about the Tories. Scepticism and cynicism were enough at that point; the tremors of 1968 still lay a long way in the ideological future.

The Conservative Party's disarray was further revealed in January 1964, when Iain Macleod wrote a damning exposé of Home's selection in *The*

* Andrew Osmond (1938–99) was a contemporary of Robin Butler. In 1961, when Willie Rushton and Richard Ingrams, whom Osmond had known at Oxford, were planning to launch *Private Eye*, they approached Osmond for financial help. To their astonished delight, he signed a cheque for the princely sum of £300 to get the magazine started. His obituaries speak of him as 'the original Lord Gnome'.

Spectator. After a calm and dispassionate account of the events surrounding Macmillan's retirement, Macleod concluded that the Conservative Party 'for the first time since Bonar Law is now being led from the right of centre' and that the Tories had 'confessed that [they] could not find a Prime Minister in the House of Commons at all'.[7]

These were instructive years for a new entrant in the Civil Service. The popular perception of Whitehall – a perception later fostered by *Yes, Minister* and similar parodies – is that its leaders are essentially conservative and doggedly resistant to innovation of any kind. In the early 1960s, over Butler's first three years in the service, there was a perceptible shift, not so much in bureaucrats' attitudes as in the disparity between the service and the government. At a time when modernity was increasingly fashionable, the Tory government appeared provocatively out of touch.

There was, in fact, an unusual anomaly: the supposedly reactionary Civil Service found itself to the left of the government that it was serving. Peter Hennessy describes Sir William Armstrong, the Permanent Secretary at the Treasury in 1962, as being 'somewhat left of centre' and, in his own words, a 'Butskellite'.* Armstrong believed that most senior civil servants would have liked a government with Heath as Prime Minister and Jenkins as Chancellor.[8]

Douglas-Home far exceeded general expectations in the election of October 1964 but, to no one's surprise, Harold Wilson and the Labour Party came to power. Adopting a refrain of 'thirteen years of Tory misrule', the new government seemed to offer a new and exciting world to Britain of the 1960s. In several different ways – from the appearance of the Beatles to the birth of anti-establishment satire – a culture of youth and modernity appeared irresistible. The new Labour government was the crucible of these modern values, albeit with a majority of a mere four seats in the House of Commons.

The expected end of the long-standing Tory government was accompanied by other news of shifts and changes. The Chinese had exploded their first nuclear bomb the previous day. On the same day, Nikita Khrushchev, old and tired, had been removed by a conspiracy led by Leonid Brezhnev.

* The expression, a conflation of the last names of Rab Butler and Hugh Gaitskell, denoted a centrist political stance, and was coined by Norman Macrae in *The Economist*, 13 February 1954.

In the twenty-four hours leading up to the election, the world had changed dramatically. Wilson even wondered, had the news of Khrushchev's removal been broadcast before the polls closed, whether voters would have resisted change and voted for the security of life under the Conservatives.[9]

By the end of 1964, having lost the election, Douglas-Home was shortly to be replaced by Edward Heath; Gaitskell was dead, and the Labour Party had moved to the left; Harold Wilson, not yet fifty, was in 10 Downing Street. The media, particularly the 'new media' of satirists and weekly commentators, took credit for ushering in the '60s – or, at least, for having buried the '50s.

To his older superiors at the Treasury, Butler must have seemed a very suitable recruit in the early 1960s. A conventional public school and Oxford background; a very decent degree; head boy at school and rugby Blue at the Varsity. Yet he was well connected with the Young Turks of the new satire: friendly with David Frost of *That Was the Week that Was*,* on lunching terms with Richard Ingrams and dining terms with Christopher Booker.[10] Here was a recruit tailor-made for this disquieting new era.

The years of 1963 and 1964 were busy ones for the young Butlers. Their weeks were full of amateur dramatics, bridge evenings and a full social life. Butler's weekends were largely occupied with rugby at Richmond. In the summer of 1963, they took a trip through Austria, over the Grossglockner Pass to Caorle, Padua, Verona and Lake Garda. All this was managed on a strict budget; Butler might have been identified as a future mandarin, but a collective annual salary of £1,700 did not permit excessive extravagance. Most of their young friends were having babies in 1963 and 1964; early in the New Year they experienced a *rallentando* when Jill, too, became pregnant.

After three years at the Treasury, the year of 1964 brought changes to Butler's life. Professionally, he was identified as a 'fast streamer' and selected to attend a six-month course on economics and statistics. Thomas Balogh, the Hungarian economist who worked closely with the Labour Leader Harold Wilson, had criticised the tendency of the Civil Service to appoint to the Treasury generalist amateurs rather than professional economists.[11] To

* The satirical programme *That Was the Week that Was* ran on BBC television in 1962 and 1963. It was devised by Ned Sherrin and presented by David Frost.

counter this criticism, the service ran the course to ensure that the non-professionals would have the level of expertise of an Oxford PPE student.

The introduction of this course was a novel attempt to rebut the criticism that civil servants as a breed tended to have 'an almost unanimous reliance on intuition and a distrust of systematic argument, especially where the content is highly quantitative'.[12] The course that Butler attended was only the second to be held and, after completing it, he was earmarked for promotion. He also earned a reputation as a hard worker since, alone among those selected for the course, he refused to have a stand-in during his absence. Instead, he did his normal job, working early in the morning and late at night. As the *Financial Times* later commented, 'it was noted then and is remembered'.[13]

On being appointed private secretary to the Financial Secretary of the Treasury, for the first time he was at the 'sharp' end of the service, involved in the preparation of Treasury briefs for whichever party won the election of that year. A less professionally significant result, but one equally lasting in its effects, was that several of those attending the courses shared an interest in cricket and together formed a Civil Service team called, inevitably, 'the Mandarins'. This was to be an important element of Butler's life for several years.[14]

Labour's victory in the election and Butler's appointment as private secretary brought him into close contact with Niall MacDermot,* a successful barrister, elected MP for Derby North in a 1962 by-election. On the right wing of the Labour Party, MacDermot was responsible for handling the reforms that the government immediately introduced, including a capital gains tax. He was a demanding boss, and for a year Butler was worked hard. In September 1965, after four years on the lowest rung of the ladder, he was promoted to principal and transferred to the Public Income and Outlay division.

This was the first significant step on the Civil Service ladder and, at the age of twenty-seven, Butler found himself at the centre of the Budget-making process, as the principal was ex officio secretary of the Budget Committee,

* Niall MacDermot (1916–96) was Financial Secretary to the Treasury from 1946 to 1967. Initially MP for Lewisham North from 1957 to 1959, when he lost his seat, he returned to the Commons as Member for Derby North in 1962 and held the seat until his retirement at the 1970 election.

working closely with the Treasury's forecasters. The post also brought him into contact with Sir William Armstrong, the Permanent Secretary at the Treasury,* and with the Wilson government's economic advisers, Nicholas Kaldor and Robert Neild. The latter remembers clearly that Butler was, even at this early stage of his career, a young man clearly marked for promotion to the upper reaches of the service.[15]

'This was the high tide of Keynesian economic management', Butler recalled. By stimulating or restraining government expenditure and consumer demand, the government regulated the overall level of economic activity. It was a time of erratic industrial relations, frequent crises and lively disputes between protagonists of different economic approaches. These served to bring the young principal to the attention of powerful civil servants and politicians, including James Callaghan, the Chancellor of the Exchequer. Butler's star was decidedly in the ascendant.

Since the election of October 1964, the month in which Sophie, the Butlers' first child, was born, Harold Wilson had been impatient to call another election in order to increase the government's unworkably small majority. Tactically, it was decided that the election should be called with as little notice of polling day as possible. The Conservative Party had elected a new leader, Edward Heath, in July 1965, and Wilson wanted to go to the country before the Tories were sufficiently organised to conduct a powerful campaign.

On 28 February 1966, Wilson announced that Parliament would be dissolved on 10 March with polling day three weeks later. The law provided that there should be a minimum of seventeen days, excluding Sundays and bank holidays, between dissolution and polling day. On Sunday 27 February, the day before Wilson's proposed announcement, Butler noticed that 17 March, Saint Patrick's Day, was listed as a bank holiday in Ireland. If this was a bank holiday in Northern Ireland as well as in the Republic, the time allowed by the government would be one day shorter than the minimum prescribed.

At such moments, blind panic is generally balanced by the reassuring certainty that professionals could not make such elementary mistakes.

* Sir William Armstrong (later Lord Armstrong of Sanderstead, 1915–80) was Permanent Secretary at the Treasury from 1962 and was appointed head of the Home Civil Service in 1968. He suffered a breakdown during the dispute with the miners in 1973 and retired soon after.

Nonetheless Butler promptly telephoned the Chancellor's Private Secretary to alert him to the possible problem. He too at first reassured Butler that of course the government would have foreseen this. In the event, however, the question turned out to be more complex. The Bank Holidays Act that designated 17 March a bank holiday had been passed in 1871, before the partition of Ireland. Thus, by default, it was legally a holiday in Northern Ireland, part of the United Kingdom. Parliament's dissolution on 10 March would, therefore, be one day too late. The Queen was abroad on 28 February, and frantic efforts were made to reach her to obtain approval for dissolution of Parliament on 9 March. That approval was obtained and the legal timetable was duly observed. The Prime Minister and the staff at No. 10 were fulsome in thanking Butler for his attention to detail.

The snap election succeeded in establishing the Wilson government with a greatly increased majority. The Conservative Party suffered a swing against them of 1.5 per cent, losing fifty-two seats, of which forty-eight went to Labour. With a majority of almost 100, Wilson was in a vastly stronger position. Almost immediately, however, the government was besieged with a series of problems, which collectively gave the Prime Minister the look of a man under siege – an image that, after the summer of 1966, he never quite lost.

The Budget of 1966, with the introduction of the Selective Employment Tax, went some way to restoring confidence in sterling, but the question of devaluation was ever present, the issue that ministers wanted to go away and which they rarely addressed. Butler was involved in both matters – in the case of the SET, in devising the most efficient method of collecting the tax while, at the same time, distributing the load of a discriminatory tax fairly.

The Chancellor's presentation of the Budget to the House of Commons involved what Butler describes as 'a sort of striptease act, progressively ruling out increases in the existing taxes before coming to the announcement of the Selective Employment Tax'. Jim Callaghan was committed to avoiding increases in existing taxes – a central plank of the government's election platform – but, as his speech progressed, successively eschewing potential sources of income, so confidence in the British economy eroded. As a result there was a huge flight from sterling while the Budget proposals were being announced. Within a month, it seemed that devaluation was inevitable and when, on 4 July, the June gold figures showed a huge drain on sterling, the Treasury were resigned.

Two days later, Georges Pompidou visited London and indicated to reporters that British entry to the EEC would not be possible unless tough action were taken first. The *Financial Times* reported that 'a high French source, questioned ... on what would constitute an improvement sufficient to permit British entry into the Market, said that as an example one would no longer expect there to be a sterling crisis every few months'.[16]

Continued pressure was exerted on the government, and heavy selling of sterling continued in the second half of the year. Butler watched with concern as the Labour leaders failed to agree on the next step. George Brown, Secretary for Economic Affairs, favoured devaluation as a means to industrial expansion, and pressed Callaghan to devalue. Wilson was determined to resist such pressure; to make devaluation effective would have involved diverting real resources from the domestic market to exports at a time when resources were fully strained.[17] Throughout July, the Bank of England poured in reserves to support sterling. The Cabinet was divided, opposed to taking any action under pressure. Brown continued to argue that devaluation was essential for growth, threatening to resign unless Cabinet agreed.

In the short term, devaluation was avoided, but poor trade figures, the disruption of oil supplies as a result of the Arab-Israeli war, and a dock strike in Liverpool ultimately forced the government's hand. The inevitability of devaluation became apparent just as Butler's personal life was undergoing radical changes: he and Jill became parents for the second time when Catherine Nell was born in January 1967.

After a holiday in Sansepolcro in the summer of 1967, Butler returned during the week that the ruling triumvirate of the Labour government – Harold Wilson, George Brown (now Foreign Secretary) and Jim Callaghan – had reached the decision that devaluation of the pound could no longer be avoided. That decision was taken in July, and from then until November, when the devaluation was announced, preparations were handled at the Treasury in extreme secrecy. This required considerable agility of the government to avoid admitting that devaluation was possible, even imminent. On the morning of 16 November, a decision was taken in Cabinet to announce a devaluation of 14.3 per cent two days later. That same day, Jim Callaghan, Chancellor of the Exchequer, asked whether devaluation was the optimum solution to Britain's economic problems, replied swiftly but not altogether candidly: 'I have nothing to add to or to subtract from anything I have said on previous occasions on the subject of devaluation and, in any case, it does not arise from my original Answer.'[18]

Once the decision to devalue was taken in Cabinet, events needed to move swiftly, and Butler had the responsibility for the initial announcement that would be made on the evening of 18 November. This announcement was brief and factual, timed to be heard when the world's financial markets were closed on Saturday night. It was followed by a more comprehensive statement by the Prime Minister the following night. The operation was neatly and efficiently executed and Callaghan thanked everyone who had been involved in it, congratulating them on 'the efficiency and devotion of those who took part in the operation'.[19]

In 1967, devaluation was widely seen as an extreme measure, a statement of economic failure. Wilson and Callaghan, not unnaturally, were anxious that their action should not be seen as particularly drastic. The simple draft of the announcement, therefore, underwent seventeen redraftings before the final version was agreed. For Butler, it was his first experience of the art of 'spin'. He later recalled that he 'began to feel that the politicians were paying more attention to the nuances of the words than to the substance of the measures which were to accompany devaluation'.[20]

This was undoubtedly true – particularly as the government itself was feeling its way, hesitant to take strong steps to reduce demand. The November devaluation, therefore, was the first action taken in response to trade deficits, speculative action against sterling, and nagging balance of payments crises. Further action was needed, and this ultimately came to pass in the 1968 Budget. By then, Callaghan, to Butler's satisfaction, had been replaced at the Treasury by the more urbane and intellectual Roy Jenkins.

Butler was not alone in feeling comfortable with Jenkins at the Exchequer. William Armstrong's description of senior civil servants in the 1960s was probably still accurate in 1970. After Gaitskell's death in 1963 and Rab Butler's retirement in 1965, the two lived on in the spectre of 'Mr Butskell', that elusive politician, at once solid and dependable, innovative and dynamic. Butler remembers that 'senior civil servants were at ease with the non-polarised statist approach to government in the 1960s'. Speaking entirely personally, he recalls that he voted for the winning party in all general elections up to 1974.[21]

As secretary of the Budget Committee, Butler was principally occupied with the twin issues of government expenditure and taxation, necessary but intellectually unexciting aspects of the national economy. He was delighted, therefore, when, after three years in that position, he learned that his next job would be in the overseas section dealing with exchange control.

The 1968 Budget saw a significant 'first' when it took £900 million out of the economy. That amount is relatively unremarkable today, but at the time it was the largest amount ever imposed in public taxation. So daunting was the total that there was severe doubt at the Treasury as to whether the public would accept it. Butler accordingly proposed a compulsory 'bond issue', by which additional taxation would be levied in the form of a loan to the government. When the economy improved, this would be repaid to the taxpayer. Butler comments ruefully, with the benefit of age and experience, that the proposal was not taken seriously by his superiors at the Treasury.[22]

One further event marked 1968 as important in Butler's life. Jill and he had their third and final child – Andrew, whose arrival gave his father particular pleasure. Happy with his two daughters, he nonetheless looked forward to playing rugby and other sports with a boy.

His new posting to exchange control would bring him closer to the workings of the financial system and, in preparation for his new responsibilities, he was seconded to the Bank of England for a six-month induction course. Sir Montagu Norman, Governor of the Bank from 1920 to 1944, had decreed that exchanges with the Treasury were not in the public interest. Butler believes that this suspension of the exchanges reflected a difference in attitudes at the Bank and at the Treasury towards the sacrosanctity of the value of sterling.

In 1966, however, when Leslie O'Brien took over as Governor, he and Sir William Armstrong decided to reintroduce the practice of exchanges between the two organisations. As with the course on economics and statistics,

Butler was only the second Treasury man to be seconded.* Once again, he happened to be in just the place at the right time for his career. Armstrong, however, was careful to warn him to tread with caution as the exchanges were in an experimental stage. Butler remained on his best behaviour, despite finding the Bank's customs amusingly archaic.†

The six months were important and instructive, although not over-taxing. He discovered early that he was not expected to do any practical or constructive work; instead he was to become familiar with all aspects of the City of London – first at the Bank of England itself, later with a variety of City institutions. He not only learned how the system functioned, but, perhaps more importantly, he made contacts with men of his own age (he admits that there were very few women to be found at the Bank) who would rise in the City *pari passu* with his own rise in the Civil Service. One such contact was Eddie George, nicknamed 'Steady Eddie', who had joined the Bank in 1962 and would be its Governor from 1993 to 2003.

During the 1960s, exchange control was exercised in many forms. The economic crisis of 1961 brought a halt to the dismantling of controls and, for the balance of the Wilson government's time in office, direct investment outside the sterling area, access to the investment currency market, private purchase of overseas property, together with all forms of export of sterling, were tightly controlled.‡ The Treasury was responsible for the formulation of policy, which was then implemented by the Bank. As the 'man from the Treasury' with the power to approve or deny applications for offshore funds, Butler commanded the respect – but sometimes also attracted the contempt – of wealthy and powerful merchant bankers seeking Treasury approval for use of funds offshore.

In a 1999 lecture, Butler looked back at his Oxford years, commenting that at Univ he had dined under the portraits of Clement Attlee and Lord

---

* The first had been David Walker, the Cambridge economist who had been ranked second after Butler in the entrance exam.

† It particularly amused him that Bank officers were expected to stand up to receive a telephone call from a direct superior. The daily ritual of 'Books', each day at 11.00 a.m. involved a presentation of the Bank's assets and liabilities in a ledger with no alterations or erasures. Any error had to be corrected by scraping the ledger page with a razor blade.

‡ The allowance for travel overseas was £50 per person.

Beveridge, that Harold Wilson, then a rising star in the Labour Party, was very much a presence in the college's socialist tradition. By 1970, he had first-hand experience of Wilson's first government. Despite a natural respect for tradition, Butler was an idealist who, in common with many of his generation, had hoped for great things from the new government. In common with many of his generation, he was deeply disappointed.

The end of the Labour government and Harold Wilson's departure from Downing Street in June 1970 was a cause for celebration in the City of London. The much-trumpeted economic recovery was thrown into question by the trade figures for May, released on 15 June. A deficit of £31 million added fuel to the growing doubts about Labour's 'economic miracle'. Yet Wilson's government remained favourites – by odds of up to 34–1 on – to return to power. Watching the results in a Liverpool hotel, the Prime Minister was jolted to attention by a 5.3 per cent swing to the Tories in Guildford.[23] Tony Benn recalled that 'in a fraction of a second one went from a pretty confident belief in victory to absolute certainty of defeat. It was quite a remarkable experience'.[24]

Barbara Castle, who had held three Cabinet appointments during the six years, recalled that even though Tory leader Heath was 'stiff and uncharismatic' and was receiving an unsympathetic press, she feared that 'there is a silent majority sitting behind its lace curtains, waiting to come out and vote Tory'.[25] Wilson, too, distrusted the bookmakers' odds. 'I was one of the few who had doubts', he wrote, 'though I would have found it difficult to rationalise them.'[26] The Tory victory was, probably correctly, attributed by Wilson to an all-round decline in confidence in the Labour government, crystallised bizarrely by England's defeat by Germany in the quarter-final round of the World Cup. Rising prices, worsening industrial relations, the fear of further devaluation – all seemed to be encapsulated in the football match played in Mexico.

Another explanation, widely adopted – as it was convenient to have someone tangible to blame – was offered by Peter Jenkins in *The Guardian*. Roy Jenkins could, he wrote, have budgeted more generously for growth – a view confirmed by figures released by the Central Statistical Office. The Chancellor had, the article maintained, made the mistake of 'fighting on a balance of payments surplus when the housekeeping money was still in deficit' and had thus lost the election.[27]

Thus the decade that had begun in optimistic expectation of a quiet revolution in British *mores*, of a moderate Butskellite majority, gradually shedding the outdated philosophies of the Tories in the 1950s, ended with the hasty departure of the Wilsons by the back door of 10 Downing Street, their government not only defeated but discredited and savaged at the ballot box. Mary Wilson saw the manner of the handover of power as 'barbarous'. It was, she complained, 'like having the bailiffs in'.[28]

There was disappointment, too, among the twenty-something professionals who, in 1964, had welcomed the first Labour government for thirteen years. Butler 'was disappointed with the manipulation and backbiting'. Heath had been confident that he could lead the Tories back to power and was creating a radical free-market policy. Whether or not this was realistic, it was more congruent with the spirit of modernity that had brought Wilson to power. There was real policy, as opposed to politicking, Butler recalls. 'We all wanted "action not words".'[29]

In 1951, six years after winning a landslide victory, Clement Attlee's Labour government had yielded to a senescent Churchill. The socialist experiment, crowed the Tories, was over. Now, almost twenty years later, Robin Butler and those young centrist idealists who had come of age in the complacent years of Macmillan, might reluctantly have agreed with incoming Home Secretary Reggie Maudling's comment that 'Britain is a Conservative country that sometimes votes Labour'.[30]

CHAPTER 4

THE QUIET REVOLUTION AND THE THINK TANK, 1970–1972

IN RETROSPECT, IT IS astonishing that the Heath government lasted for less than four years, so impressive were the government's stated ambitions on entry and so tarnished its record by February 1974. In a very short time, the widespread optimism that accompanied the election of a modern, meritocratic Conservative government evaporated. The Prime Minister was not a popular leader. A loner, whom many senior Conservatives found unacceptable, he would certainly have been sacrificed if the Tories had lost the 1970 election. His position was further undermined by the very public quarrel that he was conducting with Enoch Powell, first over immigration, then ranging over the strategic direction of the Conservative Party.

From January 1970, when Heath organised the Selsdon Park conference, public perception, stimulated by the press, had been that the Tories were moving to the right and that immigration and law and order were to be legislative priorities. The apparent move to the right prompted Wilson to coin the phrase 'Selsdon Man' to characterise the senior Tories and what he described as their 'atavistic desire to reverse the course of 25 years of social revolution'.

The philosophy of the putative Conservative government was laid out in the election manifesto *A Better Tomorrow*, which marked the departure of the party from the post-war consensus and 'One Nation' Toryism. There would be 'a new style of government' and 'a fresh approach to the taking of decisions'. The government would not be compelled to operate with inadequate advice. Instead, 'it should use up-to-date techniques for assessing the situation'. It should be 'deliberate and thorough'.[1]

All of which must have sounded alarming to Robert Armstrong and his centrist colleagues in the Civil Service.* Not only was the government moving to the right; it was planning to rely on external advisers to help it move in that direction. In his Downing Street appointments, at least, Heath favoured civil servants, appointing Armstrong his Principal Private Secretary and Donald Maitland press officer.

As a guiding principle, Heath gave the impression of wanting to operate in a manner as unlike that of Harold Wilson as possible. Wilson had worked hard to identify himself with the youthful image of John Kennedy; Heath was no less industrious in setting out to demonstrate that his team was more in tune with Camelot than the 'elderly, inflated and unprepared' Labour administration.[2] To Butler, the new government offered seriousness after the capriciousness of Labour, and he hoped for their success.[3]

Heath's general strategy was to introduce fresh blood to the government's decision-making process, to impose his policies on the Treasury through a strong Chancellor, and to ensure, through continuous review, that his government remained faithful to the promises on which it was elected. He would, as he intimated in his speech to the Tory Party conference in October, 'have to embark on a change so radical, a revolution so quiet and yet so total, that it will go … far beyond this decade and way into the 1980s'.[4]

This 'quiet revolution' was to be spearheaded by bold initiatives introduced by the best and brightest in Britain. The Prime Minister's rhetoric gave the impression of a radical overhaul of the mixed economy, as Jean Campbell wrote in the *Evening Standard*: 'It was aggressive Toryism at last. A far cry from the defensive Toryism of Rab Butler which had shared room and board with Socialism for the last twenty-two years. Heath was pulling down the Butler boarding house … Instead he plans to build a skyscraper with self-operating lifts.'[5]

The most dramatic difference in Downing Street personnel was between

* Robert Armstrong (later Lord Armstrong of Ilminster) was Principal Private Secretary to the Prime Minister from 1970 to 1975, thus serving both Edward Heath and Harold Wilson.

Wilson's political secretary Marcia Williams and Heath's choice for that position, Douglas Hurd. A Foreign Office man committed to Heath's quiet revolution, Hurd recalled wistfully almost a decade later: 'I, and I believe others, thought there was a real chance in 1970 that Mr Heath and his colleagues would break out of inherited attitudes and make possible a sharply higher level of achievement by the British people.'[6] Butler and his contemporaries were looking for the new government to reverse the trend of stagnation.[7]

Several strands made up the 'quiet revolution', some institutional, others more visible and directly related to public spending and the professed 'dash for growth'. 'Super-Ministries' were created in an attempt to streamline decision-making and reduce the Cabinet load. The system of Programme Analysis and Review was introduced to reduce bureaucratic waste. This was viewed askance by the Treasury and, as Peter Hennessy recorded, 'was [removed] from the grasp of Heath's businessmen in the Civil Service Department and [drawn] into their own citadel in Great George Street from which it never emerged alive'.[8] Businessmen joined the management teams of several departments in an attempt to sharpen the bureaucracy.

Unsurprisingly, mandarins in the Civil Service reacted with suspicion to the recruitment of temporaries, amateurs who, after a brief induction course, would pass judgement on the professionals in Whitehall. William Armstrong, however, recognised that businessmen would have no more than a peripheral role and that ministers and their departments would retain 'central' control.[9]

While much of this affected the Civil Service, particularly the Treasury, little had any immediate, direct effect on the young Butler, too junior to be involved in the turf wars provoked by the Heath government. By the autumn of 1970, however, a radical innovation brought Butler into the mainstream of government planning and strategy.

The United Kingdom does not have an official Department of the Prime Minister; the question of whether or not it needs one is endlessly debated. By the time Heath became Prime Minister in 1970, he had developed the conviction that 'we needed to change the structure of government, based upon the thorough examination we had carried out in opposition'.[10] The first, immediate innovation was the reduction of the size of the Cabinet; two new departments – Environment and Trade and Industry – were created to replace five existing ministries.* The system of Programme Analysis Review was developed 'to assess the makeup of each government department, to see whether the taxpayer was getting value for money'.[11]

In Heath's own opinion, the most important and effective reform that the new government introduced was the setting up of the Central Policy Review Staff (CPRS), commonly known as the 'Think Tank'. Heath saw it as 'a group of some twenty people, mostly young and selected from the universities, business and the civil service'. Encouraged to think the unthinkable or, at least, to 'express the uncomfortable', it existed to 'keep under review the country's economic performance … to undertake studies in depth of major long-term issues which transcended departmental boundaries' and to 'provide collective briefs for the Cabinet, or sometimes personal briefs for the Prime Minister, on specific issues being submitted to Cabinet or Cabinet committees for ministerial approval'.[12]

The emergence of the CPRS had been preceded by a long germination, tracing its development to 1916, the date of birth of the Cabinet Secretariat, under Colonel Maurice Hankey, and the Policy Unit, known as 'the Garden Suburb' for its accommodation in huts in the garden of 10 Downing Street. Hankey, the first Cabinet Secretary, remained in place until 1938, when Sir Edward Bridges succeeded him.

Despite the apparent continuity of the Policy Unit, between the wars there was a void at the centre, prompting Leo Amery, when he was Secretary of State for India, to comment that 'the one thing that is hardly ever discussed is general policy'. There was, he said, very little Cabinet policy on any subject, for the simple reason that it was no one's job to coordinate its elements. 'There are', he complained, 'only departmental policies.'[13] Churchill made some progress towards changing that, bringing his personal staff from the Admiralty to 10 Downing Street in 1940. His group of approximately twenty was very similar in outlook and purpose to the CPRS of thirty years later.

In 1968, Heath had established a small working group of former civil

* The Department of the Environment replaced the ministries of Housing and Local Government, Transport, and Public Building and Works. The Department of Trade and Industry merged the Board of Trade and the Ministry of Technology.

servants under the chairmanship of Baroness Sharp.* As a Permanent Secretary, Lady Sharp had observed ministers wading through papers outside their departments' fields, which nonetheless they were expected to evaluate. She had also had a revealing exchange with Harold Macmillan, who lamented to her over lunch that he had 'the biggest job [he had] ever had and less help in doing it than [he had] ever known'. This was congruent with her view that there was a gap at the centre of government machinery. Something was needed to serve the Prime Minister and the Cabinet.[14]

The Prime Minister needed a small staff to examine proposals from the point of view of long-term national interest, offering pragmatic recommendations rather than the briefings of the Civil Service with their 'on the one hand ... on the other hand' approach. This central staff would be tasked to help ministers develop a strategy for government as a whole. Heath expressed this need bluntly: 'Cabinets often seemed to be dealing with the day-to-day problems with no real opportunity to address strategy.'[15] This weakness was particularly in evidence in the case of a new government. When Heath outlined plans to members of his first staff after the 1970 election, he commented that, for as long as it was in opposition, the shadow Cabinet was able to consider policy as a whole and to take a longer-term view of things. Once the shadow Cabinet became a government, however, that luxury evaporated. It was to re-enable that perspective that he founded the Think Tank.[16]

From the very conception of the CPRS, it was clear to the Cabinet Secretary Burke Trend that he, rather than the Prime Minister, must control the 'central capability', and that the CPRS should be a resource for the Cabinet rather than an independent unit functioning for the sole benefit of the Prime Minister. Much, therefore, would hang on the individual appointed to lead the group. Mark Schreiber, special adviser to the Prime Minister, was adamant that this be a political appointment and that control be removed from the Civil Service. Lord Jellicoe, Leader of the House of Lords and Lord Privy Seal, made a broad search for possible candidates and submitted three names – Professor Dick Ross, Ralph Turvey and Robert Marshall – to the

* Baroness Sharp had recently retired from the position of Permanent Secretary at the Ministry of Housing and Local Government.

Prime Minister.[17] Ross, an economist working for the OECD in Paris, and Christopher ('Kit') McMahon, an economist with the Bank of England, were most favoured by Heath and his advisers.[18] Initially, Heath inclined towards McMahon, a 43-year-old Australian who was not afraid to speak his mind, and a formal offer was made to him in mid-September 1970. To the consternation of Heath and his advisers, McMahon turned it down flat, preferring to stay at the Bank.[19]

Ross, it was decided by Trend, head of the Home Civil Service William Armstrong and Principal Private Secretary Robert Armstrong, 'might not have enough cutting edge'[20] – or, as Butler explains it, more pithily, 'he was vacillating and indecisive'.[21] The post was accordingly offered to Professor Hugh Ford, a lecturer at Imperial College, despite Robert Armstrong's concern that he lacked experience in the ways of Whitehall.[22] When Ford at first accepted then, suddenly, refused the offer,[23] there was panic at No. 10. Time was running out to have the unit operating by October, Heath's deadline. Then, in early October, like some *deus ex machina*, Victor Rothschild appeared at Downing Street to speak to Trend about a review of government research and development that he was conducting. Trend, who knew Lord Rothschild and was familiar with his exotic record, decided that he had stumbled on the right candidate and proposed him to Heath as the unit's director.* Heath promptly agreed. Rothschild, summoned to Downing Street, later recorded his first exchange with the new Prime Minister:

> *Mr Heath:* 'It's funny we have never met before.' Then there was a sort of row of dots. I could not think what to say; after a while, I said, rather desperately: 'Prime Minister, do you not think it would be better to have an economist in charge of this Unit?'
>
> *Mr Heath:* 'I did economics at Oxford.' Another row of dots. Again after a while, I said rather desperately: 'Prime Minister, could you give me an example of the type of problem you want the Unit to tackle?'

---

* Victor Rothschild had worked for the Security Service (MI5) during the Second World War, was by profession a biologist at Cambridge University, and had held senior executive positions with Shell and with the family business N. M. Rothschild and Company, a prominent merchant bank.

> *Mr Heath:* 'Concorde.' At that moment I thought, perhaps wrongly, that I detected some anguished vibrations emanating from Sir Burke Trend and Sir William Armstrong, as they then were, who were hovering in the background. There was some justification for their anguish, if I did not imagine it, because an hour beforehand they had told me it was precisely things like Concorde that the Government Think Tank would *not* be expected to study.[24]

In spite of the silences and 'rows of dots', Heath was confident that Rothschild was the right man, and the appointment was announced on 29 October.[25] Rothschild was about to retire as head of research at Shell, and the company's CEO urged him to take an extended holiday before starting his new assignment. Rothschild made a detour to Washington to speak to Henry Kissinger and contacts in the Office of Management and Budget about what he saw as the Prime Minister's department. He rejected not only the American model, but also the '*bons mots* of Robert Wade-Gery – "sabotaging the smooth working of the Whitehall machine" – or of Dick Ross – "thinking the unthinkable"'. Instead, 'we needed excellent analytical brains … I thought we needed about sixteen graduates, half from within the Civil Service and half from outside.'[26]

The description of the Think Tank with which Rothschild most agreed came from one of its members. Its functions were:

- Sabotaging the over-smooth functioning of the machinery of Government.
- Providing a Central Department which has no departmental axe to grind but does have overt policy status and which can attempt a synoptic view of policy.
- Providing a Central reinforcement for those civil servants in Whitehall who are trying to retain their creativity and not be totally submerged in the bureaucracy.
- Devising a more rational system of decision-making between competing programmes.
- Advising the Cabinet collectively, and the Prime Minister, on major issues of policy relating to the Government's strategy.

- Focusing the attention of Ministers on the right questions to ask about their own colleagues' business.
- Bringing in ideas from the outside world.[27]

The work of the CPRS can be summarised under three headings: (1) six-monthly review of the government's strategy, to Cabinet and, separately, to middle and junior ministers; (2) special studies requested or approved by the Cabinet; (3) collective briefs.[28]

The appointment of Rothschild was inspired. Not only was he widely talented and studiedly eccentric – not at all a typical Heath acolyte – he had also worked in MI5 during the war and did not shrink from speaking truth to power. Additionally, as a member, admittedly increasingly lukewarm, of the Labour Party, he escaped accusations of cronyism. He won respect from ministers, and maintained a distance from Whitehall's mandarins. To Butler, he was a different kind of force, 'a stimulating maverick, naive in the ways of government'.[29]

That 'different kind of force' was apparent in the memoranda that were fired, like torpedoes, from Rothschild's desk. There was never any ambiguity, as a memo to Professor Claus Moser, the director of the Central Statistical Office revealed. 'Some organisational questions require resolution', Rothschild wrote, 'before the Population Unit, group or section starts work.' He then disposed of four possible organisational steps, including a Royal Commission, a Standing Royal Commission, a unit under the supervision of the Chief Scientific Officer, and a unit in the Cabinet Office, reporting to Burke Trend. For different reasons he rejects them all. He then questions whether the terms of reference are the right ones, whether the necessary work is being done, whether the right material is available, and how many people of what qualifications would be needed to do the job. He concludes his four-paragraph memo with the question: 'Do you agree with me that the end product of the work of the population group should be recommendations for action and, if you do, would you care to give me one example of the type of recommendation you have in mind[?]'[30] This was not the circumlocution to which Butler had become accustomed in Civil Service memoranda.

After speaking to Trend, Lord Rothschild assembled his team. He saw

Britain's list of 'the great and the good' as too exclusive. It was impossible to be on the list, he complained, unless one was aged fifty-three or more, had an upper middle-class accent and a degree from Oxford or Cambridge and was a member of the Reform Club. The government, therefore, drew its advice from a very narrow group. This would not occur with the CPRS.

The assembled group comprised the director and two assistant directors, supported, predictably, by a group of young high-fliers, all with impressive academic credentials.[31] The unit included a total of around twenty, which was also the number that would fit around the conference table in Rothschild's office. Some were civil servants, from all over Whitehall, including Butler from the Treasury; there was always a brace of economists and usually one member from Shell or BP. The balance hailed from academe or industry. The average length of secondment was two years, the maximum term for which the Treasury would allow Butler to be absent; the mandarins also stipulated that Rothschild not poach anyone else from the Treasury.[32]

In normal circumstances, a 33-year-old civil servant would have little or no influence over policy, but this was not a normal group. Indeed, Rothschild saw the unconventional nature of the CPRS as central to its effectiveness. The average age was about thirty-five, and William Waldegrave was a mere twenty-five years old when he joined the group in early 1971. He describes his feelings of being 'the baby' of the group among 'colleagues [with] more *gravitas*: Robin Butler, future cabinet secretary; Peter Carey, war hero and future permanent secretary; Robert Wade-Gery, fellow of All Souls and future High Commissioner in India; and many others'.[33]

Butler's superiors at the Treasury were torn between disapproval of the 'irregular' nature of the group, and realistic recognition that, if the CPRS were to establish itself, there should be a Treasury man involved. Amid this ambivalence, Butler joined the group on 1 February 1971. At the group's first full meeting on that Monday morning, Butler recalls, 'We all sat around the table in Victor [Rothschild]'s room in the Cabinet … Victor's opening words were, "What the bloody hell do we do now?"'[34]

Such showmanship characterised Rothschild's handling of the CPRS. It was his own project, to which he gave character, informality and style. He subsidised the 'Tank' beyond the meagre government finances provided, while stressing that he was an independent operator, enjoying unique direct access to the Prime Minister. In every possible way – from privileged access to the special binding of CPRS memoranda, distinctively printed with red covers – Rothschild strove to underline the independent charter of the Think Tank. It was 'for' the government, but not a tool of the party.

To young members of the 'Tank', Rothschild's 'boys and girls', the early years of the CPRS provided an unparalleled intellectual experience. Butler quickly adapted to Rothschild's original and unconventional methods and a lasting friendship developed between the two. For the younger man, quick to identify individual talents and flaws, and a relentless pigeon-holer, Rothschild was an original – and that recognition pleased Butler greatly.

Butler's delight in Rothschild's unconventional methods was not, however, universally shared. In a minute to political secretary Douglas Hurd, Mark Schreiber* expressed concerns that illustrate the extent to which the CPRS was regarded as a potential threat to Whitehall custom and practice, needing 'rather close political direction from the top to focus their efforts onto what they alone can do rather than allowing them to diffuse their limited resources onto what departments should be doing'.[35] This was the principal focus of the assaults from Whitehall. Trend himself became involved and wrote to the Prime Minister in the first month of the life of the Think Tank, emphasising his hope 'that the CPRS will seek to work in cooperation, not competition, with Departments. Unless this is accepted – by both parties – from the outset, the experiment will fail.'[36]

The hallmark of the group was the absence of hierarchy and specialisation. Rothschild delighted in the youth of his acolytes and deliberately used younger members as his emissaries, regardless of the age and seniority of those with whom they had to deal. This access and autonomy was a novelty for an upwardly mobile civil servant, accustomed to automatically deferring to his seniors. 'One of my young men will come and see you,' he would say to his 'clients'. Several of the 'young men' were female.

The group met each Monday morning and all members were expected

* Schreiber worked for the Conservative Party Research Department and advised Edward Heath from 1970 to 1974. He was ennobled as Lord Marlesford in 1991.

to attend, if at all possible. These were important sessions, as CPRS members 'shared the feelings of being both a privileged and somewhat beleaguered group'.[37] Privileged because they enjoyed extraordinary access to the Prime Minister and Cabinet; beleaguered because they were regarded with suspicion, even resentment, by other civil servants, and had to battle with the machine if they were to do any good. Departments initially opposed the collective briefs produced by the CPRS because they were independent analyses, produced by 'a group of people uncontaminated by years of Whitehall experience'.[38]

At first the Think Tank's activities were shrouded in exceptional secrecy. Trend told Rothschild that he was allowed to admit that 'the Government's Think Tank took an interest in certain subjects, apart from a few sensitive ones', but 'in no circumstances admit that [the CPRS] had written a report on any of them'.[39] This secrecy, combined with the feeling of being a group of vigilantes, helped to build a strong sense of team solidarity. Tank members lunched together in the canteen, avoiding the Cabinet Office mess. They formed a wine-buying syndicate and a duplicate bridge team 'which competed without distinction in the lower reaches of the bottom division of the Civil Service bridge league'.[40]

As juniors, Butler and Waldegrave were thrown together from the start, working in an attic eyrie in the Cabinet Office. When Waldegrave's sister, Lady Susan Hussey, telephoned one day, Butler answered the phone in the approved manner, 'Waldegrave's telephone; Butler speaking'. Lady Susan was impressed that after just a week in the Civil Service her brother had a telephone butler.[41] The two young men worked closely together and, years later, Waldegrave recalled the thrill and unconventional nature of their work with the CPRS:

> At Chequers … we told them (the Cabinet) how the government was doing and what it should do next. Robin and I were in charge of this. We designed large charts that were not circulated in advance – against all protocol – so that departments could not brief against them in advance. 'How could we circulate them?' we would argue. 'They won't fit in the regulation secure envelopes.'

They pinned the charts to the linen-fold panelling in the upstairs drawing room at Chequers and, when they were reprimanded for this vandalism, Butler replied that they were only using holes that had already been made. 'I knew then', Waldegrave commented, 'that he would one day be cabinet secretary and head of the civil service, KG, GCB, CVO and a peer.'[42] Theirs was an association that was to develop into a close friendship – hardly surprising, for Waldegrave's description of his teenage heroes and ambitions could have been written by Butler. They had read Greats not

> because it carried most prestige, not because you wanted to be the next Wilamowitz. F. E.'s repartee was the best, and Lord Randolph's invective,* but because it was a culture of competition, pure and simple – of winning, of life as sport, with a podium finish the only thing that mattered and the top spot all that could be admitted as a possibility.[43]

Heath's vision of a group that 'expressed the uncomfortable' was quickly realised. The laudable principle of the new Tory government was to treat no issue as beyond discussion and possible reform. In this, of course, its goals were in direct conflict with the 'Sir Humphrey' methods of the Civil Service. Butler was thus positioned at the meeting point of political leaders and mandarins, and of the collective power of Cabinet and the executive power of the Prime Minister. 'Emphasis was placed on the need to brief each Cabinet Minister about matters which were *not* the concern of his or her department', Rothschild wrote, 'but on which the Cabinet was expected to take decisions.'[44] This is completely congruent with Heath's professionalism and difficult to imagine in the 'gentlemen's' Cabinets of generalists in the past.

One feature common to many of the issues tackled by the 'Tank' was that several departments were affected – a feature which had historically contributed to the apparent insolubility of those issues. Concorde was a prime example of this: it involved not only the Department of Trade and Industry

---

* The references are to Ulrich von Wilamowitz-Moellendorff, German philologist, to F. E. Smith, Lord Birkenhead, ever known to friends and colleagues as 'F. E.', and to Lord Randolph Churchill, father of Sir Winston. Though Waldegrave does say immediately following this passage, 'I think now it is a poor model for life.'

but, as a joint venture with France, it brought the Foreign Office into its orbit. Because of noise problems, the Department of the Environment was affected; for obvious reasons the Treasury was very much involved. To Rothschild's delight, the 'Tank' was located in the Cabinet Office 'because the Cabinet Secretariat is better informed than any other part of Whitehall as to what Ministers will have to attend to in the future'.[45] As an experience of working close to the centre of government, it was intoxicating for Butler and Waldegrave, even if their shared office was in the attic.

One issue that severely tested and ultimately damaged the executive power of the Prime Minister was that of the Upper Clyde Shipbuilders (UCS). In his memoirs, Heath harangues the 1964–70 Wilson government, particularly in relation to UCS. Urged by Tony Benn, the government had formed a conglomerate comprising, on the one hand, two shipyards in financial difficulties and, on the other, the Yarrow yard, a naval shipbuilder that, Heath maintained, should never have been compelled to join the merger.[46] Despite attempts by Heath and John Davies, the Secretary of State for Trade and Industry, to salvage a viable company from the ailing conglomerate, UCS went into receivership in June 1971.

Heath had set up an advisory group that worked together with the Think Tank to find a solution that would preserve two of the yards. However, the government's insistence on not supporting lame ducks destroyed confidence in UCS and the company was forced into liquidation. When the trade union leaders staged a 'work-in', public sympathy swung behind the company's putatively redundant workforce and against the government. Ultimately, cornered by the shop stewards and public opinion, Heath and Davies were compelled to step down. In its first attempt to impose a non-interventionist approach on British industry, the Heath government suffered a serious defeat.

The debacle of the Upper Clyde Shipbuilders and the consequent damage to the government's public image led Heath to charge the Think Tank with the task of identifying potential corporate disasters before they occurred. This 'early warning system', basing its work on the examples of Rolls Royce (of which more below) and UCS, ranged over the gamut of industrial companies in Britain. Other projects considered by the 'Tank' involved energy, the shipbuilding industry, the coal industry, government research and development, the British computer industry, public expenditure, nuclear reactor policy, race relations, energy conservation, worker participation, the UK population, electric cars – and the government's strategy, which, Rothschild commented, 'more or less covers everything'.[47]

The style of the reports was not mellifluous, but brutally direct. Intentionally so: the language in which they were couched was the very antithesis of that regularly used by the Civil Service. Of the reports produced during Butler's time at the Think Tank, 'The Future of the Concorde' was perhaps the most controversial. This opened in typical Rothschild style with the statement: 'Concorde is a commercial disaster.'[48] Having gained the reader's attention, it continued with the more emollient points that (1) a point of no return had already been passed, and (2) the French would sue if Britain abandoned the project. So the government should press on, complete the project rapidly, and market it aggressively. Rothschild later told Peter Hennessy that the report had contained a coda – 'And for God's sake stop bellyaching about it, just get on with it.'[49]

Another clash between commercial and political considerations arose over the supply of Rolls Royce RB211 engines to Lockheed for the new L-1011 Tri-Star aircraft. Eager to secure the Lockheed order and casually underestimating the cost of stipulated design modifications, Rolls Royce faced financial ruin in 1970 unless the government was able to intervene and either supply or secure financial assistance to the tune of approximately £60 million – an estimate which rapidly grew to £150 million.

Rolls Royce employed over 80,000 people, largely in areas of high unemployment, such as Scotland and Northern Ireland. Its products were central to British defence capabilities. The RB211 engine 'was a potential market leader in just the kind of high-technology field that [the government] was keen to encourage'.[50] In addition to the damage that a collapse of Rolls Royce would do to relations with Washington, there was concern that it would do irreparable damage to British prestige worldwide.

It was vital, therefore, that some formula be found whereby the government brought about the salvation of Rolls Royce in a manner compatible with declared Tory industrial policy. This, the Think Tank recommended, could be achieved by separating the aero-engine, marine engine and industrial divisions of the company and injecting them into a newly formed company Rolls Royce (1971) Ltd. That would allow the original company to go into liquidation, while creating an entity that could later be sold to private investors as a profitable going concern. The solution was accepted by Cabinet and by President Nixon and Congress. It was, Butler commented later, 'heady stuff'.

Heady it certainly was. The role was also ambiguous for Butler in his capacity as a representative of the Treasury. It was common knowledge that Heath wanted to reduce the power of the Treasury and, within days of the Tories' win at the 1970 election, the Treasury 'had begun a rearguard action to defend itself against any potential reduction of its power'.[51] Despite his standing with Burke Trend, who had recommended him to Rothschild, Butler needed to tread carefully in case he should be accused by Civil Service colleagues of 'sleeping with the enemy'. This became clear to him in the summer of 1971 when he had the initial responsibility for identifying future problems. The initiative could not begin to work unless all departments were prepared to share information with the CPRS; many ministers, however, jealous of the power and influence wielded by the Young Turks, were not prepared to cooperate. Margaret Thatcher's Department of Education and Science, for example, was hostile, as was the Treasury, to which Butler expected to return.

In the event, he managed to satisfy both his masters, making important contacts during the year he spent with the Think Tank. Indeed, the most important contact made was with the Prime Minister himself. One continuing task for the 'Tank' was its responsibility to keep the government on track with its strategy and election promises. Here the team divided along lines of age between Dick Ross and John Mayne, the conventional forces, and the younger, more daring and innovative members – Butler, Waldegrave and William Plowden. Instead of preparing a massive analysis, listing the government's objectives department by department, the younger faction proposed an analysis of government policy in an enormous flow chart, showing how each element fitted together and forming what Butler called 'a half-term report' on the government's performance.

When he presented this report to the Prime Minister in the garden of 10 Downing Street, Heath's preferred venue for summer meetings, Butler received general approval, tempered by Heath's comment that he really was not interested in retrospective grading, but wanted an analysis of how the government would perform in the future. Waldegrave and Butler, therefore, prepared three charts: an analysis of original strategy; a synopsis of areas where progress had and had not been made; and, most daringly, explicit forecasts of future trends and suggested responses. In Butler's words, this made for 'the largest flow chart classified secret ever to be presented to the Cabinet'. Despite its volume, the document appealed to Heath's pragmatism. By the end of 1971, Butler had good reason to be pleased with the preceding eighteen months. He was an established and respected member of the most exciting and innovative unit formulating the government's strategy. He had survived the demands placed on him by the exacting Rothschild, and had established himself with that often remote and uncompromising figure, the Prime Minister.

The three-cornered workings of Heath, Rothschild and Butler must have provided an advanced course in inter-personal relations for the ambitious civil servant. It is hard to imagine two figures with management styles as different as those of his two bosses. Something of this was expressed in Butler's inscription to Rothschild on a 'team photo' of the CPRS in 1972: 'To Victor, who reminded me that government should be fun and should deal in big ideas.'[52] The respect was mutual. When Butler left the 'Tank', Rothschild was quoted by the *Financial Times* as saying that he would have to find a replacement with the same 'intellectual skills, zest, charm and all-round sporting ability'.

In retrospect, the CPRS received a mixed report card. Colleagues and opponents of Heath, such as Enoch Powell and David Owen, admired the initiative for analysis and review that had spawned the 'Tank'. Critics, such as Sir John Hunt, who succeeded Burke Trend as Cabinet Secretary in 1973, commented that 'the programme analysis and review system created a great deal of work but not much in the way of results'.[53] Rothschild was too long in the tooth not to be aware of jealousies and cabals within the government. Years later, in a 1984 interview with Bernard Levin, he light-heartedly recalled his tactics and how he had employed Butler 'to make presentations because in those days [he was a] rather good-looking young man who looked like a well-scrubbed head prefect. And I thought that they would be more attracted by somebody looking like him, than an elderly gent like me.'[54]

From Butler's personal perspective, it had been an invaluable experience: he had learned skills in the presentation of advice to ministers, particularly in the vital technique of holding their attention. Rothschild maintained that opinion papers should be short and, most importantly, should arrive at a clear conclusion and unambiguous recommendations. To argue both sides of a case was not the function of the CPRS; moreover, it irritated busy ministers. This, Butler recalls, 'was an injunction I always tried to follow in my subsequent career'.[55]

CHAPTER 5

10 DOWNING STREET: FIRST TOUR, 1972–1974

THE CULTURAL DIFFERENCES BETWEEN the Wilson and Heath governments were a continuing source of material for political cartoonists. The image of Wilson seated at the kitchen table with a bottle of HP Sauce or with a pipe firmly stuck into his mouth recurred almost daily. Heath, by contrast, was portrayed as remote, formal, chillingly distant. Certainly, Heath strove to project an image as different from the Gannex-clad Wilson as possible; from the outset, he aimed to restore to the office of Premier the grandeur that he believed Wilson had stripped away. From the moment he arrived at Downing Street after kissing hands at the Palace, therefore, he underlined the changes that his administration would bring to the building.

These changes ranged from the very large – complete redecoration of the Cabinet Room and renovation of the living quarters at No. 10 – to the very small, such as the immediate cancellation of Wilson's television rental contract. In the selections of Donald Maitland, Douglas Hurd and other key appointments, the informality, the 'shabbiness' of the Labour government was replaced by polished professionalism and smooth formality.

On the day of the 1970 election, Heath drove from Buckingham Palace to Downing Street for an hour-long meeting with William Whitelaw and Francis Pym before driving to Windsor for the Queen Mother's seventieth birthday party. At around eight o'clock, he proposed a short break for supper and pressed a bell for the Principal Private Secretary. Told that 'everyone left with Mr Wilson and there are no supplies here', Heath acidly suggested that the secretary go and acquire some sandwiches. Twenty minutes later the latter put his head through the half-open Cabinet Room door and called out 'Grub's up'. This sent Whitelaw into paroxysms of fury. 'How can anyone behave like that?' he demanded. 'He must be sacked at once.'[1]

In response, Heath murmured the election slogan, 'Time for a change', and the Principal Private Secretary, David ('Sandy') Isserlis, was indeed very soon replaced by Robert Armstrong, at that time a senior Treasury official. When, in the spring of 1972, Peter Gregson, the private secretary for economic affairs at No. 10, came to the end of his period of secondment, Armstrong recommended a reshuffle in which Butler would go to Downing Street as the private secretary with responsibility for parliamentary questions. The Prime Minister, who had been impressed by Butler's presentation of Think Tank briefs and reports, immediately agreed. Aged thirty-four, Butler began his first term of working for a Prime Minister.

There was a slight delay in his taking up the post, however, as he had been invited to take a month-long trip to the United States. Earlier in the year, on the fifth hole of a round of golf, Steve Canner, the US Treasury representative in the American Embassy, had told Butler of a telegram he had received from Washington, asking him to recommend six up-and-coming Britons who had not been to the United States to visit as part of the US International Visitors' Program. 'I can certainly think of one', Butler replied with alacrity. Canner took the hint and Butler received his invitation soon after. Before settling into a new position, naturally enough, he wanted to take advantage of the invitation.

The terms of the International Visitors' Program were typically generous, in hospitable American fashion; the daily allowance for expenses was ample enough for Butler to include Jill on the trip and have his parents look after the children. His only obligation was to choose a subject for study; by selecting 'The relationship between Federal, State and City Government' he reckoned that he would be able to go pretty much wherever he wanted. After five days in Washington, he and Jill travelled through Virginia and south to Atlanta; then west to New Orleans and on to the Grand Canyon. After a spin through the West – Las Vegas, Los Angeles, San Francisco and Salt Lake City – they headed back via Chicago, Boston and New York to Washington.

The US State Department arranged for local hosts to meet them and show them around each city they visited, and for a month he and Jill were generously entertained in a dozen different cities and regions of the United States. In each city they visited their hosts were knowledgeable and informative about local politics and conditions; it was the beginning of an enduring friendship with America and Americans. The organisation of his visit and this form of hosted travel also impressed him, and a quarter of a century later he was in a position to offer similar travelling scholarships to young people embarking on their careers.*

Back in England in May, Butler reported for work at 10 Downing Street. He viewed his new job with some trepidation, as Heath was notoriously difficult socially and Butler, naturally gregarious, was quite the opposite. He describes his early conversations with Heath from which all small talk was absent:

> When asked a question, he would often remain silent for so long that at first I thought he had not heard. When I was halfway through repeating the question, he would answer it as originally put. But, once we adjusted to conversations in which there were long intervals between utterances, I began to enjoy them and spent comfortable times with him on journeys in the Prime Ministerial car. He was a kind man and, though long periods would pass in which he showed no great warmth, from time to time the glaze would clear from his eyes and a look of affection and even need would replace it. I found these occasions winning.[2]

Heath was not only philosophically opposed to socialism; he genuinely felt that the office had been seriously devalued during Harold Wilson's six years in Downing Street. His determination to restore not simply the fabric of 10 Downing Street and Chequers, but also the ceremonial importance of the office, was completely genuine; it also appealed to Butler's instinctive respect for tradition. On the other hand, his commitment to modern, management-based efficiency was equally appealing to the young, ambitious Treasury official. Precisely and only because these two sides of the two men

---

* Much later in life, as Master of University College, Oxford, Butler expanded the programme of travelling scholarships to the USA and Canada, for which undergraduates competed. With accommodation and basic hospitality provided by old members of the college, young scholars were able to travel extensively at little cost. See Chapter 18.

were so suited was it possible for them to work together in such unspoken harmony. By responding sympathetically to both Heath's traditionalism and his modernism, the new private secretary was able to anticipate his boss's needs and to serve him exceptionally well.

Not on every occasion, however, was Butler able to anticipate Heath's needs accurately. On the first time when he was responsible for a Prime Ministerial visit – to Yorkshire for a racing dinner and a visit to Leeds General Hospital for the opening of a new wing – he gave Heath his proposed speech as the plane descended to Leeds/Bradford airport. 'Where are the statistics about the government's hospital building programme?' demanded Heath. When Butler replied that he had not thought them relevant to a purely local visit, the Prime Minister snapped back: 'I'm meant to be the Prime Minister of this country, not the Princess Royal. Write it again.'

Fortunately, Douglas Hurd was present and able to dictate an impromptu speech to a secretary, opening with the assertion: 'In my first week as Prime Minister I decided that the government would reverse the disastrous decline in hospital building left by our predecessors.' On the following day, the newspaper headlines focused on that opening sentence and Butler's speech written for the racing dinner was not mentioned.

This experience contained an important lesson for an ambitious private secretary. It highlighted the role of the Prime Minister, the political context in which he operates, the value of a quotable sound bite and, as Butler was to find on many a subsequent occasion, the vital ability to improvise that was 'needed to keep the No. 10 show on the road'.[3]

Frequently a certain clairvoyance was required to grasp and to produce what Heath wanted. While he never hesitated to express his displeasure when a speech failed to embrace his political aims, he was frequently unable to communicate his *desiderata* in a direct and intelligible form. Butler recalls that 'something witty and persuasive' was as far as he ever went in formulating his requirements. Stories abound of how adviser and speechwriter Theodore Sorensen could assess perfectly the needs of President Kennedy in every speech he made. After his initial omission, Butler, a fast learner, was able to perform a similar role for Heath.

Britain's Prime Minister from 1970 to 1974 was a man of curious contradictions. From being a widely popular Chief Whip – an achievement in itself – he evolved into a leader who rapidly and comprehensively lost the support of the very members who had promoted his candidacy for the leadership. Yet, despite his famous rudeness, exemplified by his inability to offer the simplest word of thanks to those who performed a service for him, he commanded affection and respect from his closest colleagues. He had remarkable qualities, yet his vision of the society he wished to create was compromised by his inability to communicate that vision. Ultimately, the support of his colleagues evaporated; the Tory Party rewrote their account of the 1970s to exclude him; there were few, after his fall in 1975, who admitted to supporting him a decade before.

In particular, it was Heath's refusal to accept the leadership of his successor, Margaret Thatcher, that showed him in a poor light, sulking at his rejection. It might easily be imagined that Robin Butler, later Mrs Thatcher's confidant, always the very incarnation of *politesse* and good manners, would have been repelled by the ill-mannered Heath, whose demeanour was frequently that of a spoiled child. Yet, the opposite was the case: he looked beyond the often boorish façade and saw Heath's isolation. He saw the rudeness as social ineptitude, free of malice. To the surprise of observers – and of Butler himself – a closeness developed between the two.

There were similarities between the elder son of a Kentish building contractor and the only son of a Lancashire paint merchant. Both Ted Heath and Robin Butler were the recipients of their parents' fervent hopes for success. Both had been president of their Oxford college's junior common room. Both had clear moral and political beliefs that, for different reasons, they had kept largely to themselves. Very early in their association, a mutual respect developed and became a positive and productive force. For a speech at Muirfield after the Ryder Cup, Butler included a joke about Mary Queen of Scots, referring to her as 'the first golf widow'. Heath effectively ignored the joke but thereafter described him as his 'sporting adviser' and used him to write speeches for all sporting occasions.

In the daily running of No. 10, too, there was harmony between politician and civil servant. Heath ran a tidy ship in Downing Street – a fact that Butler respected and subsequently deeply missed when the looser regime of Harold

Wilson and Marcia Williams returned to No. 10. As a sportsman, he was shocked by the unfairness of the treatment to which Heath was subjected. As he later wrote to Heath, the Premier had pursued the only course open to him and had been criticised for his actions. The government was playing with an unfair handicap.

Butler arrived in Downing Street soon after the disastrous miners' strike of February 1972. The government had attempted to stand firm; power cuts followed; the inquiry chaired by Lord Wilberforce, who was under pressure to end the dispute, made an unreasonably generous award, which steered the government towards a tougher stance next time round. The seeds of the fall of the Heath administration were already sown. Yet before the Sophoclean drama of 1973–74 unrolled, Heath and Butler worked closely together on a wide range of issues, finding that their views on policy were congruent. Mutual acceptance and similarities of outlook were important when it came to what was perhaps the greatest test of the Heath government and certainly the issue in which the Prime Minister demonstrated the greatest courage of his political career. As it happens, the crucial events in Northern Ireland in the early 1970s were played out in the two years that the two worked together at Downing Street.

In August 1969, Wilson's government had sent troops to Northern Ireland but, on coming to power in 1970, Heath was confident that the crisis was temporary and that the reforms and concessions made would, in due course, remove the flashpoints of sectarian violence. His appointment of Reggie Maudling as Home Secretary, and his decision to leave responsibility for Northern Ireland with the Home Office, reflected his certainty that Northern Ireland, given time, would solve itself. This was a serious miscalculation. The Irish historian J. J. Lee commented succinctly that Maudling was 'from a Northern Ireland point of view … probably an unfortunate choice'.[4]

Maudling who, together with Iain Macleod and Enoch Powell, was considered the most cerebral of the post-war intake of Tory members, matched his ability with an outward calm – so calm was he, indeed, that *Private Eye* cartoons portrayed him in a nightshirt and nightcap, somnambulant and carrying a candle as he groped about. Fond of fine claret and something of an arbiter of elegance, he undiplomatically made no secret of his disdain for

Ulster. Lee wrote that 'his reputed comment on the plane back to London after his first visit to the North, "What a bloody awful country!" testified more to his intelligence than to his sense of responsibility'.[5]

During the first eighteen months of Heath's government, with the hated system of internment without trial in operation, and the British Army increasingly perceived as the enemies rather than as the protectors of the Catholic community in Northern Ireland, marches and demonstrations, although outlawed, became frequent in Ulster. Internment was the running sore; on 30 January 1972 thirteen unarmed demonstrators were shot dead by British troops in Londonderry. On the following day, Bernadette Devlin, MP for Mid-Ulster, incensed by Maudling's assertion that the troops had fired in self-defence, attacked the Home Secretary in the House of Commons, screaming at him: 'You murdering hypocrite'.[6]

Recognising that 'the estrangement between the two communities had become virtually complete' and that 'the political situation and the security situation alike were deteriorating',[7] Maudling proposed to the Cabinet that responsibility for law and order be transferred to Westminster; that there be an immediate referendum concerning the border; that power-sharing be instituted in Ulster; that the number of internees be progressively reduced; and, most importantly, that a Secretary of State for Northern Ireland take over responsibility for the province from the Home Secretary. Heath broadly accepted these proposals, and on 22 March confronted Brian Faulkner, the Northern Ireland Prime Minister, with his non-negotiable decision to adopt direct rule. Two days later, after the resignation of Faulkner's government, Heath appointed Whitelaw Secretary of State for Northern Ireland.

Such was the unpromising state of affairs when Butler arrived at 10 Downing Street. The responsibility for briefing the Prime Minister on Northern Ireland lay principally with Christopher Roberts, the economic affairs private secretary, but the entire question of Northern Ireland had become a highly explosive issue by the time that Butler took up his post. He thus saw at close quarters the sequence of events, the carnage, the virtual civil war that challenged British control of Northern Ireland. He also had a close-up view of the determination of a Prime Minister to solve, in Northern Ireland, what at first he viewed as an issue of law and order, but came to see differently.

The 'Troubles' that disrupted Ireland for thirty years began with the Londonderry civil rights march on 5 October 1968 and the Wilson government's response to riots in August 1969, by sending in troops. In 1969, thirteen people were killed in the province, a number that rose to twenty-five in 1970, to 174 in 1971 and abruptly to 467 in 1972. That year proved to be the bloodiest in the entire thirty-year struggle, and it was in 1972–73 that desperate and ultimately unsuccessful attempts were made to find a solution. Unlike many of his successors in Downing Street, Heath saw it as his duty to strive for a lasting settlement. His government devoted endless hours and, ultimately, its own credibility, to doing so. Not content to utter platitudes through the mouthpiece of a Secretary of State, Heath put himself in the forefront of the battle. His private secretary for economic affairs watched with fascination. When the Sunningdale Agreement was signed on 9 December 1973 a photograph shows a very stern but satisfied Butler surveying the scene as Heath, Brian Faulkner and Taoiseach Liam Cosgrave signed. There is no trace of the detachment of 'Sir Humphrey', only of shared pride in having done, as far as possible, the right thing.

The days spent in Sunningdale Park in Berkshire turned out to be, in Butler's memory, 'one of the most extraordinary weekends in Ted Heath's premiership'. Preliminary work between the Irish government and the leading political parties in Northern Ireland had continued through the summer and autumn, and a basic agreement had been reached at a meeting in Scarborough. It remained only to iron out final details, for which a meeting was arranged for Friday 7 December at the Civil Service Training College in Sunningdale. It was expected that this would be a fairly short affair and the Irish visit would be wrapped up with dinner at 10 Downing Street.

Unfortunately, the final agreement took longer to thrash out than had been expected, and it was arranged that talks would continue on Saturday morning. Meanwhile, a bibulous dinner, accompanied by quantities of Bushmills whiskey, was held on Friday. Talks were resumed on Saturday morning but, as the Italian Prime Minister Mariano Rumor was visiting Heath at Chequers for the weekend, time was severely limited. In the event, it was arranged that Signor Rumor would be received at Chequers and given lunch in Heath's absence. Thereafter, in somewhat quaint recognition of Italian custom, he would be allowed time for a siesta. Once the talks were concluded at Sunningdale, the Prime Minister would fly by helicopter to Chequers, some twenty miles distant.

This carefully planned timetable was disrupted when Heath and John Hume, the leader of the SDLP,* became locked in discussion. The SDLP, with its twin goals of social democracy and Irish reunification, fascinated the Prime Minister, and he was in no hurry to leave before he had learned all that he could from Hume. As the afternoon wore on, Tom Bridges, the foreign affairs private secretary at Chequers, telephoned increasingly shrill warnings to Butler that the Italian Prime Minister's siesta could not be extended indefinitely without diplomatic incident. At the same time, the helicopter pilot was warning him that as the light faded, only a few minutes of flying time remained. Finally Butler succeeded in separating Heath from Hume and bundling him into the helicopter.

The difficulties were still not entirely solved, however, as there remained fundamental issues – principally the question of a Council of Ireland and the responsibility of the police forces on each side of the border – that needed to be resolved. Heath flew to Chequers for dinner with Rumor; Butler drove to Richmond, where he was scheduled to speak at a rugby club dinner. At 10.30 p.m., the group gathered again at Sunningdale. They now faced a different deadline: the Ulster Unionists would be unable, for religious reasons, to take part in talks on Sunday unless these were an uninterrupted continuation of talks on the previous day. As it emerged, this turned out to be the case, as matters remained far from resolved on Sunday morning.

All parties had agreed to the existence of a Council of Ireland, but there continued to be little substantive agreement as to the powers that such a Council would wield. Faulkner staunchly resisted the proposal that the Northern Ireland security forces should lose their autonomy to a 'Council' that he considered nebulous at best. Feeling that he was being blackmailed into giving ground on policing, the Unionists resisted. Faulkner recalls:

> Heath argued with several of the speakers and grew quite irritated, raising his voice heatedly, but … our determination not to concede must have

* The Social Democratic and Labour Party, a nationalist party that stands for unification of Ireland and devolution of all power. In the 1970s it was the most popular Northern Irish party.

> been unmistakable, for he lapsed into one of his famous silences. After sitting for perhaps several minutes looking over our heads he got up suddenly and walked out without a word.[8]

Faulkner's recollection captures the commonly held view of Edward Heath – the man given to behaving like a head prefect, who sulked when he was not heeded. In that all-night marathon, when it seemed that unreason would finally prevail, it is easy to imagine Butler, himself a former head boy, sympathising deeply with the Prime Minister who had staked his political future on this conference and who now faced rejection by Faulkner, his former ally. Heath, not Whitelaw, was in the firing line. It was his own sense of responsibility that had placed him there.

Still Heath persisted. He flew back to Chequers for breakfast with Rumor, took him to church in Oxford, where they had lunch before driving to Heathrow for Rumor's return flight. Heath then returned to Sunningdale, where he accepted 'extremely reluctantly' that the control of security be in the hands of the devolved assembly, once the emergency ended. That, Faulkner commented, was the only basis on which any agreement would have been signed.[9] By eight o'clock on Sunday evening, an acceptable agreement had been reached and signed; a press conference followed. In his final act of public service that weekend, Butler loaned his suit to Attorney General Peter Rawlinson for the press conference before driving home, arriving at 1.00 a.m.

In truth, the agreement at Sunningdale was based on wishful thinking – by Cosgrave, by Faulkner and, not least, by Edward Heath. The principle according to which each side must yield something was a laudable one, endorsed by Heath as an instance of where logic must prevail. The alternative was chaos, an outcome that he and Butler refused to envisage. The problem was that Faulkner would be reviled in the North for even entertaining the possibility of a Council of Ireland – seen as the first step towards a united Ireland, while in the South, backing away from insistence on Ireland's thirty-two counties was regarded as betrayal. Under those circumstances, the agreement was bound to fail. If Heath and his private secretary for economic affairs had been more ruthlessly analytic, they would not have deceived themselves that agreement was possible. That shortcoming was, sadly, symptomatic of the last months of the Heath government.

Nonetheless, the political courage displayed by Heath and Faulkner deeply impressed Butler. The wages of that courage were paid in the general election of 28 February 1974. Brian Faulkner was branded a traitor for selling out, and eleven of the twelve seats in Northern Ireland were taken by parties campaigning under the Loyalist banner brandished by Ian Paisley and the United Ulster Unionist Council (UUUC). The principal tenet was a rejection of Sunningdale and of power-sharing.[10] Faulkner himself wrote the most accurate epitaph for Sunningdale, describing it as 'the nadir of Unionist treachery'. Designed to 'draw together all the threads of Anglo-Irish relations in a new settlement', Faulkner wrote, it contained 'unanswered questions, the loose ends of the threads, that brought about its downfall'.[11]

While Britain's problems in Ireland provided a relentless backdrop of mounting civil war, Heath's government faced two linked problems closer to the typical Briton, and which would ultimately bring it down: the economy and industrial relations. On the night after the marathon weekend that culminated in the Sunningdale Agreement, a decisive step was taken: an exhausted Prime Minister held a dinner for members of the Confederation of British Industry (CBI) to discuss how sufficient coal stocks could be maintained at power stations. It was at that meeting, Butler recalls, while Heath fought to stay awake after the all-night negotiating sessions, that the three-day week was adopted as a definite policy.

After two years in office, Heath's government found itself beleaguered; industrial relations, specifically with the National Union of Mineworkers (NUM), languished; Britain's entry into the European Economic Community, a personal priority of the Prime Minister, had been far from certain; for Heath there was a mutual connectedness of these strands of policy. Failure in either one would have a disastrous effect on the credibility of his administration.

When Butler had come to Downing Street in 1972, he had, as a member of the Think Tank, experience of the government's difficulties from a theoretical standpoint, but had had little opportunity to counsel the Prime Minister in a way that he would be required to do, if he was to serve Heath well. To fit industrial relations into broader industrial policy and the stability of sterling, all within the context of Britain's imminent membership of the Common Market – and, moreover, to recognise the pressure points of each independent issue – required a different form of mental adroitness from that needed in the Think Tank. Underlying the transition, of course, was the danger of a Treasury man becoming too 'political', as some suspected Sir William Armstrong, the head of the Home Civil Service, of being.*

As with the sequence of events leading to the Sunningdale conference, Butler's arrival coincided with a distinctly new phase of policy and preparation. The second reading of the European Communities Bill took place on 17 February 1972, and it was immediately clear that the philosophical assumptions underlying the government's policy were far from generally accepted. After a robust debate, Heath succinctly spelled out the vital importance, in his view, of Britain's joining the EEC. Britain's prosperity and position in the world, he argued, depended on membership.

In an act of great political courage, despite the uncertainty in the Whips' Office, Heath linked the continuation of his government with the outcome of the vote. If the House did not agree to the second reading of the Bill, he warned that he and his colleagues were 'unanimous that in these circumstances ... Parliament cannot sensibly continue'.[12]

The government survived the subsequent division with a 309–301 victory but, although Heath treated the win as routine and absolute, there was no doubt that the government had suffered a severe setback. In the four months between the Bill's going into committee and the third reading on 13 July, violent argument over the Bill continued. David Owen describes this time as 'one of the most unpleasant periods of my whole political career', with 'voting night after night against the EEC Bill, all on the rather absurd theory that it was up to Heath, as Prime Minister, to get his own legislation through'.[13]

Against this backdrop of Heath's constancy regarding Europe, the government was forced into a series of U-turns that highlighted the inter-dependent

* Sir William Armstrong, later Baron Armstrong of Sanderstead, had been head of the Home Civil Service since 1968 and wielded great influence in the Heath government. He suffered a nervous collapse at the time of the three-day week.

nature of policy. Butler had grasped the principles of this when the 'Tank' had considered the problems at UCS. On that occasion, only *The Economist* had questioned the wisdom of the course of action dictated by political necessity, doubting that Britain, a country of high wages, was the wisest location for the shipbuilding industry.[14]

By then, of course, the NUM had won the first round of battling with the government. Heath justified the concessions made to the miners in a broadcast, maintaining that it was not a question of whether the government won or lost; the important issue at stake concerned the real nature and value of the British way of life.[15] Almost immediately after this setback came the Budget on 21 March 1972. This was a package urged on a compliant Chancellor by the Prime Minister, in the face of opposition from the Treasury. Chancellor Tony Barber was opposed to the dramatic reductions in taxation – a view fully shared by the Treasury. The Cabinet was, at best, acquiescent. The spirit and the language, although expressed by Barber, were manifestly those of Edward Heath.[16]

At the same time, William Armstrong, Sir William Nield and Leo Pliatzky, a deputy secretary at the Treasury, were working secretly with the Prime Minister on what was to become the Industrial Relations Act 1972. It seems extraordinary, in retrospect, that Heath could have hoped for reason to prevail over politics, for problems to be dismissed by logical analysis and a measure of compromise. John Campbell describes Heath's *modus operandi* at this time as more that of a civil servant, perhaps formed by his rapport with Armstrong.

Joe Haines, Wilson's press secretary, believed that Heath's inclination to view politics in the manner of an official allowed the Civil Service to increase its power 'alarmingly' during the 1970s.[17] This power, he argued, enabled the service to prevent things being done. His complaint is a common refrain among Labour politicians and, in the case of Heath and the Civil Service, Douglas Hurd, from the perspective of political secretary, felt much the same. Hurd felt that Heath 'tended to exaggerate what could be achieved by new official machinery'. Had Heath been more sceptical, he would not have believed in the power of the Department of Trade and Industry to enforce the Industrial Relations Act.[18]

Thus, a U-turn was presented as an act of regional policy, a re-engagement of British industry to compete in the Common Market, rather than as support for lame ducks. Economic growth was mandated; overdue taxation reform was an essential element; the government was sensitive to the quality of life in Britain. How could the Barber boom of 1972 not succeed?

What followed was a descent from the idealism of the 1972 Budget to the failure of the Industrial Relations Act, to a disillusioning first year in Europe, to a second disastrous confrontation with the miners and recession caused by the end of cheap energy. Cold comfort for Butler or for Heath that Rothschild's antennae had sensed imminent oil price rises two years before. On 13 December 1973, an appeal by Heath for unity failed to rouse the public and signally did nothing to shame the NUM into cooperation. Once again, Heath's posture, placing principle over politics, could be viewed as morally inspiring but, as the country slid into the grey winter of the three-day week, few saw Heath's efforts as anything more than political manoeuvre. By the beginning of 1974 there was no doubt that a showdown was imminent and no doubt as to the issues at stake. The faithful looked to Heath for a lead, for a battle cry asserting government's right to govern. Yet that was the very call that Heath refused to give.

He disdained to do so principally from distaste for divisive and partisan politics; the notion of pitting the Conservative Party inexorably against the trade unions struck at the core of his political philosophy, his devotion to the concept of one nation. To appeal to class hatred was, for him, a retrograde and pitifully divisive ploy. When Heath's final appeal to the miners failed, it was clear that there would have to be an election – the extent of the gulf between government and unions dictated that – but it would be fought decently. On 7 February, he called an election for three weeks later, Thursday the twenty-eighth.

Between the day of the announcement, when the Tories were confidently expected to win, and the election itself, which eventually resulted in a tortuously hung parliament, the Tories remained favourites, albeit by a narrow margin. Their manifesto, however, was a doctrinaire document, replete with 'strident rhetoric'.[19] By attempting to limit the election issues to the question of 'who governs Britain?' the Tories exposed their flank to attacks based on rising prices, housing, balance of payments deficits and the Common Market. For the Prime Minister, Labour reserved their most effective barbs: Heath was portrayed as dictatorial and obstinate; as a tyrant waging a war against the working class (according to Denis Healey); as pig-headed over the miners as Anthony Eden had shown to be over Suez (according to Tony Crosland).

The sustained Labour offensive succeeded in eroding the slim Conservative majority. With 301 seats to the Conservatives' 297, the Labour majority was negligible. Yet, the Tories could only continue in power if Heath could fashion a workable coalition. In the post-Sunningdale calculus, however, the Tories could not count on any support from Ulstermen, and Heath saw an alliance with the Liberal Party as his only hope of forming a government.

Since the Liberals had won a mere fourteen seats with 19 per cent of the popular vote, their leader Jeremy Thorpe could accept no agreement that did not offer proportional representation. Heath, aware that the Tories would never countenance such a concession, weakly offered a Speakers' Conference on the issue. The British sense of fair play prompted mounting resentment towards a defeated Premier struggling to stay in power, and a violent wave of anti-Heath feeling was expressed by *The Spectator*, which harangued the departing Prime Minister five days after he left No. 10:

> Mr Edward Heath's monomania was never more clearly seen than in the days after the general election when, a ludicrous and broken figure, he clung with grubby fingers to the crumbling precipice of his power … The spectacle was ludicrous; it was pathetic; it was contemptible. And Mr Heath, having been over the weekend a squalid nuisance,* remains as leader of the Tory Party just that … Mr Heath must now depart the Tory leadership as quickly as possible.[20]

The view of *The Spectator* was prescient and shared by many of Heath's colleagues. The expectations of 1970 were quietly buried. His premiership had

* The description 'squalid nuisance' originated with Sir Winston Churchill, who used it to describe Aneurin ('Nye') Bevan.

hardly begun, James Margach later wrote, and the optimism surrounding Heath's quiet revolution had already evaporated:

> After the tantrums, bitter arguments and high tensions of Wilson's Mark-I government there was ... a sense of optimism as Heath moved into No. 10 ... Alas, power, which has the ability to mellow some of those who achieve it ... in Heath's case changed his personality overnight. When Prime Minister he became authoritarian and intolerant.[21]

Although Butler had shared that 'sense of optimism', he decidedly did not share Margach's opinion either of Heath or of the Tory defeat. From 1972 when he started work at 10 Downing Street, until March 1974, when Heath departed, humiliated after the election and its messy aftermath, there was a productive synergy and shared unity of purpose between Prime Minister and Private Secretary. Remarkably, Heath had, in Butler's case, lowered the barriers that he had constructed to shut colleagues out. Butler had become an important source of moral support for an embattled Prime Minister – not in the role of policymaker, in the manner of William Armstrong, or as a political adviser, in the manner of Douglas Hurd, who had political ambitions of his own. Instead, Butler and Jill quietly became part of the machinery of Downing Street, for, as a bachelor, Heath frequently needed a formal hostess. Jill and other secretaries' wives were regularly called on to help out.*

When Jeremy Thorpe predictably refused Heath's offer of power-sharing with a single Liberal seat in Cabinet, Heath, who had surrendered his lease on his Albany flat, was literally homeless. He had lavished time and attention on the refurbishment of 10 Downing Street and Chequers, perquisites that were now Harold Wilson's to enjoy. In the early hours of Monday 4 March, Butler and Tim Kitson, Heath's parliamentary private secretary, cleaned, tidied and prepared a flat in Vauxhall that belonged to Kitson so that Heath

---

* Edward Heath was not generally at ease with women. He had close female friends from the world of music (such as Moura Lympany) and others whom he chose for their ability to stand up to him and return his natural rudeness. One of these was Sara Morrison, former wife of the MP for Devizes, who acted as his hostess in Downing Street in the early years of his premiership.

might move in on Monday. For both men, these were actions performed for a leader who had earned their profound respect.

For the man from the Treasury, schooled from earliest Civil Service days to view politicians with cautious scepticism, Edward Heath was an exception for whom normal rules were reversed. It was the opposition that he faced that was unprincipled, determined to bring him down over membership of the EEC, over the Industrial Relations Act, over Ireland. By contrast, in the eyes of the civil servants who worked closely with him – Robert Armstrong and Butler – his successive stances were positions of principle, convictions that successively eroded his position as leader. Heath, who wanted no more than the best for Britain, was to them a resolute figure, a Roman senator in the mould of Cato the Elder. Armstrong saw his strengths in context:

> One could have great sympathy with what Heath was trying to do. He was an honest, honourable politician who earned one's respect, even affection. He was not an easy man but he was a man whom you could respect and like.[22]

For Butler, the triumph of politics was a source of regret. Few tributes could be more heartfelt than his letter to the departing Prime Minister:

> Dear Mr Heath,
>
> You will have so many letters to read at present, and perhaps it is the duty of those who worked most closely for you not to add to them. But I feel that I am doing my duties in other ways and can indulge myself in this.
>
> This is mainly a thank you letter – to say 'thank you' for having given me the privilege of working for you at No. 10. It has been fascinating and I will look back on it with pleasure all my life – that goes without saying. But there has been more to it than that. It is not just that, under your leadership and Robert Armstrong's, we have been such a happy and united team, both on the Civil Service and on the political sides. I think that all of us at No. 10 in every role have been delighted to be here over these past months and years for the same reason. We have believed wholeheartedly

in what you wanted to do for this country and supported you with all our hearts in trying to do it.

This must have been a terrible time for you, and no doubt you will have thought much over the events of the last months. If it is worth anything as a support at this time, I can see no alternative viable course you could have taken. There was no escape from introducing a statutory incomes policy and, when the miners were about to defy it successfully, you had no alternative but to appeal to the electorate to support the government. Nor do I think that anyone has previously been in such a strong position to ask for that support. A policy to stop wage inflation was never more necessary, it had the backing of the law and it was not repressive to the miners – quite the reverse.

That is why it has been so profoundly depressing that the British people did not give you that support. I believe that I can honestly add 'regardless of party politics'. I shall now do my best for your successor for as long as he wants me to do so – the problems facing the country have not changed. But nobody can disguise from themselves that the British people have made things much more difficult for themselves. It may be that now only the suffering that will come from a major economic collapse will show the British people where they have been going. I only hope that, if that time has to come, you will be there for them to call on.

In the meantime Jill and I send you all our best wishes and thanks for the personal kindness which you have always shown to both of us.[23]

On the evening of 4 March, with Edward Heath installed in Tim Kitson's flat in Vauxhall, Butler stood in the hall at 10 Downing Street to await and greet his successor, Harold Wilson.

CHAPTER 6

INTERMEZZO: BETWEEN TORY GOVERNMENTS, 1974–1979

FROM 1964 TO 1976 the two principal party leaders, young meritocrats, each claiming to know the formula that would bring Britain up to date, took their turns in 10 Downing Street. Butler, who served both Edward Heath and Harold Wilson as Private Secretary, continually marvelled at the contrasts between the two men. In 1974, the outgoing Prime Minister may not have been in the Old Etonian mould of his immediate predecessors – Douglas Home, Macmillan and Eden – but the atmosphere in No. 10 had been 'something of a gentleman's club'. With the arrival of Wilson's entourage he saw it as

> a hotbed of intrigue and high temperament, sometimes of hysterics. The leader in this was Marcia Falkender.* She hectored Harold like a fishwife. If she wanted to be driven in the Prime Minister's car to do her shopping, she took it, regardless of whether the Prime Minister needed it or not. She made the diary secretary's life a misery by fixing appointments for Harold without concern for the official engagements. I was shocked that what I regarded as the serious business of government could be treated so irresponsibly.[1]

This was the first time that he had experienced a change of Prime Minister during his service at Downing Street, and he found the cultivated objectivity

* Harold Wilson's personal and political secretary Marcia Williams (née Field) was created Baroness Falkender in the Birthday Honours List of July 1974.

of *le roi est mort; vive le roi* stilted and artificial. Marcia Williams, later Lady Falkender, herself had only contempt for permanent civil servants, whom she damningly referred to as 'the Whitehall Establishment'.[2]

She was not alone. Joe Haines and Bernard Donoughue, two of the new Prime Minister's inner circle, were intensely suspicious of anything to do with the Civil Service and even before arriving at No. 10 were busy discomfiting Robert Armstrong, the Principal Private Secretary in Downing Street. At the suggestion of Marcia Williams, when Wilson emerged from the Palace, Haines jumped in the car with him and Mrs Wilson to ride to Downing Street. 'That', recalled Haines, 'meant Robert Armstrong would have to make his own way back. There were few men wiser in anticipating trouble than he. He had a spare car waiting.'[3]

This boisterous, adolescent gesture reflected the almost obsessive belief of Wilson's entourage that the Civil Service was determined to obstruct any Labour initiative. Haines viewed the weekly meeting of Permanent Secretaries as a kind of clandestine alternative Cabinet 'that very few people in Whitehall know anything about'.[4] From Haines's memoir, it is clear that Wilson and his entourage were prepared for a power struggle with Sir William Armstrong, widely known as 'Deputy Prime Minister' during Heath's government. In the event, that confrontation was avoided when Armstrong was compelled to retire for health reasons.

Donoughue, as much an academic as a political operator, saw both sides of the apparent divide:

> In the 1960s the Civil Service didn't fully understand how you could achieve growth and the Wilson team was hostile to them when they returned in 1974. I listened to Joe Haines and Marcia Williams because they both had experience of Wilson's first term, but the team at Number Ten was brilliant. Once they saw that I understood their language they treated me well, Robin especially ... I had been an academic and most academics know bugger all.[5]

For Butler and his colleagues at No. 10, the adjustment required was considerable and complex. Civil Service discipline required that the staff at

No. 10 be apolitical, that Butler and his colleagues move seamlessly from working long hours writing speeches for Heath on the necessity of resisting the miners' demands to writing speeches for Wilson, arguing that the dispute had been wasteful and unnecessary. When Butler handed one such speech to a Garden Room typist, he was sure that he saw her contempt for his 'turncoat' behaviour. The experience of being distrusted by the new guard and despised by the old while simply doing one's job must have seemed unwarranted.

From the first day of the new government's tenure, Butler was closely involved in the settlement of the miners' strike, the ultimate cause of Heath's fall. In a 'Note for the Record' during the first week of Labour's term, it is clear that he enjoyed the new Prime Minister's trust and that he would work as assiduously as before to achieve industrial harmony, even though the price to be paid was quite at variance with the economic absolutes in force the week before. His notes are objective, detached and revealing in their clarity and brevity.[6] Nor was he beyond a little obfuscation of the economic implications, as a handwritten note on a letter from the Secretary of State for Energy to Joel Barnett at the Treasury proposes.[7]

Donoughue draws a perceptive picture of the lineup and the realities of power at No. 10. Of the hundred or so people working there, only nine had frequent access to the Prime Minister, half of whom were civil servants on loan from other departments – Armstrong, Bridges, Butler, Mark Forrester and Nick Stuart. From the 'Kitchen Cabinet' were Joe Haines, Marcia Williams, Albert Murray and Donoughue. 'It was', he said, 'a good balance between bureaucrats and pirates, and on the whole it worked well.'[8]

The two groups circled each other warily at first, but soon established a *modus operandi* based on mutual confidence, as Donoughue recalls:

> When I set up the Policy Unit everyone told me that the Civil Service would undermine me. The Private Office stood back and watched to see how we would perform. When we began to have influence on the PM they took the view, 'if you're part of the machine, then we'll work with you'. It was the first time that there had been independent economic advice at Number Ten and the Treasury naturally, was suspicious of it. Wilson

> wanted alternative economic advice and so he hired Andrew Graham and Gavyn Davies who could take on the Treasury and present proper economic alternatives. They worked closely with Robin Butler, while it took longer for the Treasury to come round. Some civil servants tried to shut out special advisers, which was silly, but Leo Pliatzky summoned me to the Treasury and said, in effect, 'If we can't beat you, we'll join you.'[9]

Butler and Wilson, despite their widely different backgrounds, had an Oxford college in common. Wilson had been a research assistant at University College during the war, and had taught economics there until he was elected to Parliament in the 1945 Labour landslide. This affinity initially persuaded Butler that the relations between the Civil Service staff and the Prime Minister and his political staff need not be as hostile as they had been during the first Wilson administration of 1964–70.

Indeed, Butler found Wilson easy to deal with: he, unlike Heath, was able to indulge in small talk and moments of levity. The Univ connection served them well, as did the subject of sport. He did suspect, however, that Wilson had a number of prepared passages – on Huddersfield Town football club, on Oxford, on a number of subjects. At the time, he believed that these were 'tapes' that the Prime Minister played to avoid difficult questions. In retrospect, he suspected that they could have been signs of the onset of dementia that affected him later.

Even if he managed to project a wholly apolitical front, Butler was far from certain that his services would be required for long after the change of government. A few months before the election, at a dinner party hosted by William Plowden, former colleague in the CPRS, he had had a 'lively discussion' over Heath's stance on the miners' strike with Bernard Donoughue, not knowing that he was a Wilson insider. Immediately after the election, when Donoughue joined the Prime Minister's inside team, Butler, in common with the other private secretaries, was apprehensive about his own future. His fears were misplaced, as Donoughue later explained:

> During the 1974 election campaign I had dinner at William Plowden's. Robin was there and we had a difference over something or other. He was

> worried when he realised that I was in charge of the Policy Unit, but he need not have worried. I was pleased to see him in the welcoming group when we returned to Number Ten from the Palace. I understood his position after working so closely with Ted Heath.[10]

In the event, they and the incoming Prime Minister's staff (with some exceptions) shared the goal of settling the strike as rapidly as possible. Butler overcame his initial feeling that his role was akin to that of a mercenary. He was able to establish good working relations with Wilson's intimates at No. 10, with the notable exception of Lady Falkender. He was impressed by Donoughue, Haines and the enthusiastic team of young economists, including Andrew Graham (aged thirty-two) and Gavyn Davies (aged twenty-four).* Donoughue's initial task was to create Wilson's Policy Unit, 'against the scepticism and occasional hostility of some of the regular civil servants'. The unit was an innovation; there had previously been no systematic policy analysis in Whitehall separate from the Civil Service machine, working solely for the Prime Minister.[11]

A year after Wilson's return to office, Robert Armstrong's tour of duty at Downing Street came to an end. During those twelve months, aided by Butler and his colleagues, he had transformed Donoughue's view of the value of civil servants in Downing Street. Donoughue's diary entry for 16 April 1975, when Wilson gave a farewell dinner for Armstrong, reflects his changed views. Armstrong, he wrote, 'is really a remarkable public servant, one of the best I have dealt with'. There had been mistrust, he admitted, commenting:

> He is of course quite conservative and very attached to the traditional institutions of the Establishment – monarchy, Church, public schools etc. ... not because he wants favours from the Establishment, but because he thinks those values, that stability is the very best of the Establishment. I don't actually agree with all that. But I do think he is the very best of the Establishment. Robin Butler and Pat Nairne are junior ones of his calibre.[12]

* Andrew Graham was to be Master of Balliol College, Oxford from 2001 to 2011. Gavyn Davies went on to have a successful career with Goldman Sachs and was chairman of the BBC from 2001 to 2004, when he resigned after criticism of the BBC in the Hutton Report.

Donoughue had been impressed by Butler since his first day in Downing Street. 'He was immediately warm to me', Donoughue recalled. 'Straight, wickedly humorous, and a real team man, he became one of my most valued personal friends.'[13] Good relations with Donoughue and Haines turned out to be invaluable a few months after the 1974 election, when Armstrong told Butler that Wilson wanted to remove him and bring in another person from the Treasury. The individual behind this sudden decision, Butler established, in talking to Donoughue and Haines, was Marcia Falkender. Soon after the 1974 election, *Private Eye* ran a series of articles implicating Lady Falkender in apparently questionable land deals in which she had allegedly used her influence with Wilson to the benefit of her brother Tony Field and land speculation in the Midlands, even forging a letter ostensibly from the Prime Minister.[14]

Butler had, of course, been at Harrow with Andrew Osmond, one of the original investors in *Private Eye*, and in his Oxford years had shared tutorials with Richard Ingrams, the editor of the magazine. Invited to one of the famous *Private Eye* lunches, he had been astounded at the 'malice and inaccuracy' with which those present attacked Nicholas Bethell, another Harrovian contemporary. He defended Bethell and resolved to avoid *Private Eye* luncheons in future. On one occasion, talking during a car ride with Marcia Williams, he mentioned the luncheon to illustrate how savage the satirical magazine could be.

Williams had stored this nugget and used it as a reason to importune Wilson to remove Butler – a request Wilson initially received sympathetically, as *Private Eye* was consistently critical of him and his government. The true reason for Williams's request, however, according to Donoughue and Haines, was that Butler had been too prominent behind Wilson at the TUC Congress in the autumn of 1974. It appeared that, upset at the visibility of a civil servant at the very centre of press photographs, she had approached Wilson with the story that he regularly attended these scurrilous luncheons. This, she knew, would discredit him with the Prime Minister. In the event, Donoughue and Haines intervened with Wilson on his behalf and he was spared the potentially damaging embarrassment of being returned to the Treasury before the end of his posting. Nonetheless, Donoughue recalls over forty years later, 'Robin should not have gone to lunch with those snakes.'[15]

This incident apart, relations between Wilson and his Private Secretary were friendly. In briefings for parliamentary questions, Wilson proved to have very different needs from his predecessor. Heath wanted facts and would deal with them in a rather wooden manner. Wilson was, for his part, less interested in facts than in diversionary tactics. Writing speeches for him was, therefore, much more difficult, particularly as he took an intense personal interest in the speech – or at least in the press handout. Wilson often recycled material for speeches, working on the principle that the congenitally idle reporters would base their reports solely on the press handouts.

When totally new speeches needed to be composed, the Donoughue-Butler-Haines triumvirate operated smoothly and effectively. Donoughue and the Policy Unit provided the policy items. Butler massaged these into 'technically correct form', bringing, according to Haines, 'astonishing energy and rigid discipline to his work'. The final brushstrokes, patina and palette were provided by Haines. Butler recalls that Haines saw his skill as akin to that of Hans van Meegeren – the skill of imitating Wilson as the Dutch artist imitated Vermeer, producing versions that were indistinguishable from the work of the master.[16] In the October 1974 election campaign, analysts divided Wilson's speeches into two distinct sections: the first ten days of the campaign and the final stretch. The Prime Minister was dull and unconvincing in the first ten days, the press reported, because his speeches were written by Haines. When, thereafter, Wilson took over, the speeches had more brio. The truth, however, is the opposite; it was Haines who took over from Wilson.

One project on which Butler worked closely with both Haines and Donoughue was the development of a new housing policy to incorporate a fair deal for council tenants who were at a severe financial disadvantage during periods of inflation. The plan to offer council houses for sale was a key plank of Labour's housing policy, but the Conservative government had appropriated the plan, proposing to sell council houses at a substantial discount reflecting the length of time the occupier had lived there. Such a plan, however, was unacceptable to Labour local councils. Haines accordingly developed a plan to offer council houses to tenants of ten years' standing. They would enjoy all the benefits of home ownership, except that, on the death of the tenant and/or dependent relative, ownership of the house would revert to the local authority.

The proposal, as Haines was the first to admit, was merely an outline plan, designed to meet the demands of the tenant, of local government and of the central government. Butler, shown the outline by Haines, immediately identified the principal drawback from the tenant's point of view: there was no opportunity to pass on an asset to the tenant's children, in the form of either bricks and mortar or accumulated equity in the value of the property. Butler took away Haines's proposal to consider how to overcome this drawback. A day or two later, he sent Haines a minute with his solution, 'designed to complement [Haines's] original proposal rather than supersede it'. Butler retained the 'life-lease' principle and proposed that a tenant have the right to buy his house 'with the cost calculated on a different formula, one that would allow him to sell it back to the local authority and to receive part of the enhanced value that might have accrued during his ownership'.[17]

Haines was clearly impressed, not only by Butler's acuity of perception, but also by his ability to avoid the political issues involved in home ownership and to focus on broadening the acceptability of a scheme that had engaged the Prime Minister's interest. It was this cooperative detachment that most impressed Haines and Donoughue – as well as the Prime Minister himself.[18]

As Robert Armstrong's departure from No. 10 approached, all three discussed his replacement as Principal Private Secretary. Their first choice was for an internal promotion, whereby Butler would take over directly from Armstrong. The Civil Service, however, responded that he was 'too young' and appointed Kenneth Stowe* to the post.[19] Possibly the closeness between Butler and Wilson's inner circle was a source of resentment at the Treasury, as a curious incident came close to undermining their mutual trust.

Once it had been decided that Stowe would succeed Armstrong, the Treasury moved to replace Butler before the end of his three-year term and, according to Donoughue, 'tried to bounce this through [the Prime Minister] by sending him a paper in a hurry agreeing to his successor'. Wilson spotted

---

* Sir Kenneth Stowe GCB, CVO (1927–2015), Principal Private Secretary to Harold Wilson, Jim Callaghan and Margaret Thatcher (1975–79). He was knighted in 1980.

that this was a Treasury ruse and said he wanted time to think it over. In the meantime he asked Donoughue to find out what Butler wanted, as Donoughue recalls:

> Before Questions I ... told [Butler] that Robert Armstrong had told the PM this morning that he was to be moved within a few weeks, and the PM wanted to know what he wanted. Robin was stunned. He said that Robert had sent for him *yesterday* and told him that the PM had asked for Butler to be moved because he wanted somebody with more of an economic training. Robin had believed this and had been deeply saddened that the PM wanted him to go. I assured him that the PM had not asked for this – and had known nothing about it until this morning. Butler was shattered and said he felt betrayed by the Whitehall machine, and simply could not understand why they would lie to him.[20]

When Donoughue reported back to the Prime Minister, Wilson was astonished and denied that he had expressed any view about Butler's departure. Certainly he had not asked for a trained economist as he already had Andrew Graham and the Policy Unit. 'HW swore about Robert', Donoughue recalled. 'These are curious Whitehall games.'

Against the early odds, the young Private Secretary had become an integral part of the machinery of No. 10 and he was retained *en poste* through the summer of 1975. On 5 June, Donoughue recorded his regret that Butler was leaving. He criticised the Treasury for assuming that they could automatically put their appointee into the private office. 'Spies are inevitable', he wrote, 'but departmental espionage should not become a hereditary right. They must work for it.'[21]

Before his return to the Treasury, Butler was involved in an issue that solidified his standing with the Wilson team. A struggle developed between the Policy Unit and the Treasury over the proposals for an incomes policy. Officials at the Treasury were 'hell bent on having a full statutory policy backed by the criminal law'. On 19 June, the Cabinet agreed to some kind of incomes policy but, in order not to alienate the left, insisted that it be voluntary and less draconian than that envisaged by the Treasury. Pressure was then applied by the Governor of the Bank of England, Sir Gordon Richardson, who demanded an immediate full statutory incomes policy. Donoughue and Haines resisted this, supported by Butler, who was not afraid to speak out against the Treasury on behalf of the No. 10 Policy Unit. When the Treasury offered Denis Healey proposals that were essentially Heath's 1973 policy, which Wilson had denounced at the time, Donoughue and Haines sent Wilson a memorandum pointing out that to impose a statutory incomes policy was counter to policy agreed by the ministerial Cabinet Committee.[22] After an initial inclination to yield to Treasury pressure, Wilson agreed with Donoughue and Haines.

Once the trade unions had agreed to the Policy Unit's proposals, Donoughue and Butler met with Treasury officials to finalise the Treasury draft of the new policy. One item in the draft puzzled Donoughue:

> The only remaining surprise for me was when I spotted a new footnote drafted by Treasury officials and Whitehall lawyers. It said that 'fees and increments' were to be exempted from the constraints of the new pay policy. I asked Robin Butler what this meant. He gave a typical Butler chuckle and said with a guilty grin, 'Well, fees are them [pointing to the lawyers] and increments are us [civil servants].'

Thus the people creating the policy specifically excluded themselves from its provisions, a course that much amused Donoughue.[23]

Donoughue and Haines might not have changed their general perception of senior civil servants since the prank played on Armstrong in the forecourt of Buckingham Palace just over a year before, in 1974, but they had certainly altered their view of Armstrong and Butler. Donoughue manoeuvred unsuccessfully to have Butler stay on until the end of the year, but in the event, he returned to the Treasury at the end of October, as the Treasury had always planned. In November, he entertained the No. 10 Policy Unit, together with Ken Stowe and the private office, at a farewell lunch, as Donoughue recalled:

> We all went to lunch at Beotys restaurant with Robin Butler as a farewell gesture. He is enjoying the Treasury but says that he has been stuck right

> away from immediate economic policy. The Treasury always gives people a 'sterilisation' period after they return from No.10. He also said that one reason why the Chancellor is so reluctant to discuss policy matters with the PM is that he does not want Hunt to get his hands on it and start interfering with the Treasury.[24]

Try as he might to appear impartial in political matters, it is clear that, as a working environment, Butler preferred the formality of No. 10 under Edward Heath to the more casual atmosphere under Harold Wilson – despite his excellent working relations with Haines and Donoughue. Unfortunately, Marcia Williams schemed to retain her influence over Wilson and, inevitably, sought to destroy Butler, whom she instinctively but erroneously saw as a rival. Donoughue recalls that Butler was always polite to her, but he simply minimised contact between them.[25] While remaining above the fray, Butler confessed to Donoughue that Williams was 'the only totally destructive person I have ever met'.[26]

She did, nonetheless, exercise a powerful – and to Butler, incomprehensible – influence over the Prime Minister. On one occasion, Haines, Donoughue and Butler were working with Wilson on his speech to be given to the 1974 TUC conference in Brighton. Williams had coined a phrase – speaking of 'a Declaration of Interdependence' – that Haines particularly disliked. Wilson, however, was insistent that it should be included in the speech. Haines argued that it was a cheap gimmick; the Prime Minister reached for his glass of brandy and repeated his wish to include it. Donoughue and Butler joined in, pointing out that the theme did not arise from the rest of the speech, which contained three quite different themes. Wilson admitted to liking the themes, and again proposed 'a Declaration of Interdependence based on the three themes'. Donoughue had no doubt that 'Marcia has forced this in, and the PM dare not drop it. But he knows Joe is right.'[27]

Butler's broader view, very much the opinion of a traditionalist where etiquette and form are concerned, is that the return of Harold Wilson to Downing Street in 1974 represented a final break with the trappings of grandeur in government. The decade of the 1960s, he believes, saw a significant devaluation in the currency of politicians, that a sea change took place, sufficiently fundamental to ensure that Heath's 1970–74 government was the final breakwater, until it too was washed away in the late 1970s.

A kind of democratisation, Butler believes, was taking place in the 1960s, in which the press no longer accorded automatic respect to senior politicians. A turning point was the moment when *The Times* ceased to refer to the Prime Minister as 'Mr So-and-So', and merely used surnames. It was an irreverent time, when satirical revues played to huge, hungry audiences and there was general disillusion with hypocrisy in government. Britain had won the war and, in its complacency, had not adapted but rather had reverted to a Churchillian ante-bellum conservatism; other European countries were overtaking Britain. From a posture of idle complacency, the country was thrust into cynicism and self-questioning. The result was an orgy of satire.

Without doubt, there was ample scope for the democratisation of Britain's arcane institutions in the 1960s, and the sweeping away of antiquated class prejudice, of assumptions of entitlement and privilege, was long overdue. Equally certainly, the young Butler saw clearly, after the Macmillan era, that dramatic change was imminent. Since the election of John Kennedy to the presidency in 1960, calls for a younger administration in Britain had foreshadowed the Wilson revolution of 1964.

The Civil Service itself was the target of robust criticism and there were calls for its reform. In 1959, *The Establishment* was published, a collection of essays that took aim at what it perceived as an anachronistic master class, dominating the most sensitive British institutions. Once this class was swept away, Britain would reassert itself and, through the humane nature and efficiency of its institutions, return to moral leadership of the world.

An important essay in that collection was 'The Apotheosis of the Dilettante' by Thomas Balogh. In a savagely accurate criticism of the Civil Service, Balogh describes the kind of person and the qualities that were valued by the service, summing them up as 'an attitude of effortless superiority, combined with cultured scepticism'. Upon these depended 'that special mysterious art, Administrative Capacity'. Education in an arts subject was mandatory, he argued, while 'anything smacking of vocational training and technical knowledge was severely discountenanced'. Instead, the ideal candidate acquired 'a purposefully useless, somewhat dilettante, erudition which would keep "dangerous thoughts" well away'.[28]

In 1965, the Select Committee on Estimates published a report that urged research into and examination of 'the structure, recruitment and management of the Civil Service'. The upshot was the Fulton Report of 1968, which reached similar conclusions to those of Professor Balogh. This was the first comprehensive review of the Civil Service since the Northcote-Trevelyan reforms of 1854, and after such an interval there was ample scope for modernisation. The first section of the report made the point that the service of 1968 remained essentially the product of nineteenth-century thinking, and set out six specific criticisms of the *modus operandi* of the service.

First, it was still based on the philosophy of the 'amateur', 'generalist' or 'all-rounder', a tendency most visible in the administrative class. Second, the existing system of classes within the service 'seriously impede[d] its work'. The word 'class', moreover, should be abolished in favour of 'groups'. Third, many scientists, engineers and other specialists did not receive the responsibilities, authority or opportunities due to them. Fourth, too few civil servants were skilled managers. Not enough had been trained in personnel management, project management, accounting and control. Fifth, the service was insulated; there needed to be more contact between its members and the community. Finally, there were significant defects in personnel management; career planning was sketchy; officers were moved too frequently; individual initiative was inadequately rewarded.[29]

This damning set of conclusions articulated the concerns of many. While attitudes were changing fundamentally, the Civil Service seemed proof against change. Butler who, after seven years, was reasonably well established, represented the very 'generalist' at whom the Fulton Report took aim. Change would follow – and reasonably quickly after Fulton – but officials of Butler's age, already well up the ladder, would be those who ran the service in the 1980s and 1990s. As it happened, they were the last of that ilk to do so. Since Butler's time as Cabinet Secretary, no classicist, no all-rounder has held the top spot.

The intake of the service was also changing. Graduates still occupied the fast stream, but their profile was more varied. In 1961, when Butler joined, the service took 120 entrants, of whom 117 were men, predominantly from Oxford or Cambridge. By the 1970s, those figures were changing, and by the time he retired from the service in 1998, equality between the sexes had almost been achieved.

Throughout his secondment to Downing Street, Butler was aware of the changes taking place and of the inevitability of a fundamental restructuring of the Civil Service. His quarrel was not with those changes, which he broadly regarded as progressive, but with what he viewed as the unnecessary class warfare that certain of Wilson's team institutionalised. Marcia Williams, for example, had been determined to replace the typing secretaries at 10 Downing Street. Known as the 'Garden Girls', this was a group of polite, presentable, well brought-up girls, typically the daughters of lieutenant-colonels and country squires. Recruited on the principle that the upper classes are naturally discreet, they were anathema to Williams, who was determined to find a different source of supply. Her apparent fixation that the Civil Service was the enemy of democratic government was offensive to Butler and, after three and a half years, he was not entirely unhappy to be returning to the Treasury.

Even as Butler was leaving Downing Street, Williams used her influence with the Prime Minister to discomfit him, to Donoughue's disgust, when he recorded:

> Richard Graham from my Unit has not been invited to Robin Butler's farewell party – because Marcia has intervened to restrict severely the number of guests at a hated civil servant's party. Typical of the high political policy level on which she naturally operates. Private Office now call her the Princess of Pettiness. Harsh, but she has worked hard for the title.[30]

Williams herself, as Donoughue recorded, simply ignored Butler's farewell party at Downing Street:

> I went upstairs to Robin Butler's farewell party. I talked to Douglas Wass, Victor Rothschild and Robert Armstrong ... Marcia refused to come into the blue room where the party was held. She sat in the big room next door

having her photograph taken by a famous society photographer. Everybody could see this going on – it was very rude to Robin Butler.[31]

Butler's departure, however, did permit one change at No. 10 that gave pleasure to Donoughue: the educational background of the private office became more democratic. 'Robert Armstrong (Eton), Tom Bridges (Eton) and Robin Butler (Harrow) have gone', he wrote, 'and been replaced by Ken Stowe (grammar school), Patrick Wright (minor public school) and Nigel Wicks (grammar school).'[32]

As a result of the decision that he was too young to succeed Armstrong at No. 10, Butler was, perhaps fortunately, absent from Downing Street for the closing years of the Labour government. When he returned to the Treasury at the end of 1975, he had no idea that Wilson would retire in April; the question of whether he intended to resign or whether the decision was forced on him has been exhaustively debated. Numerous conspiracy theories surround his decision.*

At the heart of those theories was the allegation that Wilson was, if not a Soviet agent, at least a sympathiser. The first public hint of any such suspicion came in October 1971, when the *News of the World* attributed to Soviet defector Oleg Lyalin the assertion that the Soviet Union had arranged the murder of Hugh Gaitskell in order to force an election of a Labour Party leader, an election that Wilson could be expected to win.† The theme was taken up by *Private Eye*, where Auberon Waugh kept up an unceasing barrage of innuendo about Wilson's Soviet connections.

The accusation was not news to the Security Service (MI5), where several officers had serious concerns about Wilson's loyalty. Indeed, MI5 kept a file on Wilson, a file so sensitive that it was labelled 'Henry Worthington' and

---

* The belief that there was more to Wilson's resignation persisted and was, in fact, further inflamed by subsequent scandals involving Wilson's and Marcia Williams's cronies, notably the conviction of Joseph (Lord) Kagan for tax fraud in 1980. See also the *Sunday Express*, 13 August 1978, for the pervasive belief that Wilson's resignation had 'never been fully explained'.

† This theory was well known to British Intelligence. In fact it was another Soviet defector, Anatoliy Mikhaylovich Golitsyn, who defected via Helsinki in December 1961, who accused the KGB of poisoning Gaitskell and accused Wilson of being a KGB informer.

kept in the Director-General's safe. Peter Wright asserts, in his book *Spycatcher*, that elements of the Worthington file were systematically leaked to the press.[33] When Wilson and the Labour Party were returned to power in 1974, the campaign of smears and innuendo was renewed.[34]

The sudden nature of Wilson's resignation in April 1976 fuelled the theory that he had been blackmailed into resigning to avoid the revelation of damaging information. His biographer, Ben Pimlott, records that 'people who saw Wilson in his last month of office found him listless, tired and anxious, and with a diminishing appetite for political struggle'.[35] The official version of events is that he had decided in 1974 that he would serve only two more years as party leader, whether in power or in opposition. On that principle, he suggested to Donoughue that he take a two-year leave of absence from the London School of Economics 'until Easter 1976, because I will retire then'.[36]

Years after the events of 1976, Butler asked Lady Wilson, Harold Wilson's widow, what her husband had intended in 1975–76. She confirmed categorically that he had told her in the spring of 1975 that he had lost his appetite for the job. Whether or not he was assisted in taking that decision by the belief that MI5 or MI6 had damaging information about him remains uncertain.[37] There can, however, be no doubt that Butler was better away from Downing Street than involved in the allegations and counter-allegations of those last four months.

Instead, while Callaghan took over from Wilson, he embarked on what he saw as a 'purge treatment to refresh me and get the contamination of politics out of my system after the heady days at Number 10'.[38] The task that awaited him at the Treasury was in his words, 'the most back-room of back-room jobs'. In the twenty-first century, when computers are commonplace, when every adolescent is familiar with a spreadsheet and when instant calculations, from heart-rate while jogging to mileage per gallon of fuel in real time, are available, it seems inconceivable that Whitehall was unable to calculate the rate at which the national government was spending cash. As Chancellor of the Exchequer in 1956, Harold Macmillan described economic forecasting based on historical numbers as akin to 'looking up a train in last year's Bradshaw' (a railway timetable).[39]

With the goal of devising a system of gathering information and forecasting expenditure rather than collecting data retrospectively, Butler was appointed to lead a team of Treasury officials alongside consultants from Arthur Andersen, the Chicago-based company that was at the time one of the 'big five'. The project was given the name FIS1* and was known in the Civil Service as 'Fizz'.

The new task appealed to him greatly, as it had a specific target, a clear deadline of 1 April 1977, and a precisely defined budget. Unsurprisingly, for such a wide-ranging project, whose scope was initially impossible to predict with accuracy, costs seemed certain to exceed the budget in the final months, when Arthur Andersen needed to bring in more staff. Reckoning that, since this was the first important project in which the Treasury had used outside consultants, Andersen would see it as an important precedent, he was able to hold the accounting firm's fees to the original quote. For both Andersen and for Butler personally, it was important that the FIS project be completed as forecast and budgeted. Both sides, he recalls with a chuckle, 'were on trial'.[40] In the event, the project was completed on time.

The eighteen months that Butler spent on 'Fizz' turned out to be of enormous significance in 1976 and 1977 when Britain was compelled to seek help from the International Monetary Fund. Denis Healey, the Chancellor of the Exchequer during the difficult months of 1977, was the beneficiary of the much tighter control that the Treasury now exercised on the public sector borrowing requirement. He records that, after the frenetic activity and panic when the government first approached the IMF, he was credited with achieving a miracle in turning the economy around. In all candour, he admits that this credit was undeserved. It was principally excessive caution in Treasury forecasts that had caused the IMF's stringent controls; Britain, he claims, could in fact have managed without the IMF loan. Forecasts were too pessimistic and Britain was 'still describing our public expenditure in a way that was immensely damaging to our standing in the financial markets.[41]

In April 1977, having successfully put Financial Information Systems in place, Butler returned to policy work. With the change of job came promotion to under-secretary, a notable step, as he was only thirty-nine. In

* Naturally enough 'Financial Information Systems 1'.

a posting to what he described as 'the boiler room of the Treasury' he was put in charge of the General Expenditure Policy Group. The internal Civil Service newspaper reported on the project with some fanfare in April 1977:

> From next week the Treasury's general expenditure division will be run by Robin Butler.
>
> Butler, an Old Harrovian, Oxford Rugby Blue and classical scholar, who succeeds the Wykehamist John Anson on the latter's promotion from under-secretary to deputy secretary, has spent the past 18 months in the kind of job not normally associated with the *jeunesse dorée*.
>
> Perched in a turret above the rooftops of the Treasury Chambers, the former billet of the Ministry of Defence aerial reconnaissance library, he has helped develop, with a battery of computer experts, what the Treasury men call 'Fizz'.
>
> Butler and his boffins have had the task of tightening up the gap in the government's control of public spending with the introduction throughout Whitehall of a new Financial Information System, to give it its proper title, which measures spending flows on a monthly basis, a distinct improvement on the quarterly returns previously available.
>
> Tall, fair-haired, athletic with an infectious enthusiasm for his esoteric work, Butler in his new job will be deeply involved in that annual cycle by which Treasury men live, known as the Public Expenditure Survey.
>
> His most glamorous job to date was his membership of the team of Whitehall fliers who make up the private secretaries' office at Number 10 Downing Street. For all his junior rank, there was talk of his succeeding Robert Armstrong as Principal Private Secretary in 1975.[42]

The language of the article is revealing. The reader is immediately made aware of Butler's social background – Harrow and Oxford, replacing a Wykehamist. The notion of specialism in something as vulgar as economics is lightly brushed over and the system by which 'Treasury men' live is mildly ridiculed. However quaintly phrased, it is clear – particularly clear from the last paragraph – that the tall, fair-haired, athletic Butler is being trained and put through a careful job rotation to equip him for the very top of the service.

The eighteen months in 'the back-room' may, as Butler suggests, have put him on trial. The promotion in April 1977 underlined the importance of the project that had occupied him since his return from Downing Street, and projected him into a greatly more visible role, mixing with expenditure controllers at international conferences. One such conference took place in Washington in 1978. A photograph among Butler's papers shows a somewhat overawed civil servant shaking hands with President Jimmy Carter at the White House.

Butler headed a group whose doings and achievements were very much in the public eye, even if its members necessarily remained off the radar screen. As the Labour Party became locked in an internecine fight between its centre and its far left, as Wilson's reputation was increasingly impugned and Callaghan made a series of disastrous errors in relations with trade unions, Butler must have been content to be involved in policy rather than the 'political' side of the Civil Service. The Treasury was a distinctly safer place to roost than 10 Downing Street.

In October 1978, Callaghan decided against an election, preferring to postpone it until the following spring. This turned out to be an expensive error, as the trade unions, contemptuous of the 5 per cent limit to pay rises, orchestrated widespread disruption of public services during what became known as the 'winter of discontent'. The timing was unfortunate; the Conservative Party under Margaret Thatcher campaigned on promises to halt inflation and to curb the trade unions. This ensured a huge swing from Labour to the Tories. With the Liberal Party in disarray as allegations of conspiracy to murder swirled around Jeremy Thorpe, the Tories were elected with a comfortable majority.

CHAPTER 7

MIDPOINT, 1979

MATHEMATICALLY, THE YEAR OF 1979 was always going to be the midpoint of Butler's Civil Service career, provided that he followed the normal practice of staying with the service until his sixtieth birthday. After his first eighteen and a half years of service he turned forty-one and could look forward to a further eighteen and a half years before he retired at the end of 1997. Such, in the event, was the precise shape of his career.

Since 1961, his life had followed a conventional course. He and Jill had married in August 1962 and moved into a small flat in Dulwich. In October 1964, Sophie was born and, when Jill became pregnant again in the spring of 1966, they moved into a house in nearby Sydenham Hill. Their lives were busy: they acted together with the Dulwich Players and with the Old Harrovian Players. In May 1964, a production of *The Tempest* at Harrow included Butler as Ferdinand, 'a superbly languid and effeminate young prince', and Jill as a nymph.[1] Butler continued to play rugby at weekends and took part in a Richmond tour of Kenya in May 1963.

Early in Butler's Civil Service career, Rab Butler, First Secretary of State and Home Secretary, worked in the same building and, to avoid possible security problems if Rab's post was misrouted, a system was instituted that all correspondence addressed to 'R. Butler' would go first to Rab and would then be forwarded as necessary. On one occasion, Rab received a curious notice from the Richmond Rugby Club that at first alarmed him: 'You have been selected to play for the First XV against Bath ... Position: Wing-forward. Please attend training on Wednesday night and reply by return.' Rab, by then a portly sixty-year-old, put the card in the internal mail to Butler with a note reading simply: 'Dear Robin, I am not free on Saturday. Please could you deputise for me? Rab.'[2]

Soon after Sophie's birth, however, Butler decided to take a significant step and give up playing rugby.[3] In moments of candour, he admitted that the decision was helped by the arrival in Richmond of Tommy Bedford, a South African wing forward.* Four critical years younger, it seemed very likely that Bedford would take Butler's place in the Richmond XV, and he decided that this was a suitable moment for him to bow out with dignity.

Catherine Nell was born in January 1967. In the growing modern trend, her father was present at the birth; the experience was one that he found 'moving', but one that he had no desire to repeat when Andrew was born in June 1968. The Butler family of five was then complete. The names of the three young Butlers were each derived from a Greek virtue: Sophie for wisdom, Catherine (although she was known by her second name 'Nell') for purity, and Andrew for manliness. Looking after the three was a full-time job, and it was to be twelve years before Jill returned to teaching.

Both Butler and Jill had developed a love of travel in their Oxford days, and they have continued to travel all their lives. Neither saw a holiday as an opportunity to sit on the beach minding children. Holidays were to be enjoyed, of course, but were also to pose challenges – rock climbing†, hiking, rounds of golf. Accordingly, they and friends developed a system of taking holidays together, accompanied by two or three au pair girls to look after the children and take them to the beach during the morning, while the parents did what they wanted. It was a system that worked and lasted for many years; even after the children were grown, the couples continued to take holidays together; a Cornish house between Rock and Polzeath on the north coast of Cornwall became the holiday destination for the Butlers and their friends every Easter after 1970.

Not only were their frequently vigorous, physically demanding holidays

---

* Tommy Bedford, who played both as a wing forward and number 8, won twenty-five caps for South Africa and was captain of the national team. His international career came to an end as a result of his continued criticism of the South African government's policy of apartheid.

† On one occasion, on holiday in the Lake District, Butler enquired about the best rock climbing in the area. The hotel owner obliged with some suggestions, ruefully adding that every year some damfool Londoner managed to kill himself. Butler wisely revised his plans.

important, but their choice of travelling companions was also critical. By travelling with friends who were not civil servants, they were able to make a complete break with Butler's working life. This came to be a very important part of their routine, and Jill estimates that they spent over a hundred holidays together with the small group of their close friends.

These Easter holidays were interspersed with expeditions overseas in the summer. Yugoslavia, Italy and Greece featured at different times in their holiday plans. One additional activity was forced on Butler by his wife and daughters, who missed no opportunity to reproach him for spending his weekends playing male sports. Surely there was a sport that the whole family could engage in – sailing, for example. Despite having very little experience and certainly no expertise in dinghies, Butler was persuaded, press-ganged perhaps, into buying a Mirror dinghy. After a disastrous maiden voyage, the family acquired the knack of steering the craft and, full of enthusiasm, joined the Civil Service Sailing Club. In time, the children wanted their own boat, so a second dinghy was acquired, a purchase that ensured that at least one Butler craft was able to avoid finishing last in the club races. For many years thereafter, sailing was an important part of family weekends and holidays.

From the time of their marriage in 1962 until Butler's retirement from the Civil Service at the end of 1997, Dulwich and the surrounding communities provided a home base for the family. It made sense, therefore, for them to consider sending all three children to schools within the Dulwich group.* A further consideration was that Jill had taught for three years and was keen to return to teaching at a secondary school. 'I missed the experience of seeing children develop, as one does observe in a secondary school', she explained.[4] This was an important factor in Jill's decision to teach at Alleyn's, a post she took up in 1976. As it turned out, only Nell spent her teenage years at Alleyn's, but it was a decision that Jill never regretted.

After leaving Harrow in 1956, Butler had kept up his connection with the school beyond appearing for the Old Harrovian Players, and in 1975 he was invited to become a governor. It was a critical time for the school:

* The group includes Alleyn's School, a co-educational school, Dulwich College, a boys' school for ages seven to eighteen, and James Allen's Girls' School.

during the 1960s, the headmaster, Dr Robert ('Jimmy') James, was reluctant to implement any significant change, incurring the accusation that he was intimidated by the school's governors, whose stooge he had become. In the following decade, the governing board recognised its tendency to be over-conservative and agreed that some younger members were needed. Butler, at the age of only thirty-seven, joined along with three other 'youngsters', Evelyn de Rothschild, Geoffrey Simmonds and Roger Boissier.

Although the young Robin Butler had decided in 1956 that schoolmastering would not be his career, he developed and retained a passionate interest in education. It certainly influenced him that Jill was a teacher; reform of Britain's school system was a very live topic in the 1970s and the future of the public (independent) schools was uncertain. The presence among the Harrow governors of an apparently progressive young mandarin of somewhat Whiggish tendencies had a leavening effect on the traditional direction of the governing body.

Since Butler's departure in 1956, Harrow had become leaden-footed in adapting to a new era. There were a few innovative and forward-thinking housemasters, but most were deeply conservative and unadventurous. A handful of stimulating, mostly younger masters ran the literary and cultural societies* but, for the most part, the old, outdated values of a Victorian boarding school prevailed. The governors were symbols of that era and Dr James was their willing agent.

In the early 1970s, there had been periodic calls for reform of all kinds on Harrow Hill and, symbolically, the governors' meeting in November 1970 that agreed the terms of a new headmaster's appointment also agreed that the wearing of formal dress – morning tailcoat, striped trousers and all the trimmings – at Lords for the Eton and Harrow match should be discontinued. Thus ended the veneer of perhaps the most sacred event on the Harrow calendar, a social date that had been revered by Bertie Wooster as well as by Stanley Baldwin.[5] This was just one of the proposals for modernisation that were being entertained.

It is unclear whether it was Butler's experience of negotiations with the Irish,

* There was one notable exception: the Revd H. L. ('Bush') Harris was an iconoclastic polymath whose wide-ranging knowledge of literature and the arts was a stimulus enjoyed, unfortunately, exclusively by boys in the upper stream. His ability at once to represent and question authority was unique among the school's senior common room in the 1960s. There were a few up-and-coming younger beacons, of whom Butler's contemporary Jeremy Lemmon was a leading light.

his years at the Treasury, his urbane and conciliatory manner blended with a certain ruthlessness, his relative youth, or the simple fact that he had once been head boy, that marked him out as a school governor. At all events, once projected into this potential minefield, he quickly established his role as the voice of reason, overlaid with a realistic approach to the future. He had kept up a regular, if loose, connection with the school, returning to act in performances by the Old Harrovian Players and for occasional Old Boys' rugby and Harrow football matches. The appointment of new governors, each of whom brought a record of early success in his field – in finance, business and the Treasury – signalled a move away from the country Tory atmosphere that Butler found to be 'pretty stuffy'.

R. A. A. 'Bimby' Holt, chairman of the governors, was an old Harrovian whose son had been at the school in the 1960s, a decade in which over 40 per cent of school entrants were sons of old Harrovians.[6] He tended to dominate and get his own way with his fellow governors; Butler recalls that 'this may have irked other members of the Board'. This delicate understatement undoubtedly conceals an autocracy and resistance to change from a man whose name was synonymous with legendary athletic success in his youth.*

When, in 1980, Holt, a solicitor, ran into trouble for drafting a client's will from which he stood to benefit – an action that ran counter to Law Society's rules – he asked Butler to sound out the opinion of the other governors as to whether he should step down. Butler consulted his colleagues and had the difficult task of communicating to Holt that the majority felt that he should go. The episode – and the part that Butler played in it – were illustrative of his skills as a diplomatist and of the respect in which he was held by Holt and other governors. Predictably, in due course, after thirteen years as a governor of the school, he had the satisfaction of capping his boyhood success by becoming chairman of the Harrow governors in 1988. The appointment, in the year that he became Cabinet Secretary, had a pleasing symmetry.†

* He was an outstanding cricketer and racquets player in his schooldays. His son Chris played cricket for Harrow against Eton at Lords from 1963 to 1965 and also represented Harrow at racquets.

† Further symmetry is offered by Andrew Butler's career: following his father as head of the school, he too read 'Greats' at Univ, almost won a rugby Blue and joined the board of governors at Harrow.

At the beginning of 1979, at the midpoint of his career, he could not have predicted the importance of the coming year. It was to be the year in which the Conservatives won the general election, bringing to an end the Wilson-Callaghan administration that had first come to power fifteen years before; it was the year in which the first female Prime Minister moved into Downing Street, with unforeseeable consequences for Butler's career. It was also the year in which Robin and Jill moved from the small Dulwich townhouse into a more substantial family home.

The family was now quite at home in South London and they scoured Dulwich for a suitable house. In the late 1970s, London property was beginning to command higher and higher prices, and their attempts to coordinate the sale of 6 Rockhill and the purchase of a house both large enough for five and within their budget proved frustrating. When they stumbled on 28 Half Moon Lane, across from Brockwell Park* and around the corner from Herne Hill railway station, despite its several shortcomings, they leapt at it.

The house in Half Moon Lane was one of a variety common in the 1970s. Built in 1895 and originally occupied by a middle-class Victorian family with, perhaps, one live-in maid, it had fallen from popular favour as the area became less *petit bourgeois* between the wars. After the Second World War, the house had been divided into several units and bore the marks of low-cost conversion by the owners. Butler was about to change jobs in the Treasury, moving from his role as controller of public expenditure to that of Principal Establishment Officer, effectively director of personnel, and the imminent move entitled him to take a month's special leave. With the aid of an enthusiastic but erratic contractor, he set about restoring and redecorating the house, room by room.

The contrast between the small, modern, utilitarian townhouse that they had occupied before and the spacious Victorian pile at Half Moon Lane was, at first, daunting. As young graduates and upwardly mobile professionals, Robin and Jill had occupied flats in gently decaying bourgeois neighbourhoods. Married, they had moved from basic flat to basic house, each functional, neither a place that they would cherish as a family home. As they moved up the ladder,

* When Sir Robin Butler was honoured with a barony in 1999 he chose the title 'Lord Butler of Brockwell' to the consternation of Garter King of Arms who felt that it was inappropriate to take one's title from a public park. See Chapter 18.

another child arrived until, with three children over ten, they moved into a property that they could make their own, a solid, enduring structure that would be home for more than a year or two. In the event, they lived there for the next eighteen years.* Butler's career was prospering. At the very least, barring some massive indiscretion, he would retire as a Permanent Under-Secretary with a knighthood; as for the most he could expect, with a little luck...

One other life-changing bonus came Butler's way in 1979. Viscount Waverley, chairman of the Royal Opera House from 1946 to 1967, knowing how conspiratorial the arts could be, had asked for someone from the Treasury to take minutes of meetings; first Sir Denis Rickett and then Robert Armstrong, an opera lover, had taken the job. When he became Cabinet Secretary in 1979, Armstrong did not feel able to handle the entire task himself, so he, Butler and two other civil servants handled the minutes in rotation. The task was hardly taxing, and brought the reward of two tickets for every Royal Opera House production. While Jill had enjoyed ballet, Jeremy Lemmon, Harrow contemporary and an accomplished singer, said of Butler that 'he didn't have a note in him'.[7] With assiduous preparation – in the days before projected surtitles, when every libretto needed to be studied beforehand – he and Jill became devoted opera-goers, an interest included in his *Who's Who* entry.

That same year of 1979 brought the events that most affected Butler's career in the Civil Service – the May election and the arrival of Margaret Thatcher in Downing Street. At the beginning of the decade, Butler had been in close contact with Heath's 'inner Cabinet' – Whitelaw, Carrington, Prior – and had not imagined Thatcher as a future leader. Symbolically, her elevation to the highest office came to pass in the same year as the Butler family established itself in their first lasting family home.

The first half of Butler's Civil Service career – the arriving – came to an end in 1979. Now he had arrived, both professionally, as the youngest Under-Secretary in the Service, and as a father, *paterfamilias* of a family with three children in a spacious family home. The curtain was about to rise on

* By the time that Butler retired from the Civil Service, he and Jill had bought a house in Norfolk. The move from Half Moon Lane was complicated as the assorted chattels of thirty-five years of marriage were moved either to Norfolk or to the Master's Lodgings at University College or to their London flat.

the second half of his career which, from 1982 until his retirement, was to flow naturally, almost inevitably, from the earlier years. In retrospect, the symmetry of his career path, with 1979 at its centre, is remarkable.

That is with the benefit of hindsight; at the time, the immediate future was much less clear. As the breakdown of diplomatic relations between Thatcher and Heath became increasingly public and increasingly poisonous, Butler must have wondered how his immediate career would develop. Would he be a marked man as a result of his earlier closeness with Heath? Would he be allowed into the inner counsels of the Thatcher government? Was that in fact a place where he wanted to be? In his eighteen years in the Civil Service, he had accumulated experience that the new Prime Minister would find invaluable. Indeed, if Providence had decided to mould him for the role of Cabinet Secretary and head of the Civil Service, it could hardly have done a better job. He had reached the age of forty as the Labour government ran out of steam; the activities of youth gradually became memories as heavier responsibilities weighed.

When the Tory government came to power, Butler had run the General Expenditure Division of the Treasury for two years. His family was increasingly independent; his recent appointments had been handled with timeliness and efficiency. He was now eminently qualified and ready for the appointment denied him in 1975. Whether he was to receive it was in the gift of a Prime Minister not known for her tolerance of opposing views.*

* In the event, Butler described Mrs Thatcher's attitude to him in 1979 as 'understanding'. She accepted more readily his close relations with Edward Heath than she did those of his predecessor, Sir Robert Armstrong. Butler remained on friendly terms with Heath. When Heath's autobiography was published in 1998, he invited the Butlers to the launch party and presented Butler with a copy inscribed 'To the man who stopped me writing this book for 25 years and has now been overcome.' Letter to Nora Butler, 19 October 1998.

CHAPTER 8

FOUR BUSY YEARS, 1979–1983

THE TORIES CAME TO power in 1979 on a promise to control inflation and to curb trade union power. Also high on the government's agenda was the reduction of direct taxation, principally by reducing the highest rate of income tax from 98 per cent to the European average of about 60 per cent.[1] 'Pay as you spend' was to replace 'pay as you earn' in the government's glossary of terms. Such a change of policy would involve significant savings in government expenditure and necessitated an almost immediate Budget. The election was held on 3 May; on 8 May, the Cabinet met for the first time and agreed the date of 12 June for Chancellor Geoffrey Howe to announce the first of the widely expected cuts.

In preparation for the announcement, Howe indicated to Sir Douglas Wass, the Under-Secretary at the Treasury, that he proposed to announce cuts of £800 million in public spending. Wass promptly consulted Butler and, together, the two were able, with some difficulty, to arrive at a total reduction of that amount. Well-satisfied, Wass accompanied Howe to Downing Street to inform the new Prime Minister, but returned to the Treasury soon after 6.00 that evening and, considerably shaken, informed Butler that Mrs Thatcher had demanded a further reduction of £400 million and that these should be agreed to before 9.00 the following morning. Taking the Treasury telephone directory home with him, Butler contacted all the Under-Secretaries in charge of Treasury expenditure control groups. Where, he asked, could further significant reductions be made? After what he described as 'like obtaining underwriting for a flotation in the City', he had extracted promises of a further £400 million.

After the Budget, Mrs Thatcher invited Howe and his junior ministers, together with the Treasury team, to a drinks party at No. 10. Butler reminded her tactfully that the Treasury had managed to find her extra £400 million overnight. 'I know', the Prime Minister replied deadpan. 'I should have asked for more.' This typical Thatcherism masked a considerable gratitude, for Margaret Thatcher never forgot a favour or disfavour. Butler is sure that his prompt and effective response to her demands marked him out for her support and patronage on several occasions in the future.

The business of reduction of expenditure was to recur almost immediately when he settled into his new job as Principal Establishment Officer at the Treasury. There was no mystery about Mrs Thatcher's views on public expenditure, and there were few candidates for pruning as tempting as the Civil Service. In that context, the decision to transfer Butler was seen as significant by the *Financial Times*, who predicted an imminent reshuffle, noting that 'Mr Robin Butler, one of the most highly regarded officials, is to become establishment officer responsible for personnel at a time when the staff numbers are being squeezed tightly'.[2]

There had already been reductions in the size of the Civil Service; 21,000 jobs had been cut since 1976, bringing the total complement to 735,000. In 1979, Mrs Thatcher set in motion a further reduction of 100,000 by 1983. Her approach, Butler recalls, was tactically sound. Previous attempts to reduce staff had failed because several ministers demanded specific reductions, thus galvanising their officials to demonstrate that it would be impossible to cut those specific jobs. Now, the Prime Minister effectively said: 'I don't care how you do it. I want the total staffing to be at 635,000 within four years.' She did, however, make one stipulation: the cuts had to be applied at all levels; it would not be enough simply to reduce numbers of junior staff.

The request met with predictable resistance from Permanent Secretaries, all of whom were invited to Downing Street to receive their instructions. Ultimately, as they recognised, they could do nothing but obey the directive, and it was agreed that cuts would be made in direct proportion to the size of each department. As the official in charge of human resources at the Treasury, Butler drew the short straw to implement the cuts.

Counter to the Prime Minister's concern that no real progress would be made and that senior staff would be retained at the expense of expendable junior staff, in the Treasury it proved vastly easier to shed officers in the senior grades. Typists and messengers, on the other hand, were needed as much as ever; the paper load had not diminished. Part of the messengers' job, however, was to prepare coffee and tea twice a day and to wheel this from office to office around the Treasury. If everyone prepared their own tea and coffee, Butler reasoned, it would be possible to achieve the cuts required.

With the approval of the Permanent Secretary, Butler took his proposal to the trades union, whose officials pointed out that it was scarcely sound economics to replace junior, inexpensive staff with senior, higher-paid staff to perform the same function. Nonetheless, he was resolved to be seen to be doing something, and he addressed how staff would behave if there were no tea/coffee service. In true bureaucratic style, he circulated a questionnaire to all staff, asking:

> Do you currently use the messenger tea service in the Treasury? If the answer is no, tick this box and ignore the rest of the questionnaire.
>
> If the answer is yes, please say what you will do when it is replaced. Will you:
>
> a. Go without?
> b. Get your secretary to make it for you?
> c. Bring in a flask from home?
> d. Use one of the hot water dispensers located around the building?
> e. Join a tea club to share the task?

Predictably, the initiative was met with facetious and ribald responses; an article in *The Guardian* pilloried the entire enterprise.[3] The most effective satire, however, came from within, when a further questionnaire was circulated, informing staff that, with the withdrawal of the tea/coffee service, there would be less need for lavatory facilities and that a charge would now be introduced. In pitch-perfect parody of Butler's memorandum, the spoof questionnaire asked:

Do you currently use the toilet facilities in the Treasury? If the answer is no, tick this box and seek urgent medical advice.
If the answer is yes… *

The 'questionnaire' continued in the same style – would the respondent go without, get his secretary to do it for him, bring in a flask from home? – and concluded by warning staff that, if the survey were leaked as the previous one had been, a leak inquiry would be conducted. Conscious that he had been responsible for making the Civil Service look like the setting for a *Carry On* farce, Butler duly abandoned the project and sought economies in other areas.

During Butler's time as Principal Establishment Officer, one long-running issue came to centre stage. The Fulton Report of 1968 had recommended the creation of a Civil Service Department, and this had been introduced by Harold Wilson in the same year. The department was something of a political football throughout the 1970s; a 1977 report recommended that many of its functions be returned to the Treasury. Unsurprisingly, James Callaghan, then Prime Minister, refused to be pressured into taking action on an issue that he considered political rather than bureaucratic.

Soon after the Tories came to power in 1979, the Commons Treasury and Civil Service Committee made a number of recommendations concerning the department. The Prime Minister responded by abolishing it altogether in late 1981. By an Order in Council of 1 December 1981, its functions were redistributed between the Treasury, which assumed control of manpower, pay, superannuation and allowances, and took responsibility for the Central Computer and Telecommunications Agency, the Civil Service Catering Organisation, Her Majesty's Stationery Office and the Central Office of Information. The new position of Second Permanent Secretary in the Cabinet Office was created with responsibility for management, organisation, staff efficiency and personnel recruitment.

The abolition of the department resulted in massive internal disruption accompanied by a severe loss of morale in the service. For Butler, the exercise

* Much later, Butler discovered that the author of the spoof questionnaire was Alex Allan, later Principal Private Secretary to John Major and Chairman of the Joint Intelligence Committee.

was a crash course in personnel management, a fairly new responsibility for officers of the administrative grade. It also served to convince him of the importance of a long-term approach to human resources. To develop and maintain the highest levels of operating efficiency in the Civil Service, Butler came to believe, involves planning ahead in order to train and effectively to deploy the talent at the disposal of the service. This approach – which he unashamedly describes as 'paternalistic' is directly at odds with the more 'modern' method of advertising for applications for senior management positions.

In the task of deploying retained staff of the Civil Service Department, restoring morale, meeting the Mrs Thatcher's demands for staff reductions and maintaining good relations with senior civil servants in other departments, Butler was by and large successful. His handling of the transition was praised by Sir Douglas Wass, by then Permanent Secretary at the Treasury, who wrote:

> Dear Robin,
>
> We had so much to talk about yesterday at lunch that I quite failed to do what I most wanted to: that is to express my great gratitude to you for the marvellous way that over the past couple of years you have handled the P.E.O. job. It has been a period of great difficulty. First the study for the merger and then the absorption of half the C.S.D. Quite apart from these organisational upheavals we have had the ongoing problems of morale, internal audit, management accounting, not to mention the Crown Agents Tribunal. I cannot remember a time when we have had more to cope with on the management front … I believe that your two years as P.E.O. will in the long run stand you in good stead. I wish that when I was your age I had had a comparable experience.[4]

In fact, Butler was happy to have responsibility for human resources, rather than for public expenditure, as the Prime Minister was relentless in seeking out areas where cuts could be made in Civil Service costs. On 28 January 1981, she paid a visit to the Treasury, an event that both he and Wass viewed with some concern, as he wrote to his parents:

> Mrs T's visit to the Treasury seemed to go well on Wednesday; anyway Douglas Wass was very pleased. She is in a great fury about public expenditure at the moment – thank goodness I'm out of the firing line! … I kept out of her way until she took tea with a representative group as the last item in her visit, and then I had a talk with her and escorted her out of the building.[5]

By the end of 1981, the Butlers were well enough established at Half Moon Lane to have a family Christmas, inviting Bernard, Nora and Diana and, after some pressure, to yield to Nell, who had mounted a campaign to adopt a family dog from the Battersea Dogs and Cats Home. Robin and Jill finally capitulated and Tess, a blend of collie and Alsatian, joined the family. Tess became an important part of family life and routine; her morning walk introduced the family to other local residents, including Anthony Lester (later Lord Lester of Herne Hill), whose morning conversations with Butler became an important part of the latter's day.

Diana, however, was not well and, as the weather was snowy, Bernard and Nora decided against driving down from Lytham St Annes. Diana's health had been deteriorating for some time; indeed, she had well outlived the initial prognosis of four years, given in 1959 when the hole in her heart was discovered. Butler recalls that she was increasingly sad to be in worsening health as her nephew and nieces were 'growing more capable and energetic as she declined'. On Diana's fortieth birthday, 12 January 1982, Nora went into her bedroom in the morning to find that she had died in her sleep.

Nora had long been concerned about Diana's future after her own and Bernard's death. She saw the obvious difficulties of Diana's living with Robin and Jill and there was, accordingly, a certain resignation, an acceptance of her death. Her brother had been a devoted friend and had spent time with her whenever possible; he and Jill had taken her, for example, on a week-long trip to Paris when Sophie was a baby. He had taught her to drive and to play bridge, which she later played to a very high standard. The short, unhappy life predicted for her as a young girl had turned into four decades in a family she loved. She had retained all her faculties and died painlessly in her sleep. The sadness of loss was tinged with a sense of liberation.

During his years in the Civil Service, Butler had worked and become friendly with Sir Robert Armstrong.* Armstrong had resisted the suggestion that Butler succeed him as Principal Private Secretary in 1975, and had proposed Kenneth Stowe for the job. The quiet and unassuming Stowe, after spending two hours unsuccessfully trying to persuade Harold Wilson that he was the wrong man for the job, served Wilson, Callaghan and Thatcher until he was succeeded by Clive Whitmore in 1979.

As part of the same move, Armstrong became Cabinet Secretary; three years later, Sir Frank Cooper, the Permanent Under-Secretary at the Ministry of Defence, retired. On 22 July 1982, Downing Street announced new appointments that set insiders predicting who would succeed Armstrong five years down the road. Undoubtedly the appointment that set most tongues wagging was that of Butler to succeed Whitmore as Principal Private Secretary to the Prime Minister. Suddenly, there was speculation, in Whitehall and in the press, that the choice for the top job in 1987 had already boiled down to Whitmore or Butler.

During his time in Downing Street, Whitmore had made himself indispensable to Mrs Thatcher, who reportedly depended on him for advice on all major decisions.[6] His promotion to the rank of Permanent Under-Secretary at the age of forty-seven was seen as a strong endorsement of him as a future head of the Civil Service. On the other hand, his successor at No. 10 was three years younger and at forty-four was assembling impressive credentials. Both men suddenly attracted press attention, and the public image of Robin Butler took shape. Beyond the personal profiles that appeared of the two men, there was the excitement of a horse race. A short piece in *The Guardian* was typical:

> Mr Robin Butler (44), Treasury under-secretary has just become the new principal private secretary to the prime minister and the most eminent 'minder' in the land. Mr Butler knows all about minding prime ministers. He was on the team of Sir Robert Armstrong, then principal private secretary to the prime minister, during the tricky transition in the mid-1970s

* Later Baron Armstrong of Ilminster GCB CVO. He was created a life peer in 1986.

> from Mr Edward Heath to Sir Harold Wilson. A big, fair-haired man, he is a familiar sight pedalling down Whitehall on his battered bicycle. He looks like an ageless head boy. If that makes him sound guileless, he is not. Too subtle to be tainted by devotion to a single economic theory, he has a gift for disagreeing without causing offence.
>
> This summer's dispositions have enabled Whitehall betting men to appraise the field for the Cabinet Secretaryship, when it falls vacant in 1987. The card reads: Whitmore and Butler, joint favourites. But keep an eye on Hancock, the dark horse in the race.[7]

By that time, Butler had completed a twenty-year induction course in the Civil Service, had handled delicate and possibly incendiary issues at the Treasury, and had worked successfully as Private Secretary to two Prime Ministers. Now, having made a good impression on the Prime Minister and with solid support from the Cabinet Secretary, he was a clear first choice to succeed Whitmore. At the time of his summons to Downing Street, he commented that he found Thatcher easy to talk to and he was confident that he and she would work well together.[8]

Typically, the Prime Minister reminded him not only of his fine performance in cutting government expenditure but also, as a warning note, of a remark he had made in a strategy presentation to the Cabinet at Chequers, while he was with the CPRS in 1971. Had he not said, unwisely: 'If we can't beat inflation, we've got to learn to live with it'? Eleven years later, she chided him: 'You said inflation was endemic. I've never heard a more shocking remark from a young man.'[9] She had, she assured Butler, forgiven him his youthful indiscretion.

Suitably cautioned and assured that he had been forgiven this heresy, he returned to Downing Street in September 1982. Robert Armstrong had doubtless briefed him comprehensively on the nature of the job, but even so the range of his responsibilities must have been daunting. In the few days between his arrival at No. 10 and his departure with Mrs Thatcher on a trip to Japan and China, Butler was confronted by a bewildering array of issues:

- plans for a meeting with the Scottish TUC;
- details of a seminar on the international banking scene;

- dealing with Jim Molyneaux and the boycott of the Northern Ireland Assembly by the SDLP;
- a meeting with senior Conservative Ministers and members of the CPRS to discuss strategy;
- arranging a meeting between Thatcher and Francis Pym to discuss cuts to the FCO vote in 1983–84;
- arranging a dinner for leading figures in the Falklands campaign;
- arranging for Field Marshal Bramall, the incoming Chief of the Defence Staff, to visit the Prime Minister;
- discussion with Robert Armstrong of the desirability of asking Lord Franks to suppress the record of meetings between Nicholas Ridley and the Argentinian Deputy Foreign Minister in September 1980;
- a meeting of the Liaison Committee at No. 10. On the agenda were papers on social security priorities and education priorities, both complicated and detailed documents that will have taken time to master;
- arrangements for the Prime Minister's schedule of meetings in Japan and China;
- communicating to the Prime Minister the details of a report from the Governor of the Bank of England on the international financial situation, with particular reference to Mexico, Bolivia, Argentina and Denmark;
- fine tuning the guest list for the Falklands dinner on 11 October;
- recommendations to the Prime Minister for the distribution of life peerages by party;
- handling a request from Lord Zuckerman that Mrs Thatcher should accept the offer of a female giant panda, if the Chinese were to make such an offer;
- making final changes as requested by Robert Armstrong to the guest list for the Falklands dinner; discussing with Armstrong the proper dress for the dinner.[10]

After his spell in personnel management, Butler recognised the importance of creating a friendly and efficient ambience in the private office at No. 10. When Ferdinand Mount joined the team as head of the No. 10 Policy Unit, he realised early on that the private secretaries' room was the hub of the place, as there is not a Prime Minister's office as such; different PMs, he observed, use different rooms.[11] Then, when he was taken to meet the private office, he was impressed by the stamp that Butler had put on his team: '[John Vereker] took me down to meet Robin Butler and the other private secretaries, Michael Scholar and Tim Lankester. Suddenly from my austere isolation I became part of a lively band of clerks, handpicked from the Treasury for quick-wittedness and good humour.'[12]

Margaret Thatcher is commonly portrayed as an aggressive, confrontational woman. While no one would deny the 'Iron Lady' side of her character, the converse is also true. She was a dependable friend and those whom she saw as members of her political family were admitted to a working intimacy that was singularly effective. Butler quickly established himself as such a member.

Almost immediately after his appointment, Butler joined the Thatchers for their annual weekend as guests of the Queen at Balmoral. The programme, repeated each year that he held the post, was to attend a political event on the Friday, then to stay overnight with their friends Hector Laing, chairman of United Biscuits,* and his wife Marian at Dunphail, near Elgin. Laing, described in an obituary as 'a flamboyant competitor', had no inhibitions in making his feelings known. At a City luncheon, he was offered biscuits made by a rival company. Leaving the table, he threw the offending biscuits out of the window.[13]

This charismatic businessman made an immediate impression on Butler. He owned a plane, and employed a professional pilot, but enjoyed landing his plane himself, swooping down over the trees to a clearing in the forest, apparently missing the treetops by a small margin. This daredevilry appealed to Butler the competitor, and the two became good friends. It fell to him, however, to reassure Civil Service officials that the Prime Minister's annual visit to Dunphail was not life-threatening, as word had spread of Laing's hair-raising qualities as a pilot. Butler stretched the truth and assured the authorities that the professional pilot always handled take-offs and landings.

---

* Laing (1923–2010), later Lord Laing of Dunphail, was chairman of the company from 1972 to 1990.

On Saturday morning, the Prime Minister's party would travel along the whisky trail, past Speyside distilleries – The Macallan, Aberlour, Tamnavulin, Knockando – to Balmoral. A firm believer in ordered schedules, Butler was awed by the established Balmoral procedure.

On arrival, the Prime Minister, her husband and Butler would have luncheon with Sir Philip Moore, the Queen's Private Secretary,* to establish what issues the Prime Minister wished to discuss with the Queen. Moore would use the afternoon to brief Her Majesty. During the afternoon, while the PM worked, Butler and Denis Thatcher would play a round of golf. The Thatchers would then take tea with the royal family while Butler stayed with the Moores. There was usually a formal dinner on one evening, and on the other a barbecue at a Finnish chalet that the Queen had given Prince Philip for a silver wedding present. Butler became used to the procedure whereby he was invited to each of these in alternate years – amounting to two dinners and one barbecue. The latter was an unusual event at which the Queen and Prince Philip cooked, served and washed up after the meal without the help of servants. Butler, as the one person in the party whom Her Majesty did not know, sat beside her and found her easy to talk to and 'great fun'. After eating, he helped the Queen by drying dishes, clad in a plastic Balmoral apron. He wrote to his parents that he returned to London, 'walking on air'.[14]

After the morning service at Craithie church, Sunday afternoon was unstructured, and Butler found it a delightful, albeit surreal, experience to drive around the estate in a Land Rover with Moore, as he later recalled:

> He and I would drive around the estate, which was like travelling through a theme park in which actors were impersonating members of the Royal Family, except that in this case they were the real thing. We would go round one corner and encounter the Queen walking her corgis; round another and meet Prince Philip driving his ponies; round another and see Princess Diana pushing the young princes in their pushchair. I had to pinch myself to be sure I wasn't dreaming.[15]

* Sir Philip Moore, later Baron Moore of Wolvercote (1921–2009), Private Secretary to HM the Queen from 1977 to 1986.

After this gentle induction to his new job, Butler was soon introduced to the realities of working with Margaret Thatcher during a trip to Japan, China and Hong Kong, returning via Delhi and Bahrain. From the moment that they touched down in Tokyo after an eleven-hour flight from London, the Prime Minister drove her staff, as well as the British ambassador, relentlessly. The task, after dinner with the ambassador, was ostensibly a simple one: to hit upon a Japanese proverb as a closing sentence to a speech that the Prime Minister would make on the following evening.

Sir Hugh Cortazzi, the ambassador, produced a number of possible proverbs, all of which Mrs Thatcher rejected. The problem, in Butler's opinion, was that she had taken an immediate and profound dislike to Cortazzi. It is easy enough to imagine this, as the ambassador, every inch a diplomat, president of the Asiatic Society of Japan and a student of Japanese customs, was the antithesis of the determined woman whose manners he would have deemed 'pushy'. For over five hours the unhappy diplomat strove to find the right expression until, at 2.00 a.m., the Prime Minister accepted a suggestion from the ambassador's butler, almost certainly an action intended as a snub to Cortazzi. Having slept little that night, or the subsequent two in Tokyo, Butler was beginning seriously to doubt whether he would be able to stand the pace of Thatcher's Downing Street. Fortunately, a good night's sleep on the fourth night, and his resolve that he could outlast a woman ten years his senior, combined to shore up his resolve.

Over time, Butler became used both to Thatcher's resolute refusal to admit to exhaustion and to the fact that she, too, was human. Ferdinand Mount described a typical weekend at Chequers and Butler's tactful efforts to preserve her reputation for indefatigability:

> There is to be no resting, let alone recreation. Meetings continue all afternoon and sometimes long after dinner throughout the weekend, until even her beautifully coiffed head begins to sink on to her briefing papers. It is at this moment that the celebrated tact of the higher reaches of the British Civil Service comes into play. As it is a publicly declared dogma that the Iron Lady requires less sleep than other mortals and is never ever exhausted, it is Robin Butler's role as Principal Private Secretary to rise to

> his feet, give a yawn and stretch his arms in an extravagant manner like a man using a chest-expander and say, 'Prime Minister, I'm afraid you'll have to excuse me, I'm feeling extraordinarily tired' – at which the rest of us emit various yawns and say that, for some unaccountable reason, we feel a bit knocked out too.[16]

The Tokyo visit was also his first experience of Thatcher's infectious, fierce determination. The principal purpose of the visit was to secure a commitment from Nissan to invest in building a manufacturing plant in north-east England. The area had been through three decades of industrial decline with the closure of shipyards and the Durham coalfield mines. Unemployment was high; a new factory in the region would be a substantial boost to the region's economy. With a sizeable potential workforce available and an attractive agricultural price of £1,800 per acre for the proposed site of 800 acres, the package was designed to be attractive to Nissan. Against those incentives, however, was the notoriously poor state of industrial relations in Britain. As Butler himself had witnessed at first hand, the previous two governments had been humiliated after savage struggles with the unions.

It is a testament to the Prime Minister's resolve and her ability to transmit that certainty, that she was successful in persuading the company's president Takashi Ishihara to proceed with investment in Britain rather than in another European country with more stable labour relations. It is a testament to Ishihara's wisdom that he went ahead, insisting on a single union in the plant to encourage flexible working and to avoid demarcation disputes. His decision has been justified by the remarkable record of Nissan's United Kingdom operation that has encouraged continuing investment over the following three decades.[17]

Of less diplomatic importance was another example of Thatcher's determination. At the end of their negotiations, Ishiwara presented her with a top-of-the-range Nikon camera, at the same time presenting Butler with a good but lesser model. Butler pointed out that she could not accept so grand a gift while engaged in negotiations but that, if she wished, she could take his camera instead. Such diplomatic offers are not intended to be taken at face value and he was dismayed when the Prime Minister accepted it.

From Tokyo, the party continued to Beijing where Mrs Thatcher's resolve was again tested, this time by Deng Xiao Peng who stated simply and aggressively that on sovereignty there was no leeway for China:

> Sovereignty was not a matter that could be discussed ... It should be clear today that in 1997 China would certainly recover sovereignty over Hong Kong. It was under this pre-condition that China and the United Kingdom would hold talks between the two sides on formulae for the future of Hong Kong and on policies for maintaining Hong Kong's prosperity.[18]

Once more, Butler was impressed with the Prime Minister's poise under pressure and her success in blunting Deng's aggression. He was under no illusion that progress over Hong Kong would be tough, but he did not doubt Mrs Thatcher's ability to persevere on the issue.[19] At this meeting, after agreeing to a communiqué that assured the world of both countries' desire for the continued stability and prosperity of Hong Kong, the two leaders set aside theatrical bellicosity.

This trip, the first of many that he would take with Thatcher, was illustrative of the Prime Minister's relations with her staff and officials. She made her views clear on every issue and it was impossible not to be aware of her position. In discussion or dispute with her, an interlocutor might react in one of three ways. First, one could be deferential, agreeing with her unthinkingly. This was the manner that Cortazzi had adopted in Tokyo, an attitude that earned Mrs Thatcher's contempt. Second, one might disagree, finally be persuaded, and later attempt to obstruct implementation of her decision. That she regarded as disloyalty tantamount to enemy action. Third, one might disagree, volubly and robustly and, provided she believed that opposing counsel was being offered for her benefit, she was prepared to listen and did not hold the disagreement against the adviser. Robert Armstrong recalls the first occasion on which he strongly believed Thatcher to be following an unwise course:

> Once when I said to her, 'No, Prime Minister, you are wrong', she asked me to explain why. When I had finished, she said simply, 'Thank you, Robert. You're quite right; I was wrong.' She respected strongly held views.[20]

Butler was to fall not infrequently into the third category, a tendency that he believes secured his position as trusted counsellor. John Major also was impressed by her taste for a robust exchange of views, recording that after he and Thatcher had crossed swords violently, 'her husband Denis came up to me. "She'll have enjoyed that", he remarked and drifted off happily, clutching a gin and tonic.'[21]

The first few months of Butler's time at No. 10 saw him involved with the Prime Minister in several lively differences of opinion. These ranged from a difference over the leak to *The Economist* of a paper prepared by the Think Tank to fundamental policy matters.

The leak involved a paper that, on Butler's authority, was circulated to the Cabinet. The document contained radical suggestions for saving money in the public expenditure review, one of which proposed 'hotel charges' for patients in NHS hospitals. Predictably, as with any controversial proposal concerning the NHS, this was leaked, and the resultant outcry in Cabinet and in the national press embarrassed the Prime Minister. Butler apologised for his *naïveté* and, under pressure to tighten security around future radical proposals, accepted Mrs Thatcher's argument that the usefulness of the Think Tank had run its course. After the 1987 election, it was abolished and its functions were given to the No. 10 Policy Unit.

Even more central to policy and the principles of government by Cabinet was a disagreement that grew out of the Falklands War. To avoid future failures of diplomatic intelligence, Mrs Thatcher demanded the establishment of a foreign policy unit at No. 10. To take charge of the unit, she wanted Sir Anthony Parsons, the Permanent Representative to the United Nations at the time of the invasion of the Falklands.[22] Robert Armstrong was violently opposed to this, arguing that a unit run by a man with Parsons's seniority would be viewed as being in competition with the Foreign Office. Butler initially supported Armstrong's objections, but was ultimately overruled by Mrs Thatcher. At that point, yielding to the inevitable, he spoke to Alan Walters, who ran the No. 10 Economic Unit, in an attempt to formulate a job description similar to Walters's own that would be both realistic and acceptable to the Foreign Office.[23]

On both occasions, there was what Butler described as 'robust disagreement', and subsequent cooperation without resentment once the disagreement had been settled. He took on the task of persuading the Foreign Office that there was merit in the Prime Minister's proposal. He pointed out that the Economic Unit actually reduced, rather than provoked or exacerbated, conflict with the Treasury. Parsons retired from the FCO in 1982 and acted as special adviser to Margaret Thatcher on a part-time basis. Butler concluded that he was an 'effective bridge' with the Foreign Office and that, in spite of his and Armstrong's objections, the Prime Minister's instincts had been correct.

Towards the end of 1982, Sir Douglas Wass, the Permanent Secretary at the Treasury, neared retirement. He proposed to make a speech to the Royal Institute of Public Administration, the Civil Service professional body, on 2 December. The subject was to be the state of the Civil Service. Wass sent Butler a copy of his proposed address as a matter of courtesy. At a time when the Prime Minister was demanding cuts in public expenditure, Butler recognised that this would be scrutinised by the media for any potential divergence from government policy. Accordingly, he was punctilious in submitting the text to the Prime Minister with suggested amendments; additionally, he asked Bernard Ingham, her chief press secretary, to look over the speech with a journalist's eye. Where, he asked, were the key issues on which the press might seize?

To Butler's relief, Thatcher wrote a two-sentence reply: 'Sir Douglas is free to say whatever he wishes. I shouldn't dream of trying to stop him.'[24] Ingham was more analytical in his response, warning Butler that the press would swoop on any indication of complacency, and suggesting that Wass project a picture of 'a Service which, far from being complacent, is lacking in self-assurance … we must try to secure not merely more informed criticism but also a more balanced approach to some very serious questions which do in fact affect all our citizens'.[25]

Butler duly wrote to Wass, complimenting him on the style and tenor of his address, and passing on the suggestions that he had received.[26] The care and concern with which Butler handled this public report on the state of the service are truly impressive. Without in any way projecting himself, he ensured that a distinguished civil servant, joint head of the service, gave a retirement speech that showed both the speaker and the service in the best possible light.

At the end of 1982, Butler had completed a somewhat hectic four months as the Prime Minister's Principal Private Secretary. In common with the most exacting roles, the nature of the job is comprehensible, in principle, to an observer, but the true demands are beyond imagination. So Butler found. He wrote to the Thatchers, whom he felt able to address as 'Margaret and Denis', on 28 December, first thanking them for their gift of a Christmas hamper, praising the quality of the smoked salmon, and continuing:

> I have been thinking of you at Chequers and have been hoping that you were getting a rest. I did not realise how fast the pace had been until I stopped ... But I want you to know how much I have enjoyed my first four months ... I hope that all of us can help you make it another memorable and successful year and give you 100 per cent support in the work you are doing for our country.[27]

In the months following the Falklands War, the Prime Minister impatiently awaited the report of the Franks Committee, specifically its assignment of responsibility for the Argentine invasion and subsequent fighting. On 6 July 1982, Mrs Thatcher had indicated that a committee of inquiry would report within six months;[28] that deadline was approaching. The publication of the report was eagerly awaited, as the Foreign Secretary Peter Carrington had taken full responsibility for Foreign Office complacency prior to the invasion and promptly resigned. In the autumn of 1982, the question of how far up the tree the Franks committee would go exercised Mrs Thatcher a great deal. The widespread anger that Britain had been unprepared for the invasion was countered by equally widespread patriotic pride in the outcome. The Franks report would tip the balance.

The report is, as Jim Callaghan described it, 'a splendid picture, delineat[ing] light and shade', for 338 paragraphs until, in paragraph 339, Franks 'chucked a bucket of whitewash over it'. The Prime Minister who, as Butler frequently asserts, had to be made to read beyond the headline, behind the soundbite, was comfortable simply to read paragraph 339. He remembers her taking a deep breath and saying: 'I think that's all right.' When the report was published in January 1983, the debates in the Commons passed off without problem.

Mrs Thatcher was particularly anxious about the conclusions of the Franks Report, as it would affect her strategy before the next general election. On Friday 7 January 1983, amid extreme secrecy, she, her husband, press secretary Bernard Ingham, John Coles, the foreign affairs secretary at Downing Street, and Butler all drove in separate cars to RAF Brize Norton and boarded a VC10 for the first leg of a flight to Port Stanley. It was a potentially dangerous trip, as Argentina was still nominally at war with Britain. The visit had enormous public relations value, however, and it was assumed by Butler and colleagues that, in addition to boosting morale in the Falklands, it could be profitably employed to boost the Prime Minister's image at home. When the party's return to London, on 12 January, was followed by the release of the conclusions of Lord Franks's committee, it was an effective piece of theatre, entirely congruent with the Prime Minister's plan to call an election in May. For Butler, the trip was a moving experience, although he confessed to a sense of unreality in touring battlefields, the scenes of a struggle to maintain control over an area with the 'population of a small English village'.* It was also a valuable lesson in the Prime Minister's methods of handling public relations.

In March, he had his first tenuous contact with William Hague, then a 21-year-old recent Oxford graduate, who was to become leader of the Conservative Party fourteen years later. In 1977, as a sixteen-year-old schoolboy, Hague had spoken at the party conference in Blackpool, urging smaller government, and warning of the growth of socialism in Britain. In 1983, he offered his services as a special adviser to Geoffrey Howe, the Chancellor of the Exchequer, and there was strong support for his appointment. John Kerr, a senior Treasury official, wrote in his favour to the Prime Minister on 17 March, recalling his performance at Blackpool, where he had been photographed with her.

---

* The population of the Falkland Islands in 1982 was approximately 1,800, of whom 1,000 lived in Port Stanley. Butler described the trip vividly in a letter to his parents on 16 January 1983.

The idea of employing an untried youth, even one with a first-class degree in PPE, struck Mrs Thatcher as a gimmick that 'would be deeply resented by many who have financial-economic experience'. Butler completely agreed with this view, writing to the Prime Minister that 'promising though William Hague is, it is a bit difficult to see what a 21-year-old will contribute as a special adviser in the Treasury'. This was distilled into a formal response to the Treasury in which she suggested that 'if the Chancellor and the Chief Secretary wanted Mr Hague to help with speeches, he should be employed by the Conservative Research Department or some other private sources'.[29] As it happened, the story had leaked, and it was widely reported that Hague was to work at the Treasury. It was left to Bernard Ingham to deny that any such 'gimmick' was planned.

As the anniversary of Butler's appointment to Downing Street approached, the Prime Minister prepared for a general election. She took the opportunity to demonstrate her satisfaction with his work to date by recommending that he be promoted to the rank of Deputy Secretary, a signal honour for a man of forty-five. He was to remain at Downing Street for the remaining year of his posting.

As the Prime Minister moved towards a decision for the date of the election, Butler achieved a certain visibility as an eccentric by Whitehall standards. Needing to go from No. 10 to Buckingham Palace to discuss the dissolution of Parliament and other election matters with Sir Philip Moore, the Queen's Private Secretary, he was concerned about the number of journalists in Downing Street. Judging that, if he were seen climbing into an official car and being whisked to the Palace, obvious conclusions would be drawn, he discreetly closed the front door and went out by the back. Climbing onto his bicycle, he rode the short distance to the Palace and sought the Queen's approval of the election timing through Moore.

Shoving his notes on their discussions into his pocket, he rode back along the Mall, only to be stopped by a policeman as a rehearsal for the Trooping of the Colour was taking place. No one, not even the Prime Minister's aide, was allowed to pass. Butler and his rusty bicycle were diverted by back streets; and he added a detail to his growing dossier in Fleet Street. He maintained, however, that this was not eccentricity but a practical decision. While official cars tend to get stuck in traffic, over the short distances in Whitehall and Westminster, his bicycle was more efficient.[30]

On 9 June 1983, the Conservatives romped home with a comfortable majority. Rising discontent over unemployment and recession was neutralised by a wave of patriotism. There had been no serious doubt that the Tories would win, but it must have been gratifying for Butler to contemplate a further spell at No. 10 working for Mrs Thatcher rather than for Michael Foot.

Almost immediately after the summer parliamentary break came the party conference in Blackpool, where the Prime Minister was to make the keynote speech on Friday 14 October. Butler's memories of writing, editing and assembling speeches for Mrs Thatcher are not particularly happy ones:

> She would only address a speech 48 hours before it was due. Six weeks out she would ask for contributions from her 'Brain Trust' people such as Hailsham. She would then put all the contributions on the floor and complain that there was no structure. We would assemble it and she would go through it line by line. We would work long into the night – until 3.00 or 4.00 a.m. She micromanaged until people like me lost the will to live.
>
> It was a chaotic, wearing way of composing speeches, but by putting intensive effort into it she would internalise bits of the speech and make 'off-the-cuff' remarks from these. Occasionally she would nod off and, waking up, demand, 'Where are we?' I would assure her suavely, 'We're on the last page, Prime Minister.'
>
> One contributor, Ronnie Millar, had some first-class phrases but, sadly, had no grasp of policy and I frequently had to rewrite his material. This produced a sequence in which a speech was ronnified, then deronnified, and finally reronnified.[31]

The speech for Blackpool was principally a product of Ronnie Millar's remarkable ability to find the resounding phrase. His, for example, was the memorable Tory punch line: 'There is no such thing as public money. There is only taxpayers' money.' The speech shows the signs of joint authorship, as it contains the occasional Ciceronian passage, the attention to symmetry of a classicist – of Robin Butler. As the Prime Minister enumerated policies, each preceded by the words 'We were elected to', and spelled out the solutions applied, there is more than a hint of classical Latin oratory, rising to the Millar-inspired crescendo: 'Protecting the taxpayer's purse, protecting the public services – these are our two great tasks, and their demands have to be reconciled.'

The result was a forty-seven-minute oration, not perhaps one of her most dramatic speeches, but a characteristic, polemical attack on the wasteful nature of socialism. For Butler, it was a very different process from composing a speech for either of the Prime Ministers he had served before.

While he was working on the speech with Mrs Thatcher, he was called away to be told that *The Times* was publishing a statement by Sarah Keays, former secretary of Cecil Parkinson, Secretary of State in the newly-created Department of Trade and Industry, in which Keays stated that she was pregnant by her former boss and that he had abandoned her once he learned of her condition. Parkinson had admitted the affair ten days before and Mrs Thatcher had supported him. Now, with a broader scandal brewing, it was clear that Parkinson would have to resign.

Butler was in a quandary. Knowing the Prime Minister's *modus operandi* in composing speeches, he decided not to interrupt the process, but rather to speak to her husband, immediately calling a meeting with Denis Thatcher and Parkinson. The three agreed that Parkinson should resign immediately.[32] The thrust of Keays's accusation – that Parkinson had been less than frank in his statements to the press – made his position untenable. Denis Thatcher took Parkinson's place in unveiling a plaque at the new Blackpool heliport, and the former Secretary of State left the conference. Butler succeeded in defusing the incident without disrupting the Prime Minister's schedule.

Ten days after the party conference, on 25 October, the United States launched an invasion of Grenada following the removal from power and subsequent murder of Prime Minister Maurice Bishop by a so-called Revolutionary Military Council led by General Hudson Austin. Two days earlier, at 2.30 in the morning of Sunday 23 October, President Reagan had been notified of the destruction of a Marine barracks in Beirut by a car bomb. Reagan and his Secretary of State, George Schultz, felt it vital to show force against any threat in the Caribbean and, once the Organisation of East

Caribbean States (OECS) requested American support, they determined to invade.* Ostensibly, the reason for the use of force was to ensure the safety of 1,000 American students in Grenada. By the evening of Monday 24 October, the Pentagon had drawn up a detailed set of steps for a rescue operation to be launched from the United States.[33]

The set of ten steps is an extraordinary document as, although Grenada was a member of the Commonwealth, no reference is made to discussion of the plans with the British government. Indeed, the Commonwealth is briefly mentioned in point seven and the Governor General is considered (whether alive or dead) in point ten. Clearly the special relationship was not to be allowed to impede the unilateral American invasion of a Commonwealth country.

On the same evening, the President's briefing of congressional leaders was interrupted by a phone call from the Prime Minister with a message that was 'negative and uncompromising'.[34] She knew nothing, she said, of any request for help from the OECS. She was clearly furious but, in Butler's opinion, reluctant to make the call. Reagan, he observed, was equally baffled when she indicated that she did not want to speak on the secure line but would be sending a written memorandum. As he later recalled: 'So, with bemusement at his end and distrust of technology at hers, the exchange ended. The fact was that she didn't want to have an embarrassing conversation with him.'[35]

A later conversation between Prime Minister and President, after the operation had been launched, supports the view that Mrs Thatcher was subdued and careful to avoid any unpleasantness. This exchange, along with Butler's comments, suggests that she was aware of the nature of the Washington jungle and keen to avoid any personal unpleasantness with the President. Nonetheless, she roundly condemned the American rescue operation:

> We in the western countries, the western democracies, use our force to defend our way of life. We do not use it to walk into independent

---

* Reagan consistently denied the accusations from Speaker of the House Tip O'Neill and others that the invasion of Grenada was carried out in response to the Beirut bombing. It is true that contingency plans for Grenada had been drawn up, but planning moved into top gear on Sunday 23 October. It is difficult to believe that the Beirut bombing was not a factor in the decision to launch the operation.

> sovereign territories. ... If you're going to pronounce a new law wherever communism reigns against the will of the people, even though it has happened internally, there the USA shall enter, then we are going to have really terrible wars in the world.[36]

Thatcher's warnings were more than mere platitudes. Relations between the USA and USSR were chilly in late 1983 after the shooting down of Korean Airlines flight 007 between Anchorage and Seoul. By then, General Secretary Yuri Andropov was critically ill, and there was uncertainty concerning the future leadership of the Soviet Union. In February 1984, Andropov died, and Butler accompanied the Prime Minister to Moscow for his funeral. This took place in the morning, and a meeting with Andropov's successor, Konstantin Chernenko, was arranged for 7.00 that evening. In the meantime, the Prime Minister and her party sat in the British Embassy. As it was Butler's first visit to Moscow, he was acutely conscious of valuable sightseeing time being wasted. At length, a messenger arrived with an invitation from Chernenko to visit parts of the Kremlin that were not open to the public. The Prime Minister, living up to her reputation as a workaholic with no time for frivolous pursuits, demanded: 'Does your President think we have come here for tourism? I am busy preparing for my meeting with him.' Butler confesses, 'I could have strangled her.'[37]

In the event, Chernenko was to survive just one year in office. From the moment of his accession, Western strategists were studying the likelihood of a very different General Secretary in the near future. Mikhail Gorbachev had been Andropov's choice to succeed him but had been judged too young by the politburo. For Reagan and Thatcher, the questions surrounding the succession were critical.

CHAPTER 9

VISIBILITY, 1984–1985

WHEN SIR BURKE TREND had initially summoned Lord (Victor) Rothschild to meet him and Sir William Armstrong in Whitehall to discuss the formation of the Think Tank, Rothschild later confided to a friend that 'until this week I never realised the country was run by two men whom I'd never heard of'.[1] In the following decade, the air of mystery and secrecy surrounding senior civil servants had largely dissolved and the Civil Service was comfortable that 'faceless bureaucrats' were being replaced by talented individuals with defining characteristics and foibles. Butler fitted perfectly into this modern image. It also appealed to the media, delighted to have a subject to lionise, a figure more colourful than the shadowy Robert Armstrong.

Prima facie, there was little unconventional in his background: Harrow and Oxford were scarcely surprising training grounds for a rising mandarin. But he added individuality and zest to that conventional curriculum vitae: head boy of his school, a rugby Blue, mountain climber, cricketer, cyclist, hiker, supporter of Crystal Palace FC.* Above average in height, burly and good-looking, possessor of a double first-class honours, a 'brain-box', but not an airy-fairy intellectual, here was a thoroughly modern man, with a weekly date for squash against Permanent Secretary Sir Michael Quinlan, a reassuring symbol of the superiority and permanence of Britain's ruling class.

Beyond concrete attributes, a measure of adventurous originality also shone through in his methods: when he requested that his windows in the Treasury be cleaned, and nothing happened, he let it be known that if they

---

* Butler was reputedly the first senior civil servant who admitted to supporting a football team.

were not cleaned by a certain date, he would clean them himself. When the day came, and the windows had not been cleaned, he made sure that he was firmly tied on, stepped out onto the ledge, and went round the outside of the building, cleaning the windows as he circulated.[2] His windows were always cleaned on time after that demonstration.

Peter Hennessy, close observer of Whitehall matters, charted Butler's upward progress with interest and, after his first ten months at No. 10, wrote 'Head Boy of Downing Street' for *The Times*, a profile that became the gold standard for the many Robin Butler profiles that were to follow. Two days before the general election of 9 May 1983, Hennessy perfectly captured his pivotal role in the Downing Street hierarchy. Quoting from Joe Haines's perceptive description of a Prime Minister's welcome at No. 10 after an election, and noting that Butler had been present at the last election and would be there again at the next, he turned to his subject. 'Mr Butler is superb at managing Prime Ministers', he said, adding:

> It must have been infuriating to have been at school with Mr Butler – he is the kind who gets blues and firsts and makes it look effortless. A big fair-haired man pedalling down Whitehall on his bicycle, even at 45 he still looks like a perpetual head boy (which he was at Harrow in 1956). His conversation brims with infectious school-boy exuberance.[3]

Hennessy, speculating on the possibility of Butler's rising to the very top of the service, quotes one friend's comment that Butler 'tends to side with officialdom, even in a non-Whitehall context'. At the time of Watergate, the friend recalls, he felt that Nixon had done 'nothing untoward'. That was hardly a fashionable stance in 1983 and it certainly reflected Butler's distaste for the hysterical bloodlust of journalists hunting in a pack. At all events, it served as a clear pointer that he was capable of expressing thoroughly unfashionable opinions. 'He has a gift of disagreeing', Hennessy wrote, 'without causing offence.'

All seats of power are surrounded by an inner circle and in Mrs Thatcher's No. 10 in 1982, Bernard Ingham, the Prime Minister's press secretary, was the gatekeeper. He and Butler became allies and their close working relations with the Prime Minister can be gauged from a light-hearted project initiated by Ingham. In January 1984, Mrs Thatcher was asked to present an award to *Yes, Minister*, her favourite television programme. Ingham was keen that this occasion should be more than a simple presentation speech, and he devised a sketch in which she would play herself and two of the principal actors of *Yes, Minister*, Paul Eddington and Nigel Hawthorne, would play their customary parts as Jim Hacker and Sir Humphrey Appleby. Ingham wrote the script, helped by Butler and by Ingham's deputy, Romola Christopherson; Mrs Thatcher unwillingly rehearsed the sketch with Butler and Ingham. The substance of the sketch was that the Prime Minister planned to abolish all economists, a proposal that she presented to the minister and Permanent Secretary, each of whom reacted predictably – the first with enthusiasm, the other with studied mandarin caution.[4] Thatcher was concerned that the entire sketch might fall very flat and embarrass her as Prime Minister. In the event, however, it was a resounding success.[5]

By 1984, Butler had become the man beside the Prime Minister, with whom, according to one newspaper, she spent more time than with her husband Denis, and as such was a highly visible and popular subject for journalists. A growing cult of personality, combined with a wider interest in 'the officials behind the scenes' added to his visibility. This resulted in Butler's being one of the '80 people for the 1980s', a feature run by *The Observer*.

Thatcher herself attracted attention as a handsome woman. As the first female British Prime Minister, she carried a frisson of sexuality in media portraits. François Mitterand's comment that she 'had the eyes of Caligula and the mouth of Marilyn Monroe' fed that voyeurism.[6] Butler's athleticism, good looks and muscularity gave him a certain status as Thatcher's 'minder'. All these qualities were to add appeal to his public image over the difficult year of 1984.

The year began badly, with a report in *The Observer* of a questionable business deal between Mark Thatcher and the Sultan of Oman. In May 1981, Mrs Thatcher had flown to Oman and allegedly promised the Sultan preferential government finance terms if Cementation, a company with which Mark Thatcher was associated, was awarded the contract to build a new university in Oman. When the story of possible corruption in Oman broke, the responsibility for handling the explosive situation fell to Butler.[7] On 3 February 1984, he was on the point of leaving with the Prime Minister on a visit to Hungary, but

> Each Friday for the last three weeks we have had the press harassing us about Mark Thatcher and Oman, and the PM and I agreed that I would help her best by staying behind and fending them off.[8]

Sir Clive Whitmore, Butler's immediate predecessor as Principal Private Secretary, singled out Mark Thatcher for criticism, commenting that in the Oman contract he had been 'driven by greed'. Butler's criticisms ranged wider, involving both son and mother. There was, he believed 'a whiff of corruption' in her wanting to see Mark right. Her insistence on secrecy, he felt, gave the wrong impression. In short, he suspected the worst.[9]

Returning to London from Moscow later in February, Butler was immediately immersed in the miners' strike and what became an epic struggle between government and unions, between Thatcher and Arthur Scargill of the National Union of Mineworkers (NUM). He was a close observer and periodic adviser to the Prime Minister, but was less involved in the tactics of union confrontation than in wider policy and the supportive role, as he puts it, of 'holding MT's hand'. He was in a position, however, to observe the Prime Minister in action and was impressed not only by her resolution, but also by her commitment to justice.

> We were returning from a lunch in the City during a bleak moment in the miners' strike, when the dockers had begun industrial action in support of the miners, threatening the import of oil and coal supplies. On a newspaper hoarding we saw that Mr Justice Glidewell had found against the government in a judicial review of the decision to ban trades unions from GCHQ. Margaret Thatcher immediately said, 'We will appeal but of course we must accept the decision of the court. We cannot stand for the rule of law in one context and try to subvert it in another.' As judicial reviews became more prevalent, I suggested to Mrs Thatcher that we should organise joint courses of judges and civil servants so that judges

could understand the problems of government better. She wouldn't hear of it, regarding the idea as a potential incursion on judicial independence.[10]

Such observance of the rule of law, when the other side was consistently defying it, surprised and impressed Butler. His own instinct was less legalistic and more solidly practical than that of the Prime Minister, particularly when Robert Armstrong informed him that the NUM, in common with the IRA, was receiving financial subsidies from Colonel Muammar Gadaffi of Libya.[11]

On another occasion in early 1984, he took a harder line than Armstrong and was solidly behind Thatcher. In January, Sir Geoffrey Howe announced that, after eight occasions of disruptive industrial action that might have had serious implications for national security, the government was resolved to ban trade unions at GCHQ in Cheltenham. Unsurprisingly, the announcement encountered resistance from staff members who belonged to the Civil Service union. According to Lord Gowrie, Butler was 'hawkier than thou' on the issue. He later recalled to Charles Moore his concern that Armstrong was too acquiescent to the demands of the Civil Service union, and so he made notes in the margin of Armstrong's memoranda to Thatcher, urging her not to be trapped into any kind of climb-down.[12] Determined not to be humiliated by the unions as Heath had been, Thatcher held the line, and by March 1984, 90 per cent of GCHQ staff had given up union membership.[13]

It was Armstrong who had been responsible for implementing the policy. The legacy of the deunionisation of GCHQ, inevitably, was to become Butler's concern three years later when he succeeded Armstrong.

Butler was also suspicious of the increasing number of special advisers – SPADs in political jargon – appearing in the Thatcher government. These 'temporary civil servants' differed from permanent civil servants insofar as they were political appointments. Indeed, Stephen Sherbourne, the head of Mrs Thatcher's political office,* was active in arranging a reception at No. 10 early in 1984 for all SPADs who had worked for the Tory Party during the election.[14] At this point, there were a total of fifteen such SPADs, a number that was to increase exponentially in future administrations.

* Later Chief of Staff to Michael Howard; became Lord Sherbourne of Didsbury in 2013.

Butler ensured that he was firmly in the loop in matters relating to pay and conditions of special advisers. His twin concerns were that discrepancies in pay would arise between SPADs and civil servants, adversely affecting civil servants' morale, and that previously apolitical positions would be filled by political appointees. This was anathema to him – and a development that he was later to oppose vigorously as head of the service in 1997.[15] An interesting feature of the exchange is the growth of Butler's self-confidence over the first fifteen months as Private Secretary. He appears to gain stature within the Civil Service itself, a development reflected in the manner of his correspondence with Robert Armstrong. Without presuming to speak to the Cabinet Secretary as an equal, he addresses his superior with markedly more authority than before.[16]

The miners' strike of 1984–85 contributed substantially to his self-assurance in dealing with complex and sensitive issues. From July 1984, when he addressed the problems caused by simultaneous dockers' and miners' strikes,[17] until the end of the miners' strike the following year, he played a role akin to that of a senior staff officer at GHQ, coordinating the efforts of different departments, clearing proposed action with the Prime Minister in advance, and issuing recommendations.[18] He foresaw the possible need to reach ministers absent from London during the month of August, and contacted Robert Armstrong to ensure that communication would be easy;[19] he became an active and skilled proponent of the public relations weapon;[20] his considerable tact, discretion and charm placed him, still a young man at forty-six, in a position at the very centre of planning the government's campaign. At the same time, because he was a relatively junior member of the General Staff, he perforce maintained a low public profile.

Butler's manner of handling strategy and communicating with his superiors is reminiscent of the wartime role of Brigadier Vivian Dykes who, at the age of forty-two, as Director of Plans, worked with General Bedell Smith* to found and build the secretariat for the Combined Chiefs of Staff in Washington. General Hastings Ismay wrote of him as 'a grand man in a tight place – never flustered, always courageous, absolutely dependable'.[21] Throughout

* General Walter Bedell Smith, a blunt and irascible American, is best known as General Eisenhower's Chief of Staff, and Director of the CIA under President Truman. He and Dykes became fast friends, a tribute to Dykes's ability to work closely with all colleagues.

the strike, Butler understood the relative importance and interconnectedness of the different campaigns, in particular the gladiatorial combat being waged between the Prime Minister and Arthur Scargill.[22] He gave the Prime Minister the information that she needed, always on one or two sides of paper, stating issues crisply and clearly. The similarity between his *modus operandi* and that of Dykes, as revealed by his wartime diaries, is remarkable. Butler can always be certain that he, too, would have been a highly competent wartime staff officer.

It was during the summer of 1984 that Butler was most challenged by the job and by the Prime Minister's unceasing work schedule. In a letter to his parents, normally a regular Sunday missive, he wrote:

> I'm sorry that you haven't had a letter from me in a couple of weeks, what with Sunday evenings at Chequers and the weekend at Balmoral. Even this weekend I would have been in Malaysia if the PM's far east trip had not been cancelled. Anyway, that gives us a breathing space, even if it will be largely taken up with the problems arising from the miners' strike.[23]

It was the last item, the miners' strike, that proved most wearing, as Butler felt that Scargill was winning the public relations battle. It frustrated and baffled him that 'the British lean over backwards to see even the most unreasonable person's point of view'; he was bitterly disappointed that David Jenkins, the Bishop of Durham, was hoodwinked by the miners' leader and spoke out publicly for him.[24]

The event that catapulted Butler into the public spotlight occurred on 12 October, during the party conference at Brighton, where he, the Thatchers and most of the Cabinet were staying in the Grand Hotel. As at Blackpool the year before, the evening before the Prime Minister's speech wound long into the night as the paragraphs were meticulously taken to pieces and reassembled. On this occasion, the speechwriters finished 'quite early', as he recalls:

> Mrs Thatcher used to work long into the night to complete her party conference speech and on this particular occasion she finished quite early by 2:30 in the morning and I had a document that Number 10 wanted a decision on by breakfast the next morning, so I said to her would she take

> this and look at it overnight and let me know what she thought in the morning. By this time all the speechwriters had left the room and it was just she and I in the sitting room in the Grand Hotel. She asked if I'd mind if she dealt with it that night as she wanted to concentrate on her speech.[25]

Prime Minister and Private Secretary sat in their armchairs, dealing with the last piece of business that day, Butler thinking how pleasant it would be to get to bed soon, although knowing Mrs Thatcher's ability to function perfectly on four hours of sleep, he was not confident of getting a decent night before the onslaught of the next day. As the Prime Minister underlined phrases in the paper – dealing with the future of the Liverpool Garden Festival Site, hardly urgent government business – there was a loud explosion. There was no doubt as to what had occurred:

> I had heard several bombs in my time at Number 10 … so I knew at once what it was and thought here I am, alone with the Prime Minister and someone is trying to blow her up, so you'd better do something sensible. So I said to her 'I think you ought to come away from the windows in case there's another bomb.' … She said, 'I must see if Denis is alright' … What I should have done is said, 'Stand back Prime Minister. Let me go through; I'm more dispensable that you are', but not wanting to stand between a lady and her bedroom I let her go in.

Butler accompanied the Thatchers into the corridor and tried to persuade the Prime Minister to leave immediately for London. She, however, was adamant that she should stay in Brighton and, once she was able to account for everyone, she and the evacuated ministers met at Hove police station. Rooms were found for the Thatchers at the Lewes Police Training College and, when they had left, he began to assess the damage. Remarkably, the hotel had not been destroyed by the nine kilograms of gelignite used by the IRA in the explosion. Five people, however, had been killed.*

* These were Conservative MP Sir Anthony Berry, Roberta Wakeham, the wife of Parliamentary Treasury Secretary John Wakeham, local Conservative Party official Eric Taylor, and Jeanne Shattock and Muriel Maclean, wives of local party chairmen.

When Butler turned on the television, he learned that the carnage was worse than at first supposed. Nonetheless, the Prime Minister insisted that the conference open as planned at nine o'clock. Butler, appalled, urged her not to continue. 'We must show that terrorism can't defeat democracy', she replied. The conference did start on time with the Prime Minister 'looking like a new pin, shaken but not daunted'. 'It was', said Butler, 'a marvellous gesture of strength.'

On the morning after the attack, newspapers seized on the story of the memorandum that Thatcher had been reading at the time of the explosion, and ran headlines such as 'Maggie saved by piece of paper' and 'Work on just one more paper saved Thatcher'.[26] From this factual detail grew the much-repeated story that, by keeping Mrs Thatcher working, Butler had saved her life. Certainly, her safety had been assured by her presence in her sitting room rather than her bathroom, where she might have been if they had stopped work five minutes earlier, but Denis Thatcher survived unhurt in the bedroom, so there is no certainty in that hypothesis. It did make for great camaraderie under fire, however, and the Christmas card sent by the Thatchers to Robin and Jill that year said simply 'A happy and a *quiet* Christmas, Margaret and Denis'.

The IRA, disappointed in the Brighton attempt, indicated that they would continue to target Mrs Thatcher, and promptly issued a statement. 'Today we were unlucky', it read, 'but remember we only have to be lucky once. You will have to be lucky always. Give Ireland peace and there will be no more war.'[27]

Two months after the bombing, on 3 and 4 December, there was a European Union summit meeting in Dublin Castle and, not unnaturally, there was considerable concern for the Prime Minister's safety. Over the two days, Butler recalls, there was also 'a good deal of gallows humour'. The Prime Minister's party remained in Dublin Castle rather than staying in the embassy. 'We turned on the television with cautious trepidation', Butler recalled. He and Denis Thatcher debated who should be the first to taste the Irish whiskey provided. A macabre touch was added by a plaque in the room where Bernard Ingham and he were billeted: 'In this room James Connolly, as a prisoner of the British, spent his last night on earth before being taken out and executed.' Despite gloomy predictions as to their likely fate in Dublin, the British delegation returned to London without incident.

A quality of the Prime Minister that Butler found remarkable was her stamina. Apart from her tendency to work late into the night, her resolute determination to prepare herself in depth for every meeting, irrespective of the physical toll involved, evoked his admiration and concern in equal measure. Later that month, on a round-the-world trip to Beijing, Hong Kong and the United States, the itinerary called for fifty-five hours in the air as part of a total journey of 130 hours. When they arrived back in London on 23 December, Butler asked the Prime Minister if she felt tired. 'Good heavens no', she responded. 'Why ever should I?'

The five and a half days had included two important meetings – with Deng Xiao Peng and with President Reagan. The discussions in Beijing concerned the signing of the agreement for the handover of Hong Kong to China, and the Washington talks, for which Mrs Thatcher prepared between Beijing and Washington, concerned the Western stance on nuclear disarmament and the proposed Strategic Defense Initiative (or 'Star Wars'). Not only did the Prime Minister disdain to sleep between Beijing and Washington; when her plane landed at Honolulu to refuel, she asked the welcoming admiral if there would be time to visit Pearl Harbor. On being told that it was too far to drive – a pity, as it was just on the other side of the airfield – she pulled her torch from her handbag* and led her staff and the welcoming military brass across the airfield, arriving at the harbour as dawn broke.

Taking off from Honolulu shortly after dawn, the party arrived at Washington at 9.00 a.m. and proceeded to Camp David, the President's retreat in the Maryland hills. The visit, Thatcher's first time there, was a full-dress affair to which Reagan brought George Schultz, the Secretary of State; Caspar Weinberger, the Secretary of Defense; Robert ('Bud') McFarlane, the National Security Adviser, and defense adviser Richard Perle. Talk soon turned to the future of Anglo-American relations with the Soviet Union.

The Prime Minister had met Mikhail Gorbachev at Chequers during his

* Since the Brighton bombing, the Prime Minister carried a torch in her handbag in case another bombing extinguished the lights wherever she might be at the time of the explosion.

visit to Britain earlier in the year. Gorbachev had risen in the Communist Party hierarchy during Yuri Andropov's term as General Secretary and Andropov had wanted Gorbachev to succeed him but Konstantin Chernenko had been appointed, a more conservative choice by the politburo than the 52-year-old Gorbachev. As Chernenko was not expected to survive for long,* Western leaders were already preparing for Gorbachev's accession to power.

Strategic Arms Limitation was the first item on the meeting's agenda, and Butler, the formal civil servant, was astounded by the opportunism with which Charles Powell and John Kerr† handed a note to the Prime Minister, setting out the four principles of deterrence. She read the note and passed it to the President. 'I could go along with these', he said, passing the note down the American side of the table. 'So', the amazed civil servant later wrote, 'the stance of the Western world towards its defence was formulated.'[28]

The Prime Minister and Butler kept up a full and demanding travel schedule during the early months of 1985. Tactically, this had the value of conveying the impression that she had more important matters to deal with than the miners' strike. In February, she was back in Washington, and in early April she undertook a ten-day trip, including Malaysia, Singapore, Brunei, Indonesia, Sri Lanka, India and Saudi Arabia. Butler thought the itinerary too demanding, a view supported by a speaking error in Indonesia, when she expressed her pleasure at being in Malaysia, and by the loss of her voice during a speech to the Sri Lankan Parliament.

Once the Prime Minister's party arrived back in England, Butler urged her to slow down and succeeded in making her promise not to undertake any overseas trips during the Whitsun recess. She agreed to spend the ten-day break at Chequers, allowing her staff to enjoy a brief respite. As Whitsun approached, however, she proposed several seminars to Butler, frankly admitting that she 'would die' if she were forced to honour her promise not to work for ten days. A compromise was reached whereby each member of the

---

* Chernenko died on 10 March 1985 and was succeeded as General Secretary by Gorbachev.

† Charles Powell, foreign policy adviser to Margaret Thatcher, pronounces his name 'Pole'. His brother Jonathan, Chief of Staff to Tony Blair, pronounces his name more conventionally to rhyme with 'howl'. Kerr was, at the time, head of chancery at the Washington embassy. Later Baron Kerr of Kinlochard.

private office would organise a day's event during the five days after Whitsun. Butler, as head of the office, would take responsibility for two days.

Mrs Thatcher proved quite unable to deal with leisure time. She suggested that on the second day of his care they visit St Christopher's, a hospice run by Dame Cicely Saunders in Sydenham.[29] Robin and Jill planned to follow the visit with an evening at the theatre. *Coriolanus* was playing at the National Theatre, but Butler felt it would not be appropriate to suggest a play where the protagonist is toppled by his own people. To his surprise, Mrs Thatcher suggested a 'relaxing evening' and invited herself and Denis to dinner at the Butlers. It was the first act of simple friendship between the two families, and it marked a significant step in the nature of the relations between Prime Minister and her confidential adviser.

Jill pointed out, however, that for her as hostess, entertaining the Prime Minister in her home would be far from 'relaxing' and she insisted that, after she had spent a full day teaching and time helping at the tennis club, she needed two hours of calm before dinner. Butler accordingly arranged to keep the Thatchers busy. He arranged a visit to the show house for a housing development that Barratts were building adjacent to the Dulwich and Sydenham Golf Club. Mrs Thatcher was delighted by the show house and they asked to see another house that was almost complete. As the lease on their house in Flood Street, Chelsea, was coming to an end, she and Denis decided to buy a house on the estate.

It turned out to be an unfortunate decision. The drive from Westminster to Sydenham runs through the centre of Brixton, a drive that deeply depressed the Prime Minister. That area of London was forever associated with the riots of April 1981. Unemployment of over 50 per cent among black youths, combined with disgracefully sub-standard public housing had created an incendiary atmosphere which was ignited on 10–12 April with 5,000 local residents confronting over 2,500 police. More than a hundred vehicles and several buildings had been destroyed in three days of widespread violence, arson and looting.[30] The Brixton riots had provoked other outbreaks of violence, particularly in Liverpool, where the Toxteth area saw nine days of rioting in July.

Mrs Thatcher's reaction, in the teeth of compelling evidence that the police were institutionally racist and that they behaved like an army of occupation, was to condemn the rioters as criminals, rejecting any attempt to explain or mitigate. Brixton served as a permanent reminder of the first in the series of riots in the 1980s and, of the thirty-minute drive from Westminster to Dulwich, Butler noted that she found the experience 'disagreeable' for herself and her guests.

The Dulwich and Sydenham Golf Club, moreover, posed a security nightmare as its flank was exposed to potential bombers. Given these drawbacks, the Thatchers used the house very little and sold it soon after they left Downing Street in 1990. Despite the short tenure, *Private Eye* had fun, cobbling together unrelated facts concerning the Thatchers' move into quiet suburban Dulwich Village. In his barbed satirical social news, the columnist 'Grovel' noted that a second off-licence had opened in the village. There had been a John Barnett shop for some time and this appeared to satisfy the needs of the villagers. The governors of the Dulwich Estates, however, Grovel wrote, decided otherwise. Possibly Butler, one of the Estates' governors, had realised that one off-licence could never 'hold sufficient stock to satisfy the needs of his convivial golfing companion Denis Thatcher, whose arrival in the village is expected imminently'.[31]

The Dulwich Estates took up much of Butler's time. Indeed, he once remarked that the pile of Dulwich papers was taller than the pile relating to the Irish talks. The Estates had a complex organisation involving assets of £20 million that the Dulwich schools wanted to liquidate, arguing that the Estates' governors were retaining an excessive amount of the Estates' assets. A commission was set up in the 1990s with Butler as chairman in an attempt to resolve, without resorting to litigation, the question of releasing funds from the estates. It was a thankless task in which he strove to reconcile the incompatible attitudes of two sides with entrenched positions.

Later, looking back at the saga of the Dulwich house, Butler was amazed at the thinking – or lack of it – behind the purchase. Mrs Thatcher had decided, quite unilaterally, that it would be most suitable for Denis because of its proximity to the golf course. Denis, however, loathed the course, as it was too hilly and wet. For his part, Denis persuaded himself that his wife would enjoy walking around the Dulwich College playing fields to watch school rugby matches. 'I wondered', Butler wrote, 'how two people who had been married so long could know so little about each other's tastes!'[32]

By the time Butler's posting to Downing Street came to an end in the late summer of 1985, he had forged a relationship of mutual trust with the Prime Minister. Despite being a centrist with views very different from those of Mrs Thatcher, he was able to play the role of a loyal and disinterested civil servant. He was consistently motivated by his wish that the Prime Minister should be served to the best of his ability, whatever his personal view regarding her policies. He was careful to be quite certain of his position before venturing to disagree with her, and he ensured that she always had the best advice and support.

Naturally enough, he began his posting at Downing Street with severe first-night nerves. Gradually, however, he realised that Mrs Thatcher's apparent confidence, even over-confidence, was a tool that she used to hide her own uncertainties, a fact that she later admitted at a dinner given by John Birt, the Director-General of the BBC, after she left Downing Street. Recognising this tendency, Butler saw his role as one of ensuring that, whenever she performed in public, she arrived 'with just the right amount of adrenalin flowing'. This might involve calming her down or 'psyching' her up, depending on her mood.

He knew her moods well; he did not always agree with her – differences over Britain's relations with the European Community were a prime example – but he understood when to press a point and when to finesse a position. He also understood the language in which to frame factual reports. A classic Butlerism occurred when he sent her a report of a supper meeting she attended with senior Tories. 'My impression', he wrote, 'is that [Willie Whitelaw] has reservations about a "Night of the Long Knives".'[33]

That close working relationship with the Prime Minister enabled him on occasion to display a certain levity. In Paris in November 1984, after a summit dinner with Mitterand, Thatcher gathered ministers and officials at the Paris embassy for drinks. To general surprise, she began to speak favourably of the fixed-link Channel tunnel. Bernard Ingham was astounded and asked Butler: 'When did this conversion on the road to Damascus take place?' 'About 17 minutes ago', he replied.[34]

The Prime Minister had an unfortunate reputation for having no light side, no sense of humour. On one occasion in 1983, the *Private Eye* columnist Grovel mentions that Cecil Parkinson's secretary Sarah Keays had 'only recently returned from an exploration of the jungles of Uganda with Sir Marcus Fux MP'.[35] When Thatcher heard of this, she protested that it was an outrageous slur as she knew that Sir Marcus Fox had not been to Africa. It fell to Butler to explain to her that the code word 'Uganda' indicated adulterous sexual activity in *Private Eye* parlance. On other occasions, however, she was able to laugh at the magazine's satirical column 'Dear Bill'. This was a spoof letter purportedly written by Denis Thatcher to 'Bill', one of his golfing and drinking buddies. Replete with disdainful and contemptuous comments on Cabinet members, journalists and politicians in general, the letters, like the column's predecessor, 'Mrs Wilson's Diary', were hilariously accurate. On a few occasions, Butler read the column to the Prime Minister and Denis. 'She was amused', said Butler. 'He was not.'[36]

As to the content of a speech or the formulation of specific policy, Butler soon recognised that she was intolerant of advisers who had not examined issues in the greatest detail, and contemptuous of those who simply agreed with her. In the face of disagreement, she would argue her point of view forcefully but respected the positions of those who disagreed, provided that their case was soundly researched and logically thought-through. Once Butler came to understand this, he was greatly more valuable to her and, for his own part, came to 'admire the clarity of her principles and the courage with which she stood up for them'.[37] As Bernard Ingham described her, 'she was in the back row when tact was handed out and at the head of the queue when a propensity for a knock-down argument was distributed'.[38]

The respect was mutual, a critical element of Butler's competence during his Downing Street years. Before he returned to the Treasury in 1985, the Thatchers gave him a dinner party on 1 August in No. 10, to which they invited Butler's parents, together with Jill and the children. To cap the success of his time at No. 10, the Prime Minister continued the custom she had created of appointing her Principal Private Secretaries to the rank of Permanent Secretary when they moved on.* Unlike Stowe, who went from

* Mrs Thatcher had established this custom with Sir Kenneth Stowe and Sir Clive Whitmore, both of whom became Permanent Secretaries after a spell as her Principal Private Secretary.

Downing Street to the Northern Ireland Office, for Butler the transition was a natural one, as the obvious appointment was available. After three years in a job that he had initially viewed with some concern, he now left it on the crest of a wave. He returned to the Treasury as Second Permanent Secretary in charge of public expenditure.

Since 1982, in just three years of his Civil Service career, he had emerged from the small group of 'high-fliers' and staked his claim to the highest positions in Whitehall. He had, moreover, a staunch ally in the Prime Minister, to whom he had become an invaluable, confidential aide. His presence at the moment of the Brighton bombing had branded him permanently as the man who saved the Prime Minister's life and, while that label rested on certain assumptions, it had an element of truth and great popular appeal. Now, a 47-year-old Permanent Secretary with a public profile, he was a symbol of how government could work effectively when Prime Minister and mandarins were thus disposed. This principle was underlined when he was succeeded at No. 10 by another Treasury man, Nigel Wicks. 'Treasury connections with the Prime Minister's office are being reinforced', wrote Sarah Hogg.[39] In the 'Men and Matters' column, the reporter for the *Financial Times* mischievously traced the circular progress of the different Whitehall players as the musical chairs of employment and promotion played out. 'Small world, isn't it?' the article concluded.

Butler's return to the Treasury as Second Permanent Secretary in charge of public spending was widely reported. There was sober reflection in national newspapers. *The Times* commented that having worked in Downing Street seemed to be a *sine qua non* for promotion. Moreover, 'it does not seem to matter which prime minister they served'.[40] Not only national newspapers recorded the appointment of the new Permanent Secretary, however. Local Lancashire papers claimed him as their own, referring to him as 'a member of Royal Lytham and St Annes' (golf club), and even as a former student of Lawrence House preparatory school, which he had attended at the age of seven. He was interviewed by *Palatinate*, the magazine of the Durham University Students' Union, in January 1985 – an honour that it is difficult to imagine being accorded to any of his predecessors in the role of Second Permanent Secretary. The author of the subsequent article, Richard Calland, was clearly captivated by the notion that he had the opportunity to speak to someone so close to the centre of power.[41]

The more cynical *Financial Times* referred to 'the Whitehall snakes and ladders',[42] adding, in a separate article, that 'there were 599,000 civil servants on April 1, less than 2.5 per cent of the working population and 133,000 fewer than in 1979'.[43] The subtext is clear: one possible reason for Butler's excellent relations with the Prime Minister was that he, as Principal Establishment Officer, had presided over a drastic reduction in the number of Civil Service employees before his 1982 posting to No. 10.

Butler had succeeded in a delicate series of three-cornered negotiations. He was well aware that Mrs Thatcher was determined to reduce public expenditure, and that she was looking hard at the Civil Service as the entity that would experience the greatest reductions. This called for considerable diplomatic and personal skills to achieve the reductions demanded by No. 10 while maintaining good relations within the Treasury and with the Civil Service trade union. A ringing endorsement from Douglas Wass and the evident gratitude of the Prime Minister indicate that he succeeded in implementing her policy in the Treasury without causing lasting resentment in Whitehall.

The responsibility of a Principal Private Secretary involves finding a delicate balance between serving the Prime Minister and remaining remote from the business of the party leader. Few counsellors close to the Prime Minister are able to remain totally apolitical, but Butler succeeded in remaining distant from party politics, while retaining Mrs Thatcher's full confidence. Beyond this was the almost unprecedented exposure given to him as her saviour at the Brighton conference; as a young 'high-flier' reaching the upper reaches of the service before his fiftieth birthday; and as a mandarin with an almost film-star-like quality. As Peter Hennessy's 1983 profile pointed out, according to one Permanent Secretary, he was 'everyone's idea of a complete man'.[44] To cap it all, moreover, he had the endearing, slightly eccentric foible of riding a bicycle along Whitehall. A Renaissance Man might have seemed too perfect to the British public; a Renaissance Man on a bicycle was perfectly acceptable.

Two and a half years later he was to return to Mrs Thatcher's Downing Street as Cabinet Secretary. In this post, his responsibilities were naturally greater and more far-reaching than they had been as Principal Private Secretary. At the same time, he was to find that the closeness of being on the same team as the Prime Minister, if necessary *contra mundum*, was not part of the Cabinet Secretary's brief. He would maintain and develop his relations with Margaret Thatcher, but the unique nature of his first three years in her service would not be repeated.

CHAPTER 10

CONSOLIDATION, 1985–1987

SINCE EARLY DAYS IN his career, Robin and Jill had travelled extensively, taking a holiday each summer, except in 1968, when Andrew was born. From 1971 onwards they added an Easter holiday, usually in Britain, most frequently in Cornwall. Summer holidays were often energetic affairs – cycling in Burgundy, trekking in Kashmir, walking in Norway – and they were vital aids to recharging the batteries after intense periods of work. Many of the places where they went on holiday, Butler recalls, 'were places that I had visited with Margaret Thatcher and made a note to revisit as we flashed by in a speeding car'.[1]

The summer of 1985 was no exception. Butler negotiated an extended holiday before returning to the Treasury. With all three children fully occupied – Sophie in her final year at the University of Warwick, Nell between school and university, and Andrew entering his last year at Harrow, where he, like his father, became head of the school – there were few responsibilities at home, and Robin and Jill were able to set aside a month for a trip to Israel and Egypt.

In 1976, Treasury business had taken Butler to Israel and, after a brief visit, he determined to return with Jill. Now they had time to travel extensively; from Israel they drove through Gaza into Egypt, stopping first in Cairo, then travelling by overnight train to Luxor. He recalled that a highlight was a six-day journey on a felucca, a traditional Egyptian sailing boat, from Luxor to Aswan:

> We were with a number of young Antipodeans in three boats. Ours was the greybeard boat with no illegal substances aboard. We slept on the deck

> by filling in the hull of the boat with boards. I never saw so many consecutive sunsets and sunrises as I saw in those six days. Yes, it was quite arduous, but it was a great adventure.[2]

It was a memorable trip that succeeded in restoring him physically, but also in stimulating his and Jill's interest in the Middle East. At Easter in the following year, they returned to the region, taking Andrew with them, to visit Jordan and Syria. This was a rather more alarming trip, as Hezbollah had recently taken a British hostage,* and apparently Robin and Jill attracted the interest of the Syrian security service. In the event, despite apparently being followed by three men and later hearing gunshots and a late-night knock on their door in Aleppo, they came to no harm and returned safely to Damascus and home.

During the trip, Butler had time to reflect on his situation and on the evolution of his career to date. As Sir Edmund Compton had counselled him in his Oxford days, he had gone to the Treasury and that path had proved fruitful. When he returned to the Treasury in 1985, a Second Permanent Secretary at the age of forty-seven, he could be confident that, barring serious missteps, he had as good a chance as any of his colleagues of reaching the very top of the service. The probable succession, he calculated, would put Clive Whitmore, by then Permanent Under-Secretary at the Ministry of Defence, in line for the top job before him; it was clear that he would not be far behind.

There was, however, the ritual 'cleansing' to be performed. Returning to the pure waters of the Treasury after three years in No. 10, he had first to re-establish his credentials as a civil servant. Fortunately, in a complex reshuffle, a suitable slot had been found for him. His new position, succeeding Alan Bailey in charge of the Treasury's public expenditure divisions, was congruent with his previous experience in the engine room of the operation. From that perspective, he had been able to observe how others handled the job; the appointment held a measure of challenge without being daunting.

* The hostage was Terry Waite, the assistant for Anglican Communion Affairs to the Archbishop of Canterbury, Robert Runcie. Travelling to Lebanon to negotiate the release of four hostages, he was himself taken hostage by Hezbollah.

As Second Permanent Secretary, he was not at the head of a department, but he enjoyed at least the same status as the Permanent Secretary at the head of a less important ministry.

As for future prospects, Robert Armstrong, Cabinet Secretary since 1979, would reach the mandatory retirement age of sixty, two years later, in 1987; as Armstrong had wanted Butler eventually to succeed him at Downing Street, so he could now hope to follow him as head of the service.* He had good patrons in Whitehall and Downing Street. He also had two years to stake his claim for the top job. The position of Second Permanent Secretary, which demanded constant negotiation with Treasury ministers and the Cabinet, would provide him with valuable experience.

As Butler remembers, looking back over the final two years that he worked at the Treasury, conditions can never have been more favourable to the role of the watchdog on public expenditure. Thatcherism and Treasury parsimony were perfectly aligned, and the job of his department – the paring down and planning of expenditure by each government department before the Autumn Statement and Spending Review – was prima facie painless, simplified further by the committee of ministers chaired by Whitelaw. This committee, popularly known as the 'Star Chamber', was an effective means of settling disagreements between spending ministers and Permanent Secretaries, as it was cumbersome to settle such matters in Cabinet. From the Treasury perspective, moreover, it was unwise to hold discussions in a forum in which spending ministers outnumbered Treasury officials, as the former would close ranks and support each other.

So the 'Star Chamber' came into existence, presided over by a very senior neutral minister, with other non-departmental ministers on the board. They would hear a minister's case and the Treasury case and make recommendations to Cabinet. Various techniques were employed to ensure that the Treasury won such disputes: there was always a fixed total amount in the Budget, and a contingency reserve for which ministers would compete. There was also an incentive to settle early, as Whitelaw let it be known that

* In fact, Sir Robert Armstrong recommended Whitmore to succeed him. Butler commented that this would also have been his choice.

if ministers could not agree with the Treasury but came to the 'Star Chamber', they could expect to end up with a worse settlement than if they had reached agreement with the Chief Secretary in the first place. In the climate of Thatcherism, when the tendency of ministers was to reduce rather than increase public expenditure, Butler's job was greatly facilitated.

His first ministerial boss as Chief Secretary of the Treasury was John MacGregor, returning to the Treasury, where he had served as Lord Commissioner between 1979 and 1981. He had worked at the merchant bank Hill Samuel early in his parliamentary career and was a firm supporter of Thatcherite monetarism. Butler found him a decent man, personally friendly, popular with colleagues and a good negotiator.* In the two years leading up to the 1987 general election, this was an agreeable posting, involving important decisions, but relatively calm after the exciting but exacting years in No. 10.

It is customary for the Prime Minister's Principal Private Secretary to receive an honour at the end of the appointment, and Butler was duly included in the New Year's Honours List. In early December, he received a letter from the Secretary of the Royal Victorian Order, informing him: 'I am commanded by The Queen to inform you that Her Majesty has been pleased to announce her intention of appointing you to be a Commander of the Royal Victorian Order, on the occasion of the New Year.'

Early in 1986, Butler's role in launching the Thatchers on the purchase of the Dulwich house threatened to come back to haunt him. They had bought the five-bedroom, mock-Georgian house in Hambledon Place, a gated community, for £400,000, principally as insurance against losing the 1987 election. They were reputed to have received 'a hefty discount' from Barratt Homes, the developers.[3] In April, *Private Eye* published an article larded with innuendo, suggesting a financial arrangement between Sir Lawrie Barratt, the company's founder and chairman, and Mrs Thatcher.[4]

The thrust of the article was that Barratts had produced a glossy brochure, entitled 'Homebuyer', with a prominent feature under the heading 'Award-winning luxury – A Truly Premier Choice', an article showcasing the Thatchers'

* MacGregor has the unusual distinction among politicians of being a magician. He is a member of the Magic Circle.

home and quoting Mrs Thatcher as brimming with ecstasy at her fine country kitchen. 'As soon as Mrs Thatcher saw the superb kitchen in the Dulwich Gate showhouse', the article gushed, 'she decided it would fulfil all the busy demands she would make upon it. It was, she said, "a dream kitchen".' The suggestion was that this had been a payment in kind for Barratts' providing an aeroplane for Thatcher during the election, and that the award of a knighthood to Lawrie Barratt was somehow tied into the deal. That suggestion, at least, is unmerited, as Barratt was knighted in 1982, long before the purchase of the house. A more dangerous allegation was that there were severe faults with many houses on the estate which, naturally, were not mentioned in the brochure.

As with many accusations of Faustian pacts in politics, there was little or nothing sinister about the transaction. The implication of kick-backs and the suggestion that the name of the Prime Minister was being used to promote houses with design faults or shoddy workmanship might have become a *cause célèbre* and could easily have involved Butler, who had originally introduced the Prime Minister to the development. In the same issue of *Private Eye*, there was a report of a share deal involving a mining company in Australia. Mrs Thatcher owned some shares in the company and, although insignificant sums of money were involved, the Labour MP Dennis Skinner raised the matter to embarrass Mrs Thatcher in the Commons. Once again, there was no apparent conflict of interest, but just a few years later similar suggestions of 'sleaze' contributed substantially to the Tories' downfall.

In the event, neither issue had enough substance to become a scandal. Butler saw the purchase as a simple decision to have a stake in the property market to keep pace with the rise in house prices when the Thatchers left Flood Street. As for the whiff of scandal,

> I knew nothing of her dealings with Lawrie Barratt, but I wouldn't be at all surprised to hear that he gave her a discount on the house; to have Margaret Thatcher as a satisfied client buying one of his luxury houses was tremendous publicity. I don't think that was anything improper.[5]

The purchase of the Dulwich house turned out to be unnecessary when the Tories won the 1987 election. In the subsequent reshuffle, John Major succeeded MacGregor as Chief Secretary.* Major had come under public scrutiny in January that year when, as Minister of State for Social Security, he was criticised by the *Sunday Times* for implementing a 'shabby and mean' plan to provide support for the elderly during a severely cold winter.[6] As the article pointed out, 'The baptism of fire accorded to Mr John Major, the new social security minister, will no doubt do him good.'[7] Major's handling of the affair was observed with approval from No. 10, and his promotion after the Tories' crushing victory in the June election was a significant reward.

Bids for departmental budgets were submitted in the summer before the parliamentary recess. Negotiations ran through the summer and conclusions were reached in the autumn. Major took up his new position on 13 June, and the process of negotiating budgets was a severe test for him, with much to be done in a very short time. Inevitably, he relied a great deal on Butler during those early months, and a friendship developed between the two. Butler watched with growing admiration the way in which the new Chief Secretary negotiated with his Cabinet colleagues. He was junior to many of them, but never overawed, Butler recalls. 'Instead he always took a sympathetic approach, finding out what they really wanted and helping them to get what they wanted. It was a two-way process; he would always help them provided that they helped him.'[8]

This appointment in 1987 was, effectively, the boost that enabled John Major eventually to bid for the leadership of the Conservative Party. From the relatively lowly position of Minister of State for Social Security, he occupied, three years later, two of the great offices of state.† This Treasury appointment, which brought him into contact with Butler for the first time was, therefore, enormously important; Butler was impressed by the new Chief Secretary's application and determination to grasp the nettle in his first Cabinet post. This mutual confidence was to serve them well when first Butler was appointed Cabinet Secretary less than a month after Major's arrival, and when, two years later, Major himself was promoted with bewildering rapidity

* The Chief Secretary of the Treasury is the government's second-in-command, usually with a position in Cabinet. This appointment was a significant step for John Major.

† John Major was Foreign Secretary from July to October 1989 and Chancellor of the Exchequer from October 1989 to November 1990, when he succeeded Mrs Thatcher as party leader and Prime Minister.

before taking over as Prime Minister in November 1990. By then, of course, Butler was *en poste* and able once more to act as Major's guide and mentor.

The years from 1985 to the summer of 1987, then, were important but relatively untaxing years for a senior civil servant who had already made his mark in critical appointments. Control of government expenditure was a priority for the Conservative government; the Chief Secretary of the Treasury was keen to steer a conventional course without making waves. In comparison with the Wilson years, when Downing Street and the Treasury co-existed at a hostile distance, the period of Butler's tenure was one of a fast growing economy, backed by dramatically reduced public expenditure. In 1988/89, public spending fell to below 40 per cent of national income – the first time that it had done so since 1966, and the last, too, before another twenty-five years had gone by.

During this period, Butler's relations with No. 10 remained good. Despite being 'on the outside', Butler still acted as an informal adviser to the Prime Minister, as he recalled:

> I remember over the Westland affair, which happened after I left Number Ten, I wrote Margaret Thatcher a letter on the day of the Westland debate when we thought she might be forced to resign – and might have been if Neil Kinnock had argued the case more effectively over the leak of the Attorney-General's advice. I wrote to advise her on two points. Thirty years later I don't remember with clarity what those two points were, but I tell the story to illustrate that I still felt linked to Number Ten, attached to her, and wanting to help. Also I retained close connections to Number Ten in my Treasury job as she kept a very close eye on public expenditure.[9]

Butler's relations with Mrs Thatcher, while consistently good throughout this period, were guarded. Charles Moore quotes him as saying that talking to her socially was 'like feeding a wild animal'.[10] Butler chuckled at this description and recalled:

> I always felt when I was going into her study to give something to her that it was like going into a cage with a leopard. You gave the leopard its meat

> and hoped that the leopard is in a docile mood and would be friendly but you might suddenly find that there was something deficient in the meat – in the issue you were putting to her you had forgotten something – and the leopard would suddenly bite your arm off. There was always adrenalin flowing when I took an issue in to her.[11]

The year of 1987 was a year of changes in the Butler family. Bernard, Butler's father, was diagnosed with inoperable pancreatic cancer a few weeks before his eightieth birthday in July. The prognosis of six months to live seemed incredible to his son, as over Whitsun his father and he had played four rounds of golf, his father winning all four. In the event, he died less than three months later.

The passage of time was underscored, too, by the reality of Robin and Jill's children growing up. Sophie had completed her undergraduate degree at the University of Warwick and had started work as a research assistant with the Consumers' Association. The constraints of moving back with her parents after the relative freedom of university were proving difficult and, in an inspired moment, Robin and Jill hit on a solution that would satisfy all parties. The three children should jointly buy a house, for which their parents would underwrite mortgage payments.

At the time, joint buyers of a property could each claim tax relief on £30,000 of investment, so the family looked for a house that Sophie, Nell and Andrew could buy for a price tag of about £90,000. They soon found a suitable house, 8 Aquinas Street, close to the Southbank Centre. The children proved to be compatible joint owners and conflict was avoided. All went according to plan with one minor variant. Originally, it had been planned that Robin and Jill would acquire the house from Andrew when he, the last of the three, was ready to move on. In the event, they decided against this step and moved close to Westminster Cathedral instead.*

Victor Rothschild, a man whose contacts were as valuable as his intellect,

* Butler maintains, only partially in jest, that the proximity of his flat to the Roman Catholic cathedral of Westminster has probably been a deterrent to the IRA's blowing him up. His predecessor, Robert Armstrong, swept his car each morning for IRA bombs and one morning was rewarded, finding one attached to the underside of his car (private source).

made it a tradition to keep in touch with the 'boys and girls' who had worked with him in the Think Tank. On 21 July 1987, he staged one of the regular reunion dinners, after which, amid much hilarity, spoof telegrams were 'sent' from guest to guest. These tended to be somewhat riotous parties, and Butler was not at his best at breakfast the next morning, when Charles Powell phoned from 10 Downing Street to summon him to Mrs Thatcher's presence at nine o'clock. Surprised by this unusual invitation, he asked Powell the reason for the summons and was told to ready himself for an important appointment. He was to succeed Robert Armstrong as Cabinet Secretary and head of the Home Civil Service.

The issue of Robert Armstrong's retirement and the question of his successor had been under discussion for some time. Due to retire on his sixtieth birthday at the end of March, Armstrong had remained at his post while the question of a general election was discussed. The second Thatcher administration, elected in June 1983, might have run its course until 1988 but, as the economy surged, it seemed increasingly likely that Thatcher would call an election in 1987. In that eventuality, it would be sensible for Armstrong to remain, allowing a new government to choose his successor, if the Labour Party were to achieve a surprise win.

In the event, with a small swing against them, the Tories were returned in June, and Armstrong's retirement was planned for the end of the year. His probable successor, in the eyes of senior civil servants, was Sir Clive Whitmore who, in the orderly Civil Service progression, was expected to precede Butler in the top job. Critically, aged fifty-one to Butler's forty-nine years, a senior Permanent Secretary and head of department, he exuded more gravitas.

In fact, not only was Whitmore the popular choice, he was also the personal recommendation of the outgoing Cabinet Secretary.* It was the Prime Minister, exercising her personal preference for Butler, who went against Armstrong's recommendation. Butler, too, felt that Whitmore was the more natural choice, recalling:

---

* Butler remembers that Charles Powell told him that Whitmore was Armstrong's personal preference as his successor.

> My interview with Margaret Thatcher was short but memorable. I told her of my surprise and said that I felt young and junior. She did not contradict me but said that she believed I could give effective leadership to the Civil Service. For want of something else to say, I asked her how long she envisaged continuing in office. She said, 'Only another year or so because Denis isn't getting any younger'. In the event she stayed another three years and left under compulsion.[12]

Peter Hennessy, that peerless Whitehall insider, cites 'a prescient senior man' who predicted at the time of the 1983 election, out of line with the general expectation, that the younger man would succeed Armstrong in 1987. But, he said to Hennessy, it would be a close-run contest. Comparing the two, he concluded:

> Robin is a better all-rounder than Clive … He's a more eager beaver … Robin is a get-up-and-go man all the time. And he's different from Robert. Although Robert has a good manner with people, he doesn't identify with the rank-and-file in the manner that Robin does. Ken [Stowe] and Clive are at heart both big managers. Their *forte* is management. Robin's and Robert's *forte* is policy – it's partly their genesis in the Treasury – and the Cabinet Office is really a policy department.[13]

Butler himself felt that Whitmore was simply better qualified, having been Permanent Secretary at an important ministry. He enjoyed, Butler recalls, a very high standing among the Whitehall mandarins. As to the other candidates, Peter Middleton may have seen himself as a candidate, but his expertise was financial – more so than Butler's – and so the Treasury was the obvious place for him.

Butler foresaw a potentially thorny meeting with Middleton, his former superior at the Treasury. Middleton, a dedicated monetarist with a can-do approach,[14] was a favourite of the Prime Minister and could quite reasonably have expected to be joint head of the service, a role that Douglas Wass had performed with Armstrong. This had, in fact, been proposed to Mrs Thatcher, who had rejected it as a 'Pinky and Perky arrangement'.[15] It was certainly much more in her character to want one person in charge, one potential head on a charger. Butler had consistently impressed her in his Downing Street years and had overseen both strategy and tactics; her decision was, in retrospect, predictable. Like Whitmore, Middleton was friendly and wholly supportive, despite his reasonable disappointment. He, too, knew Mrs Thatcher and recognised that power-sharing was not likely to receive her seal of approval.

'I think he may have felt passed over', Butler recalls, 'at not being at least made joint head of the Civil Service. Other people felt that too. I wouldn't say that this embittered him, but it left a sour taste in the mouth. Clive must have been particularly disappointed. His wife certainly was and she never spoke to Mrs Thatcher again.'[16]

There were a number of reasons posited for the preferment of the junior man, one of which was the antipathy of Mrs Thatcher towards Whitmore because he had failed to control Michael Heseltine over the Westland affair. When Heseltine resigned, he incurred Thatcher's undying enmity, greatly exacerbated by the manner in which he handled it. Not only did he walk out of a Cabinet meeting but he also deviated from normal convention by not announcing his resignation in the Commons. Instead he called a press conference for four o'clock that afternoon. Even more unorthodox was his decision to attack Thatcher in his statement and to do so on government premises, at the Ministry of Defence. Since Heseltine by resigning had forfeited his right to use the building for his own purposes, the argument goes, he needed approval from Whitmore, whose decision to allow Heseltine to use the ministry for the press conference permanently dished him with the Prime Minister.[17] This is certainly the view of Robert Armstrong, who recalls cautiously: 'I suspect that Whitmore's closeness to Michael Heseltine may have worked against him. I have no evidence for that, but I think that he may have been tarred with the Heseltine brush.'[18]

That may have been a contributing factor; and it would not be accurate to see Butler as a more wholehearted Thatcherite than Whitmore. Both enjoyed the Prime Minister's confidence; both had proven their ability as managers. Hennessy's Whitehall contact correctly identified Butler's 'people skills' as a crucial factor. Above all, perhaps, it was Butler's ability to handle and grip several problems simultaneously that clinched the appointment in his favour. In the skill of guiding business from ministerial wish to reality, working out its implications and smoothing its path through different departments, Butler had no peer. Bernard Donoughue felt strongly that Butler was the best man for the job, as he recalls: 'I thought that Robin should be Cabinet Secretary, but I was afraid that the machine would appoint a machine man. I was pleased to be proved wrong. Robin is a great public servant because he genuinely believes in public service.'[19]

After his meeting with Thatcher, as he left Downing Street, bound for the regular Wednesday meeting of Permanent Secretaries at ten o'clock, Butler decided to walk first to the Ministry of Defence to talk to Whitmore. In what might have been a sticky conversation Butler said frankly that Whitmore would have been his first choice. To his relief, Whitmore responded with honest congratulations and promised his full support as they walked together to the meeting. Good to his word, he was never anything but a willing ally of the new Cabinet Secretary.

Butler and Middleton were always going to be closely involved over Civil Service pay and conditions. Both were also aware that the Next Steps initiative, proposing attenuation of Treasury control of departments, was about to be completed. The Treasury, understandably, was extremely sceptical about the proposals and was resisting the empowerment of departments which, they felt, should not be given this responsibility.* Middleton, in Butler's view, took a cynical view of departments and public expenditure: if you delegated responsibility to them, they would let you down, because they knew that in the end the government would have to pay up. For that reason, he felt strongly that the Treasury should keep a firm grip on them. That view was a source of tension between him and Butler from the outset.

The opposing view, strongly held by Butler, was that it was not sensible to have four or five very junior officials, however bright they were, in the Defence division of the Treasury, with a stranglehold on the multi-billion Ministry of Defence budget. Butler believed in settling the Budget and then giving those concerned the responsibility for running it. It did not produce

* Next Steps is covered in more detail in the following chapter, Chapter 11.

the best results, he argued, to allow people at the Treasury, good economists but limited in their knowledge of defence strategy, to decide what tank or what jet fighter the military should be allowed to possess.[20]

All in all, Butler was reasonably confident that he could handle the Civil Service side of his new appointment. In 1985, when he had become Second Permanent Secretary at the Treasury, some of the Permanent Secretaries were men of stature, ten or eleven years older than himself. He had dealt with them as an equal for two years, but now he was to chair their meetings. He was sure that he could command their support, but he was conscious of their possible apprehension. What was the new man going to be like? Everything settled down quite quickly, but Butler, perhaps unsure of himself, nearly made a serious strategic mistake in his first few weeks on the job.

In August, an issue arose concerning further reallocation of resources between the Cabinet Office and the Treasury. Butler's instinct was to allow the Treasury to have what it wanted. Richard Wilson, Permanent Secretary at the Home Office and Butler's successor as Cabinet Secretary, intervened and told him that this would be a grave error. 'You must keep your leverage on the Treasury', he said, 'and retain your powers.' Butler quickly recognised that Wilson was right and that he had prevented him from yielding the initiative to the Treasury on the matter of running the Civil Service.[21]

His relations with the inner circle at No. 10, by contrast, had perforce changed during his two-year absence. There had been a gradual but insistent discontent with Mrs Thatcher's leadership among senior Tories. She was a notoriously difficult and strident leader, prone to humiliate colleagues; her abrasive manner was summed up in the commonly used term for one aspect of her character – the TBW (that bloody woman) factor. From 1984 to 1987, there had been erosion, promptly checked in the interests of pre-election unity. After the election, the whispering began again. The problem for the whisperers was that there was no obvious replacement.

There was Douglas Hurd, whose disadvantage was that he was southern and an Etonian; there was Michael Heseltine, 'a big beast', but a highly divisive one, to whom Thatcher was implacably opposed. Cecil Parkinson and John Moore were stars that had shone and faded. Nigel Lawson was brilliant, but too abrasive. The Prime Minister grew distant from her Cabinet colleagues and increasingly isolated in the two years after Butler's return to the Treasury; by 1987, she was dangerously dependent on Charles Powell, her Principal Private Secretary, and Bernard Ingham, her Press Secretary. This dependence, which Butler regarded as decidedly unhealthy, was to lead, a year later, to his most difficult confrontation with the Prime Minister.

Meanwhile, the condition of Bernard Butler had deteriorated much more quickly than had been predicted, and the six-month prognosis had shortened. To his son's pleasure he survived long enough to learn of his appointment and he asked Butler if he would now be knighted. Butler, familiar with the protocol of honours in the service, could respond honestly and without elaborating the truth that, unless he gravely blotted his copybook, he could be certain of becoming Sir Robin. This, he said, was a very important thing for his father.

Less than a month later, on 18 August, Bernard died. To Butler's acute disappointment, he was unable to reach the hospital in time, for which he reproached himself. Bernard's nurse's view, however, was that he would not have known his family. Nonetheless, Robin felt that he had failed his father, a dominating force in his life who had been

> always supportive and proud of what I did. I believe that it was a principal motive in my life not to disappoint him. As he was essentially a conservative and conventional man, so too have I been. But he had the qualities which went with his conventionality – honesty, patriotism, duty and kindness. People who knew him loved him. He was a model to me.[22]

CHAPTER 11

CABINET SECRETARY: THE FIRST YEARS, 1987–1990

ON 8 JULY 1987, the Press Office at No. 10 announced simply that Her Majesty the Queen had approved the appointment of Mr Robin Butler to succeed Sir Robert Armstrong GCB, CVO as Secretary of the Cabinet and head of the Home Civil Service.[1]

The announcement followed some careful fact-checking of the age of earlier Cabinet Secretaries when they were appointed. Once more, it appears, as in 1975, there was a body of opinion that he was too young for the job. At forty-nine years old, Butler was younger than all preceding heads of the Civil Service with the exception of Sir Warren Fisher, who was a mere forty when he was appointed in 1919. Cabinet Secretaries, by contrast, had been younger, ranging from Sir Maurice Hankey (thirty-eight), the first to hold the title, to Sir John Hunt (fifty-four) appointed in 1973. Three individuals – Sir Norman Brook, Sir Burke Trend and Sir Robert Armstrong – had been appointed Cabinet Secretary before becoming head of the service.[2]

It was not only relative youth that was an issue within the Civil Service; there is also evidence that the press relations office of the service was on the defensive regarding a number of questions. The question and answer brief, covering matters likely to be raised by journalists, is guarded and terse on certain issues. The second question addressed in the brief is 'Was Sir Clive Whitmore not chosen because he was Mr Heseltine's Permanent Secretary at the Ministry of Defence?' The suggested answer ('That had nothing to do with it') is revealing in its brevity.[3]

Beyond the question of alternative candidates, as one reads through the question and answer brief, it seems that there were several possible bases on which Butler's appointment might be challenged. The question of his age is brought up and dealt with; his status as a Second Permanent Secretary, rather than a head of department is raised and dismissed. More dangerous issues, however, were raised by the two questions: 'What motivated the Prime Minister in choosing a man who has ten years to serve?' and 'Does the Prime Minister recognise that by appointing someone with so long to serve she could be accused of perpetuating her regime beyond the period when she is Prime Minister?'

The press office of the Civil Service was apparently concerned that journalists would seize on the history of the association between civil servant and Prime Minister and suggest that the new Cabinet Secretary has been somehow 'politicised', that he had become an apparatchik of the incumbent in No. 10 – at a time when Mrs Thatcher was coming under increasing criticism for behaving autocratically. Whereas in 1985, when Butler had left Downing Street with a promotion, the association with No. 10 was seen as an asset on a curriculum vitae, three years later there was a clear effort on the part of the service to distance the Cabinet Secretary from the Prime Minister, to dismiss the possibility that he might be a Trojan horse for an outgoing Premier.

Question number sixteen in the brief suggests a very different interest on the part of the press, anticipating the question: 'Can we expect a reorganisation of the machinery of Government at the time of the changeover, its having been planned by Sir Robert Armstrong and Sir Kenneth Stowe?' The press office proposed a simple *nolle prosequi*, such as 'Cannot help you', but enjoined the responder to 'discourage speculation on this front without giving a flat denial'. In retrospect, there may have been concern about a different Trojan horse. Could there have been a possibility that Mrs Thatcher, in cahoots with the new head of the Civil Service, would renew her efforts to wield an axe around Whitehall?

Political opponents and left-wing media based their opposition on such questions. Alan Beith, the deputy leader and Chief Whip of the Liberal Party, was outspoken in his criticism of Mrs Thatcher's choice, focusing on her decision to appoint the same man to be both head of the Home Civil Service and Cabinet Secretary. Several newspapers carried his criticism that:

> It is characteristic of the Prime Minister's determination to concentrate power at the centre ... She has ignored the view of the Treasury Select Committee, which recommends that these two posts should not be combined and could not properly be fulfilled by one person. It is quite wrong that Robin Butler should be put in the untenable position of attempting to fulfil these incompatible responsibilities.[4]

A similar objection was raised by Michael Mates, a senior Conservative backbencher, in an interview on BBC2. Recent events, he maintained, had shown that the two jobs were incompatible. There was a permanent risk of conflict of interest, which had caused several committees to recommend separating the roles. The experience of Butler's predecessor Sir Robert Armstrong during the Westland inquiry – in which he was both the Prime Minister's inquisitor and shop steward to the Civil Service – should, Mates argued, be ample precedent.[5]

In general, however, response from press, from politicians and from colleagues was extremely positive. A *Financial Times* article commented that he had a 'probably unique distinction – he is respected and liked by Mr Edward Heath, Lord (Harold) Wilson and Mrs Margaret Thatcher'.[6] He was widely described as 'a civil servant for all seasons' and his career, from Harrow, through Oxford, and his 'meteoric' rise in the Civil Service endlessly repeated. Amusing characteristics ('he speaks no foreign languages; he doesn't do foreigners') and endearing eccentricities ('his rusty bicycle with a squash racquet in the basket') did solid service in projecting Butler firmly into the public gaze. Such opposition as was expressed to the appointment was not in any way *ad hominem*. There was simply concern that the Prime Minister was hijacking power to the centre and that her new Cabinet Secretary, despite his acknowledged ability to speak truth unto power, would unwittingly become her accomplice.[7]

Against this background, the position that Butler had taken regarding the deunionisation of GCHQ in 1984 threatened to present a dilemma. As head of the Home Civil Service, with a clear responsibility to maintain service morale, his uncompromising support of the Prime Minister as Cabinet Secretary would be put to the test. Butler himself had stated the nub of the problem:

> Leaders of the Civil Service, in representing the interests of the service to Ministers, are obliged to make their submissions in the same private way as the rest of their policy advice to Ministers. For that reason, civil servants do not always feel as strongly defended by their top managers as they would wish.[8]

Fear of a shift of power to the executive lay behind the comments of Alan Beith and possibly those of Michael Mates. Yet, while Members of Parliament speculated that the combination of two roles might be too large a job, and while newspapers enumerated the endearing eccentricities of the new Cabinet Secretary, Butler's own views on the relative roles of No. 10 and the Cabinet remained under his hat. He did, in fact, have very clear opinions on the subject, opinions that he sensibly kept to himself until he retired from the service.

He did, on occasion, express his own views in public, as in the 1999 Attlee Foundation Lecture, by which time he was Master of his – and Attlee's – Oxford college, University College.* In an inspired moment, he chose to speak on how Cabinet government had developed since Clement Attlee's time in Downing Street from 1945 to 1951. Opening with Attlee's famous remark that 'in Cabinet the most important thing is to stop people from talking', he developed his theme.

The principal compromise in forming a Cabinet lay in its being large enough to be comprehensive, yet small and streamlined enough to be efficient. Attlee arrived at the optimum size of the Cabinet as sixteen members. In the full years of Attlee's premiership (1946–50) there were, on average, eighty-seven Cabinet meetings and 340 circulated papers annually. By the early 1970s, when Butler first 'sat in a corner of the Cabinet room', these numbers had fallen to sixty meetings and 140 Cabinet memoranda. By the end of the Thatcher administration, the annual number of meetings had fallen to forty and in only one year after 1989 were more than twenty memoranda circulated.

* Lord Butler was originally invited to lecture on the subject of 'Cabinet Government' in 1996. He asked for a stay of execution until after he retired in 1997. This lecture was given at the Mansion House on 18 March 1999.

Cabinet had in that half-century reverted from being the government's executive committee to being akin to eighteenth-century meetings of political colleagues.* Certainly, there were still decisions of major importance taken in Cabinet, but a great deal of business was increasingly handled by Cabinet committees, by bilateral negotiations between ministers and by collective agreement. The machinery of Cabinet consensus – paperwork and late-night boxes – had increased, while attendance at collective meetings had diminished.

Despite continuing assertions in the media that the role of the Prime Minister was becoming more 'presidential', and that the Cabinet was unwieldy, Butler was – and remains – convinced that, adapting the words of Mark Twain, 'reports of the death of Cabinet government are greatly exaggerated'. In common with Lord Hailsham, he saw Cabinet government as 'one of the permanent gifts conferred by British political genius on the science and art of civilised government'. Also in common with Hailsham, he saw the need for constant vigilance to avoid the erosion of the Cabinet's authority.[9]

The new Cabinet Secretary was fully aware of the rapid and far-reaching changes wrought on government by information technology; he was acutely conscious of the increasing need for rapid decisions by the executive; he was also determined to preserve the collective authority of Cabinet government. Equally, as head of the Home Civil Service, he saw the need for the service to advance *pari passu* with government. If modernisation was needed, he would be no Luddite; reform for the sake of reform, however, he abhorred.

Reform of the Civil Service, a topic that has occupied national leaders since Augustus Caesar, had been high on the agenda of every Prime Minister since the end of the Second World War. As Peter Hennessy stresses in his study of Whitehall, for any initiative to succeed, it must have the wholehearted support of the Prime Minister. Wilson, originally committed to reform, lost interest. Thatcher did not.[10]

Relations between government and business are generally excellent under a Conservative government, and both Edward Heath and Margaret Thatcher

* Nigel Lawson wrote in his memoirs that Cabinet meetings were, 'apart from the summer holidays, the only period of real rest that I got in what was a very heavy job'.

brought managers to the business of improving Civil Service performance. One hardy perennial in this sphere was Derek Rayner of Marks & Spencer, who served both Heath and Thatcher during his career. Rayner and his chief of staff Clive Priestley, both dedicated to the ideal of a 'well-managed state', led a crusade against waste and inefficiency, and aspired to introduce a new style of management in the service. This delighted Mrs Thatcher, who detested the idea of uniquely privileged institutions and was deeply biased against civil servants as a breed. One Permanent Secretary captured her attitude perfectly in a *bon mot* to Hennessy: 'She doesn't think clever chaps like us should be in here at all', he said; 'we should be outside, making profits.'

Rayner was succeeded by Sir Robin Ibbs, who presented Thatcher with his comprehensive proposals, Next Steps, shortly before the 1987 election. The document contained some radical proposals, notably that Whitehall departments were large enterprises with different and special needs. They should, therefore, be managed by independent chief executives, operating outside Treasury control.* Unsurprisingly, as elements of the document were leaked, Treasury officials marshalled their forces in opposition.[11]

The controversial nub of Next Steps, a conclusion that Thatcher was naturally keen to conceal, was that over eight years, her famous Whitehall revolution had achieved remarkably little. The proposals that it contained, principally to devolve power from the Treasury, were watered down before the report was published. Treasury power remained intact.[12]

When Butler took over from Robert Armstrong as head of the Home Civil Service, he made it very clear that attempts to remove power over budgets, manpower and national pay bargaining from the Treasury were not going to be successful. A month later, he testified to the Civil Service Select Committee and gave the clear impression that any recommendations

---

* The paper included proposals intended to streamline the Civil Service and make it a responsive, up-to-date organisation, the performance of which was permanently under review. This required radically changed approaches to the central staff, agencies, service delivery, the machinery of government and the relations between the service and Parliament. The Treasury would need to adopt a broader set of criteria. Ultimately, the newly formed Office of Public Service and Science (OPSS) should become 'the real focal point for the reform process, pulling together wayward barons and forcing them to integrate their efforts' (*The Next Steps* (Ibbs Report) pp. 10–12).

of Next Steps were tentative at best and that no major changes were being considered. Thatcher might have talked of a general direction, but each department would need to consider its own situation and its needs. There was not to be devolution of authority or the creation of outside bodies to change the nature and responsibilities of Civil Service officials.[13]

The announcement, on 8 July, coincided, entirely by chance, with an example of what the *Sunday Telegraph* described as Butler's 'robust loyalty'. Lord Rothschild was awaiting a decision from the Director of Public Prosecutions on whether or not he would be prosecuted for an alleged offence under the Official Secrets Act in connection with the *Spycatcher* affair.[14]

While the issue was being weighed by the DPP, Butler planned a grand dinner, inviting Rothschild and about sixteen former Think Tank colleagues and friends of Rothschild for an evening of Chinese food, spoof telegrams and Cabinet minutes.[15] Those present included Sir Peter Carey, Sir Robert Wade-Gery, Sir Adam Ridley, William Waldegrave and Tessa Blackstone, recently created Baroness Blackstone.[16] At a time when his own position was the subject of widespread controversy, as the *Sunday Telegraph* article pointed out, this was an act of considerable loyalty on his part. Rothschild was deeply moved by the gesture, and he wrote to Butler thanking him for allowing him to spend just under four hours 'not thinking about what I euphemistically call "my problem"'.[17]

In a piece of classic understatement in his memoir, Butler wrote that 'the role of the Head of the Civil Service is a tricky one'. There can be no doubt that this was so – and particularly in his own case, as he had managed to impress the several teams that he had worked with in Downing Street, as Private Secretary to Heath, Wilson and Thatcher. We have seen how he established excellent relations with these Prime Ministers and, also – a more remarkable achievement – developed first-class working relations with their close aides, a species that is hesitant to allow access to anyone outside their kitchen cabinet.

In a climate where the Prime Minister was stridently demanding change in the service, there were few candidates for the post of Cabinet Secretary who would satisfy Downing Street and the Treasury at the same time. The 'prescient senior man' whom Peter Hennessy quoted in his forecast had identified in Butler his directness of character, combined with his quality as 'an all-rounder'. The sporting metaphor for a Rugby Blue and captain of the Mandarins XI is apt. Hennessy explains a quality that impressed Haines, Donoughue and Thatcher: 'He never grew grand, either, remaining what in fact he had been, an enthusiastic public school head boy whose conversation was peppered with "goshes" and "supers".'[18]

In the context of a society still dominated by the old school tie, Hennessy's profile for *The Times* in 1983 was accurate as far as it went.[19] Butler represents tradition, respect of institutions, cherished public school values. Yet he is not a slave to them. In a pinch, he is likely to come down on the side of officialdom, but he is his own man. He is friendly with Richard Ingrams of *Private Eye* and makes jokes with him. He is youthful, agile; he rides a bicycle and plays cricket at the age of fifty.* But he is not a swinger; he is British to the core. He is progressive without being dangerous. Not a stick-in-the-mud but not a firebrand either. Safe pair of hands. Just the sort of chap we need at the top of the modern Civil Service. Qualities that Hennessy identified in 1983 had not vanished in 1987. Butler had enough of Armstrong's virtues to be sound, but was enough of a moderniser for conservative Armstrong to favour Whitmore.

From the outset, Butler set out to fulfil this seemingly contradictory role of conservative moderniser. This required considerable diplomacy and the ability to secure the confidence of both the service and the government. From all sides he heard the refrain that morale in the service was lower than it had ever been. At the same time, he was expected by a Tory government to institute reforms proposed by Ibbs. This would involve the creation of 'agencies', each under a chief executive, whose function would be to deliver services required by the minister.

The task, in essence, fell into two parts: selling the concept to civil servants and, simultaneously, determining the shape of the agencies – how delegation would operate, the extent of empowerment and responsibility.

---

* By the age of fifty, Butler accepted that his cricket career was coming to an end. On 27 May 1986, however, he took the wicket of Mike Brearley (the former captain of England), which convinced him that he had a few more matches in him (letter to Bernard and Nora Butler, 1 June 1986).

The first part was squarely down to him; for the second, he was fortunate in finding an officer with the right blend of experience in and outside the Civil Service. Peter Kemp, a deputy secretary at the Treasury, had qualified as an accountant before joining the Civil Service as a late entrant. While handling pay negotiations at the Treasury, he had gained the confidence of the trade unions in addition to having worked in the 'real world' of commerce. Butler was also confident that he had both the commitment and the energy to drive through reforms to which it was certain there would be initial resistance.

His own immediate task was to explain the proposed reforms to the service as a whole and, as head of the service, to gauge the mood and likely reactions of civil servants at all levels. He therefore made sure that he had time to visit outstations, setting up a programme for visits the length and breadth of the country. To achieve this, he delegated a function of the Cabinet Secretary's job that Armstrong had found important. Armstrong recalled: 'I acted as Sherpa at economic summits for Thatcher. Robin did not do that, but delegated the role to Nigel Wicks. I enjoyed the role and found the Sherpa experience valuable and very useful.'[20]

This trimming of his role allowed Butler to spend almost 50 per cent of his time on visiting outlying departments, twice as much time as Armstrong had devoted to this task. He described this as an important part of the job, one that was facilitated when the Prime Minister was on an overseas trip.[21] Greatly more comfortable than Armstrong in the role of visible head of the Civil Service, he symbolised the new emphasis on delivery rather than pure policy formulation. In the opinion of Gus O'Donnell, at the time press secretary to John Major, his determination personally to observe the Civil Service outside Whitehall in operation was one of his greatest contributions to the service.[22] His accessibility and pragmatic approach to problem solving were vital elements in the rebuilding of confidence within the service and redefining its purpose in the context of Next Steps.

Aware that the issue of 'hiving off' civil servants to agencies was symbolic of a far wider political philosophy, Butler took nine months to acquire the fullest possible understanding of the service before publicly addressing the question. In a speech in late September 1987, he gave a balanced analysis of the need for a different management style.[23] As many as 580,000 Civil

Service employees might be employed by agencies over the next decade, he said, but there were substantial areas of government that could never be handled by a commercial regime. The Cabinet Office was responsible for Next Steps, and would probably recommend that 100 Whitehall sections become agencies. It should be borne in mind, however, that the service had on its own initiative improved efficiency, set performance targets and made the salary structure more flexible to enable performance to be recognised.

As head of the Home Civil Service, then, his vision of his role was generally congruent with attitudes at No. 10. As Cabinet Secretary, on the other hand, his relations with the Prime Minister had changed of necessity. William Whitelaw, that wise elder statesman, described how the Cabinet Secretary can work closely with the Prime Minister but how his loyalties are not to No. 10, but to the Cabinet as a separate entity. 'Of course', he conceded, 'successive Secretaries to the Cabinet have naturally become close advisers and friends of the Prime Minister of the day.' But the outstanding Cabinet Secretaries he had worked with – Burke Trend, John Hunt, Robert Armstrong and Robin Butler – had followed the tradition that they served the whole Cabinet.[24]

Thatcher had unhesitatingly appointed him to the dual role, perhaps not realising how much his loyalties would differ from those of Principal Private Secretary. His responsibilities were to the Cabinet at a time when the Prime Minister was behaving more autocratically, with diminishing respect for collective responsibility. As he simply expressed it, 'I was on the other side of the green baize door.' There were, moreover, other difficulties. Her intellectual grip was as strong as ever, but she had come increasingly to depend on Powell and Ingham, to the exclusion of her political colleagues, particularly Sir Geoffrey Howe and Nigel Lawson. Additionally, Whitelaw had been compelled by ill health to retire at the end of 1987.[25]

Mrs Thatcher's Downing Street, he might have said, was now being controlled by a 'kitchen cabinet'. With memories of Harold Wilson's second administration (and, incidentally, foreshadowing the style of the next Labour government), Butler was surely distressed at the degeneration of ordered democratic principle. Personifying this slippage was the figure of Charles Powell, whom he had recommended to Thatcher in 1984 as her foreign affairs private secretary. By the time that Butler became Cabinet Secretary, Powell had been in that post for nearly four years, longer than a normal secondment. Butler's concerns that prompted limitation on the length of secondments – that there was a growing danger of politicisation of the Civil Service – were coming to the fore.

Foreign Office opinion was that the Prime Minister was too dependent on Powell for advice on foreign affairs and that the positions of the Foreign Secretary and his department were being eroded. Sir Percy Cradock, a foreign affairs adviser to Thatcher, commented that 'it was sometimes difficult to establish where Mrs Thatcher ended and Charles Powell began'. He continued:

> To the Foreign Office, ... his employers, and to the Cabinet Office in the person of the Cabinet Secretary, Charles began to present a ... formidable problem. His closeness to the Prime Minister and his influence with her, his willingness to venture into the political world, came to seem as a threat to the balance between No. 10 and Whitehall and even to the constitutional division between ministers and civil servants ... Charles and the Press Secretary, Bernard Ingham, portrayed as Mrs Thatcher's praetorian guard, underlined the dangerous dominance, and loneliness, of their mistress. Ministers and Members of Parliament as well came to resent their influence.[26]

Not only was Powell assuming powers that traditionally belonged to the Foreign Office; he and Thatcher did not plan to include Butler in talks during President Reagan's visit to London. Not unnaturally, Butler made it clear to the Prime Minister that this would greatly damage his credibility.[27] It was, in short, time for Powell to move on. Accordingly, he was offered the post of ambassador to Switzerland, a position that he had indicated that he would like.* Despite his initial enthusiasm, he ultimately refused the offer.

Butler was, however, determined that Powell should be moved and, when Thatcher indicated that he would be happy to become ambassador to

---

* His socialite wife Carla grew up in Valle Vigezzo, the valley between Domodossola and Lake Maggiore. Her childhood and youth, before she went to university in Turin, were spent just a few miles from the Swiss province of Ticino.

Spain, he set the wheels in motion. This in spite of the fact that the Madrid embassy was a more senior post than Powell's status justified, and despite the fact that the current ambassador was not due to retire for another year. Thatcher asked him to make the necessary arrangements with the Permanent Under-Secretary of the Foreign Office and, not without difficulty, the transfer was arranged. Thatcher duly approved Powell's appointment to Madrid to take effect in June of the following year.

During the autumn of 1988, either the Prime Minister or Charles Powell or both had second thoughts about the transfer and, in December, Mrs Thatcher informed Butler that she wanted Powell to remain in Downing Street and to be available for the Commonwealth Heads of Government Meeting in Kuala Lumpur the following October. Butler accordingly delayed the retirement of the ambassador in Madrid that he had, with some difficulty, advanced. By June 1989, the situation had changed once more and the entire project was cancelled; Thatcher wanted Powell to stay at No. 10 and not go to Madrid.

Considerably vexed by this chopping and changing, Butler's first reaction was to tell the Prime Minister that, if Powell's appointment to Madrid were to be reversed, then he would feel obliged to resign. Predictably, this raised the stakes between Prime Minister and Cabinet Secretary and, on reflection, he reached the decision that he had been acting improperly in applying pressure to the Prime Minister in this way. Her new Principal Private Secretary, Andrew Turnbull, moreover, told him frankly that the Prime Minister had the right to appoint the Private Secretary she chose.[28] Nonetheless, Butler maintained his position that Powell should leave No. 10 and take up the appointment as ambassador in Madrid. His advice was ignored and Thatcher informed him, through Turnbull, that Powell would remain in Downing Street. The changed nature of relations between Butler and the Prime Minister were writ large.

Not only were relations different; the role of the Cabinet Secretary involved him in a surprisingly varied range of business. During the first eighteen months in the job, he was closely involved in performing two very different roles – as arbitrator and diplomat – in each of which he personified the national spirit.

In January 1988, investigators at the Department of Trade and Industry (DTI) reported that the investment company Barlow Clowes, run by Peter Clowes, was not 'a fit and proper' company to handle funds on behalf of investors. On 1 March, they followed this up with a report that Barlow Clowes was operating a Ponzi scheme,* investing new clients' funds to cover shortfalls in existing client accounts; the report recommended that the company be wound up. By promising abnormally high returns, coupled with no risk as the company claimed to invest only in gilt-edged securities, Barlow Clowes had attracted £189 million from investors, a considerable amount of which had been used to purchase four private jets, a yacht, a French château and a farm in the Peak District for Peter Clowes.

When it emerged that the DTI had initially told Clowes that he did not need a licence to do business and later had issued a licence without adequate investigation of the company's operations, the question of government culpability – and, therefore, its possible obligation to compensate defrauded investors – was studied by the Cabinet Secretary. Initially both he and Sir Brian Hayes, the Permanent Under-Secretary at the DTI, saw no reason why the government should effectively underwrite Barlow Clowes's activities, particularly as it would set a dangerous precedent for future disappointed investors to turn to the government to reclaim losses.

A report by the Ombudsman was highly critical of DTI officials, and the government's attitude hardened in favour of challenging the report, yet favouring payment of compensation – a position that Butler considered illogical. In the event, he accepted that public opinion in favour of the government's paying compensation was too strong to ignore, and 90 per cent of the missing £193 million was repaid by the government. Over the following twenty-one years, £156 million was recovered and, in February 2010, two decades after the event, Butler's judgement that the government had an obligation, and that the obligation could be limited to the single scandal under

* A Ponzi scheme is a fraudulent investment operation in which investors' money is appropriated by the organiser and returns to original investors are made by using funds invested by subsequent investors. It is named after Charles Ponzi, a Boston financier, who initiated such an investment scheme in 1920.

consideration, was supported by public opinion, thanks to the satisfactory financial outcome.[29]

Another, very different, mission that Butler undertook as Cabinet Secretary had little to do with politics but much to do with British prestige. Baron Hans Heinrich Thyssen Bornemisza de Kaszon, the billionaire son of German industrialist Heinrich Thyssen, had added to his father's enormous collection of pictures until the 600 Old Masters and 900 modern works overwhelmed his home, the Villa Favorita on Lake Lugano. Thyssen was concerned that the collection be kept together after his death, and had approached the Swiss government to fund an enlargement of his museum. When the Swiss offered a mere $3 million, he began a round of bargaining with different countries to make the best possible deal for the future of the pictures. He had at one point hinted to Thatcher that he would favour Britain as a future guardian of the collection. As Britain had not acted sufficiently rapidly to secure the Gulbenkian Collection,* the Prime Minister urged prompt action, including a three-month time limit to be placed on any offer made.

The Prime Minister obtained Cabinet approval for a proposal to be made to Thyssen, incorporating three possible sites for a purpose-built gallery – in Birmingham, in Hampshire or a new museum in London's Docklands at a cost of £150 million. She also invited him to Downing Street and, to initiate discussions, asked Butler to prepare a proposal and take it personally to Baron Thyssen in Lugano. With the help of Sir Peter Smithers, a neighbour of Thyssen (and the model for Ian Fleming's James Bond),[30] Butler arranged a meeting with the baron and flew out with Sir Claude Hankes-Drielsma, a financier and friend of Smithers, on 21 May 1988 to open negotiations.[31]

From the outset the journey was ill-fated. Arriving late after a delayed flight, in time for a postponed luncheon, Butler was given a tour of the villa and its collection, which he described as 'unforgettable'. Particularly striking was the Renoir *Woman with Parasol in Garden*, which was hung above the baron's bed. For good measure, the bedroom also contained another Renoir, a Manet, a Morisot and a Picasso.[32] The villa and the adjacent

* In 1936, Gulbenkian had loaned thirty paintings to the National Gallery and his collection of antiquities to the British Museum. The remarkable collection was ultimately left to the Calouste Gulbenkian Museum in Lisbon.

gallery contained a remarkably eclectic collection, ranging from Dürer, El Greco and Tintoretto to Munch and Pollock. Of particular British interest was Holbein's *Henry VIII*. Estimates of the likely cost to Britain were in the region of £200 million, but the value of the collection as estimated by Sotheby's was a massive £1.2 billion.[33]

Butler knew that Britain was only one of several countries with which the baron had entered into discussion, and he was concerned when the baron's fifth wife, Carmen 'Tita' Cervera, was unable to join the group for luncheon; apparently the illness of her dog made it impossible.* As it was known that the baroness, a former Miss Spain, wanted the collection to be housed in the proposed Thyssen-Bornemisza Museum in Madrid, Butler felt – correctly, as it turned out – that this was a bad omen. He used the three-month deadline of the British offer to apply gentle pressure on the baron, but, after nine months of negotiation, agreement was reached for the collection to be loaned to the Spanish foundation. The Prime Minister later described the failure of Britain to secure the collection as her 'greatest disappointment'.[34]

By the time that Butler took over as Cabinet Secretary, Margaret Thatcher had been leader of the Conservative Party for thirteen years and Prime Minister for nearly nine. Her style had always been more abrasive than conciliatory and, with each election victory, her certainty in her own methods increased – even as her personal popularity sank in opinion polls.

This led to an increasing alienation of the Prime Minister (and her office) from the Tory Party and her own Cabinet. As Charles Powell extended his influence as her foreign policy adviser, upsetting the Foreign Office in the process, so tensions grew between Sir Alan Walters, the Prime Minister's economic adviser, and Nigel Lawson, the Chancellor of the Exchequer. Thatcher's increasing support of her advisers at the expense of her Cabinet colleagues not only prompted open disagreement in Cabinet, but also led to constitutional difficulties that inevitably involved the Cabinet Secretary.

In selecting Butler for the post, Thatcher had been guided by her experience of having him as her Principal Private Secretary from 1982 to 1985,

* The credibility of this somewhat improbable excuse was, in fact, bolstered when the baroness's dog died soon after.

during which years his primary loyalty had been to her. Now his loyalties were different and, as she increasingly imposed her will through her private office and her own team of advisers, she further distanced herself from her Cabinet. Butler recalls that this distance became alarmingly clear in June 1989, when Walters made no effort to conceal his disagreement with Lawson over exchange rate policy:

> In this he may have been emboldened by the increasingly distant relations between the Prime Minister and the Chancellor ... The Prime Minister was unwilling even to discuss [the European Exchange Rate Mechanism] with Sir Geoffrey Howe and Nigel Lawson and they finally secured a meeting only by threat of resignation ... The issue was on the agenda for an EU Summit in Madrid* and, during the flight to Madrid, the Prime Minister refused to speak to her Foreign Secretary and Chancellor of the Exchequer, keeping the curtain closed between her compartment on the aircraft and theirs.[35]

Under pressure, Thatcher agreed in Madrid to enter the Exchange Rate Mechanism ('ERM') once five conditions were met: when inflation had gone down in Britain; when the European Community removed capital controls; when competition was introduced in financial services; when European competition policy had been strengthened; and, perhaps the most vague condition, when progress was made in completing the internal market. There was a quality of 'when pigs can fly' inherent in her undertaking. In the following month, an undeterred Thatcher dealt with Howe by replacing him with Major at the Foreign Office and giving Howe the largely ceremonial titles of Leader of the House, Lord President and Deputy Prime Minister.

To this atmosphere of strong mutual suspicion – so strong that Butler believed a Cabinet crisis to be imminent – Walters contributed an incendiary bomb when he wrote an article for the *Financial Times* describing the ERM as 'half-baked'. For Lawson, this was the final straw; he demanded that Walters resign and, when Thatcher refused to dismiss him, on 26 October 1989 he himself resigned and was replaced as Chancellor by John Major. From the

* On 26–27 June 1989.

position of Chief Secretary to the Treasury, Major had advanced to Foreign Secretary, an office he held for ninety-five days, and then to Chancellor of the Exchequer. On each occasion, his appointment filled a gap left by a hostile resignation. Major, positioned, like Thatcher, outside the aristocracy of the Tory Party, clearly was the PM's chosen successor. As Butler noted in characteristic understatement, 'the atmosphere at the centre of Government was not easy'.[36]

By late autumn, there was mounting discontent with Thatcher and with her authoritarian style, particularly on divisive issues such as the community charge (commonly referred to as 'the poll tax') and the extent of Britain's involvement with the European Community. On 23 November, the Prime Minister was formally challenged for the leadership by Sir Anthony Meyer, a wealthy baronet and passionate pro-European. Meyer had no illusions about the likelihood of his being elected leader, but he hoped that a challenge to Thatcher might bring a better-known pro-European such as Michael Heseltine or Ian Gilmour into the ring. In the event, it did not, and Thatcher won the election by a massive margin.* Beneath those numbers, however, were spoiled ballot sheets and abstentions, revealing that almost 20 per cent of the Tory Members of Parliament had not supported Thatcher. The implication was clear: a more prominent candidate might have unseated her.

The government's situation at the end of 1989 caused Butler considerable concern. Nominally apolitical, but of a centrist disposition, he was in the middle of a rift capable of destroying not only the Prime Minister but the whole Tory Party. The increased power of the Prime Minister's office had alienated many senior ministers; now her determination to introduce the community charge in the face of equally determined opposition put Conservative backbenchers in fear of losing their seats at the next election. Meanwhile, the Prime Minister, convinced of her popularity after the dismantling of the Berlin Wall, became increasingly strident.

During the summer and autumn of 1990, the fissure between Prime Minister and Cabinet, the breakdown of collective government that Butler had foreseen, became overt. After Saddam Hussein's invasion of Kuwait in

---

* The margin of victory was 281 votes (314 for Thatcher; 33 for Meyer).

August, the Prime Minister excluded the Cabinet Office from servicing a ministerial group that she chaired and which oversaw the Iraq crisis. Butler and Sir Patrick Wright, the senior Foreign Office official concerned, were reduced to holding their own meetings at which officials pooled such information as they had. Wright and Sir Percy Cradock exchanged limericks that made light of Thatcher's autocratic manner.* Butler, 'a less whimsical figure than Wright or Cradock', was deeply disturbed at the constitutional implications and refused to join in the fun.[37]

Worse was to follow. Over the weekend of 27–28 October, a European summit conference was held in Rome. When the Prime Minister reported on the conference in the Commons on 30 October, she came under attack from Neil Kinnock, the Leader of the Opposition, who, suggesting that she lived in cloud-cuckoo land, criticised her method of negotiation with European leaders over farm subsidies. Her manner was so aggressive and authoritarian, he claimed, as not only to upset heads of other governments, but also to alienate members of her own party. 'Tantrum tactics' would do nothing to halt progress; they served only to 'strand Britain in a European second division without the influence over change that we need, the financial and industrial opportunities that we need and the sovereignty that we need'.[38] It was a reasoned and devastating broadside.

Thatcher's response, laced with sarcasm, was shrill and doctrinaire, reaching a climax in an attack on the Labour party and a rejection of a federal Europe as proposed by President of the European Commission Jacques Delors:

> Yes, the Commission wants to increase its powers. Yes, it is a non-elected body and I do not want the Commission to increase its powers at the expense of the House, so of course we differ. The President of the Commission, Mr. Delors, said at a press conference the other day that he wanted

* Wright sent to Cradock: 'Robin Butler, preparing for doom, / Called the mandarins into his room. / As he turned out the light / He said, "Let's get this right. / Who does what and with what and to whom?"' To which Cradock replied: '"Dear Robin", the mandarin said, / "There are letters that may not be read. / There are minutes as well / Which no man may tell, / And which all must be kept in the head. / And from this conclusion it's stark / That we all must remain in the dark / While our Masters decide / Without briefing or guide / Who does what and to whom in Iraq."'

> the European Parliament to be the democratic body of the Community, he wanted the Commission to be the Executive and he wanted the Council of Ministers to be the Senate. No. No. No.[39]

Two days after this exchange, she humiliated Howe at a Cabinet meeting, provoking his resignation the same afternoon. Two days later, on 3 November, Heseltine wrote an open letter to his constituency chairman, a clear challenge to Thatcher's leadership. From Downing Street, Ingham responded with a robust counter-attack, inspiring, Heseltine believes, an editorial in *The Times*:

> The attempt by Mr Heseltine to demoralise her into resignation, so that he can avoid the odium of abandoning his pledge not to stand against her, will not work. In the event of a stalking horse standing, she will fight and certainly win. Mr Heseltine is at present merely helping the Conservatives to lose the next election. He should put up or shut up.[40]

After a brief trip to Geneva for the World Climate Conference, the Prime Minister assembled her advisers; if there were to be a leadership contest, it should, they agreed, be tackled immediately. Accordingly, the date of 15 November was fixed as a deadline for nominations and 20 November as the date of the first ballot.

Butler observed these events with concern; he had great admiration for Thatcher, but her manner with Cabinet colleagues had become 'overweening'. As he considered the likely outcome of a leadership election, he faced a conundrum: Heseltine, he believed, would not beat Thatcher; Major was a possible winner but it would be unwise for him to stand, as he would wound himself by apparent disloyalty. Thus, despite the increasingly widespread opposition to the incumbent, he could not see who could mount a successful challenge.[41]

Thatcher's first instinct was to enter the fray with vigour, to renew her authority in the face of resistance. Belatedly, however, she realised that she had overstepped the limits of reasonable discussion and, attempting to put the genie back in the bottle, issued the Downing Street emollient that the dispute was one of style rather than substance. This earned scorn from Howe when he made a statement on his resignation to the Commons on 13 November.

> It has been suggested – even, indeed, by some of my right hon. and hon. Friends – that I decided to resign solely because of questions of style and not on matters of substance at all. Indeed, if some of my former colleagues are to be believed, I must be the first Minister in history who has resigned because he was in full agreement with Government policy. The truth is that, in many aspects of politics, style and substance complement each other. Very often, they are two sides of the same coin.[42]

Coming to the end of his speech, having opined that 'there is grave danger that the hard ecu* proposal is becoming untenable', he made the accusation that opened the door for serious challenge to Mrs Thatcher's leadership. The levity of the metaphor did nothing to lessen the effect of the attack.

> How on earth are the Chancellor and the Governor of the Bank of England, commending the hard ecu as they strive to, to be taken as serious participants in the debate against that kind of background noise? I believe that both the Chancellor and the Governor are cricketing enthusiasts, so I hope that there is no monopoly of cricketing metaphors. It is rather like sending your opening batsmen to the crease only for them to find, the moment the first balls are bowled, that their bats have been broken before the game by the team captain.[43]

Finally, having delivered an attack that Thatcher described as 'cool, forensic, light at points and poisonous',[44] Howe openly raised the question of the Tory leadership:

> The conflict of loyalty, of loyalty to my right hon. Friend the Prime Minister ... and of loyalty to what I perceive to be the true interests of the

---

* European currency unit.

> nation, has become all too great. I no longer believe it possible to resolve that conflict from within this Government. That is why I have resigned. In doing so, I have done what I believe to be right for my party and my country. The time has come for others to consider their own response to the tragic conflict of loyalties with which I have myself wrestled for perhaps too long.[45]

The hint was made – and understood. As Thatcher saw it, 'Michael Heseltine had been handed more than an invitation to enter the lists; he had been given a weapon as well.'[46] On the following morning, he declared his intention of standing for the leadership. His immediate campaign promise was to conduct a thorough review of the community charge, a promise that was well received by Tory backbenchers, concerned about retaining their seats if the community charge remained prominent in a Conservative manifesto.

Initially, it seemed that Thatcher would have the necessary support to win comfortably on the first ballot and she left London for the conference of the Commission on Security and Cooperation on Europe.* This enabled her to maintain a front, as Macmillan had done when three Treasury ministers resigned in 1958, of 'a little local difficulty' but, in her absence, the mood of dissatisfaction and concern as to the government's direction had weakened her position. The result of the first ballot was a win, but not a conclusive win, for Mrs Thatcher: she received 201 votes; Heseltine 152; there were 16 abstentions. There would be a second ballot.

Returning to London, the Prime Minister took stock. Denis strongly urged her to resign. One after another, Cabinet ministers assured her of their support but expressed their doubts that she could win a leadership election. It became a predictable chorus, reinforced when John Major hesitated to agree to second her nomination. Major was loyal, but he had his own ambitions once Thatcher could no longer govern.

While it was becoming clear to Thatcher that she could not even assemble a credible campaign team, the Cabinet Secretary 'remained in the

* Also known as 'the Helsinki Commission', established in 1973 and source of the Helsinki Accords of August 1975. The Paris meeting, which signed the Charter of Paris for a New Europe, was held in response to the collapse of the Soviet Union.

background'. He had felt for some time that the government was increasingly unstable and unpopular with backbenchers. Cabinet members, he believed, were honest and direct, rather than treacherous, in their assessment of the Prime Minister's position. The fact remained, however, that, in the event of Thatcher's resignation, there would very possibly be pressure for an immediate general election to ratify the position of the new Prime Minister. When it became clear that she had decided to resign, he 'gave [his] mind to stage-managing the Cabinet'.

> It was clear that, if the Prime Minister's statement told the Cabinet that she was going to resign, someone would need to respond and pay tribute to her. The obvious person to do so was the Lord Chancellor, Lord Mackay, both because he was the most senior member of the Cabinet following Geoffrey Howe's resignation and because he would not be a candidate for the succession. So, while the Prime Minister was in the Cabinet Room with speech-writers drafting a speech for a No Confidence debate which the Opposition had put down for the following day, I was drafting a statement for Lord Mackay and negotiating it with him.[47]

Much later, when six former Cabinet Secretaries met in November 2016 to celebrate the centenary of the office of Cabinet Secretary, Butler revealed that the official record of Thatcher's last Cabinet meeting contained his only falsification of Cabinet minutes. The official version, that he recorded, was that she hoped she could rely on colleagues to carry on her mission. In fact, Butler admitted, they were 'less coded'; she had, in fact, begged her colleagues: 'Please don't appoint Michael Heseltine as my successor.'[48]

The reality of life as a private citizen had already been made clear to Denis. On the evening of 22 November, the day of Mrs Thatcher's resignation, Harrow School held its School Songs in the Albert Hall. This was a grander affair than usual, celebrating the fiftieth anniversary of Sir Winston Churchill's attendance at Songs at the school in 1940. Butler, as chairman of the school's governors, oversaw the event, and Margaret and Denis Thatcher, as parents of old Harrovian Mark, were to attend. When the Prime Minister instead had to attend the No Confidence debate in the House of Commons,

Richard Daft, Robin's great-grandfather. An All-England player, he and W. G. Grace competed to head the annual batting averages. Richard Daft was captain of Nottinghamshire, the author of *A Cricketer's Yarns* and *Kings of Cricket*.
PHOTO: J. J. E. MAYALL (1813–1901)

Fred Jones, Robin's maternal grandfather, founder of Leyland Paint and Varnish. He pressured his son-in-law, Robin's father, to choose between playing rugby and a career with Leyland Paint. At the age of sixty, he left his wife for a younger woman.
COURTESY OF LORD AND LADY BUTLER

Robin's parents, Bernard and Nora Butler, at Robin and Jill's wedding, 25 August 1962.
COURTESY OF LORD AND LADY BUTLER

Robin's younger sister Diana, born four years after Robin. Nora had German measles while she was pregnant and Diana was born with hearing disabilities and, as was later discovered, a hole in the heart. She far outlived her prognosis and died on her fortieth birthday, 12 January 1982.
COURTESY OF LORD AND LADY BUTLER

Robin, aged three in Lytham St Annes, 1941.
COURTESY OF LORD AND LADY BUTLER

Friends exchanged photographs when they left the school. Note that Robin's is signed 'Freddy', the name he went by through his schooldays.
COURTESY OF MR JEREMY LEMMON

About to deliver his *Contio Latina* at Harrow Speech Day, June 1956. The speech was delivered in Latin to the school governors. The young Butler wrote his own Latin version, the first Head of School to do so since 1907.
COURTESY OF LORD AND LADY BUTLER

The Oxford University Blues team at Twickenham, 8 December 1959. Cambridge were the pre-match favourites, but the Dark Blues won by three penalty goals to one. Robin is in the back row, fifth from the left.
COURTESY OF LORD AND LADY BUTLER

Summer Eights on the river at Oxford, where Robin and Jill met in June 1960. Robin (at 5, fifth from the left) rowed in the 'Rugger Eight', a light-hearted version of the real thing.
COURTESY OF LORD AND LADY BUTLER

Robin continued to play rugby after Oxford, turning out as a wing forward for Richmond until family commitments persuaded him to retire.
COURTESY OF LORD AND LADY BUTLER

Robin and Jill's wedding, 25 August 1962.
COURTESY OF LORD AND LADY BUTLER

FAR LEFT Acting with Jill in *The Rivals* in a 1963 Dulwich Players production.
COURTESY OF LORD AND LADY BUTLER

LEFT With Harold Wilson and Clive Jenkins of ASTMS (the Association of Scientific, Technical and Managerial Staffs).
COURTESY OF LORD AND LADY BUTLER

At the signing of the Sunningdale Agreement, 9 December 1973.
COURTESY OF LORD AND LADY BUTLER

The photograph that almost ended Butler's time at No. 10. He believes that his proximity to the Prime Minister was the true reason that Marcia Williams angled for his dismissal.
COURTESY OF LORD AND LADY BUTLER

In Lytham St Annes with Jill and Sophie, 1966.
COURTESY OF LORD AND LADY BUTLER

With President Jimmy Carter in the White House, 24 May 1980.
COURTESY OF LORD AND LADY BUTLER

An undistinguished appearance at the Oval, playing for a 'Lords and Commons' team and bowled out for two, 11 July 1975.
COURTESY OF LORD AND LADY BUTLER

With Margaret Thatcher and President Mitterrand at the Elysée Palace.
COURTESY OF LORD AND LADY BUTLER

With Mrs Thatcher and President Reagan in the White House.
COURTESY OF LORD AND LADY BUTLER

Robin and Jill turned their proposed around-the-world trip in 1998 into a goodwill tour to extend the 'Univ family'. On their way back from New Zealand they stopped in Washington to visit Bill Clinton, a University College alumnus. Jill, initially reluctant to see Clinton because of his dalliance with Monica Lewinsky, overcame her hesitation and was, naturally, charmed by him.
COURTESY OF LORD AND LADY BUTLER

'Feeding the leopard', as Butler described sessions with the PM.
COURTESY OF LORD AND LADY BUTLER

LEFT Knight of the Garter at Windsor, 2003.
COURTESY OF LORD AND LADY BUTLER

ABOVE A familiar sight, the Cabinet Secretary on his rusty bicycle.
© PETER MACDIARMID / GETTY IMAGES

Doctor of Civil Law at King's College, London.
COURTESY OF LORD AND LADY BUTLER

Builders of The Millennium
Lecture Series

Speaker:
The Prime Minister,
The Rt. Hon. Tony Blair MP

Tony Blair was one of the speakers in the lecture series to commemorate the 750th anniversary of University College.
COURTESY OF LORD AND LADY BUTLER

Tony Blair was impressed by Bill Clinton's 1992 campaign for the presidency and studied his tactics closely, imitating them in the 1997 British election. Four weeks after the election, on 29 May 1997, President Clinton visited the new Prime Minister in Downing Street.
COURTESY OF LORD AND LADY BUTLER

PAUL FOOT

PRIVATE EYE

No. 1111, 23 July – 5 August 2004, £1.30

BUTLER REPORT NO SHOCK

It's an insult to the intelligence

Private Eye on the release of the Butler Report.

REPRODUCED BY KIND PERMISSION OF *PRIVATE EYE* MAGAZINE

Younger daughter Nell repays her father for the 'harum-scarum schemes' he inflicted on her as a young girl.

REPRODUCED BY KIND PERMISSION OF NEWS SYNDICATION AND NEWS UK

Six Cabinet Secretaries gathered on 9 December 2016 to celebrate the centenary of the office. Pictured (*from l. to r.*) Lord (Gus) O'Donnell, Lord Butler, Sir Jeremy Heywood, Lord (Robert) Armstrong, Lord (Richard) Wilson, Lord (Andrew) Turnbull.

COURTESY OF LORD AND LADY BUTLER

an employee of the Albert Hall telephoned Butler that afternoon to tell him that, in the absence of the Prime Minister, her husband would not be allowed to use the VIP entrance. Butler exploded and, promising dire consequences if the Albert Hall persisted with this insult, secured the reversal of their edict.

Six days later, on Wednesday 28 November, after nearly sixteen years as Tory leader and eleven and a half as Prime Minister, Margaret Thatcher left Downing Street. Her departure was low-key and matter-of-fact. Butler walked down from the Cabinet Office to the hall to say goodbye, but she had already left the building. *Sic transit gloria mundi.* That evening he threw a small party for the Thatchers, the Permanent Secretaries and members of the Cabinet Office who had worked closely with her. 'I wanted to show that we all felt for her', he recalled, 'and to say something appropriate.'[49] Presenting her with a complete set of *Yes, Prime Minister* and a pass to the Cabinet Office to enable her to write her memoirs, he said that 'the thing that will be most interesting about us in our later years is that we worked with Margaret Thatcher'.* A quarter of a century later, he had not changed his mind.[50]

* Mrs Thatcher enjoyed the compliment. She was less pleased, however, with the gift of a key to the Cabinet Office, presumably because this underlined the reality of her departure from 10 Downing Street.

CHAPTER 12

CIVIS BRITANNICUS SUM, 1990–1991

THE ARRIVAL OF JOHN Major in Downing Street was a milestone in Butler's career. Far gone were the days when he was the brilliant young prospect of the upper ranks of the Treasury. For the first time, the Prime Minister was younger than he was and Butler had a broader advisory role. 'I was really grateful to him for being a father figure', recalled Sarah Hogg, then head of the Policy Unit at No. 10. 'He was very good at finding the right person to work with the Policy Unit.'[1]

He also had played a different role with Major than with Thatcher. Whereas she was Prime Minister when Butler first worked with her, he had been Second Secretary at the Treasury when Major first joined the Cabinet in 1986 and by November 1990 had been *en poste* as Cabinet Secretary for almost three years. He had worked closely with Major and was able to do so in a much more relaxed fashion than with Thatcher. There was more open-ended discussion of issues; the new Prime Minister was solicitous of Butler's views and always treated his advice with respect, although he did not always follow it. Sarah Hogg commented that 'Major was a remarkably inclusive Prime Minister and he had a natural affinity for officials', and this further contributed to harmony.[2]

There was an immediate bond between the two men as both shared a love of cricket. At Cabinet meetings, Butler sat on the Prime Minister's right. If a test match was being played, he would have the scores brought to him at regular intervals and solemnly pass them to Major.[3] For his part, Major delighted in introducing him as Richard Daft's great-grandson rather than as the Cabinet Secretary.[4]

This was exactly the kind of light-hearted mischief that appealed to Butler. The levity was merely superficial, however. The new Prime Minister had inherited an unpopular government together with the unflattering – and pitifully inaccurate – sobriquet 'son of Thatcher'. With limited experience as a minister, and fearful of opposition from the right of his own party, John Major recognised that his principal goal should be rapidly to distance himself from Thatcher's abrasive and autocratic style.

His agenda was governed by one overriding consideration: he had eighteen months to establish his own government before leading it into the general election due no later than June 1992. While he could take a strategic view of long-term projects – building a fairer society, reversing Thatcher's policy towards the EEC – there were immediately pressing issues on which either binding decisions had already been taken or Major was unable to alter the momentum already gathered.

The overriding issue occupying him in the days after his coming to power concerned Kuwait. Saddam Hussein had invaded Kuwait in August, achieving a swift and comprehensive victory in two days. The Kuwaiti royal family fled and Saddam installed his cousin Ali Hassan al-Majid as governor. The United Nations passed Resolution 661, imposing economic sanctions on Iraq, and Resolution 665, authorising a naval blockade to enforce the sanctions. During the last months of 1990, Saddam made a series of attempts to link withdrawal from Kuwait to other concessions, particularly in relation to Israel. The United States continued to reject such proposals, and refused to enter any negotiations until Iraq withdrew from Kuwait. When Major took office, the decision to commit 30,000 British troops to the Gulf had already been taken; immediately after he took office, the UN Security Council passed Resolution 678, setting a deadline of 15 January 1991 for Iraqi withdrawal. Failing such withdrawal from Kuwait, 'all necessary force' might be used to implement the resolution.

As Britain was committed to the US-led coalition, an early meeting between Major and President Bush was arranged for 21–22 December at Camp David. The President, who had been Vice-President during the eight years of Ronald Reagan's presidency, had developed a close friendship with Major, continuing the excellent relations that had existed between Reagan and Thatcher. Each man was conscious that his public persona was less charismatic than that of his predecessor. Each, in Butler's view, had a deep confidence in the moral fibre of the other.

A member of the party that flew to Washington for the meeting was Sir Antony Acland, the British ambassador to the USA. Since John Major had stressed his determination to create 'a genuinely classless society in which people can rise to whatever level that their own abilities and good fortune may take them',[5] Butler found it amusingly ironic that the Prime Minister's advisers on this trip were to be Acland, recently appointed Provost of Eton, and himself, chairman of the Board of Governors of Harrow. To the relief of the duo, the press failed to pick up on the story.

The days before Christmas were devoted to meetings concerning the inevitable Gulf War that loomed beyond the January deadline. The President received Prince Bandar bin Sultan, the Saudi Arabian ambassador on 21 December, and then devoted the rest of that day and the following morning to Major and his party. For Butler, it was an emotional meeting, as he observed the immediate close rapport between Prime Minister and President – in the knowledge that Britain was fully integrated in the planning and that both countries would commit large forces to war in the following month.

For President Bush, it was important to be certain of Britain's commitment to use all necessary force in support of the UN resolution. Support from the American public and in Congress for military action was, at best, ambivalent, and the President was surprised and reassured by Major's unquestioning support. Major's sympathy for Bush's position; the relaxed atmosphere of Camp David, away from the protocol of the White House; the instinctive use of first names between the two leaders – a clear departure from the formality that Thatcher and Reagan had employed; all these details, together with the camaraderie of an evening discussion around a log fire, made for a personal bond among allies.

The patrician Bush and the less patrician Major, son of a trapeze artist and grandson of a bricklayer, in a few hours established a political and personal understanding of remarkable solidarity. In his first international mission as

Prime Minister, Major showed the characteristics that had taken him to the leadership and which Butler admired. Behind the grey, technocratic exterior was a highly sensitive understanding of the position of others and the relationship of his desiderata with theirs. This eliminated much of the preamble of discussion and negotiation. So it was at Camp David; the fundamentals needed no negotiation. After breakfast on 22 December, the British contingent departed. Butler shook the President firmly by the hand and wished him 'God speed'. It was an emotional moment.

The deadline imposed by the Security Council came and went. On 17 January, therefore, Operation Desert Storm opened with a massive air offensive. Although British participation was considerable – over 50,000 troops, the largest European contingent – the first Gulf War was a remote conflict that had little impact on everyday life in London. For the Cabinet Secretary, however, this was 'one of the most critical' periods of his tenure. The challenge was to implement the smoothest systems possible and to get the Whitehall machine functioning to maximum efficiency.[6] The aim was to facilitate Cabinet decisions by delivering information to ministers as early as possible in the day. According to the system that he introduced, the day began with a meeting of the assessment staff at 4.30 a.m., followed by a Joint Intelligence Committee meeting at 6.00 a.m. At 8.30 a.m., Permanent Secretaries would meet so that by 10.00 ministers could be fully briefed and equipped to take necessary decisions. By following this method, the lobby briefing could be held at 11.00 each morning. It was a smooth operation. Looking back on that period, Butler commented that, in many ways, the job became easier as 'trivialities fall away', facilitating focus on the important issues.

It was inevitable that comparisons would be drawn between Major and Thatcher as war leaders, and the new Prime Minister could scarcely have projected an image more different from that of his predecessor. On 5 January, he made a two-day trip to the Gulf and, according to the Commander-in-Chief General de Billière, developed an immediate and easy rapport with the troops.[7] He was 'very much his own man', capable and confident, yet modest and restrained. Back in London, *The Guardian* commented on 'an absence, even perhaps a deliberate repudiation, of that triumphalism, that vainglory, that sense of international centre-stage, which was Margaret Thatcher's hallmark'.[8]

Yet his confidence grew as he became more familiar with the levers of power, as he understood more clearly that he was indeed his own man and could fashion his own methods of achieving consensus. His consummate handling of the leadership election, in which he navigated brilliantly between betraying a dangerous loyalty to the wounded Thatcher and the equally dangerous course of calling for her removal, ensured that he gave no markers or hostages to fortune. He had no wish to impose his own ideology on the Tory Party – indeed, he was suspicious of ideology. He would restore parliamentary leadership, govern through Cabinet. Involved in a war within weeks of taking over, he instinctively understood the pivotal position that his Cabinet Secretary occupied and the importance of their close cooperation.

There was, meanwhile, growing concern that Saddam had the capability to launch a terrorist attack in London and that such an attack would involve chemical weapons.* At ten o'clock in the morning of 7 February, that concern appeared to be justified when the Gulf War Cabinet was meeting in the Cabinet Room. 'We were worried that Iraq might launch a terrorist attack in London', Butler recalls, 'and the last word I remember John Major uttering before the bomb exploded was the word "bomb".' The French windows at the end of the Cabinet Room blew in and Butler believed that it was a terrorist attack and that people were about to appear at the Cabinet Room window, spraying the occupants with sub-machine guns. Diving under the table, he found himself next to Major. The Prime Minister was removed to a safe area rapidly; everyone went through to COBRA,† and resumed the meeting. About half an hour later, Butler learned the nature of the attack; mercifully, nobody had been killed.[9]

In fact, it was the IRA, not the Iraqis, who had launched three bombs from a van parked at the junction of Horse Guards Avenue and Whitehall.

---

* British concern was justified by the knowledge that Britain had supplied the equipment to build a pesticide plant north of Baghdad that was producing mustard gas.

† COBR or COBRA, the Cabinet Briefing Room, is a crisis management centre used in the event of national or regional crisis. It fulfils the same function as the White House's Situation Room, except that is only manned as required by specific crises.

Each bomb was armed with a twenty-kilogram payload of Semtex. The firing of the first mortar, the one that had landed in the garden, shifted the van slightly so that the other two bombs overshot Downing Street and landed harmlessly on Mountbatten Green beside the Foreign Office. If the first bomb had actually hit the No. 10 building, the likelihood is that everyone attending the meeting in the Cabinet Room would have been killed.[10]

Meanwhile, the air war in the Gulf continued, amid periodic crises and concerns that Saddam would resort to chemical or biological weapons. Iraqi resistance collapsed much more rapidly than had been expected, and by 28 February Kuwait had been cleared of Iraqi troops. President Bush promptly called for a ceasefire. On the principle that only the liberation of Kuwait and not the invasion of or regime change within Iraq was legitimised by Resolution 678, the President declined to pursue the retreating Iraqi forces and began to withdraw troops.

As Major and Charles Powell were away from London at the end of February, it fell to Butler to handle the arrangements for ceasefire and withdrawal with Brent Scowcroft, the American National Security Adviser. Relations between London and Washington were remarkably close after the brief campaign, and Butler found his counterpart to be easy to work with. Most impressive to Butler was Scowcroft's punctiliously correct approach to the final stages of the war. A deeply religious man, Scowcroft showed remarkable wisdom and understanding of geopolitics, impressing Butler with his determination both to avoid involving the United States as an occupying power in a bitterly hostile land and to respect the boundaries of Iraq.* Butler was to remember that restraint a dozen years later, when President George W. Bush fell into precisely the trap that his father and Scowcroft had foreseen and avoided. Scowcroft's ability to see the world from other viewpoints than that of the Pentagon was rewarded in 1993, when the Queen awarded him an honorary KBE.

There can be few national leaders who have experienced the kind of baptism by fire that greeted John Major in November 1990. Inevitably, there was

* Scowcroft was convinced that any American occupation of Iraq would be disastrous, a position he declared publicly after the younger President Bush committed American forces there in 2003.

criticism of his resolve to drive Saddam out of Kuwait; critics painted him as slavishly following the American lead.[11] Butler was impressed by Major's handling of the war, commenting that he was well advised by Charles Powell, who also enjoyed very good relations with Scowcroft. For three months, the war dominated Major's agenda, and only in March could he begin to focus on domestic policy. There were pressing matters that he needed to attend to before the 1992 election. The retirement of Thatcher had seen a sizeable Tory gain in the polls, a surge that was further boosted by Major's conduct of the Gulf War. This, he recognised, was the time to capitalise on his popularity and to reverse the unpopular heritage of the Thatcher era.

When Major won the leadership election, Butler had been quick to offer his advice on how Major might learn from Thatcher's time in No. 10 and how he might avoid what he considered dangerous personnel errors. The new Prime Minister wanted his Cabinet to be inclusive, a Cabinet of all the talents that did not exclude those who had stood against him; Butler applauded this inclusive approach, but was concerned that there was no elder statesman to advise Major. It was most important, he argued, that Major appoint as his counsel an adviser who could be depended on for an objective, unbiased opinion – the role that William Whitelaw, until he suffered a stroke in December 1987, had performed for Thatcher.

After Whitelaw's departure, Butler was concerned at Thatcher's growing dependence on Charles Powell, who was irreverently known in Whitehall as 'the real Deputy Prime Minister'. This, Butler resolved, would not be repeated under Major. As Sarah Hogg pointed out, Thatcher's dictum, 'every Prime Minister needs a Willie', had a ring of truth.[12] Major saw the wisdom of this, and opted for David Waddington as Whitelaw's successor. As a former Chief Whip and Home Secretary, Waddington had the necessary stature; appointed by Major to be Leader of the House of Lords, he was sufficiently to the right of the party to reassure the Thatcherites.

Bernard Ingham, Thatcher's press secretary, had decided to step down when Thatcher retired and Major wanted Gus O'Donnell, his press secretary at No. 11 Downing Street, to take his place. It was, in truth, a curious appointment as O'Donnell, an economist by training, had few of the qualities normally associated with the job. For the Cabinet Secretary, this was a distinct mark in his favour as he was unlikely to handle the job in the somewhat pugilistic manner of Ingham. Indeed, according to Anthony Seldon, Butler gave 'clear instructions that he wanted him to lower the profile of the Press Secretary's job after Ingham's high exposure'.[13]

The principal legacy of Margaret Thatcher that Major was impatient to reverse was the deeply unpopular poll tax. While there was unanimity within the party that it should be abandoned, there was disagreement over what should replace it. By the end of March, Major had taken the initiative in launching what would be known as the 'council tax', a solution that most Tories were grateful to accept and to see included in the Queen's Speech in November – well in time for the general election due before June.

If the introduction of the council tax was one arm of Major's domestic agenda, the notion of a fair deal for the consumer was the other. The Policy Unit at No. 10 urged him to develop 'a toolkit of ideas that would apply market stimuli and private sector skills to the task of raising public sector standards'.[14] The somewhat hazy notion developed early in 1991, acquired the name of the 'Citizen's Charter',* and was announced to the public in a speech to Conservative Central Council on 23 March, when Major declared alliteratively, 'people who depend on public services – patients, passengers, parents, pupils, benefit claimants – all must know where they stand and what service they have a right to expect'.

This radical departure from orthodoxy rang alarm bells in the halls of the Civil Service, where a reprieve from the upheaval of the Thatcher years had been welcomed. Nor was the speech well received by the press; the Charter was treated as a clumsy attempt to win back voters hostile to Thatcherism; the virtues of Major's proposals were ignored; instead, an article in *The Guardian* suggested that the Prime Minister was merely cherry picking Labour and Liberal Democrat initiatives.[15]

By contrast, Butler saw the Citizen's Charter as an inevitable by-product of the 1970s, when consumer durables became widely available. Until then, people's basic needs had been provided for by the state, but as pressure built

---

* The punctuation of 'The Citizen's Charter' is important, indicating that the thrust of the Charter is to protect the citizen rather than citizens. The emphasis is on supplying services of a high quality to the individual.

for restraint of taxation, demand rose for greater residual income without a lessening of public services. Pressure therefore built on politicians to maintain, even to improve, public services without doing so by raising taxation.

Pressure on the Civil Service continued to focus on two main issues: the revolving-door used by retiring civil servants to parlay their knowledge of Whitehall into lucrative jobs upon their retirement at age sixty; and the continuing issue of aligning the service with the harsh facts of 'real life'. As late as 1993, Butler was occupied with the issues that he had addressed in 1987, and he confessed in an interview with *The Times* that it was impossible to say where the reforms might lead. 'The idea of the Civil Service as a comfortable and secure sinecure has gone', he believed. 'But it would be a travesty if that were replaced by the image of a service in which only the bottom line mattered.'[16]

In Butler's view, growth in managerialism in the Civil Service with more emphasis on outcomes and greater use of business methods of production and marketing was inevitable. It entailed a partial privatisation, putting services out to tender; emphasis on outcomes would introduce private sector management techniques. Since he had taken over as head of the Civil Service in 1987, he had been preparing for precisely this kind of initiative.

In April 1991, Major had been in office for four months; an election would be held within another twelve. Meanwhile, there had been little progress towards agreeing government policy. Sarah Hogg was increasingly concerned that Major would be caught flat-footed before he had established a clear set of priorities; she prevailed on him to devote the weekend of 23–24 March to a series of meetings with Cabinet ministers at Chequers. High on Major's agenda was the presentation of the Citizen's Charter to ministers and the securing of broad support for its principles. To his dismay and irritation, this was not forthcoming.

By the end of April, little progress had been made and Major, strongly committed to the Charter, felt personally aggrieved at the lack of enthusiasm among his Cabinet and in Whitehall. The widespread perception was that he would lose the election and that the project would duly be shelved, which during the spring seemed increasingly likely. In May, Major explained with animation how the benefits of quality control in delivery of public services would transform national attitudes. Six days after that speech, Roger Evans,

Conservative candidate in the Monmouth by-election, lost the seat to Huw Edwards in a 12.6 per cent swing away from the Tories. It seemed that the goodwill granted to Major when he replaced Thatcher had eroded.

Major's reaction to the by-election defeat was, not unnaturally, personal. He saw the result, alongside the poor reception to his Charter initiative, as a clear rejection of any movement away from Thatcherism towards the centre left. Cannily, he approached Butler for his advice and help in spreading the message that he planned a fundamental overhaul of popular attitudes to the social services. Where better to start than with the head of the Home Civil Service? Sarah Hogg saw Major's decision as 'the best thing he could conceivably have done'.[17] The Citizen's Charter, she later explained, 'was not the sort of thing you would expect Major to have consulted the Cabinet Secretary about. It was a policy initiative.'[18]

Many journalists have delighted in their pen portraits of Robin Butler, pointing to his respectable middle-class upbringing and education, teasing him gently for perceived eccentricities. We have seen how he achieved a visibility far greater than that of his predecessors at the top of the Civil Service. Yet few of these portraits explored his political leanings beyond the rather vapid observation that he tended to be conventional, a conservative.

As a long-serving and successful career civil servant, he has systematically concealed his politics. Few people would recognise the reformer beneath the frequently worn tie of University College, Oxford. Few would have imagined that he would begin his Attlee Foundation Lecture in March 1999 with a paean of praise for the 'humane college' of which he was by then Master:

> For four years as an undergraduate in the late '50s, I dined under the austere, dignified and entirely appropriate portrait of Attlee in Univ's dining hall. I shared the collegiate pride in Univ's association not only with Attlee, who was Prime Minister during my early conscious years, but also with G. D. H. Cole, with Beveridge, still at that time to be seen around the College, and with Harold Wilson, who became leader of the opposition during my time at Oxford.[19]

In that single paragraph, Butler summoned up four members of the pantheon of twentieth-century socialism. An upholder of tradition where it serves a purpose, he also has a sense of fairness to which the Citizen's Charter was bound to appeal.

Fairness was central to his assessment. If Butler thought of the Charter from the perspective of a political philosopher, he would have seen the complex inter-relationship of rights and duties bound up in the proud boast of a Roman citizen, 'civis Romanus sum'. To be a Roman citizen bestowed certain rights and protection, but it also entailed obligations. If he, as head of the Home Civil Service, expected the modern-day citizen to discharge his obligations, then he owed the citizen the best public services possible. The parallelism of rights and duties was matched by a mutuality of obligation. The Prime Minister, needing a powerful ally in Whitehall to persuade the establishment of the virtues of the Citizen's Charter, could do no better than to start at the top.

Butler proposed that Andrew Whetnall, a tenacious civil servant working in the Cabinet Office, be deputed to handle the preparation of the Charter and to maintain pressure on departments to submit proposals for inclusion in the planned White Paper. Anthony Seldon describes the candidate chosen for the job:

> Butler selected Andrew Whetnall, a mild-mannered civil servant, involved in work on Whitehall's Byzantine organisation, who proved an admirable choice, tenacious, meticulous and with an unparalleled knowledge of the tributaries and workings of Whitehall. He oversaw the process for the crucial next three months.[20]

Whetnall was a civil servant of considerable ability and experience, whose instincts and loyalty Butler trusted. As the Citizen's Charter was a matter of government policy, rather than a party political gimmick, he swung the wholehearted support of the Civil Service behind the initiative. Whetnall was the front man, while Butler operated in the background, unobtrusively disposing of difficulties and ensuring that Permanent Secretaries were doing all within their power to meet the challenge of the Charter. Whetnall's experience of working in Whitehall proved to be an invaluable asset.

With Whetnall in place, assisted by Diana Goldsworthy, also of the Cabinet Office, Butler had forged a vital half of the team leadership necessary to overcome political and official indifference. The second half was provided by Francis Maude, Financial Secretary to the Treasury who, after some canny horse-trading between 10 and 11 Downing Street, became the minister in charge of the Citizen's Charter. Maude, described by Butler as 'having a chip on his shoulder about the Civil Service',[21] overcame his suspicions of Robin Fellgett, representing the Treasury on his team, and the small group of half a dozen set about creating the framework of a White Paper in the six weeks allowed them.

Even so, it was not easy to bring about a complete change of direction in Whitehall. This was eventually achieved by the close – and openly visible – involvement of Butler and Andrew Turnbull, Major's Principal Private Secretary.* Their evident support for the Charter sent a clear message to the Civil Service that they were committed to assist Major with the project and that the Charter was therefore real, not some token dressing of the shop window.

Early in the campaign, as Sarah Hogg recalls, Butler openly demonstrated his personal commitment to the goals of the Charter:

> An early battle was over the principle that public servants dealing with the public should be ready to identify themselves. This met with strong resistance from some quarters. It was argued that it would make staff more 'vulnerable'. In fact, there was evidence pointing in quite the opposite direction: angry clients or claimants were more inclined to treat faceless bureaucrats as human beings if they could put a name to them. To the Prime Minister's delight, the Cabinet Secretary turned up for the Number Ten launch wearing a name badge prepared by his secretary. It read: 'I'm Robin – can I help you?'[22]

The gesture, typical of Butler, contained a measure of showmanship. It also reflected a profound desire to be of assistance, and to be of assistance

* Andrew Turnbull, later Lord Turnbull, was Cabinet Secretary and head of the Home Civil Service, succeeding Sir Richard Wilson, between 2002 and 2005.

one needs to know the facts. One of Butler's most endearing qualities is his ability to 'walk with Kings nor lose the common touch', a quality that he demonstrated most clearly at a Buckingham Palace Reception. Jill was unable to attend, so Butler, rather than bother his driver, drove up to town himself. He reported to his mother that, after talking at length to Edward Heath and James Callaghan,

> I think I was the only person at the Reception to arrive without a chauffeur and I got some funny looks as I walked across the road in all my finery to get my car. But it did enable me to have a few words with the drivers and detectives whom I knew.[23]

That concern served him well in his determination to understand as much as possible about every department of the Civil Service, and was central to the purpose of the Citizen's Charter.

The Charter's success was critical to Major, not only to his authority and status within the government, but also to his own ethical evaluation of his administration. It was his 'big idea', a fact which all his close staff – and the head of the Civil Service – realised. By the time that the proposals were presented at a Cabinet meeting on 11 July and explained in detail to the Commons on 22 July,[24] Major had recovered his confidence enough to make a solid and serious presentation. The groundwork for this second growth of Prime Ministerial authority had been carried out in March by Butler, who could hardly have rendered more important service to Major at a more critical time. The Tory Party was able to proclaim in its election manifesto:

> The Citizen's Charter is the most far-reaching programme ever devised to improve quality in public services. It addresses the needs of those who use public services, extends people's rights, requires services to set clear standards – and to tell the public how far those standards are met.[25]

It is important not to take the Charter out of context. It was simply one of several components of a policy that maintained the general thrust of Thatcherism: privatisation of key industries and extension of home ownership continued to be highly symbolic to the right of the party. But for Major, the missing element was the issue of measurable service to the consumer. He confessed himself to be angered by 'the lofty views of well-cosseted politicians [who] made little use of public services in their own lives, and had no concept of their importance to others'.[26]

It was this conviction, along with commitment to the needs of the individual, that Butler scented – and welcomed – in Major.

The Prime Minister's other significant break with the legacy of his predecessor occurred over Britain's relationship with Europe. Rejection of the Delors proposals and her public spat with her former Foreign Secretary had played a part in her rejection by the party. It fell to John Major to address the issue of the terms of British membership with an election to be held at some unspecified but imminent date.

Major and Butler were aware of how much hung on the Maastricht summit. Accused by Mrs Thatcher of being a deviant in his attitude to Europe, arrogant in his refusal of a referendum over the European Economic and Monetary Union, and unrealistically optimistic in his confidence that he could opt out of unwelcome treaty clauses, Major recognised that his prestige depended on routing the Eurosceptics. Until a fortnight before the conference, he was still unsure of the likely outcome.

In the Commons debate on 20 November, Major set out the issue frankly and clearly. He laid out the parameters of what would be acceptable at Maastricht. Those who believed that Britain would argue against many proposals before accepting them at the last minute were mistaken. 'I urge them not to make that misjudgment', he said. 'It would be fatal.'[27]

The government's method was accurately described by Norman Lamont as 'constructive but cautious: cautious to ensure that British Governments retain the freedom to act in the national interest, but constructive in preparing Community arrangements which are practical and which, if they come into being, will work'.[28] It was also persuasive. After setting out his modest agenda, holding firm and refusing to yield in the debate, Major, solidly supported by the majority of the Tory Party, received the endorsement he sought with a 351–250 majority. Six Tories voted against the government; there were nine abstentions. The first hurdle had been cleared.

There remained specific concerns among ministers, in particular concerning Britain's control of its own borders and immigration, and concerning the Social Chapter, incorporating the European Works Councils' Directive and the directive concerning parental leave. Michael Howard, Secretary of State for Employment, was particularly adamant that Britain should not be compelled to agree to the Social Chapter, despite its having been voluntarily accepted by a number of large British companies. In the days immediately before Maastricht, Major strove to include all Cabinet ministers in discussions and to make them aware of the negotiating stance he proposed to adopt. Butler was impressed by Major's candour. The Prime Minister described himself to the Cabinet Secretary as 'the fourth most Eurosceptic member of the Cabinet'. 'He was fully aware of the deficiencies of the EU', Butler recalled, 'but he never questioned Britain's membership.'[29]

The Prime Minister continued to discuss Britain's position on sensitive issues with ministers during the conference; at the same time he was candid and direct in stating agreed positions to the conference. Simply put, his goal was to achieve full membership of the nascent European Union while specifically opting out of the single currency and not agreeing to Britain's being bound by the Social Chapter. By achieving those two objectives, and at the same time mending fences with Helmut Kohl and stating his government's position clearly and unequivocally to Ruud Lubbers, the Dutch premier, Major achieved a significant diplomatic triumph.

By that point, Major had been in office for a year and Butler was both satisfied with the Prime Minister's handling of the Cabinet and impressed by his negotiating ability. His approach to the Maastricht conference, in particular, struck him as a prime example of rational negotiation, effective because Major genuinely wished to achieve the best result for all sides. The contrast with the confrontational manner of his predecessor was marked – and most effective in rallying the country as the election approached.

On the surface, Major was supremely, even irrationally, confident that the Tories would win the 1992 election. In that mood, he urged more transparency; there was growing public opinion in favour of more open government and increasing pressure for the introduction of a Freedom of Information

Act. The Tory leadership was broadly inclined to be less secretive, but was opposed to the introduction of such an Act, while Major was resolved that open government should form part of the 1992 manifesto. Unsurprisingly, it fell to Butler to square the circle by listing measures that would be introduced to create greater transparency, while stopping short of a formal Act.

For the Cabinet Secretary, this was a disagreeable task as, in his view, no package of measures could take the place of a Freedom of Information Act. Moreover, the move to more open government in the lead-up to a general election was perilously close to party politics. After the election, when Major sought to 're-launch the government's domestic agenda after the crisis management of the past few months',[30] Butler took care to remain uninvolved in the discussions, a position that was doubtless correct, but which removed the Cabinet Secretary from the centre of policy-making.

Major retained his outward pre-election optimism despite the deepening recession in the early months of 1992 and the consistent, if modest, Labour lead in opinion polls. Butler was more circumspect, admiring Major's skills as a campaigner, but unsure that Thatcherism had been adequately banished in public perception, and concerned that Major would pay the price for her fall with the electorate.[31] Accordingly, in the interests of continuity and as an objective and impartial civil servant, he sought to prepare for a possible change of government, a step that involved an important revision of pre-election procedures.

Margaret Thatcher first became Prime Minister in 1979 and subsequently held elections in 1983 and 1987 – at four-year intervals, in the fourth year of her administration. At the time, the convention was that Permanent Secretaries would meet and brief Opposition shadow ministers during the six months preceding the presumed date of an election. On Thatcher's timetable, however, the elections were held six months before such discussions were due to start and, as a result, the briefings never took place. Butler identified this as a shortcoming of the system, and obtained Major's permission for discussions to begin fifteen months before the last date for an election.

This was a sound precaution and Butler arranged extensive, though ultimately unnecessary briefings with Charles Clarke, then head of the Leader of the Opposition's office and son of Sir Richard (Otto) Clarke, who had been a second Permanent Secretary when Butler joined the Treasury.* Butler produced a grid of decisions that Neil Kinnock would have to take if Labour won: the structure of departments and ministerial posts, seniority of ministers, allocation of ministerial residences, staffing of No. 10. Clarke later told him that Kinnock spent part of polling day completing his questionnaire, only to discover, as the results came in, that it would be fruitless.[32]

Clarke put to Butler the argument that, if the Tories were to win with a hugely reduced majority, then they would have lost the moral authority to govern and that, in those circumstances, the Queen would be obliged to ask Kinnock to form a government. Butler stonewalled this suggestion with the bald statement that a Prime Minister remained in office until he or she resigned. Nonetheless, to be prepared for all eventualities, he prepared not only for a Labour Party victory but also for a situation in which Major won with a majority too small to allow him to govern. Having been closely involved in 1974 when Edward Heath was confronted with that obstacle, he dusted off the 'golden rules' formulated in 1974 to dictate correct procedure in such an event.[33] Sarah Hogg believes that confidence in the Tories among officials had seriously eroded. 'There was considerable preparation by officials for a loss of the 1992 election', she recalled. 'They expected it, even if they didn't want it.'

As it emerged, the Tory victory, ushering in their fourth term, was a significant personal victory for Major. Despite a majority reduced from 100 to twenty-one, the Tories received an unexpectedly large majority in the popular vote,† which the media attributed to the emergence of the Prime Minister as an effective leader in his own right. For Butler, Major's win satisfied his

* Otto Clarke was one of the originators of ROBOT, a controversial plan presented to Rab Butler, Chancellor of the Exchequer in 1951. The scheme would have restored convertibility of sterling against the dollar, but at a floating rather than a fixed rate. The scheme's name was derived from the names of its originators, Sir Leslie *Ro*wan, Sir George *Bo*lton and *Ot*to Clarke. Charles Clarke worked so closely with Kinnock and was so strongly identified with the 1992 election strategy that, after Labour lost, it was widely assumed that Clarke would go down with Kinnock's ship. He rebounded, however, and, after winning Norwich South for Labour in 1997, was successively Minister Without Portfolio, Secretary of State for Education and Skills, and Home Secretary between 2001 and 2006.

† The Conservatives received a total of over fourteen million votes, the highest number received by any party in a general election.

sense of fair play. Since 1979, Thatcherism had dominated Tory policy. Not only was the shift towards the centre desirable but, in his view, 'it would have been sad for [John Major] if he had become Prime Minister as the unexpected and, to some, unwanted successor to Margaret Thatcher and had fallen at the first hurdle'.[34]

Instead, Major was able to make a number of overdue changes and impose his own stamp on the government. He was to enjoy a brief period of tranquillity before the euphoria of the election victory evaporated in the autumn, By September, the thrill of victory had worn off and Gyles Brandreth wrote in his diary: 'The party is profoundly divided, our economic policy is discredited, we're on the brink of being dragged into a Balkan war, and the PM talked about the Citizen's Charter.'[35]

CHAPTER 13

ANNUS HORRIBILIS, 1992

IN THE PROLOGUE TO his biography of John Major, Anthony Seldon paints a picture of 'the three most powerful official members of the British state' dining together on 1 May 1997, the Thursday that John Major's government came to an end. The three men were Robin Butler, the Cabinet Secretary, Robert Fellowes, the Queen's Private Secretary, and Alex Allan, John Major's Principal Private Secretary. Allan was known to Butler of old; it was he who had circulated the spoof questionnaire in the Treasury in June 1981.[1]

As Major settled into his office, greatly more confident after the May election, so too Butler's working life became easier, as individuals with whom he was comfortable were appointed to posts that formed a vital part of his round. It may be strictly incorrect to refer to an 'old boys' network' at the summit of power in Britain, but there is no doubt that things can function much more smoothly when information is exchanged in a confidential, unflustered, essentially informal manner.

An example of close friendship assisting the smooth operation of government came through the friendship between the Cabinet Secretary and Sir Robert Fellowes, the Private Secretary to the Queen since 1990.* Lady Jane Fellowes (née Spencer) was an older sister of Lady Diana Spencer, who had married the Prince of Wales in 1981. As a good friend of Fellowes, Butler was able to communicate informally and give Fellowes advance warning of

* In June 1999 Sir Robert Fellowes received a peerage and became Baron Fellowes of Shotesham in the County of Norfolk.

potential minefields on an informal basis when it became clear that the marriage of the Prince and Princess was breaking down.

Other appointments that smoothed the way for him were that of William Waldegrave as Chancellor of the Duchy of Lancaster with responsibility for the Citizen's Charter and the Civil Service, and Sir Terry Burns, who succeeded Sir Peter Middleton as Permanent Secretary of the Treasury in 1991. In each case, a close friendship made for a direct and totally frank working relationship such as would have been difficult to achieve with another person.

In the case of William Waldegrave, the friendship stretched back to 1970, when Butler, aged thirty-four, had shared an office with the long-haired graduate who had come down from Oxford the previous year. Perched in the attic of the Cabinet Office, the two young men had worked for Victor Rothschild in the Think Tank. They had maintained that friendship over the intervening years, sharing 'the same outlook' with 'no inhibitions in dealing with each other'. They both supported the Prime Minister's objectives of making public services as good as possible.[2]

In the case of Terry Burns, he was a golfing partner (as was Robert Fellowes) and he and his wife Anne were close friends of Robin and Jill. His appointment as Permanent Secretary made communication between Cabinet Office and the Treasury vastly easier. Middleton, Burns's predecessor, had hoped to succeed Robert Armstrong as head of the Home Civil Service and, Butler recalls, had serious reservations concerning the extent to which Next Steps agencies would remove economic control from the Treasury. That combination of circumstances tended to inhibit communication, an inhibition that was quite removed by Sir Terry's appointment in 1991.

As Butler surveyed the landscape in the Civil Service, at the Palace and in Downing Street, he felt confident that he was on firmer ground than in the last years of Margaret Thatcher. His appointment stretched five years into the future, until his sixtieth birthday, a few months after the last possible date for a general election. He was well aware that the life of a Cabinet Secretary is rarely a quiet or passive one, but he could reasonably forecast relatively plain sailing. In the event, this was not to be, as John Major's term of office from 1992 to 1997 brought a series of body blows to the government and set the stage for what rapidly became the most difficult period in the job, during which Butler made the greatest error of judgement of his career.

On 7 February 1992, the twelve member states of the European Community signed the Maastricht Treaty, the agreement that created the European Union and led to the introduction of the euro on 1 January 2002. Major, a fervent supporter of Britain's membership of the European Community, faced opposition from Eurosceptics within the Tory Party; accordingly, he had negotiated at Maastricht a remarkable position whereby Britain, although a full member of the Community, opted out from the single currency and was exempt from the provisions of the Social Chapter. Major was privately triumphant, although he betrayed little of his satisfaction. A member of press secretary Gus O'Donnell's staff foolishly referred to the Prime Minister's diplomatic triumph as 'game, set and match for Britain'.[3] This tactless, crowing remark was attributed to John Major, a mistake that not only upset the Prime Minister, but also was much resented by Helmut Kohl and Ruud Lubbers, who had both, by accepting Major's negotiating position, helped to make the outcome possible.

Butler was impressed by the success of the Prime Minister's negotiating technique, describing Major as 'the best negotiator of the Prime Ministers I worked for because he was clear about his aims and was able to convince those he was negotiating with that he was trying to secure the best for both sides'.[4] He had observed this when Major was Chief Secretary to the Treasury and continued to be impressed, particularly in negotiations over Northern Ireland. In the case of the ratification of the Maastricht Treaty, however, that characteristic nearly cost him the passage of the Bill. In deciding to defer the final stages of the Bill until after a Danish referendum on the treaty – a rational step for a genuine seeker of consensus – the government allowed Tory opposition to Maastricht to consolidate. This was the source of almost near catastrophe the following year.[5]

The year of 1992 was a testing period for Major. After his win at the election in March, he made strenuous efforts to achieve consensus within the Tory Party, an attempt that was seen by many Tories as a sign of weakness. Major himself makes a revealing remark in his autobiography, an admission of the supremacy of party over individual, even the Prime Minister: 'I never forgot that it was the party's will to win, and the belief that Margaret Thatcher would lose, that had made me Prime Minister.'[6]

Criticism of Major in the media did not abate after his win at the polls in April. In July, David Mellor, the Secretary of State for National Heritage, warned him that *People* was running a story linking Mellor in an affair with an actress, Antonia de Sancha. The Prime Minister promptly spoke to Butler, who took the view that, although Mellor was a member of the Cabinet, his position was non-sensitive and that, therefore, there was no security risk involved, no reason for which Mellor should be required to resign.

Unfortunately, Mellor was violent in his criticism of the media's intrusive activities and, when the opportunity arose, this violence prompted retaliation. In September, the story broke that in August 1990 he had accepted the gift of a family holiday in Spain from Mona Bauwens, the exotic socialite daughter of the Treasurer of the Palestine Liberation Organisation.[7] A barrage of anti-Mellor stories, exacerbated by the apparent desire of the media to deflate and destroy him, forced the Prime Minister to take action. Again, he consulted the Cabinet Secretary; this time Butler advised requiring his resignation. 'Thus', Major commented in his autobiography, 'the first scalp was taken.'[8]

The first scalp, that is, to be taken by allegations of 'sleaze'. In the five years between 1992 and 1997, the last gasp of the Conservative administration that had begun in 1979, accusations of sleaze would become commonplace. The autumn of 1992, however, was to bring a series of crises, some avoidable, that collectively set the scene for the five-year-long decline of the Major government.

When Britain eventually joined the Exchange Rate Mechanism (ERM) after Thatcher's initial opposition, the government made a commitment to maintain the parity of sterling at within 6 per cent of the existing rate of 2.95 Deutsche Marks. When, following unification, Germany borrowed heavily and raised its interest rates, Britain was experiencing high inflation and a weakening economy. On 2 June, Denmark voted in a referendum to reject the Maastricht Treaty and, as a result, currencies close to the lower limit of ERM-permitted parity came under pressure. One foreign investor, George Soros, convinced that sterling had entered the ERM at an unrealistic and unsustainable parity, sold sterling short on a massive scale.

When Soros began selling sterling on 15 September, the Bank of England intervened the following morning before trading began and bought £600 million in a desperate attempt to prop up the pound. As selling continued throughout the day, it became clear that all efforts to shore up sterling were futile, and Norman Lamont, the Chancellor of the Exchequer, announced that Britain would leave the ERM. The attempted rescue operation had been an expensive failure, costing the taxpayer £3.3 billion,[9] while Soros, selling short, made a profit of over £1 billion.

Butler recalls that the conditions surrounding 'Black Wednesday' were surreal. As No. 10 was being rewired, the Prime Minister had temporarily moved operations to Admiralty House, an elegant house with elegant rooms ideally suited for eighteenth-century life but with no modern means of communication.* The most senior members of the government were gathered there with no television, radio or other links to the outside world. 'This made little practical difference', said Butler, 'because they were powerless to resist the force of the markets. The Chancellor of the Exchequer regarded the decision to leave the ERM as freeing the economy and laying the foundation for its future recovery but it was a crippling blow to the Government's authority.'[10]

The Cabinet Secretary was not closely involved in the unfolding crisis, but was able to observe at first hand the government's determination to stay in the ERM and to experience the inevitable descent into the abyss when it became clear that Germany would not help, that determination was not enough. Whether or not Black Wednesday was the catastrophe that Major's critics allege, or whether it prepared the ground for an economic revival, allowing New Labour to take credit for an improved economy in 1997, the crisis of September 1992 started an erosion of confidence both personally in the Prime Minister and in the Tory government.

This erosion was accelerated a month later when the planned closure of thirty-one coal mines was announced. The closures, involving the loss of over 30,000 jobs, were to be immediate and there was a storm of public outrage against their speed and scale. The National Union of Mineworkers,

---

* 10 Downing Street was undergoing extensive repair as a result of the IRA mortar bomb of the previous year.

supported by other trade unions, successfully sought a High Court ruling to declare the closures illegal. This, however, was a limited victory in that the ruling applied only to the manner of the closures, in violation of a consultation agreement that required prior independent review.

Butler was appalled by the sequence of events, both by the apparent callousness of the government's action and by the manner in which a decision had been reached between the government and the Coal Board. Most offensive to him was Major's decision to keep the plans secret and not to consult the Cabinet before making the announcement. Senior ministers would have pointed out the risks and that immediate redundancies on the scale demanded would severely alienate the public at large. Major's unwillingness to consult the Cabinet is evidence of his insecurity and fear that his enemies would weaken his position by leaks; to Butler it was a classic example of the hazards of operating without Cabinet agreement. Several years later, both Butler and Kenneth Clarke lamented the atmosphere that pervaded Major's Cabinet by 1992. Butler referred to it obliquely in a lecture: 'I used to think that the phrase "too sensitive to discuss in Cabinet" would make some of my predecessors turn in their graves, but I heard it used on more than one occasion during my time as Cabinet Secretary.'[11]

In common with the Queen, he refers to 1992 as '*annus horribilis*'* for the government as well as the royal family. It was a year that, in the view of the Princess of Wales's private secretary, was 'one of inexorable decline from the relatively optimistic pragmatism of its opening to the open bloodshed and separation that marked its end'.[12] The defining point of the decline in relations between the Prince and Princess of Wales came in May, with the serialisation in the *Sunday Times* of Andrew Morton's book, *Diana: Her True Story*. Published the following month, the book caused 'damage too deep to enable a reconciliation to take place, not just between the Princess and

* Queen Elizabeth II used the expression in a speech at the Guildhall on 24 November 1992 to describe a year in which the Duke and Duchess of York had separated, the royal family was under pressure to pay income tax (which was imposed a few days after the speech), and four days before the speech, a fire broke out in Windsor Castle. Her Majesty was personally shocked first by the pressure exerted upon her to pay tax, and later by the public resistance to the nation paying for repairs at Windsor.

her husband but also between the Princess and the role she had made for herself'.[13] At first, the Palace denied that the Princess had cooperated with Morton concerning the revelations that the book contained, but the Cabinet Secretary had reliable information that this was not so, and was able to use his back channel of friendship with Fellowes to warn the Palace.

The Palace was thus forewarned, but nonetheless powerless to stamp out what was to become the most scandalous story of 1992. In late August, *The Sun* published a front-page story, claiming that a conversation between the Princess of Wales and James Gilbey, her friend since childhood, had been recorded by an electronic eavesdropper. The conversation was, ostensibly, proof of a sexual relationship between them. In November, the *Daily Mirror* published transcripts of telephone conversations between the Prince of Wales and Camilla Parker-Bowles. Both couples had spoken in embarrassingly intimate detail, and the transcripts provided juicy gossip for several months. Butler's immediate task was to discover how the records of the telephone conversations had been obtained, and to prevent a repetition.

Once both the Prince and Princess resorted to using the media to score points off each other, vying for public attention, each striving to attract more coverage than the other, it became obvious that there was no hope of a reconciliation and, in December, the Palace announced that the two would separate. Butler drafted a statement for the Prime Minister, which Major delivered to the House of Commons on 9 December. Knowing that the Princess was much loved by the public, he attempted to avoid suggesting that she had severed her bonds with the royal family, and disingenuously inserted a sentence that played down the finality of the separation. After stating the facts and offering the sympathy of the House, Major emphasised that the separation had no constitutional implications, that the succession was not affected and that there was no reason why the Princess of Wales should not be crowned Queen in due course.[14]

At a meeting of ministers before the announcement in the Commons, Douglas Hurd, the Foreign Secretary, questioned the wisdom of stating that the Princess might yet become Queen. Nonetheless, it was decided that the statement played down the gravity of the matter, and it was made as Butler proposed. Hurd's doubts were later proved to be valid.

For the Cabinet Secretary, as for any observer of the royal marriage, there was sorrow, tinged with a sense of complete powerlessness as the truck ran away down the hill. Unlike the situation in a political scandal, there were no sanctions to be applied. Politicians live in fear of the press camping on their doorstep; the Princess of Wales, by contrast, delighted in feeding increasingly shocking pieces of intelligence to reporters. She was very happy to set in train what became known as 'The War of the Waleses'. Butler was able to keep reasonably well informed and one step ahead of the next outrage. This and his friendship with John Birt, the Director-General of the BBC, enabled him to have advance warning of an interview that the Princess gave to Martin Bashir on 20 November 1995. It was a potential public relations disaster for the royal family, as the well-rehearsed Princess succeeded in painting herself as an oppressed saint and her husband as the oppressor.

It was in this interview that the Princess spoke openly of her husband's relations with Camilla Parker-Bowles, giving the press the perennially quoted line, which Butler considered the most damaging, that 'there were three of us in this marriage, so it was a bit crowded'. She also expressed her opinion that 'a campaign was being waged against [her]' out of fear; she admitted that her friendship with James Hewitt had gone 'beyond a close friendship'. Towards the end of the interview, she said winningly, 'I'd like to be a queen of people's hearts, in people's hearts, but I don't see myself being Queen of this country', and dealt a final blow to her husband, implying but stopping short of saying that he was consumed by demons and that it would be better if the crown passed directly from the Queen to her grandson Prince William.

Learning of the interview two days before it was broadcast, Butler asked Birt for leave to speak to Fellowes about the content, and was able to forewarn him. The information was given in the strictest confidence, but Butler was realistic and imagined that Fellowes would warn the Queen. The course of events was now beyond the control of the Palace, however, and the couple divorced in August 1996.

Throughout the events of 1992, Butler operated in the background without being subjected to any pressure from Buckingham Palace.[15] His sole overt responsibility at that point was to explore the constitutional implications of divorce and to advise the government on its role, although he was able to act as a vital liaison between Downing Street and Fellowes. Divorce was a recent phenomenon in the royal family, but it was no longer unknown. The Queen's sister, Princess Margaret, had divorced Antony Armstrong-Jones, Earl of Snowdon, in 1978. Her divorce, shocking to the public at the time, served to facilitate the subsequent divorces of the Queen's children.

The first of these was that of Princess Anne from Mark Phillips in 1992. Four years later, in May 1996, Prince Charles's brother, the Duke of York, and his wife were also divorced. In each case different constitutional issues were involved, but none so complicated as in the case of the Prince and Princess of Wales. In that most public divorce, the future of Prince William, second in line to the throne, was involved, and the Princess of Wales was in a strong position.

The third crisis in three months of the autumn of 1992 came with the opening salvoes of a campaign that was to involve Butler deeply and call into question his and the Civil Service's handling of a sensitive issue. The government's case against a company called Matrix Churchill, prosecuted for illegally exporting machine tools to Iraq, collapsed. This led to accusations that, to conceal its own complicity, the government was prepared to see innocent directors of the company jailed. 'This allegation was absurd', Butler recalls, 'but its very absurdity led to some hasty decisions, to which I was a party.'[16]

In December 1984, during the Iran–Iraq war in which Britain attempted to remain impartial, the government, 'in order to reinforce [its] policy of doing everything possible to see this tragic conflict brought to the earliest possible end', had applied the following guidelines on the supply of arms:

> (i) We should maintain our consistent refusal to supply any lethal equipment to either side;
> (ii) Subject to that overriding consideration, we should attempt to fulfil existing contracts and obligations;
> (iii) We should not, in future, approve orders for any defence equipment which, in our view, would significantly enhance the capability of either side to prolong or exacerbate the conflict;
> (iv) In line with this policy, we should continue to scrutinise rigorously all applications for export licences for the supply of defence equipment to Iran and Iraq.[17]

When a ceasefire was agreed in August 1988, the conditions that had occasioned the sanctions no longer applied. Thus, logically, the guidelines had no reference to reality and were meaningless. There were huge opportunities for British companies in the post-war reconstruction of both countries and the government was keen not to miss any opportunity to secure work for British firms. Indeed, for the two ministries most involved in the promotion of military equipment and British industry – the Ministry of Defence and the Department of Trade and Industry – it was a short step from engineering equipment to weaponry. Naturally, both ministries maintained, any weaponry supplied would be of a purely defensive nature.

The third ministry involved was the Foreign Office, where both politicians and officials were firmly opposed to lifting sanctions and arming two hostile and ambitious regimes. How sustainable was the ceasefire? Was it wise to have dealings with either regime? How could exporters be sure that weaponry was strictly for defensive purposes? Finally, after lengthy discussions between officials at the three ministries, agreement was reached that the guidelines, with slightly altered wording to accommodate the defensive purpose of future exports, would remain in place, even though fighting had ceased. At the Foreign Office, the Minister of State William Waldegrave 'thought the Foreign Office had scored a signal victory'.[18]

So satisfied was Waldegrave with the outcome, that he rather too casually accepted the suggestion from the Department of Trade and Industry that, since the *status quo ante* still applied, there was no need to inform the House of Commons of any new arrangements, that sanctions had effectively been lifted. Waldegrave then compounded this error by writing to thirty-eight MPs to inform them that the policy of sanctions remained unaltered. He later explained this on the grounds that the Foreign Office 'could continue to reject every straightforward request for an arms export licence, and that is exactly what we did'.[19]

On 14 February 1990, the religious authorities in power in Iran decreed a fatwa against novelist Salman Rushdie, condemning his novel *The Satanic Verses* as blasphemous, and offering a reward for his murder. At this point, all negotiations with Tehran concerning machinery or weaponry were impolitic, as they could be interpreted as a complex barter involving Rushdie. Equally, if exports to Iran were to be halted, then, in order for Britain's dealings to appear even-handed, so should exports to Iraq.

The shift in attitude at the DTI and the MOD coincided with Saddam's going on an arms-buying spree and, in April 1990, components for Project Babylon, the construction of a 'supergun', were seized by customs officials. The barrel parts had been falsely declared as 'petrochemical pressure vessels'. Subsequent prosecution of the directors of the exporting companies was unsuccessful and, in Butler's words, 'left the Customs and Excise with egg on their face. Thereafter they were looking for the opportunity for a successful prosecution.'

In November 1992, that opportunity appeared to have come, like manna from heaven, when it was discovered that Matrix Churchill, a Coventry-based machine tool manufacturer owned by Iraqi interests, had been shipping dual-use components to Iraq. The directors of Matrix Churchill, one of whom claimed to have been working for MI6, maintained that they had been given a clear 'nod and a wink' by Alan Clark, Minister for Trade, that a declaration that the components were for peaceful purposes would be accepted at face value by the government. When the *Sunday Times* reported the Matrix Churchill allegation, Clark vehemently denied it and assured Prime Minister and Cabinet Secretary that he would sue the newspaper. This denial was at the centre of the government's case against the company.

It so happened that Butler had a weekly Wednesday morning date to play a vigorous game of squash with Sir Michael Quinlan, the Permanent Secretary at the Ministry of Defence. Sir Michael dropped in to the Cabinet Office to warn him that, if the government was relying on the testimony of Alan Clark to substantiate the case against Matrix Churchill, this would be unfortunate – in fact, they needed their heads examining. This unwelcome news put Butler in a difficult position, as the independence of the Customs and Excise as a prosecuting authority was treated most seriously; pressure from the executive would not be welcome. He passed on the substance of Quinlan's remarks to Sir Brian Unwin, the chairman of Customs and Excise, but was not surprised when the latter maintained the independence of his department and continued with the prosecution. When Clark admitted under oath, in the course of cross-examination on 15 November, that he had been 'economical with the *actualité*', the government was publicly embarrassed.* The case collapsed; Major realised that an immediate inquiry was called for. There was now much more at stake than whether guidelines had been breached. Once Clark admitted that the government had been prepared to turn a blind eye to the shipping of armaments to Iraq, the question arose of when, if at all, the government would have intervened to prevent the wrongful conviction of the Matrix Churchill directors. The government, not Matrix Churchill, was now on trial.

On the day that the case was dropped, Major was hosting a dinner for Boris Yeltsin in the Painted Hall at Greenwich. Before the meal began, Major asked Butler for ideas for a statement that he would make the following morning. The Cabinet Secretary stayed at Greenwich for the dinner and worked on the statement later. After the meal, he took the opportunity to speak to Waldegrave, who was also at the banquet, to alert him to the imminent inquiry.

On the following morning, when Major and Butler discussed the affair, they were fully aware of the need for the government to emerge untarnished from the inquiry. The suggestion of government conspiracy was dynamite and, if it were exploited by the opposition – as it later was, to great effect – the result could be catastrophic for Major. In their desire to make certain that justice was seen to be done, Butler admits that he and Major made two mistakes.

First, they appointed Sir Richard Scott as judge to the inquiry. Scott had found against the government over the *Spycatcher* affair and was highly regarded by the liberal establishment.† He was a Chancery judge, however, with no experience of government. Second, under pressure from the opposition, and wanting to be seen as whiter-than-white, they agreed to grant Scott wide terms of reference and to allow examination of the history of the export

---

* Alan Clark's bon mot passed into the public record but it is, in fact, a perfect example of 'franglais'. He intended the word to mean that which is actual, the truth. In fact, the French word means that which is current – news, current events.

† Sir Richard had much in common with Butler. A Cambridge rugby Blue and keen bridge player, he also cycled to and from work, like Butler explaining that it is more efficient and that it got him to appointments on time.

of arms to Iraq. Waldegrave was travelling to Oxford in his ministerial car when Butler called him to suggest that the terms of reference be narrowed. Waldegrave later admitted that it was with a certain arrogance that he replied that they should be 'as wide as possible'. It was a response that he came to regret.[20]

Butler and Major had estimated that the Scott Report would be published after three months and that it would exonerate the government. In the event, it took over three years. Sir Richard Scott trod carefully, determined to ensure that the government was not acting *ultra vires* but, in the process, allowed Alan Clark to appear more a virtuous whistle-blower than a cynical capitalist. The leaking of draft conclusions, stating that Waldegrave had lied, fed the left-wing press with material. The massive report of over a million words ultimately did clear the government of conspiracy and cover-up, but, as the Cabinet Secretary commented, 'much blood had been spilt in the meantime and the Opposition had a field day'.

The blood was largely spilled in robust questioning by Presiley Baxendale QC, counsel to the inquiry. Butler assured senior civil servants that they would receive moral and material support, but in the media circus, in which counsel treated the press as her jury, that assurance was small consolation. Butler was concerned that the *modus operandi* of Scott and Baxendale was more suited to a courtroom than to a public inquiry. When he himself gave evidence on 9 and 10 February 1994, he was scathing about the manner in which the inquiry was being reported, referring to 'gross distortions' of the truth, particularly in the implication that the government used public interest immunity certificates as 'gagging orders'. Distinguishing between the inquiry and the media coverage, he called on Scott to censure the press in his report:

> I repeat that I neither make nor imply any criticisms of the procedures of this enquiry, but I register my concern and my confidence on behalf of the civil servants involved, that the enquiry will in due course put the record straight and undo, so far as is in its power, the damage which has been unfairly done to our system of Government, to the reputation of the civil service and to individuals.[21]

From his peers, Butler received appreciative comments on his candour and his criticism of the media. Sir Christopher France, Permanent Under-Secretary of State at the Ministry of Defence, wrote simply: 'I have just seen your public statement to Scott about the conduct of the Civil Service – and the Press – during the Inquiry. I am full of admiration and gratitude. I have rarely seen anything more robust, more accurate or more appropriate.'[22]

Butler himself narrowly avoided being damaged by the inquiry. Just as his predecessor Robert Armstrong had admitted in the *Spycatcher* case that he had been 'economical with the truth', so Butler was widely criticised for what was presented in the media as his assertion that ministers were entitled to use half-truths and evasions on the grounds that there were always confidences that they were obliged to protect. It was, he argued, 'acceptable in some circumstances for a statement to disclose only part of the full picture'. Sir Richard Scott, unused to the ways of Whitehall, took issue with the proposition, commenting that 'if part of the picture is being suppressed and the audience does not know it is being suppressed, the audience will be misled into believing the half picture to be the full picture'.

There were several points of difference between Butler and Scott, all of which can be subsumed under Butler's comment that Scott was a Chancery judge with no experience of government. While he accepted Butler's distinction between accountability, which could not be delegated, and responsibility, which could be passed on to officials, there were significant disagreements between the two. Scott waged a running battle with Whitehall over procedures and the principles of secrecy. In March 1993, at his lone press conference to describe how he intended to conduct the inquiry, he released his correspondence with the Cabinet Secretary on the question of closed sessions.

Butler had proposed to him that the hearings should go into closed session when, in Scott's view, disclosures in public would be damaging to the public interest; in other cases, government witnesses should be instructed to request a closed session when, in their view, the disclosure of information might be damaging. Scott, by contrast, wanted closed session only when openness might 'cause serious damage to the interests of the nation'. The media, quick to scent this disagreement, enlarged it to dramatic significance.

'Waldegrave suicide statement' trumpeted one tabloid newspaper. 'It's right to tell porkies to Parliament.'[23]

The impression transmitted by Scott and the legal team of Presiley Baxendale and Christopher Muttukumaru was of mandarins and ministers conspiring to conceal acts of negligence, incompetence and deceit. Such salacious themes encouraged headlines that stimulated the self-appointed guardians of probity to further grandstanding. Ultimately Butler, no admirer of the press, accused the media of pre-judging matters which, seen in context, would appear innocuous.

Butler was certainly not extending the culture of secrecy unreasonably, in his view of the purpose of closed sessions. He did, however, cause eyebrows to be raised when he drew the distinction between accountability and responsibility. Surely, civil servants and their union, the First Division Association (FDA), argued, the acceptance of the distinction allowed ministers to claim credit for successes and to blame civil servants for less successful ventures. Despite protests from the FDA that civil servants were left in an exposed position, the government declined to offer statutory protection.

Another small controversy involved Butler. Before the Matrix Churchill trial, Alan Moses QC, lead counsel for the prosecution, had been granted access to Cabinet papers relating to exports to Iraq, to exports of machine tools and to the activities of Matrix Churchill. Shown into Butler's empty office, he was confronted by massive piles of papers that he and his junior counsel needed to sort. Furious at this treatment, Moses complained to Scott that 'nobody has any doubt that this was not a proper opportunity to look at documents'. Butler later explained to Scott that he had been absent from his office and had had no prior warning of Moses' visit. He had, moreover, 'no knowledge at all about what papers are necessarily admissible in legal proceedings' as that was 'a matter for the prosecution and the defence'. The fact remains, however, that Butler's protestation of ignorance of discovery had more than a suggestion of disingenuousness.

After a year, the legal grandstanding had lost its initial appeal to the media. Journalist Simon Jenkins described the inquiry's lawyers as 'high on politics, publicity and paperwork' and 'determined to keep their show running for ever'.[24] In an article shortly before the report was eventually published, Geoffrey Howe was blunt in his criticism, stating that 'the Scott inquiry is not a tribunal upon whose judgment the reputation of anyone should be allowed to depend'.[25]

There was one light-hearted sequel to the Scott Inquiry. When the report was released, and Major held a meeting to discuss his response, it was decided that one passage concerning the history of exports to Iraq needed to be edited. The task was handed to Butler, with Waldegrave's assistance. While the new version was being typed,

> William and I … turned on the television. The BBC was showing, undoubtedly not by accident, an episode of *Yes Minister* called 'The Arms Inquiry'. This episode had been written and broadcast long before any of the events covered by the Scott Inquiry but it was so apt and funny that it might have been written with the Inquiry in mind. William and I laughed until tears ran down our cheeks. Since William's political career was hanging by a thread … I thought that this showed admirable detachment on his part.[26]

Ten days after the release of the report, on 26 February 1996, three and a half years after the inquiry was set up, the Commons considered the Scott Report.[27] The government was acquitted by Scott; Ian Lang, the president of the Board of Trade, savaged Robin Cook for 'misleading the country' in an 'odious smear campaign' and for behaving in a manner unworthy of a shadow Foreign Secretary.[28]

After a lively debate, the government won a vote clearing it of any wrongdoing. The final tally, a win by 320 to 319, illustrated the extent to which the inquiry had been used as a weapon by the opposition. Major's government had survived the day, but was badly wounded.

While the Scott Inquiry was dealing with a sequence of events that had been brought about by Alan Clark's economy with the truth, Butler had dealings with Clark on an unconnected matter. Clark, no longer a member of Major's government, was preparing to publish a volume of his diaries covering the period from 1983 to February 1991. The Cabinet Secretary already knew of Clark's intention, and was pleasantly surprised when, on 28 May 1993, a Friday afternoon, Clark walked into his office – from the corridor, naturally, rather than through his private secretary's office – and dumped a cardboard box on his desk. The diaries had already been accepted for publication by Weidenfeld and Nicolson, and Clark was conforming to the accepted – but unenforced – convention that ex-ministers submit diaries to the Cabinet Secretary before publication.

Butler had no doubt what the box contained, and he asked Clark when he would like to receive his response. 'Monday morning', came the brusque reply. He pointed out that it was already 4.00 p.m. on Friday and that the Monday was a bank holiday. They settled for a reply by the following Monday, and Butler took the box home for weekend reading.

By Saturday morning, his reading was complete and, with a week's grace at his disposal, he cleared a few factual points with the departments to which Clark had been attached. Then, on Sunday 6 June, the *Mail on Sunday* announced that it would be serialising the diaries in a manner that made it clear that they had the full text. Action was needed sooner than he and Clark had expected. Butler, no admirer of Clark's treatment of women in general and female civil servants in particular, 'amused [himself] by drafting a letter to Clark in a form which the newspaper would not want to publish':

> Dear Alan,
>
> I am required to comment on your text under three headings. First, disclosures damaging to national security: I could find none of these. Second, passages damaging to Britain's international relations: there are a number of disobliging remarks about our close allies but I think that the countries concerned are unlikely to notice or be surprised by them. Finally, breaches of confidence within Government: there are many passages in which you make personal observations about those whose duty it was to entertain you, advise you or accompany you. I attach a list of these, together with some factual corrections, and I should be grateful if you would remove them.[29]

No reference to the letter appeared in the newspaper, but Clark replied that, while he had made corrections as requested, he would not remove any of the references to civil servants that Butler had identified. The diaries were, therefore, published with Clark's irreverences intact.*

An amusing sequel occurred a week or so later. Len Appleyard, a deputy secretary in the Cabinet Office, protested to Butler about two references that Clark had made to him ('that toad Len Appleyard' and 'that runtish little underling of Robin Butler's in the Cabinet Office').[30] Appleyard pointed out that both he and Clark were members of Brooks's Club, whose rules prohibited a member from publishing offensive remarks about fellow members and that Clark's membership might be revoked. Butler, aware that backgammon at Brooks's was an important part of Clark's routine, told him of Appleyard's complaint. Clark, in typical teasing hyperbole responded: 'Dear Robin, I am filled with remorse and self-loathing. Please pass my abject apologies to Mr Appleyard and assure him that the references to him will be corrected in the second edition.'[31]

There was a postscript, too, in Waldegrave's dealings with Sir Richard Scott. During the inquiry, Waldegrave had been shocked by the apparently biased dealings between Scott and Alan Clark. It was, he felt, as if Clark were the virtuous whistle-blower who had opened the way to investigating a corrupt government. His disillusion with the processes of the inquiry persisted and, while he was smarting at the treatment he had received, at being accused in a leaked draft of lying, and of imagining revenge on Scott, the opportunity to be avenged presented itself. 'The still-ubiquitous Robin Butler came to me', he wrote, 'and said that the Lord Chancellor … wanted to make Scott Vice-Chancellor, head of the civil courts. … For a moment I had power over Sir Richard. But what was the point? It gave me some satisfaction *not* to object; it made me feel magnanimous.'[32]

The report of the Scott Inquiry highlighted several issues that should have made the Cabinet Office distinctly uncomfortable. Paul Foot seized on these in an article for *Socialist Review*.[33] While accepting that the Department of Trade and Industry and the Ministry of Defence were more villainous than

* The first volume of the diaries, published in 1993, became a bestseller. The diaries are witty, candid and blunt in their assessment of colleagues. They are frequently compared with the recordings of Sir Henry 'Chips' Channon, although Clark's candour and occasional profanities are the more shocking.

the Foreign Office – although the FCO had its own axe to grind in its subservience to Saudi Arabia – he drew attention to the inquiry's focus on the 'tilt to Iraq' that had, apparently, existed throughout the Iran–Iraq war. This revelation, which ran counter to strident government denials, was not stressed as, naturally enough, a High Court judge hesitated to point the finger at the Prime Minister and the Cabinet. The rather too close connection between government and the arms industry was brought to light but not bruited about too loudly. There were criticisms aplenty of Major's government, but the argument that Major – and, indeed, Thatcher – knew nothing of the entire affair was broadly accepted. Scott's indictment was of the cosy relations that exist in the higher reaches of the establishment. It is, in retrospect, remarkable that little attention was paid to the tendency of ministers and civil servants to close ranks against suggestions of incompetence.[34]

To the public the Matrix Churchill story was the more sensational headline. To the Cabinet Secretary there were fundamental questions about the responsibility of ministers to Parliament, about the relations between armaments manufacturers and government – the 'military-industrial complex' against which President Eisenhower had cautioned a quarter of a century before.

On 18 June 2009, a memorial service for Sir Michael Quinlan was held in Westminster Cathedral. Quinlan, Butler's regular squash partner, had first tipped Butler off that the Matrix Churchill case would fail. Appropriately, the eulogy at the service was delivered by Butler, the defender of the half-picture-as-truth equation of fifteen years before. A lesson was read by Sir Richard Mottram, former Permanent Secretary, Intelligence, Security and Resilience in the Cabinet Office, and famous as 'one of the few mandarins who thrive on tackling problems head-on and admitting mistakes'.[35] This was appropriate, as Mottram had anticipated Butler's truthful response to Scott by almost a decade. During the trial of Clive Ponting in 1985, he was asked whether answers to parliamentary questions should be truthful and not deliberately ambiguous. After a long silence, Mottram replied that 'in highly charged political matters, one person's ambiguity may be another person's truth'.

Butler did not have sole ownership of unconventional definitions of truth.

CHAPTER 14

IRELAND: TENTATIVE STEPS, 1993

FROM THE BEGINNING OF his time in office, John Major saw the achievement of a lasting ceasefire in Northern Ireland as one of the principal priorities of his administration. The Northern Ireland Office saw his arrival in Downing Street as an opportunity to reopen talks which had been effectively suspended for some time. An Anglo-Irish agreement had been signed by Thatcher and the Taoiseach Garret FitzGerald on 15 November 1985, and the ferocity of opposition from both sides of the border had underscored the complexity of the Irish question. Ulster Unionists, led by Dr Paisley, rejected the accord on the grounds that, for the first time, it granted the Irish Republic a say in the affairs of Northern Ireland; Republicans rejected the basis of any agreement with Britain, the country that claimed sovereignty over the six counties of Ulster.

In the intervening six years, only slight progress had been made. FitzGerald had been replaced by Charles Haughey; Haughey, a controversial and provocative individual, had an extravagant lifestyle. He owned racehorses, a private island and a substantial yacht, and invited widespread speculation as to how he had acquired such wealth on a government salary. The telephone tapping of two journalists in 1982 had become a *cause célèbre*, and Haughey realised that he would be forced to resign. At first, he agreed with Albert Reynolds, who would succeed him, that he would do so at a time of his choosing. Reynolds agreed to this curious arrangement; Haughey's resignation was hastened, however, when a member of his Cabinet threatened to make public details of his dealings with a colourful Saudi Arabian businessman.[1]

Amid the dramatic shifts in Dublin, there was continuity in the position of Secretary to the government, where Dermot Nally provided a reassuring presence as one Taoiseach succeeded another. It was Nally who had established working relations with Robert Armstrong leading up to the 1985 agreement and who was still in that job when Major discussed with his Cabinet Secretary the three strands of his plan for peace in Northern Ireland.

For Butler, the achievement of peace in Ireland had long been a vitally important goal. He had been closely involved with Edward Heath during the Sunningdale talks; he had been with Margaret Thatcher when the IRA blew up the Grand Hotel in Brighton. Most recently, he had come close to losing his life when the IRA loosed off three mortars at Downing Street. There was also a personal loss that impelled him to work harder for a solution to the Irish question. His close friend Ian Gow, MP for Eastbourne and former Minister of State for the Treasury, had been killed by an IRA bomb in July 1990. They had become friends when their careers overlapped at Downing Street, where Gow was parliamentary private secretary to Thatcher between 1979 and 1983.*

Butler's determination to find a solution was shared in equal measure by his counterpart in the Irish Republic. Nally was a talented and dedicated public servant, very much the Dublin equivalent of himself in London. He had occupied the position of Secretary to the government since 1980, and was totally committed to finding a widely acceptable solution in Northern Ireland. He and Butler were in contact from the first days of Butler's appointment and, recognising that their expressed commitment to peace went further than the casual clichés of political sound bites, developed good working relations during the summer of 1991.

Notwithstanding Haughey's 'lame-duck' status, Major and Butler met him and Nally on 4 December 1991. Despite a shared feeling that agreement

* When Gow left Downing Street in 1983, he took all the private secretaries out for drinks at his London club. After a bibulous evening, Butler and Gow returned to Gow's house in Kennington, where quantities of brandy were consumed. It was not until the following morning that Butler realised he had left his briefcase, containing classified papers, at the club. Fortunately, he retrieved the briefcase, which was sitting where he had left it, and avoided the discovery of an error that might have ended his career.

between the UK and the Republic was a possibility, there remained the abiding difficulty of reaching an agreement that would be acceptable to the Ulster Unionists. When Reynolds succeeded Haughey early in the New Year, he created a radically new government, demonstrating the distance between him and Haughey. The new Taoiseach believed that Major was a man with whom he could do business, and was cautiously optimistic that the two new Prime Ministers would bring fresh minds to the perennial problems.

Sobered by the reaction of Paisley and the Ulster Unionists, whose members had resigned *en masse* from the Commons in 1985, Major had developed an approach that would, if successful, bind the three interested parties – the UK, the North and the Republic. Three sets of talks were to be held simultaneously: one between the UK and representatives of the North to discuss the re-establishment of a Northern Ireland Assembly; another to address relations between North and South; and the third to focus on relations between the UK and the Republic. It was an ambitious proposal, the success of which was conditional on the success of each of the three strands of negotiations.

There was also the forthcoming general election to consider, which meant that Major should not appear to be considering any concessions to Sinn Féin until the much talked-of ceasefire was a reality.* The central conundrum – that any meaningful proposal that might achieve a ceasefire would, by definition, be unacceptable to either the Provisional Irish Republican Army or Paisley and the Unionists – was made even more dangerous in the context of a spring election. Nonetheless, the two officials, Butler and Nally, were insistent that there should be no backing away, either in the light of Haughey's impending departure, or in the build-up to a British election. A necessary short interlude should not dim the determination of either government to press forward with the peace process. This insistence from the civil servants that the politicians be held to the substance of their rhetoric was a critical element throughout the lengthy negotiations.

The year of 1992 began with an explosion of violence in January, prompting

---

* Sinn Féin is active in both Northern Ireland and south of the border. It is a democratic socialist party, committed to the independence of a united Ireland.

The Guardian to predict that, if that rate of murder continued, it would be the worst year since the 1970s.[2] It did indeed prove to be a particularly bloody year, but desultory talks continued in the three strands. In early 1993, however, an initiative from Sinn Féin encouraged the hope that progress might bring an end to the continuing violence. Martin McGuinness* made a speech to the Ard Fheis (annual conference) of Sinn Féin that appeared to urge talks between the British government and Sinn Féin:

> The British government's policy is crucial if there is to be a just settlement on this island. The other parties to the debate can have but a limited influence on the situation and it is essential if there is to be any hope of peace that the British government lead the way by outlining its plan for a final resolution of the problem. Britain cannot be allowed to abdicate its responsibility by standing by like Pontius Pilate washing its hands of a problem it created.
>
> If they continue with their present policies there will be no settlement, no peace. Britain must also publicly accept, as I believe they now privately do, that an essential ingredient in the search for a solution is the acceptance of the need for inclusive dialogue as a vehicle towards a final settlement.[3]

This speech and the presidential address by Gerry Adams were forwarded to the government Northern Ireland Office. According to the official British version, the document was accompanied by a message from McGuinness that read: 'The conflict is over but we need your advice on how to bring it to a close. We wish to have an unannounced ceasefire in order to hold a dialogue leading to peace.'[4] The existence of such a note is denied by Sinn Féin; it is easy to see both why the British government would maintain that an overture had been made by Sinn Féin and why Sinn Féin would vehemently deny that they had attempted to treat with the hated British.

Whether or not an overt approach was made, there was a danger that a positive response from Major's government would be used to drive a wedge

* Martin McGuinness, a former IRA commander, was a Sinn Féin politician in 1993. He was later MP for Mid Ulster in 1997 and Deputy First Minister of Northern Ireland from 2007 to January 2017.

between the Tories and the Ulster Unionists. There had been a sharp cooling of relations between the Conservative Party and the Ulster Unionist Party since 1985, but the UUP now decided to take part in negotiations on the constitutional future of Northern Ireland. To maintain their cooperation, it was vital that Major not be perceived to be dealing with terrorists. Some senior ministers believed that the speech was a trap to reopen the breach between the two parties, and strenuously urged against any action that could be interpreted as weakness until the Irish Republican Army openly agreed to a ceasefire.

Major's reaction greatly impressed and encouraged Butler, for he looked beyond the question of appearance or the effect of a positive response on his negotiating position. If the overture were genuine, he argued, the British government had an opportunity that they would be callously stubborn to ignore. Instead, the government should keep an open mind and judge the IRA by its actions, ready to discuss the long-established principle that only with consent from North and South could any agreement regarding unity be reached. A secret exploratory meeting was held between representatives of Sinn Féin and the British government and, on 26 February 1993, the British replied to Sinn Féin, stressing that they understood and appreciated the seriousness of what had been said. Events would prove whether or not it could be accepted at face value. In the meantime, the British government was working to give a substantive response as soon as possible.[5]

There were further contacts during the next couple of weeks, and on 19 March London sent a concrete message to Sinn Féin. The message, which came to be known as the 'nine-paragraph letter', was drafted in the Northern Ireland Office and was discussed in detail by Major and Butler before it was dispatched. It contained several central points, starting from the principle that both sides had suffered greatly; there was no 'monopoly of suffering'. Both sides should approach the talks without deception, with a positive desire to move forward. No dialogue could be held without a halt to violent activity. All legitimate parties should be eligible to share in the exercise; the British government had no prior objective of 'ending of partition'. A united Ireland might be the outcome, but it could only come about with the consent of the people of Northern Ireland. Reduction of violence would result in reduction of security forces, on the understanding that the level of security forces would need to take into account the threat of violence from both Republican and Loyalist groups.

Confidentiality was vital for the success of the talks. At this point, apart from the Prime Minister and Cabinet Secretary, the only members of the government who knew of the initiative were Patrick Mayhew, the Secretary of State for Northern Ireland, and Douglas Hurd. It seemed that genuine progress was being made towards holding high-level talks when, on 20 March, there were two bomb blasts in Warrington, injuring fifty and killing two children aged three and twelve. The peace process was immediately suspended when the IRA claimed responsibility, but Gerry Adams, the president of Sinn Féin, made an emollient statement referring to the two boys:

> Republicans, not least because we have also buried our children, know the agony of the families of Jonathan Ball and Tim Parry. Children are always innocent. None of the rest of us stands guiltless.
>
> Those who are now exploiting the understandable emotion and human reaction to the Warrington explosions know this. Yet they are manipulating the genuine grief and deep sadness of people throughout Ireland to channel public opinion in one direction – against republicans.
>
> Republicans have nothing to fear from a genuine peace movement. Sinn Féin has been engaged in developing a peace process for some time now. I welcome any positive approach to building peace but I appeal to those who really wish to end the conflict to beware against letting themselves be cynically used.[6]

The British acknowledged the sentiments behind Adams's statement, but continued to insist that all violence must cease before talks could begin; Sinn Féin replied, maintaining that only through talks could the violence be stopped, as 'the purpose of dialogue about peace is to bring all organised violence by all parties to the conflict to an end'. While this difference of emphasis kept the sides apart, the Irish Taoiseach Albert Reynolds requested an urgent, secret meeting with Major. A meeting between the two was rejected on the grounds that it would be impossible to keep secret. Accordingly, on 6

June, Butler flew to Casement Aerodrome, the Irish Department of Defence airfield at Baldonnel outside Dublin, to receive a message from Reynolds.

The substance of the Taoiseach's message was his conviction that the IRA could be persuaded to call a halt to the violence by a joint statement issued from London and Dublin, the text of which he showed to the Cabinet Secretary. Well-intentioned the *démarche* may have been, and it was clear that Reynolds was most encouraged by the IRA's acceptance of the principle of consent, namely that agreement by a majority in the North was a precondition of a united Ireland. Nonetheless, it was immediately obvious to Butler that Reynolds's proposal, essentially the position reached by Gerry Adams and John Hume, leader of the Social Democratic and Labour Party, would be unacceptable to the British government.

Butler's assessment was accurate; there were simply too many points in Reynolds's proposal that Major could not address. Butler flew back to Casement to inform Reynolds of the *impasse*. At this point, the Taoiseach suggested that a respected, neutral individual such as Robin Eames, Anglican Archbishop of Armagh, amend the proposal to make it more acceptable to the Unionists. At a London meeting with Major on 16 June, he repeated this proposal, stressing the political risks that he had taken in holding talks with the IRA at all. Major, accepting the delicacy of the Taoiseach's position, continued to work towards a joint declaration, but rejected the text proposed by Reynolds. Over the next four months, Butler and Nally strove to find a formula that sufficiently acknowledged British sacred cows: self-determination for the North and constitutional guarantees.

Major was increasingly conscious of the risk of leaks damaging both the negotiations and the cooperation of the Unionists with the government. He, therefore, decided that he should inform Jim Molyneaux,* the leader of the Ulster Unionists, of the negotiations in progress. Butler, abidingly distrustful of the intentions of the Unionists, doubted that this could do anything but expose the Prime Minister. To his surprise and Molyneaux's credit, however, confidentiality was maintained. As expected, the Unionist leader rejected the

* James Molyneaux (1920–2015), later Lord Molyneaux of Killead KBE PC, was a blunt Orangeman who led the Ulster Unionist Party from 1979 to 1995.

revised proposal, but fully accepted that Major was in indirect contact with Sinn Féin. This acknowledgement, by itself, was a breakthrough.

In October, Dublin produced a new draft of the proposed joint declaration that seemed greatly more promising. Despite Major's initial enthusiasm, however, Mayhew made it clear that he had little faith in Dublin's intentions, a view shared by MI5, who discounted the likelihood of a ceasefire. Once again, Butler was dispatched to Casement on 19 October with a broad brief to find other ways forward, even through constitutional talks, a direction that Dublin did not welcome.

While the third strand of Major's strategy, the strand focusing on relations between London and Dublin, had made gradual, if jerky, progress through the summer of 1993, there had been activity, if not progress, in the second, concerned with North–South relations. Since 1988, John Hume, the leader of the Social Democratic and Labour Party, had been talking in secret with Gerry Adams. On Saturday 10 April, by accident or by design, Adams was spotted while visiting Hume at his house in Derry. On the following day, the news of the meeting broke in an Irish Republic newspaper.[7] After the initial shocked surprise, the talks between the two assumed their own momentum and later that month a joint statement was issued. By September, talks had progressed to the point that the Hume-Adams Initiative was drawn up; early in October, the IRA approved the proposals that it contained.

On 23 October, nine bystanders, all Protestant civilians, were killed when a bomb being planted by the IRA exploded prematurely in a shop on the Shankill Road, Belfast. This bombing caused the greatest loss of life in Northern Ireland since November 1987 and brought immediate violent response from Loyalists. Thomas Begley, the IRA bomber, was killed in the explosion; Major and Butler were outraged when Adams acted as pallbearer at his funeral.

Major's colleagues were beginning to despair of making any progress when, on 15 November, the Prime Minister took a bold step in a speech at the Lord Mayor's Banquet. Encouraged by Molyneaux's attitude, he publicly acknowledged that Sinn Féin might become involved in discussions on the future of Northern Ireland. An essential precondition, of course, was that there be an end to violence.[8] In the light of the recent Shankill Road bombing, that announcement took considerable political courage.

At this point, rather than attempt to edit an already edited, unacceptable proposal, the Northern Ireland Cabinet Committee was sufficiently encouraged to begin anew and to produce a fresh proposal. Major attached a letter to the proposal with the comment that it 'goes as far in my judgment as the market will bear'.[9] Butler flew to Casement once more on 26 November to take the proposal to Reynolds. With 'barely a glance at it' the Taoiseach rejected it, accusing the British of ignoring a historic opportunity to end violence.[10] Sean Duignan, one of Reynolds's advisers present at the meeting, recorded scornfully: 'Albert gives him hell. Tells him he doesn't have a clue. He also tells him that Major's proposal, which involves the two leaders finding some kind of middle way, won't wash.'[11]

Intermittent contact was maintained between the government and Sinn Féin into the autumn. On 2 November, the IRA had sent a message ostensibly urging an end to violence but warning that 'we believe that the country could be at the point of no return'.[12] Inevitably, *The Times* learned of the government's responses to messages apparently from the IRA – for to assume the bona fides of any message thus far received would have been dangerous – and published the story on 28 November. Predictably, there was a horrified outcry from several quarters – from Unionists, from the right wing of the Conservative Party, from Reynolds, who felt that Major had been hypocritical in his dealings with Dublin. Butler and Nally promptly applied themselves once again to salvaging the planned meeting between Major and Reynolds in Dublin on 3 December.

On the following day, Mayhew made a statement to the House of Commons, laying out in detail the course of events since the first message, purportedly from Sinn Féin, had been received in February. The version presented by the British government differed in certain details from the account that Sinn Féin later published, but in most substantive matters the two accounts were in accord. Mayhew repeated that an end to violence – not a temporary ceasefire – was a necessary precondition of serious talks. The government would not cease its efforts to bring violence to a permanent end. The way was still open for Sinn Féin to enter the political arena after a sufficient interval to demonstrate that they mean it. The key to peace, he insisted, was in the hands of the IRA.[13]

Butler had been deeply concerned about the possible results once confidentiality was lost. Now, to his surprise, the candour of the Secretary of State was answered by respectful acceptance by the opposition and, more importantly, by Jim Molyneaux on behalf of the Unionists. After Molyneaux's moment, however, the Revd Ian Paisley rose and robustly attacked Mayhew, accusing him of 'rubbishing' any suggestion of talks. He then demanded that Mayhew explain 'why he issued falsehoods himself, got officials to issue falsehoods and got Downing Street to back up those falsehoods'.[14]

After the Speaker reproved Paisley for accusing Mayhew of 'falsehood' and Paisley refused to withdraw the accusation, a division (Ayes 272, Noes 25) compelled Paisley to withdraw from the House, and business continued in a less impassioned manner. Seamus Mallon, Deputy Leader of the SDLP, added the endorsement of his party to that of the Unionists. There remained the difficulty of re-establishing meaningful discussion with the IRA and Sinn Féin, but Major was substantially released from the permanent pressure that Northern Ireland politics placed on him.

With the fear of a Tory–Unionist schism removed, Major felt able to proceed, a decision he took at a 'tense but encouraging' meeting in Dublin.[15] Unresolved points were referred to discussions, at which Butler led the British group. Working from the original Irish proposals, balanced by Unionist input from Archbishop Eames, all parties contributed pragmatically. Paisley's behaviour in the Commons and the subsequent rebuke from the Speaker's chair may, bizarrely, have contributed to the working atmosphere. In a remarkably short time, there was the basis of an agreement on the outlines of a plan for multi-party talks. Not an agreement yet, but the spectre of total non-communication and mutual accusation might, just might, at last be removed. At the final hurdle, before Major and Reynolds met on 15 December, as Butler remembers, four points had to be settled between the Prime Minister and the Taoiseach through a telephone call. Reynolds opened breezily: 'I'm glad that everything has been settled, John.' Fortunately, the Prime Minister was sufficiently well briefed to say: 'Not quite, Albert.'[16]

Despite the four remaining obstacles, both sides were conscious that huge strides had been made in a short time. They had been over the ground so many times that everyone knew what had to be settled. Perhaps the greatest irony is that Major's fervent concern for secrecy, a political consideration of minuscule weight in the broader balance, turned out to be misplaced. With the exception of the Democratic Unionist Party led by Ian Paisley, who predictably protested at a 'sell-out to Dublin', aside from the inevitable posturing and righteous indignation, all parties fundamentally wanted talks to go forward. When Reynolds and Major delivered the outlines of the plan, there were significant concessions from all sides. Underpinning what became known as the Downing Street Declaration was a clear commitment to peaceful methods. The declaration was presented as a statement of principles that depended on democratic process for the mandate to bring about any changes.

Inevitably, the twelve-paragraph document contained more than a few abstracts and depended on considerations beyond the control of either the Prime Minister or the Taoiseach. It was, however, a masterpiece of common sense with which it is difficult rationally to take issue. Precisely because emotions had tended to outstrip rational discussion, the first nine paragraphs were devoted to broad principles, and not until the tenth paragraph was the issue of 'paramilitary violence' addressed. From the first paragraph, instead of speaking of the United Kingdom and the Republic of Ireland, the document talks of two islands. This served to play down – or at least not to highlight – the isolation of the Unionists in the North. While no settlement could be imposed, 'the Taoiseach and the Prime Minister ... recognise that the ending of divisions can come about only through the agreement and co-operation of the people, North and South, representing both traditions in Ireland'.[17]

With many such efforts not to isolate any extreme elements and, above all, not to stimulate a renewal of violence, the declaration appealed 'to both traditions ... to grasp the opportunity for a fresh start and a new beginning, which could hold such promise for all our lives and the generations to come'.[18] The genuine feelings of all traditions in the North, the Taoiseach maintained, must be recognised and acknowledged. Scenting a trap, concerned that the traditions of the North were to be defined by the Prime Minister of the Republic, alarmed that the language of the declaration was too 'green', Ian Paisley and the Democratic Unionists were determined to destroy the declaration. Molyneaux, on the other hand, worked hard to bring the UUP in line behind it.[19]

Success in the peace process depended on a settlement of three sets of relationships: between the two communities in Northern Ireland; between Northern Ireland and the Republic; and the political relationship between Dublin and London. The novel element in the declaration was that it accepted that the future of Ireland would be determined by the people of Ireland as a whole, an issue that had been a trigger for violence in the past. Acceptance of the principles entailed parallel acceptance of the demand of Irish Republicans for a decision taken by the Irish and respect for majority opinion in the North. By itself, this was no guarantee that issues would be definitively resolved, but for the first time it ushered in the possibility of settlement without protracted violence.

The declaration, a clear statement of principles, was not an agreement for a ceasefire, nor was it a political document that bound either side to specific action. As such, it could not, by itself, achieve peace – in spite of the optimism of Albert Reynolds. It was, nonetheless, hailed as a milestone in the media; the language of the agreement transcended the typical platitude of joint statements, and there were significant pointers that went beyond 'laying the foundations for a more peaceful and harmonious future'.[20]

Most significant was the statement that 'it is for the people of the island of Ireland alone … to exercise their right of self-determination'.[21] To speak of 'the island' as an entity represented enormous progress. Based on that premise, the statement that the British government had 'no selfish strategic or economic interest in Northern Ireland' passed into the lexicography of the Irish question. The commitment to the peace process of the two Prime Ministers led directly to the ceasefire of August 1994.

For Butler, the declaration was of enormous significance and the signing of the document in the Cabinet Room a moving occasion. He had been intimately involved in the process throughout the ten months of germination and had led the British team that ultimately formulated the framework on which future talks could hang. The grit involved in his collaboration with Dermot Nally was of critical importance. In intellect, commitment and pertinacity he was matched by his Dublin counterpart and, once engaged, his competitive instincts found expression in his determination to make the agreement a reality. Without the determination that he and Nally brought to the clearing of a path, it is unlikely that significant advances would have been made. At one point, frustrated by lack of progress, Major urged his Cabinet Secretary to 'kick it into the long grass'. The temptation to do so must have been almost overwhelming.

Across the Irish Sea, Dermot Nally's contribution to the Downing Street Declaration was not forgotten. When he died in 2010, an obituary described him in words that could as aptly have been spoken of his counterpart in London: 'an outstanding civil servant with exceptional talents, ideally suited to that key role in our public administration'.[22] Amid the posturing and politics that dictated the conditioned responses from both sides of the border in 1992–93, the political courage of John Major and James Molyneaux stood out in Butler's analysis of events. Major himself claimed that 90 per cent of the Good Friday Agreement of 1998* was incorporated in the Downing Street Declaration.[23] Butler endorsed this analysis and was proud of his own contribution, later reflecting: 'Although there were many bumps and bruises along the way to the Good Friday Agreement of 1998, I share John Major's view that the Downing Street declaration was a turning-point, and I am happy that I played a part in it.'[24]

* The Good Friday Agreement was signed on 10 April 1998 and brought the 'Troubles', which had lasted for thirty years, to an end.

CHAPTER 15

THE MOST DIFFICULT MOMENTS, 1994–1995

INTERVIEWED AFTER HIS RETIREMENT from the post of Cabinet Secretary, Lord Butler was asked by Anthony Seldon what his 'most difficult moment' had been. Without a moment's hesitation, he replied:

> The most difficult moment for me personally was when I had to investigate allegations made by Mohamed al-Fayed against Cabinet Ministers and MPs about various forms of corruption. It was made particularly difficult by Jonathan Aitken. I was foolish enough to say publicly that I believed his story and then, of course, in a court case, his story turned out to have been untrue.[1]

The last years of John Major's government will be most remembered for the accusations of sleaze that surrounded it.[2] Butler, as Cabinet Secretary, became involved in advising the Prime Minister on whether the Ministerial Code had been broken. It was a delicate role, as there had been allegations against ministers and Members of Parliament, and there was evidence in government files. These were not accusations of criminal behaviour – any such would have been referred to the police – but allegations that involved internal evidence and which, therefore, were referred to the Cabinet Secretary.

Mohamed al-Fayed, the owner of Harrods in London and the Ritz hotel in Paris, incensed by an uncomplimentary Department of Trade and Industry Report into his takeover of the House of Fraser group, was nursing a grudge against the government. In June 1993, he gave information to Peter

Preston, the editor of *The Guardian*, concerning allegedly shady dealings that Mark Thatcher was conducting with Arab clients. Additionally, al-Fayed tipped off Preston that during his takeover of the House of Fraser group he had paid Tory MPs Neil Hamilton and Tim Smith to ask questions in the Commons that would assist him in his bid.

Four months later, al-Fayed was able to feed Preston a still juicier story. Over the weekend of 18–19 September, he claimed, he had seen Jonathan Aitken, the Minister for Defence Procurement, together with Prince Mohammed bin Fahd and Mark Thatcher at the Ritz in Paris, allegedly sharing the commission on an arms deal.[3] It emerged that there was nothing in the story, as neither Prince Mohammed nor Thatcher had been at the Ritz that weekend. Aitken had been at the hotel, however, and had dined with Said Ayas, Prince Mohammed's business manager. This, al-Fayed commented, was like seeing the Attorney General dining with Al Capone.

There was a corruption angle, al-Fayed maintained, as Ayas had paid for Aitken's stay at the Ritz. Al-Fayed, of course, as owner of the hotel, was able to substantiate this claim and he did so, showing Preston a bill for about £1,000 for Aitken's stay, which had been debited to Ayas.* As Ayas was godfather to Aitken's daughter Victoria, Preston was not convinced that there was a corruption story to be unearthed. David Pallister, however, a *Guardian* journalist, followed up with a letter to Aitken, asking him how his weekend in Paris related to his job in government.[4] Aitken replied with a bland denial that there was any commercial significance to the Paris meeting. The trip to Paris, he maintained, had been in connection with Victoria's new school in Switzerland.

Preston now began to be interested by the story and, employing a ruse, obtained a copy of Aitken's hotel bill from the Ritz. A further letter to Aitken received the reply that it was not Ayas but Aitken's wife who had settled the bill. This was manifestly untrue and, after further investigation, *The Guardian* established that Aitken's wife had not even been in Paris that weekend.

Meanwhile Aitken, without consulting Butler, wrote to Preston, denying that there was any truth in the story and, as putative proof of his innocence,

* The bill was for 8,010 French francs – about £1,000.

saying that he had sent details of Preston's allegations to the Cabinet Secretary to investigate. When Preston sent Butler a copy of that letter, it was the first that the Cabinet Secretary had heard of the matter. At first sight, the question at issue appeared simply to be whether Ayas or Aitken had paid the hotel bill; Butler's view was that, even if Ayas had paid it, there had been no violation of ministerial rules. The two were friends of twenty-five years' standing. There was nothing improper, prima facie, in such a favour. The Prime Minister agreed, and the Cabinet Secretary duly communicated this opinion to Aitken. As far as Major and Butler were concerned, the matter was 'done and dusted'.[5]

In July 1994, Aitken joined the Cabinet as Chief Secretary to the Treasury. For Preston, whose interest in the affair had quickened, he immediately became a more important target. In October, *The Guardian* published a story that resuscitated the issue of the hotel bill. Facing questions on economic strategy on 27 October 1994, Aitken was asked by Gordon Brown whether 'the Chief Secretary [would] now take the opportunity to tell us that at no time was any part of his bill last year in the Ritz hotel in Paris paid for by a Mr. Ayas'.

The Speaker intervened swiftly to forbid Brown's line of questioning, suggesting that he pursue it through the Privileges Committee. Remarkably, betraying the arrogance that characterised his behaviour throughout the affair, Aitken stated his desire to answer in order to put an end to 'the scurrilous accusations that have been made'. One such allegation was that Aitken had lied to the Cabinet Secretary; in rebuttal, Aitken quoted from a letter Butler had written him, saying that he did not regard Aitken as having lied to him. 'I hope that the House, which is a very fair-minded place,' Aitken concluded, 'will accept both my assurance and the Cabinet Secretary's assurance and put an end to the hysterical atmosphere of sleaze journalism by *The Guardian*.'[6]

Butler had offered that opinion, giving Aitken an ostensible clean bill of health, after Aitken had shown him a doctored bill from the Ritz. Aitken had cut a crucial sentence from the correspondence and continued to assert that his wife had paid the bill. Somewhat ingenuously, Butler commented that 'since there was no apparent motive for Aitken to be untruthful about this, I told Preston that I believed Aitken's story'.[7] Even if Butler had been too trusting, it nonetheless baffled him that Aitken continued to maintain that his wife, not Ayas, had paid the bill. 'We had already concluded', he said, 'that even if Ayas had paid it, there was nothing wrong. Why should Aitken tell a lie?'[8]

At the end of 1994, Preston retired and Alan Rusbridger took over the editor's chair and, as part of Preston's legacy, the pursuit of Aitken. Other hounds had also picked up the scent and the television programme *World In Action* was to air 'Jonathan of Arabia', a documentary focusing on Aitken's involvement in arms sales to Saudi Arabia while he had been Defence Procurement minister. On the afternoon of 10 April 1995 Aitken, once again demonstrating remarkable hubris, gave a press conference of quite extraordinary self-righteousness.

Declaring that he had issued a writ for defamation against *The Guardian*, Peter Preston and David Pallister, he denied allegations of pimping for Prince Mohammed bin Fahd; of engaging in 'improper commercial relationships' with individuals who were helping British companies to sell defence equipment to Lebanon and, of course, of any impropriety in relations with Said Ayas. It was a bombastic performance, replete with sarcasm and threats, ending on a flight of oratory that was later to be widely repeated with malign relish:

> Here in Britain we have both the best media in the world and the worst media in the world ... If it falls to me to start a fight to cut out the cancer of bent and twisted journalism in our country with the simple sword of truth and the trusty shield of British fair play, so be it. I am ready for the fight. The fight against falsehood and those who peddle it.[9]

Three months later, Aitken resigned. Concern mounted at *The Guardian* that his lawsuit would embrace suggestions that he had been hounded from office by the media. The broadening of the accusations against Aitken – that he was a pimp, a taker of bribes, a sexual pervert – all added spice to the public's voyeuristic curiosity and diverted attention from the simple fact that Butler had been hoodwinked and had made a severe error of judgement in appearing to subscribe to Aitken's explanations. It was an error of which he remained acutely aware and which, two decades later, he viewed as the most difficult moment of his time as Cabinet Secretary.

In the event, the action brought against *The Guardian* by Aitken collapsed. In the manner of a Perry Mason case, Aitken appeared confident and unshakeable when the case opened in June 1997. Little by little, however, cracks appeared in his testimony and, thanks to relentless investigative work, hotel registration cards, air travel vouchers and car rental documents were produced to show conclusively that Mrs Aitken could not have been in Paris when Aitken claimed that she, not Ayas, had paid the bill at the Ritz. Indeed, documents obtained from British Airways proved that she had flown directly to and from Geneva and had never set foot in Paris over the weekend in question.

Clearly, Aitken had lied not only consistently to the Cabinet Secretary, but also under oath. The nemesis that followed his hubristic, over-confident posture came in May 1998 when he was charged with perjury, conspiring to pervert the course of justice and perverting the course of justice. In January 1999, he appeared at the Old Bailey and was eventually sentenced to eighteen months in jail, of which he served seven. By the time he was released from jail and he finally paid *The Guardian*'s legal costs, over eight years had passed since the Paris weekend.*

Understandably, the public perception of the affair was that the Cabinet Secretary had been guilty of naive incompetence and that there was no governmental machinery to follow up alleged ministerial misconduct. Such judgements flow from a misconception of the Cabinet Secretary's role. On the one hand, the Cabinet Secretary performs the role of a Whitehall head prefect and Butler, like Armstrong before him, was given that responsibility by the Prime Minister. On the other hand, that responsibility is effectively circumscribed by the lack of investigative resources. The Cabinet Secretary cannot behave in the manner of a journalist or a Scotland Yard detective. The Prime Minister, a politician, can lay off on a civil servant the broad questions

* When this came to pass, the editor and journalists at *The Guardian* were understandably jubilant. Articles summarising the affair were published on 6 March and 8 June 1999. A helpful timeline of events can be seen at *The Guardian*, 4 March 1999.

of ministerial propriety, but the civil servant depends on the candour of the minister, another politician, unless there is contrary documentary evidence.

In the case of Jonathan Aitken, this imprecision was complicated by the regrettable truth that Major regarded him as 'a talented buccaneer'; Butler, less diplomatically, describes him as 'a chancer'.[10] He had that reputation with the press and, given the gossip that circulated about his amorous adventures, the media were always on the lookout for a lurid story. By giving Aitken 'a clean bill of health' Butler exposed himself to ridicule as an *ingénu* and obloquy from the left for protecting Tory ministers and Members of Parliament. After his initial blunder, it seemed that whatever course he took only invited further criticism.

When the Cabinet Office did not launch an immediate investigation, there inevitably followed the suggestion by *The Economist* that Butler had 'let himself be drawn into providing public cover' for Major.[11] The proper course of action, the article argued, would have been for Butler to decline to involve himself on the grounds that he was being asked to involve himself in party politics. Curiously, the very opposite is true. Were the Cabinet Secretary to be responsible for investigating accusations of impropriety, he would be much more deeply immersed in political issues than under the present arrangement. His error was not one of criminal negligence or concealment of malfeasance. It was, as he would readily admit, a regrettable error of judgement.

During the preliminary stages of the Aitken affair, in the summer of 1994, a story broke, according to which two reporters from the *Sunday Times* had approached two Tory MPs, Graham Riddick and David Tredinnick, and offered them each £1,000 to table questions in the Commons concerning a non-existent drug.[12] The reporters, members of the newspaper's 'Insight' team, had posed as lobbyists offering inducements for MPs to ask the Secretary of State for Health about a drug named 'Sigthin' (an anagram of 'insight'). When the story broke, Major promptly instructed that the MPs be suspended, pending an investigation, and made known his determination to hold an inquiry and to ensure that the highest standards in public life were maintained.[13]

In that context, the next allegation of sleaze was the more wounding. In October, *The Guardian* ran a story, inspired by accusations from al-Fayed, alleging that two Conservative MPs, Neil Hamilton, Member for Tatton and Trade and Industry minister, and Tim Smith, Member for Beaconsfield and junior Northern Ireland minister, had accepted cash payments in exchange for asking questions in the Commons. The accusation was made on 19 October because al-Fayed 'felt it was now [his] public duty to make these facts known'.

The essence of al-Fayed's story was that the lobbyist Ian Greer had approached him and proposed that he pay a fee of £50,000 plus a fee to Hamilton and Smith for asking questions. Greer, he alleged, had told him that 'you need to rent an MP just like you rent a London taxi'. Al-Fayed added that every month he received a bill of between £8,000 and £10,000 for 'parliamentary services'. Additionally, Hamilton enjoyed free shopping at Harrods with his wife and had telephoned al-Fayed to request a stay at the Ritz in Paris. 'I agreed', said al-Fayed. 'I am a generous man. But he ran up such a big bill, even coming back for afternoon tea.' When Hamilton asked for another free stay at the Ritz, al-Fayed 'told the manager to tell him the hotel was full. There are limits to my generosity.'[14]

Both Hamilton and Smith were questioned by the Cabinet Secretary. Smith confessed, while Hamilton continued to deny the allegations. Butler submitted a report to Major within three days. The Prime Minister communicated the contents to the Commons in a Written Answer on 25 October. Smith, the report confirmed, had taken payments between 1987 and 1989 but, the Cabinet Secretary's report alleged, 'did not declare the necessary information in the Register of Members' Interests until just before the end of this period, and he acknowledged that he should have done so earlier'. Hamilton, on the other hand, continued to deny that he had received any payments from al-Fayed, as the report summarised:

> I have found no evidence which controverts Mr. Hamilton's assurances on these matters. He acknowledged that he had received hospitality from Mr. Al Fayed, as a private guest (as he believed), at a time well before he entered the government. He had not thought it necessary to declare this in the Register of Members' Interests, for reasons which he explained in a letter to the Editor of the Guardian of more than a year ago, a copy of which he gave me.[15]

Butler's investigation, the Prime Minister assured the House of Commons in a written answer, had examined a number of allegations. Both the Cabinet Secretary and the Chief Whip had put allegations in detail to the ministers concerned and had found nothing that threw doubt on the validity of the ministers' denials.

Butler's credulity, as he later admitted, led to a certain ribald mockery in the press and he was dubbed 'Inspector Clouseau of the Cabinet Office'.* The sobriquet is not altogether justified. Smith resigned immediately and, as Butler points out, 'no subsequent inquiry succeeded in disproving Hamilton's denial but he was later forced to resign as Minister for Corporate Affairs when it turned out that he had received payments from a lobbyist named Ian Greer, contrary to assurances he had given to his Secretary of State, Michael Heseltine'.[16]

Once again, Butler may have been too ready to accept Hamilton's assurances at face value. Heseltine, Secretary of State at the Department of Trade and Industry, had immediately contacted him to ascertain how Hamilton had answered the accusations. When he learned that he had denied receiving any money from al-Fayed, Heseltine pressed further. Had he received money from anyone associated with al-Fayed? Again Hamilton answered in the negative. When it emerged that Hamilton had been retained as a consultant by Greer, who had clear connections to al-Fayed, Hamilton claimed that he had misunderstood Heseltine's question. It was then agreed that Richard Ryder, the government Chief Whip, and Heseltine should speak to Hamilton. When they did so, pointing out that his position would be undermined daily by accusations and innuendo, Hamilton saw the logic and immediately resigned.[17]

In the climate of that time, with writs being issued and the very real threat of substantial damages being awarded for libel, one can hardly blame politicians or officials for a certain caution in airing conclusions. The Members' Interests Committee opined that Hamilton had been 'imprudent' in accepting and not registering his stay at the Ritz; Hamilton did eventually admit to receiving money from Greer. It was a lengthy process but, ultimately, a

* Inspector Clouseau was a fictional character, an incompetent and bungling officer of the French *Sûreté* in the farcical series *The Pink Panther*.

form of justice was done. It was, moreover, handled more adroitly than the Aitken affair. The Cabinet Secretary questioned the two MPs; one confessed and resigned; the other was dealt with by his superior minister and the Chief Whip. The party business was dealt with by the party.

To Butler fell the larger issue of public scrutiny of ministerial conduct. On 21 October, the Prime Minister asked him to propose how best to reassure the public as to the ethical standards observed by Members of Parliament. He considered the options open to Major, and recommended an advisory committee reporting to the Prime Minister. Without delay, Major announced this to the House, ruling out a committee composed solely of Privy Counsellors as too narrowly drawn; a Speaker's Conference as this should be concerned only with electoral law; and a formal board of inquiry or judicial inquiry as this was suitable for specific investigations. The purpose was to consider rather broader issues and make recommendations to the government.

Arguments could be made for any of these bodies, Major continued, but he was confident that there was a better way to proceed. Rather than create an ad hoc body to investigate allegations, he proposed 'to establish standing machinery to examine the conduct of public life and how best to ensure that standards of propriety are upheld'. Lord Nolan, a Lord of Appeal, would chair this committee.[18] With this somewhat grandiloquent phraseology, Major attempted in one ambitious move to defuse the mounting criticisms of his government.

Simply put, Nolan provided what Butler termed 'a lightning conductor' by appointing an independent body to investigate potential scandals. In some instances, where the evidence was likely to be found among government papers, it made sense for the Cabinet Secretary to investigate. In Butler's time, there was a clear distinction between such matters and scandals involving possible criminal behaviour; in these cases the police conducted the investigations. It is revealing that Butler's predecessor Robert Armstrong believes firmly that it was decidedly not the job of the Cabinet Secretary to do the job of the police,[19] but that Gus O'Donnell, who became Cabinet Secretary in 2005, reluctantly accepted that by then the responsibility had decidedly shifted.[20]

The great majority of potential scandals, however, were questions of not satisfying the highest standards, and Major refused to be drawn into every such allegation. The Nolan Committee was modelled on the Security Commission, set up in 1980, when there were allegations of a spy scandal. Rather than have the government investigate, the Security Commission was charged with the task, and the original concept was that the Nolan Committee would be dormant much of the time, activated only when there was a specific problem to investigate. In fact, Nolan soon assumed a permanent life, which was not at all what Major and Butler had originally envisaged.

Instructed to report within six months, the Nolan Committee released its first report on 11 May 1995. It contained fifty-five recommendations, divided by category of public servant (MPs, Ministers and civil servants, quangos) and further sub-divided according to the perceived urgency of implementation. It also listed the 'Seven Principles of Public Life', under which headings – Selflessness, Integrity, Objectivity, Accountability, Openness, Honesty and Leadership – it set out the ethical standards that should guide public servants. On a more practical level, it made detailed recommendations as to how these principles might be enforced.

Both the theoretical and practical considerations were of fundamental interest to Butler. On a personal level, he was anxious to see the role of the Cabinet Secretary clearly defined, as the 'Inspector Clouseau' label chafed. His view, supported by Nolan, was that the Cabinet Secretary's responsibility was to advise on the application of standards, not to investigate alleged violations of them. Nor, he argued, should the Cabinet Secretary be the sole source of advice for the Prime Minister, a view again echoed by Nolan, who recommended that 'the House should appoint a person of independent standing, who should have a degree of tenure and not be a career member of the House of Commons staff … [with] independent discretion to decide whether or not a complaint merits investigation or to initiate an investigation'.[21]

That recommendation worried Butler deeply. He was concerned that what might happen – and indeed did happen – was that whenever there was a story in the press alleging misbehaviour by an MP on the government side, the opposition would exploit the story, demanding that it be referred to this Commissioner for Standards (as the post was to be named). If the government refused, they would be accused of covering up and damned accordingly. If the government agreed, the poor victim would be hung out to dry while the Commissioner for Standards conducted a lengthy inquiry. Major agreed with this analysis, but felt that he could not reject the recommendation, and so the post was created.[22]

On the broader question of what constituted lobbying, consultancies or conflict of interest, however, Nolan's recommendations were tantalisingly imprecise. It was clearly impossible to outlaw all questions from a member who was a paid adviser or consultant to an organisation concerned, as that would muzzle any trade union MP. Despite the obvious problems in applying the recommendations, however, the commissioning of the report and its speedy delivery (the Scott Report on the alleged arms sales to Iraq was still awaited) went some way to dispelling the air of sleaze surrounding Major.

Sadly for the Tories, however, the affair followed a string of scandals and came to a head in time to influence the 1997 general election. The election had been uppermost in the mind of senior Conservatives for some time, effectively since Mrs Thatcher's resignation. By 1995, however, the Tories had been in power for sixteen years and, Butler recalls, there was none of 'the will to govern' that had characterised the party in 1979. Having been in office so long, backbenchers were no longer hungry for power. That lethargy eroded the feeling that they needed to stick together; instead, the party gave ample evidence of its schisms and factions.[23]

Major's style of leadership sat ill with the Tory grandees; MORI polls during 1994 consistently showed Labour leading the Tories by more than 30 per cent; although during the first six months of 1995 the gap narrowed, Labour still led by twenty-two points at the end of June. Local elections in May had been disastrous for the Conservative Party, and a by-election in Perth & Kinross on 25 May saw the Scottish Nationalist candidate win, while the Conservatives suffered a swing of 18 per cent against them. With the Tories' majority in Parliament halved in the three years since the 1992 election, and growing opposition within the party from Eurosceptics, discontent among Tory backbenchers was mounting and there was open talk of removing Major before the 1997 election.

With the objectivity of hindsight, Butler recalls the atmosphere in the spring of 1995 and its effect on Major:

> For all his virtues John Major had a thin skin and was sensitive to what the media and his colleagues were saying about him. More hardened politicians would have ridden through it or dealt with their enemies in another way. Think of Harold Wilson … I thought that all the criticism had got under his skin … Because he liked political correspondents he would ask why someone was criticising him, not realising that the correspondent would go back to the editor and say 'We've really irritated him this time'. And this created more irritating stories. Fortunately, I was not the main recipient of his agonising about stories in the press. Sarah Hogg had that job.[24]

During the month of June, the Prime Minister decided to confront the issue head-on and, before announcing it to the Cabinet, informed Butler of his decision to resign and stand for re-election. Butler was sceptical and urged him to carry on, as any recognition of this discontent would suggest weakness. Brushing aside Butler's objections, on 22 June Major held a press conference in the garden of 10 Downing Street, at which he put his cards squarely on the table, blaming the situation on 'a small minority in the party'. 'The Conservative Party must make its choice', he said, which was why he was 'no longer prepared to tolerate the present situation. In short, it is time to put up or shut up.'[25]

He repeated these sentiments in Huntingdon on the following day. In a virtuoso performance of his trademark plain speaking, he condemned 'the fevered mutterings that we've had that have excited so many people over the last two or three years'. The real political agenda, he said, 'on education, on health, on the economy, on jobs, has just been absolutely extinguished by the chatter we've had about the leadership of the Conservative Party. Well, I've had enough of that to be frank.'

Major's obvious potential challenger was Michael Heseltine, at the time president of the Board of Trade. Heseltine, however, remained loyal to Major insofar as he did not challenge the Prime Minister in the first round of the contest. This, surprisingly, was left to John Redwood, the Secretary of State for Wales, who resigned from the Cabinet and announced his candidacy on a platform of reclaiming powers from Brussels. To the consternation of Butler, of Major's supporters and of the City of London, Mrs Thatcher commented that both Major and Redwood were 'sound Conservatives'. While she did not go so far as to endorse Redwood, her lack of enthusiasm for Major alarmed the Cabinet Secretary and the Prime Minister's supporters; on the stock market, £15 billion was wiped off companies' market capitalisation.[26]

In the event, Major's tactics were effective. On 4 July, he won convincingly in the first round of voting, defeating Redwood by 218 votes to 89 and obviating the need for a second round. Heseltine, as a result, was denied the chance to run for the leadership. Major had retained Heseltine's support thus far in the contest by offering him the deputy premiership, with the title of First Secretary of State, if he defeated Redwood. While the voting was in progress, Major and Heseltine met to discuss various proposals that Heseltine had made about the structure of government, in particular a proposal to merge the Department of Education with the Department of Employment. Major suggested that, in the first instance, Heseltine should discuss the plan with Butler.

The two met in the Cabinet Secretary's office. In his memoir, the Cabinet Secretary suggests, with a touch of disingenuousness, that he was unaware of the implications of the election, that if Major were wounded in the first round, as Thatcher had been in 1990, then Heseltine would enter the contest and very likely win on the second ballot. When he and Heseltine, talked, therefore, Butler believed that he was talking to the next Deputy Prime Minister, not to a potential PM. At the end of their talk, Heseltine surveyed Butler's room and announced that it would suit him well in his capacity as Major's deputy. Butler, determined not to give up his traditional – and agreeable – space, temporised rapidly, assuring Heseltine that something much grander would be found for him. Somewhat doubtfully, Heseltine proposed that, if Major won the ballot, then he would return at 10.30 the following morning to inspect the office that Butler proposed.

In truth, Butler had no office in mind for Heseltine; he had instinctively defended his own space. He now asked his private secretary where he might accommodate a Deputy Prime Minister. 'Well, there's Conference Room B on the second floor', his secretary replied, 'but it's huge and it has a massive conference table in it.' Extreme measures were called for. 'Even if you have to bring in the Royal Engineers', said Butler, 'get the table out and a desk in by 10:20 tomorrow.' When Heseltine returned on the following day, the last pieces of the table were being removed. Butler escorted Heseltine upstairs to show off a vast space with a single desk in the far corner. 'I can see that you and I are going to understand each other', said Heseltine with a smile.*

In fact, they did understand each other well, even if that understanding was far from agreement. As the minister with responsibility for the Civil Service, Heseltine saw innumerable possibilities for privatisation. His memoirs positively throb with excitement as he recalls the staff cuts achieved, the entities sold off to private ownership. While many of those disposals made eminent sense, his philosophical starting point was diametrically opposed to that of the head of the Home Civil Service. Butler prepared for a long campaign.

Opening his account of his tenure, Heseltine, successful entrepreneur and chief executive officer, states bluntly: 'The Cabinet Office at 70 Whitehall was home to a glorious confusion of responsibilities',[27] including two immediate targets for Heseltine's pruning knife: Her Majesty's Stationery Office (HMSO) and the Civil Service training college at Sunningdale. On the question of HMSO, Butler could hardly argue with the figures; an overstaffed division with operating losses in excess of £50 million, it was an obvious candidate for privatisation.

Concerning the college at Sunningdale, on the other hand, Butler was adamant in his resistance. Heseltine marshalled his arguments for privatisation carefully and presented them with skill. First, the college was simply not training officials to an adequate standard. Second, except at the higher levels, it was open exclusively to officials already in the service; there was too little opportunity for individuals from the private sector to attend. Third, the argument that Heseltine saw as the most potent, the college was a potential source not only of income but also of national prestige, as he recalled:

> I wanted to attract more overseas students, with all the benefits in terms of future influence and understanding which that would create. As the leading country in so many public sector reforms ... we had a unique

---

* Heseltine's office was 'as large as a squash court' according to a Treasury official.

> opportunity to spread our experience and earn revenues from the many countries around the world which were following our lead. The courses of the official training centre of the British civil service, which had pioneered these reforms, would be highly marketable.[28]

Despite the apparent contradiction between his first argument – that the courses were not of a high standard – and his third – that they were extremely marketable – it was a powerful attack, supported by the traditional argument that there was good money to be made by privatisation.

Butler firmly believed that the college was an enormous asset to the Civil Service, allowing rapid flexibility in training and an ability to adjust courses to fit changing government policy. To maintain this flexibility, he argued, it was essential that it remain under the control of the service. To broaden the base of his response, he circulated all Permanent Secretaries to learn their views.[29] In spite of Heseltine's allegations, he did not coach them in their responses. Responding in writing, all but one agreed with him.

Armed with this almost universal rejection of Heseltine's proposal, Butler spoke first to him and then to Major, putting the Prime Minister into the difficult position of overruling either his deputy or the assembled august mandarins. Cannily, Major compromised. He proposed a two-year review period, during which the college's performance might be assessed before a decision was taken.[30] By that time, of course, if opinion polls were to be believed, it would no longer be a concern of the Tories. There would, moreover, be a different Cabinet Secretary by then, as Butler was due to retire at the end of 1997.

As a postscript to the Butler–Heseltine clashes of 1995, Heseltine records that on the morning after the general election of 1997, after consulting incoming Deputy Prime Minister John Prescott, Butler cleared the enormous office that Heseltine had occupied. It returned to its proper function as a conference room, as Heseltine mused: 'All trace of the Deputy Prime Minister's imperial eyrie had been removed … It was as though I had never been.'[31]

CHAPTER 16

NEW LABOUR, 1997–1998

BUTLER WAS NO STRANGER to elections. He had been in Downing Street when Heath yielded to Wilson in 1973. Ten years later he had been Thatcher's Principal Private Secretary when she called an election; in 1987 he had been appointed Cabinet Secretary after the election, and had been in the thick of things five years later when Major won a fourth consecutive term for the Tories. Now, about to be at the centre of a general election for the fourth time, he was long enough in the tooth to see that there were several causes of discontent, enough widely felt dissatisfaction to bring the government down.

Throughout 1996, the last full year of John Major's government, shrill criticism in the media continued unabated. Suspicions of sleaze, lingering criticisms of Black Wednesday, the Scott Report and continuing disunity over Europe combined to dog Conservative efforts to inspire the electorate. After eighteen years of Tory rule, the Cabinet Secretary had little doubt that a change of government was certain. That change was to be of greater magnitude than at any election within his memory. Indeed, his only direct involvement in an actual transfer of power had followed the Labour victory of 1974. This had brought a fundamentally different set of policies, but nothing as radical as the changes he foresaw in 1997. The government was bedevilled by leaks, a symptom in Butler's view of chronic Cabinet disunity.

While he was sceptical about the substance of New Labour policies, he recognised their public appeal. 'I was pretty certain that the Conservatives would not win', he recalled, 'because of the great attractiveness of Tony Blair.* We all had great hopes for him. He succeeded in putting a new veneer – I say "veneer" because I don't think it went very deep – on the Labour Party and made them electable.' The excitement he generated contrasted sharply with the 'rather tired tackiness of the Conservative Government', as he explained:

> The big idea embraced youth, energy, the Third Way, compassionate efficiency ... the legacy of Thatcher was still there and many people did see the Conservatives as 'the nasty party'. Clinton was the model for Blair, which was one of the reasons why Blair appointed Jonathan Powell his Chief of Staff.† Powell had been at the Washington embassy, had followed the Clinton campaign and picked up their tricks.[1]

When New Labour romped home with a crushing victory, an 11 per cent swing against the Tories and 418 seats in the House of Commons, Butler knew that within the Civil Service some radical readjustment would be needed. The Tories had held power since 1979, and the very length of their tenure meant that there was a generation of civil servants who had known only Tory governments. The other side of that coin was that the new government was the most inexperienced group to enter Downing Street since Ramsey MacDonald. In the opinion of Bernard Donoughue, Butler saw the handling of the transition from Major to Blair as an important professional challenge.[2] No twentieth-century Prime Minister had fewer than six years' experience as a minister. The average was ten years; Blair had none.

The Labour front bench, moreover, was almost totally inexperienced. Ann Taylor had been an assistant whip in the Callaghan government; Ivor Richard had been ambassador to the United Nations from 1974 to 1979; Jack Cunningham had been Under-Secretary of State for Energy under

---

* Butler is modest in his recollection. He had won a sweepstake of fellow members of Brooks's Club – a prize of £45 – predicting that New Labour would win with an overall majority of 175 seats. In fact the majority was 177. Other wagers were placed by Lord Anthony Lloyd (174), Sir Patrick Wright (162), Lord Armstrong (96), the Right Revd Lord Runcie (82), the Bishop of Arundel and Brighton (65), Judge Verney (64), Lord Kingsdown (53) and Sir Nicholas Goodison (31). Private Information.

† Jonathan Powell, brother of Charles, who had disturbed Butler during the Thatcher years.

Callaghan; and Gavin Strang had served as Parliamentary Under-Secretary for Energy and at the Ministry of Agriculture, Fisheries and Food between 1974 and 1979. That was the total extent of the New Labour Cabinet's experience of power.

Under those circumstances, it was unsurprising that the incoming ministers looked over their shoulders with a certain personal insecurity. Added to that insecurity was the traditional left-wing conviction that the Civil Service was a reactionary body and that its members, after eighteen years of Tory ministers as bedfellows, had become incorrigibly so. The result, particularly with a Prime Minister whose natural instinct was to control all aspects of policy, was an almost insuperable gulf of suspicion between Cabinet ministers and their officials, between Prime Minister and his Civil Service staff.

By May 1997, when the Labour Party returned to power, Butler was feeling very much an elder statesman. The new Prime Minister Tony Blair was approaching his forty-fourth birthday; Butler was looking at retirement on his sixtieth birthday in the New Year. His task was a simple one: to effect a smooth transition and to share the benefit of his experience for eight months. In January 1998, he would hand over to whomsoever Blair chose as his successor.

Before that happened, however, he had to ensure that the workings of No. 10 were as efficient and harmonious as possible. In the months before the election, therefore, he attempted to anticipate Blair's wishes and needs once he arrived in Downing Street. Over dinner at Half Moon Lane, he discussed arrangements with Blair and his wife, reaching the conclusion that it would make sense for their family to occupy No. 11 and for Gordon Brown, the new Chancellor and at the time a bachelor, to move into the smaller flat at the top of No. 10.

Those physical arrangements were relatively easy. Butler foresaw much greater problems in fitting Blair's style of management and his team into the smooth-running operation overseen by the Cabinet Secretary. In the three years since July 1994, when Blair had become leader of the Labour Party, he had transformed the role of the leader, modernised the party's media and communications, creating a streamlined and modern operation at the party headquarters in Millbank.[3] There could be little doubt that he would attempt to import this operation into Downing Street. Butler was aware of Blair's management style, and when Jonathan Powell and David Miliband met with him to discuss New Labour's priorities in the context of the Queen's Speech, he insisted that these be formally confirmed by Blair.

One week before the election Blair and Butler met at Blair's Islington home. On this occasion, more substantial fare than the Downing Street living arrangements was on the menu. Concerning the priorities that Powell and Miliband had raised, Blair distractedly assured Butler that these were indeed planned.[4] When Blair expressed his wish to appoint Jonathan Powell as his Principal Private Secretary, Butler had prepared arguments to marshal against the appointment. Beyond the convention that the post required an appointee from the apolitical Civil Service, he believed fervently that the job, involving Intelligence matters and relations with the Palace, should not be held by an aide with a political agenda. The competent and experienced Alex Allan was already *en poste*; why not see how that appointment worked out over the next few months? Butler's distinct impression was that Blair had focused solely on the campaign, rather than on what was involved in being Prime Minister. Blair, he added, conveyed 'the clear sense of being fed up throughout the two hours and wanted to get rid of me'.[5]

An additional concern of Butler's was that Blair was coming to power at a time when the erosion of Cabinet authority was most marked. Conditions were ideal for a strong Prime Minister with an efficient and media-savvy team to seize executive control of central government as never before. The perceptible decline in Major's authority after his first months in office had convinced Blair that the time was ripe for New Labour to appropriate and control the levers of power from the centre. Ironically, it had been Jonathan Powell's brother Charles who had abetted Thatcher's attempt to concentrate power in No. 10. Butler describes her constitutional respect for Cabinet with approval, but adds that in the later years of her administration she became increasingly impatient with debate in Cabinet.[6] Major's intermezzo of government through a weak and leaky Cabinet was the necessary proof that New Labour, more Thatcher's legatee than Major's, could operate as it wished. Armed with that confidence, Blair agreed to Allan's remaining in the job for a three-month trial period.

Contrasting the leadership styles of Major and Blair, Michael Foley observes that 'Major's acute leadership problems with a party accustomed to leadership discipline co-existed with the transformation of the Labour Party into a conspicuously leader-centred organisation'.[7] The contrast was stark and, as Major's stock fell, so Blair became more certain that his best tactic to appeal to voters was to highlight the differences between Major and himself. A year before Blair assumed the Labour Party leadership, a Gallup poll revealed that 71 per cent of respondents saw Major as 'out of touch with the country'; 72 per cent saw him as 'shortsighted'; 68 per cent thought him 'ineffective'; and a startling 81 per cent said that he 'did not inspire confidence'.[8]

As Major appeared increasingly weak, so ministers saw Cabinet as increasingly irrelevant, and Butler became concerned that the Cabinet would cease to be the forum for discussing policy. Once again, Blair's strategy was to portray himself as the opposite in every way from the Tory brand. If Major's Cabinet was leaky, the opposition would radiate tight control and consistent messages to the media. Blair's methods in opposition translated easily into his methods in government. Once he had reshaped the Labour Party, it was hardly surprising that he set out to refashion, to 'modernise' the office of the Prime Minister. Almost immediately after the election, the debate began over the 'presidential' nature of Blair's premiership.

Having won the election with a crushing majority,* Blair was convinced that the Conservatives had made the mistake that had bedevilled Labour for two decades – that they were out of touch with the modern voter in the modern world. New Labour would continue to occupy the centre ground and push the opposition to the extremes.[9] Decisions would be taken in the inner circle of Brown, Peter Mandelson, John Prescott and chief pollster Philip Gould. Millbank methods and Millbank discipline would be introduced to central government. Butler had an early taste of Blair's intention to reform when, at the start of the election campaign, Blair pressed for his agreement that Question Time in the Commons should be reformed. In its current form, it was stacked in favour of the opposition. The Leader of the Opposition had time to devote to tricky questions, but the Prime Minister

* New Labour won 418 seats to the Tories' 165, and 12.8 per cent more of the popular vote.

had a country to run. Prime Minister's Question Time would be reduced from two sessions to one each week.[10]

Fresh from his election victory and from his interview at the Palace, Blair entered 10 Downing Street a few minutes after Major departed. Most of the staff, he remarked to himself, did not remember such a thing as a Labour government. He looked into the Cabinet room, observing the Prime Minister's chair, 'the only one with arms on'. In the chair next to that the Cabinet Secretary was seated. 'So', Butler opened, 'now what? We have studied the manifesto and we are ready to get to work on it for you.'[11]

To the surprise of Blair and his staff, Butler was speaking no less than the truth. On the following morning, carrying a large pile of briefs, he greeted the private office staff cheerily. The briefs had been prepared by the Civil Service on Butler's instructions, analysing the New Labour manifesto and preparing papers that dealt with the implementation of each of them, however far-fetched. On the morning of 7 May, six days after the election, Butler invited Blair into his regular 10 a.m. Wednesday meeting of Permanent Secretaries, the 'College of Cardinals'. When Blair said that he would run his government on the basis of ethics and not ideology, the 'cardinals' were 'hugely impressed', a fact that shocked Peter Hennessy, who had expected the more normal scepticism.[12] Blair's Chief of Staff Jonathan Powell commented that, 'far from aiming to frustrate the new government's plans, [civil servants] had to be restrained from taking each component too literally'.[13] For his part, Butler soon realised that the manifesto was no more than a means to be elected. 'They thought it was naïve of the Civil Service to take the manifesto so seriously', he recalled drily.[14]

Initially, despite fears of Blair and his inner circle that the Civil Service had worked too long with one ruling party, the transition was remarkably smooth. Jonathan Powell complimented Butler on its 'elegant' nature, and Blair wrote to him to congratulate him on the 'quite superlative' way in which the changeover had been handled.[15] Butler's greatest concern, according to Powell, was to regularise the position of Blair's principal henchmen in relation to the private office. One irritant, of course, was that Powell's brother Charles had been Thatcher's foreign policy private secretary for eight years – despite the efforts of the Civil Service to remove him by offering him ambassadorships and plum jobs elsewhere. Butler, Jonathan Powell believed, was convinced that there was going to be a similar anomaly with Jonathan aspiring to the position of Blair's Principal Private Secretary. In fact, Powell had no such ambition and, when Butler, as head of the Civil Service, said that, if Powell were to become Principal Private Secretary, he would have to resign from the Labour Party, he refused to do so.[16]

Controversy over the number and roles of special advisers in Downing Street was not new. Harold Wilson had aimed to make No. 10 the powerhouse of his 1964 administration, but the power was in the 'departmental baronies'. By the time Blair arrived, the complement of staff at No. 10 had doubled since Wilson's day, but Major and particularly Blair still believed that the Prime Minister's Office was underpowered. The private office at No. 10 was staffed by the rising stars of the Civil Service, but Butler was acutely aware of the greater demands that would be placed on the service by New Labour; he was also concerned that the younger, slicker New Labour team might outpace the private office in its grasp of information technology. A week before polling day he held a meeting of Cabinet Office staff to make them aware of the demands that a New Labour government would place on them, warning them to be on the top of their game if they were to reassure the new government that they would work as efficiently and as committedly as they had for the Tories.

Then occurred what Peter Hennessy has described as 'the special adviserdom coming into the kingdom'. The process that had started with Wilson and had been developed by Thatcher blossomed under Blair.[17] There came into being a 'new constitutional hybrid – the executive special adviser'. As special advisers could only advise but had no authority over civil servants, Butler suggested at a meeting at Blair's house that an Order in Council be issued.[18] This would create special contracts for Powell and Alastair Campbell, empowering them to issue executive orders. Predictably, Powell saw Butler's actions as reactionary and later commented that 'instead of adjusting the theory to reality, the officials wanted to protect the theory and make an exception for us'.[19]

This necessary formality led to friction with Blair, as Butler was determined that the Civil Service retain the role of the Principal Private Secretary and not allow it to be carried out by a party political fixer. On occasion, he argued, the secretary had to advise the monarch in the event of a hung parliament and it would clearly be inappropriate for that function to be handled by a political appointee. Effectively, with this adjustment of status, Blair had two political appointees and one civil servant as advisers at his elbow – Powell, Campbell and John Holmes, who succeeded Alex Allan as Principal Private Secretary.[20]

Blair succeeded in translating the systems that had worked while Labour was in opposition to his tenure of the Prime Minister's Office, which became stronger than ever before. Not only did he reduce the time given to Prime Minister's Questions; he actually spent less time in the House of Commons than other Prime Ministers. Anthony Seldon makes the perceptive point that, while he reshaped leadership of the party, he was not *of* his party.[21]

Butler observed the development of Blair's attitude towards the Civil Service with interest, initially with guarded optimism. Blair saw himself as a moderniser and planned to modernise the Civil Service, to adapt it to a world that was more political, more 24/7, more in command of the media. Accordingly, Butler recalls,

> he wanted to politicise government because that was the direction the world had taken. So he wanted the Civil Service to do what it did, but to the extent that it was supporting him, he wanted it to do it more swiftly, more light-footedly. Also, he wasn't going to rely on the Civil Service for the things that mattered to him most, that is the political conduct of the Government. Just as he wasn't going to rely on the Civil Service for that, he wasn't going to rely on his colleagues, apart from a very small group in the New Labour cell. That dictated to him that he needed to run things from No. 10 and keep a very firm grip on things there. As far as the Civil Service was concerned, apart from press officers, he was perfectly content to leave Permanent Secretaries where they were and to defend the traditions of the Service rather than attack them. He didn't actually intend to use the Civil Service very much.[22]

Explaining his *modus operandi* to Butler, the Prime Minister said simply: 'It's our job to have the vision and it's up to you, the Civil Service to carry it out.'

When Butler pointed out that it was not quite that simple, that the Civil Service would need to have the necessary resources, Blair was not particularly interested. The truth was that, in a New Labour government, the Civil Service was not intended to be involved in the formulation of policy. Butler believed that this was an inevitable result of New Labour's history as a small cell within the Labour Party. This narrow group had formulated strategy in defiance of party and colleagues and, now in power, perpetuated that policy.

The relative ease with which Blair was able to impose his leadership on No. 10 convinced Mandelson, Powell and Campbell that the antiquated, antediluvian figure of the Cabinet Secretary could be circumvented without difficulty. While they had the greatest respect for his integrity, the 59-year-old Butler, 'Buttleshanks' in their *patois*, was seen as hopelessly outdated. For example, he still believed in the value of government by Cabinet. To Powell, this was 'essentially the death rattle of the old mandarin class'.[23]

When, in New Labour's first week in office, Blair and Brown wanted to announce a decision to give operational independence to the Bank of England without authority from Cabinet, Butler protested. Then, on the Tuesday after the election, the Chancellor authorised a quarter-point raise in interest rates – to 6.25 per cent. The decision was not discussed in Cabinet; only Robin Cook and John Prescott knew, and Brown announced it at a press conference, a gesture that Butler saw as offensive and insulting to Cabinet. He had urged that a decision of such importance be discussed, but Blair and Brown brusquely rejected the suggestion.

Powell's treatise on leadership in the modern age, *The New Machiavelli*, constantly analyses the position of the 'Prince', distinguishing between the leader's role in the United States and in Britain. Unlike the American President, the British Prime Minister has no independent source of power, but depends on the party for parliamentary support and democratic legitimacy. Thus the Cabinet becomes the Premier's visible authentication and the government is only strong if it is united. Collective responsibility is cardinal to Cabinet's role.

Powell argues that a myth has grown up – that Tony Blair disposed of Cabinet government in favour of 'sofa' government, that the well-ordered system whereby the Cabinet Office kept the Cabinet fully informed on all issues and that the Prime Minister operated as *primus inter pares*, the chair of the group, was abandoned. Strong leaders tend to lead, a fact of which Butler was fully aware, having worked in two capacities with Thatcher. The difference between Thatcher and her predecessors, he maintains, was not the degree of her commitment to Cabinet supremacy but that she was a strong Prime Minister, determined to have her way; traditional civil servants' ideal of government by Cabinet was extinct by the end of the 1970s. Furthermore, Powell dismisses it as 'a singularly bad way of making decisions', involving, as it does, agreement among twenty-five people, many of whom are uninformed on the subjects at issue.[24]

On the other hand, Blair and Powell accepted that to get certain things done they needed the Cabinet Committee system. A prime example of this, Butler recalls, was the devolution agenda that Blair delegated to Derry Irvine. That succeeded because Irvine drove it in a Cabinet Committee and the Cabinet Office supported him. It was an example of Cabinet government working in the traditional way, Butler believes, 'but Tony Blair didn't want the Cabinet involved in general policy discussions'. Butler recalled:

> I went on preparing Cabinet Office briefs which were duly circulated. I gave Tony Blair a brief and he took no notice whatsoever. He gave instructions that Cabinet members had to give notice of any question they intended to raise and he would then have Jonathan Powell tell them if they could or could not raise it. In general, Cabinet Ministers were discouraged from raising questions.[25]

The appointment of Powell and Campbell caused some controversy; Blair's two closest advisers were not known for their diplomatic manners. Additionally, the use of the title 'Chief of Staff' with its trans-Atlantic overtones, reminiscent of H. R. Haldeman in the Nixon administration, was unfamiliar in British politics.* Blair later wrote that 'I could not believe, and still don't,

* H. R. ('Bob') Haldeman was the 'gatekeeper' in Nixon's White House, controlling all access to the President. He was forced to resign over the Watergate affair and his involvement in the subsequent cover-up. Margaret Thatcher had a special adviser, David Wolfson, to whom she gave the title of Chief of Staff.

that my predecessors did not have a *de facto* chief of staff, but Jonathan was the first openly acknowledged and nominated one'.[26] Butler's resistance to allowing the position of Principal Private Secretary to become political brought about a compromise. The title was taken first by John Holmes and subsequently by Jeremy Heywood, who worked closely with Powell as Chief of Staff.*

Alastair Campbell, in control of the press office, ran a tight operation. He was horrified at what he saw as amateurism in Whitehall. He, too, came into conflict with Butler as he demanded the replacement or removal by retirement of a number of heads of information in Civil Service departments. In an interview five months after the election, the Cabinet Secretary admitted that there had been 'some bumpy moments'.[27] These included a wide range of issues: Campbell's displeasure at the slowness of Civil Service press offices, Robin Cook's marital problems, and the furore over Bernie Ecclestone's contributions to the Labour Party.

The Ecclestone affair, which blew up in November, concerned the sport of Formula One motor racing, heavily dependent on tobacco company sponsorship and advertising revenue, the proposed ban of tobacco advertising, and Ecclestone's status as an important donor to New Labour. Labour had committed to ban tobacco advertising; throughout the European Union a similar ban was pending. Ecclestone contacted Powell to arrange a meeting with Blair, pointing out the considerable loss to Britain if Formula One racing moved elsewhere. Asian countries, less exercised about a ban on advertising tobacco products, were bidding for its presence. When Ecclestone proposed to make a second donation of £1 million, Blair instructed the Department of Health to 'soft-pedal' on the banning of tobacco advertising and, against Butler's advice, met Ecclestone at Downing Street.

Once the meeting had taken place and the story was leaked, the government came under pressure and a different question was asked: should it return the contribution? Derry Irvine and Gordon Brown said no. Butler and Peter Mandelson felt strongly that they should. Patrick Neill, chair of

* Heywood, in his turn, became Cabinet Secretary in January 2012 and head of the Home Civil Service in September 2014.

the Committee on Standards in Public Life, was consulted and, to Powell's surprise, said that the money should be returned. Campbell had prevailed on the Prime Minister that the donation was critical and that the fallout in the media could be handled. Powell felt simply that 'our sin in this case was largely one of naivety'; Butler, a voice in the wilderness urging caution, felt that the affair had been badly mishandled and that Blair should never have yielded to Powell's advice and met with Ecclestone.[28]

Within New Labour's system of unitary command, where media relations trumped Cabinet solidarity in importance, Cabinet was no more than a part of a network of powerful forces in Whitehall. The Cabinet Office, in Blair's view, would serve government best by operating as an adjudicator, dedicated to effective implementation of the decisions of 'joined-up' government. One member of Blair's staff saw its function as 'our Chief Whip in Whitehall'.[29] As to Cabinet meetings, they were a revelation to the Cabinet Secretary. There were reports from the Leaders of the Commons and the Lords, from the Foreign Secretary, Butler recalled. 'Then after that the discussion was principally whatever story was running in the press and how the Government was going to deal with it. Meetings lasted just thirty to thirty-five minutes and we worried that the press, noting times of entry and exit, would conclude that we weren't doing very much.'[30]

From the beginning of Blair's administration, then, two strands fused to alter dramatically the relations between the Cabinet Secretary and the Prime Minister's office. First, the private office, traditionally the preserve of the Civil Service, became more political. The tendrils of party politics crept into the most recondite corners of the service as Blair's appointed political advisers attended meetings of Permanent Secretaries at Sunningdale. After 1998, beginning a trend that Butler stalwartly resisted, senior civil servants became instruments of the Prime Minister's Office. In the case of cash for questions, Butler had made it clear that the Cabinet Secretary's role was to advise the Prime Minister; meting out punishment was not part of that role. His successor, Sir Richard Wilson, did however act as Blair's hatchet man to seek the resignation of Geoffrey Robinson over his loan of £373,000 to Peter Mandelson.

Such concentration of power in the Prime Minister's Office drew accusations that Britain no longer had a Prime Minister, *primus inter pares* in Cabinet, but a species of president. Blair and his supporters vehemently denied this, arguing that governments today cannot afford the time involved in traditional methods of government by Cabinet. To the accusation that he paid less attention to Cabinet than his predecessors, Blair would counter by citing Margaret Thatcher's disdain for Cabinet. Blair thus likened himself more to Thatcher than to Major, whose Cabinet had been inefficient, lame and leaky.

Blair's irreverence, the more offensive to Butler because it contained elements of truth, led to the accusation that Blair operated what the media labelled as 'sofa government', a casual chatty caucus of political advisers, press office and pollsters at which no notes were taken. The barb hit home and Blair was energetic in attempting to defuse the accusation:

> In the light of what later became quite a vigorous disagreement about the nature of decision-making in my government and the so-called 'sofa' style of it ... I should say that right at the outset I found Robin thoroughly professional, courteous and supportive. He didn't like some of the innovations, but he did his level best to make them work. He was impartial in the best traditions of the British Civil Service, intelligent and deeply committed to the country.[31]

Be that as it may, Butler, respectful of traditional forms of government, was offended by New Labour's decision-making process, in which the media rather than the Cabinet were informed first. This led, inevitably, to meetings between Blair, Powell, Campbell and Anji Hunter* at which decisions were taken on the presentation of issues – a more important aspect than the old-style method of obtaining agreement in Cabinet. The number of special advisers had grown gradually from a total of thirty in fifteen departments in Harold Wilson's government to thirty-eight under John Major. In

* Angela ('Anji') Hunter was a friend of Blair when both were in their teens in Scotland. She began working for him after gaining a first-class degree from the Brighton Polytechnic. She became director of government relations in 1997 and was known as the most influential unelected person in Downing Street. Colleagues have written that her closeness to Blair was greatly resented by Mrs Blair. See (e.g.) Tom Bower, *Broken Vows: Tony Blair, The Tragedy of Power* (London: Faber & Faber, 2016), pp. 49–50, 127.

Blair's first year in Downing Street, the number almost doubled to seventy. The unholy involvement of special advisers with the national press astounded the more conventional Cabinet Secretary. He watched, at once fascinated and appalled, by this *modus operandi*.

To illustrate the atmosphere in the Blair inner circle, Butler adduces not *Yes, Minister* but the greatly more hostile *The Thick of It*. This is a savage, fast-moving television comedy whose principal character, Malcolm Tucker, was modelled on Alastair Campbell. This complex individual is short-tempered, aggressive, foul-mouthed, abusive and volatile, but totally dedicated to the party line. His like had not been seen in Downing Street before.

Campbell's predecessors had been far from acquiescent functionaries. Joe Haines, Butler recalls, was a bullying press secretary, forever threatening the press. Bernard Ingham was a bruiser, but he treated the press fairly. New Labour totally changed government's relations with the media. Previously, there had been even distribution of information among the national papers. Butler was appalled as he observed the press office set itself up as monopoly suppliers, making sure that everyone had a turn at getting exclusive leaks – on the condition that they reported positively. By the time they came to power, he observed, New Labour had perfected its system for handling the press. First there would be a selective leak of information; next an announcement; then a minister on TV handling the situation (for example in a hard hat). Ingham was outraged by this style of news management. Butler, inherently distrustful of the media, was more sympathetic. One instance of news management remains particularly vivid for him:

> If a damaging story was about to break, New Labour would drown it with a better or a bigger story. Campbell was an expert at that. When Peter Mandelson said that the national minimum wage would only apply to those over 25, an outcry threatened. New Labour's response was to release a story that Tony Blair was furious with Tony Banks for describing William Hague as 'a foetus' in order to drown the story.[32]

Relations between Civil Service officials and Blair's entourage were, unsurprisingly, formally friendly but guarded. Both sides were keenly aware of the philosophical gulf that separated them and equally alert to any erosion of their position. Underlying it all was the shared knowledge that their enforced cohabitation with an inherited Cabinet Secretary would end after eight months. In Alastair Campbell's diaries, Butler is treated with respect and affection, but it is abundantly clear that Campbell had little compunction in circumventing or simply disregarding him. Like Haines and Donoughue twenty-three years before, he was pleasantly surprised not to be dealing with a dyed-in-the-wool reactionary. By 1997, however, politics had changed enough for Campbell not to need the invaluable guidance that Butler had given Harold Wilson's private office. As Butler recalled:

> There was no doubt that Tony Blair's government was more 'political' than its predecessors. One reason for this was that New Labour had been a small cell within the Labour Party and its protagonists constituted a narrow circle, which excluded most members of the Cabinet. It was further fragmented by the split between the 'Blairites' and the 'Brownites'. My relations with the inner group around Tony Blair were generally cordial – I particularly enjoyed conversations with Peter Mandelson – but I did not become one of them.[33]

Inevitably, there were tensions. At the first Cabinet meeting of the new government on 8 May, a number of ministers raised issues independently. The Prime Minister's reaction was to take Powell and Butler into an adjoining room and lambast them for allowing unscheduled issues to be raised. This must not, he told them sternly, be allowed to happen again; in future he must be briefed in advance. Thus, to the Cabinet Secretary's horror, Cabinet meetings became mere rubber-stamping of components of the New Labour message. Cabinet became, in Butler's words, 'a weekly meeting of political friends'.[34] Apart from Gordon Brown, the members of the Cabinet were subordinates; Cabinet itself was merely one element of the variegated power at the centre.

Jonathan Powell expressed the *Weltanschauung* of New Labour accurately. In his calculations, No. 10, the Cabinet Office, even the Treasury, were pieces on the governmental chessboard. The first two elements of the executive were not the sole elements at the centre, an annoyance if the Treasury is at odds with 10 Downing Street – as it was throughout the Blair administration.[35] After Butler's departure, Powell proposed an 'Office of Management and the Budget', along American lines, but did not proceed, as it would have alienated Gordon Brown. Another solution to what Powell perceived as the power vacuum at the centre was to create a separate department of the Prime Minister, capable of fighting battles with various departments. This became a live issue with Butler's successor, Richard Wilson, in 1999. Wilson, who became personally and philosophically closer to New Labour than Butler, believed that the drive to create a Prime Minister's department was the result of Butler's allowing himself to become too distant from No. 10.[36]

Wilson's comment appears to suggest that Butler was circling the wagons in a last stand against the erosion of Cabinet power. That would have been a pointless exercise; since 1993, when Blair and Gordon Brown visited the Clinton team that had recently won the American election, the Prime Minister had learned and applied the vital lesson that the leader alone must be in control of the message to the media. Out of deference to more traditional Labour elements, to avoid the accusation of class treachery, he needed to involve Brown in decisions – and the two met frequently – but it would have been dangerous to extend the policy franchise any further. Butler may not have invented the expression 'sofa government' but, in his view, the cap fitted perfectly. It was not that the Cabinet Secretary distanced himself from No. 10; rather No. 10 dispensed with the services of the Cabinet Office.

On 31 August 1997, four months after the election, the Princess of Wales was killed in a horrific car crash in a Paris tunnel. Butler, it will be recalled, was a close friend both of Robert Fellowes, Private Secretary to the Queen and brother-in-law of the Princess, and of John Birt, the Director-General of the BBC.[37] When he heard the news early in the morning, he rang Fellowes and learned that he was organising a Queen's Flight aircraft to take Prince Charles, Jane and Sarah, Diana's sisters, to Paris and to bring back Diana's body. He later spoke to Birt, who agreed to let him know if BBC journalists reported on anything which the government or the royal family should be doing but weren't. Thus, Butler learned that BBC reporters had picked up on the fact that the Princess's body was going to be taken to a private mortuary and thought that this was inappropriate. He passed this on to Fellowes, which led to the body being taken instead to the Chapel Royal. This was fortunate, Butler recalls, as 'the fuss later in the week about a flag not being flown at half-mast over Buckingham Palace showed how easy it was to put a foot wrong in the highly-charged state of public opinion'.[38]

The contrast between the reactions of the royal family and that of Blair was symptomatic of the gulf between the traditionalist generation, of which Butler was a member, and the more modern, idolising public that demanded orchestrated mourning and public demonstrations of emotion. The latter were ably activated by the Prime Minister. It was he, not the royal family, who touched the nation, whose brief eulogy was totally congruent with the public mood. 'Tony Blair', an article in *The Times* enthused, 'has this week taken on the mantle of Disraeli and Baldwin as a bridge between the people and the Palace.'[39]

The wholesale outpouring of grief at the Princess's death astounded Butler. Ensconced in the Cabinet Office, he received a call from a Permanent Secretary, who urged him to walk from his office, across St James's Park to the Mall. It was a remarkable sight: from every direction lines of people moved silently to lay bouquets and messages along the Mall. It was, he recalled, an unforgettable scene, the drama of which was heightened by the complete silence. 'I had never before been among so many people in such unbroken quiet', he later wrote.

The week that followed was a difficult one for the Queen. Her instinct to stay at Balmoral to be with her two bereaved grandsons was misunderstood; her adherence to protocol in the matter of flying the Royal Standard at half-mast was resented. The popular version of events has been much influenced by the film *The Queen*, in which New Labour – and in particular Alastair Campbell – are portrayed as unsympathetic to Her Majesty's travails. Almost to his own surprise, Butler acknowledges that friends at Buckingham Palace told him how very helpful Alastair Campbell had been. 'He may not have had a high opinion of the quick-footedness of royal courtiers', he admits, 'but in addition to helping the Prime Minister with an immediate statement on the Princess'[s] death which hit exactly the right note, he gave invaluable advice to the Palace during the week.'[40]

The few months that Butler served New Labour were lively, peppered with friction but, within the inevitable limitations, productive. The Prime Minister respected his Cabinet Secretary as an individual but, having little regard for the functions of the office, excluded him from the decision-making process. As Butler recalled, with tactful litotes, 'Blair generally looked first to his political staff for advice.' Blair went on record, in a letter and at a final Cabinet meeting, in complimenting Butler on ten years of service, adding that 'he had probably faced no more challenging task than to usher in the new Government'.

For his part, Butler recognised certain virtues in New Labour's method of operation. In an interview with Donald MacIntyre, political editor at *The Independent*, Butler compared the methods of Thatcher and Blair:

> It's a great contrast with Margaret Thatcher. Tony Blair would be very happy to say, 'Look, this is where I want to get to in a year's time; you boys go off and deliver it for me and really don't bother me more than you have to with the details.' Margaret Thatcher would absolutely be worrying about the details the whole time, too much.[41]

As he prepared to hand over his office to a successor, Butler was fully aware that the role of the Cabinet Secretary would need to change. If the trend was towards a more American, 'presidential' style of government in which Cabinet Ministers played subordinate roles, while policy and 'message' were dictated and imposed by a Prime Minister's department, then he was the last in a line of generalist, apolitical mandarins. Almost twenty years later, in 2016, Cabinet Secretary Sir Jeremy Heywood was described as 'the most influential official in Britain in the last twenty years',[42] but he operated within the Prime Minister's inner circle, a West Wing-like team overseen by Oliver Letwin, described as the 'Gandalf' of Cameron's 2010 election campaign.[43]

Before Blair would even consider the list of possible successors prepared for him, a broader question demanded attention: should the roles of Cabinet Secretary and head of the Home Civil Service be split? Butler felt strongly that they should not. Blair, undecided on the issue, asked Butler and Derry Irvine, the Lord Chancellor, to debate the question in front of him. Butler duly arranged an informal evening at Half Moon Lane, preceded by the debate, with Mandelson and Blair as the audience. Butler's argument, a pragmatic appraisal that might have been tailored for the Blair government, was that

> the Cabinet Secretary's access to the Prime Minister was an asset to the leadership of the Civil Service and that the leverage over other Permanent Secretaries which the Headship of the Civil Service gave to the Cabinet Secretary was an asset in getting the Government's policies implemented.[44]

Blair was persuaded and, after some discussion, chose Richard Wilson, then Permanent Secretary at the Home Office. A mild, cerebral man, perhaps of a less competitive nature than Butler, he was presented by Blair as a 'moderniser'. Peter Hennessy records that Wilson was chosen as most likely to appeal to Blair's style. He gave the impression of 'thinking aloud, almost elliptically', whereas Butler practised 'a terse briskness, his conversation, though engaging, driven by a capacity to speak in paragraphs in the manner of an oral memo'.[45]

Blair had initially wanted Andrew Turnbull to succeed Butler, while Powell had been urging him to appoint Michael Bichard, the Permanent Secretary at the Department of Education and Employment. Powell was confident that Bichard, who was critical of the Civil Service, would reform it along lines approved by Powell. Butler advised Blair that this would be a disaster, as Bichard had no deep background in the Civil Service or Cabinet Secretary's activities, whereas Richard Wilson had been groomed for this. 'Blair thought that this would be a safer appointment', Butler recalled. 'So this was one battle that I won over Jonathan Powell.'[46]

Nearly twenty years after his retirement from the Civil Service, Butler looked back and surveyed the succession – almost the reverse of the 'apostolic succession' that Robert Armstrong had spoken of. By 2005, Blair had appointed the Cabinet Secretary most suited to his needs. 'Gus O'Donnell was much less formal', Butler chuckled:

> In the modernity rankings there was myself; then Richard Wilson who was more modern; Andrew Turnbull, more modern still; then Gus O'Donnell,

thoroughly up-to-date. Quick on his feet, good at dealing with the press, agreeable, much more of the style that New Labour wanted. The biggest change of modernity versus tradition came with Gus O'Donnell.*

There was, in truth, a curious paradox to O'Donnell's appointment. In eight years, Blair had been served by three different Cabinet Secretaries – Butler, Wilson and Andrew Turnbull. By 2005, when the identity of the next Cabinet Secretary was a subject of obsessive speculation in Whitehall, *The Times* predicted, in remarkably prescient fashion, that O'Donnell would succeed Turnbull. The grounds for that prediction were that, aged fifty-two, he was the youngest of four candidates and that the office needed 'an element of continuity to restore its status'.[47] Between 1997 and 2005, two Cabinet Secretaries were stepping stones between the 'Old Guard', represented by Butler, and O'Donnell, emblematic of the new style favoured by New Labour.

By the time O'Donnell was appointed, the world was very different from the one Butler had known while in post eight years earlier. The explosive growth of the Internet, of social media, the 24/7 nature of news – all combined to create a very different environment. O'Donnell observed with a smile:

> Robin was appointed at a time when the Cabinet Secretary was seen but not heard. That was different by my time. The consequence of the growth of media and technology is that a lot of people are competing for media space. One's media profile is increasingly important.[48]

The handling of the media was second nature to Blair – as it was to O'Donnell. In the climate at the end of the millennium, it was increasingly difficult for the Cabinet Secretary to protest that he wanted no part of politics. O'Donnell expressed it thus:

> The Cabinet Secretary has to be good at silence when he disagrees with

* Interview, Lord Butler, 14 June 2016. The distance travelled from tradition to modernity was underscored by achievement on the sports field. Butler had won an Oxford Blue for rugby football ('a thugs' game played by gentlemen'). O'Donnell won his Blue for association football ('a gentleman's game played by thugs').

> the Prime Minister. Also he must understand the politics involved and be analytical, saying 'This is a good idea but there are several political considerations.' I would stress to Gordon Brown that there were political aspects, that he needed to talk to Ed Balls or David Miliband about the political dimension of issues.[49]

For Butler, there was little pain of parting as he reached mandatory retirement age in January 1998. Would he have resigned if his term had stretched beyond 1997? He thought not:

> I don't think so. What Blair would have wanted, I do not know. Jonathan Powell and Alastair Campbell would have pressured him to have someone more up-to-date than 'Old Buttleshanks' but Tony Blair and I got on very well. They might have offered me an attractive post, with a peerage thrown in, if they wanted to move me on, and I would not have minded if that was what they wanted. I would never have simply resigned, but I do think that the eight-month tenure suited everyone.[50]

Wilson's appointment was announced in July, and through the autumn Butler and Wilson met to introduce the new Cabinet Secretary to the scope of the job. Although Wilson had been groomed for just this appointment, he was surprised and awed by the range of the Cabinet Secretary's responsibilities – both actual and implicit.[51]

For Butler, an acquaintanceship with Downing Street that had begun with Edward Heath and had taken many different forms over a quarter of a century was coming to an end. Jill commissioned Peter Brookes to create a cartoon showing her husband, as faithful butler, serving drinks to an ill-assorted festive gathering of Heath, Wilson, Thatcher, Major and Blair.*

Butler had served the last three as Cabinet Secretary and, on his retirement, he was asked how they would react if one said something critical about them. After a moment's thought, he replied: 'Well, Mrs Thatcher would be

* Peter Brookes is a widely published English cartoonist whose work appears regularly on the leader page of *The Times*. By coincidence, Jill was teaching his son Ben, who was in the sixth form at Alleyn's.

offended and would bark back, "What do you mean?" John Major would be sad and ask, "Oh dear, do you really think so?" Tony Blair would agree wholeheartedly, but you would never know if he really meant it.'[52]

After thirty-six years as a civil servant, Butler could be fairly certain that the job he had aspired to and obtained, at the pinnacle of the service, would never be quite the same again.

CHAPTER 17

PASSING THE TORCH, 1997

WHEN BUTLER RETIRED FROM the Civil Service, he left two connected but very different jobs – head of the Home Civil Service and Cabinet Secretary. The two roles had not always been held by the same individual; not until 1981 did one man – Robert Armstrong – fill both. Butler, therefore, was the seventh Cabinet Secretary, but only the second to have such broad responsibilities. Of the two jobs, that of head of the Home Civil Service, while being the less glamorous, had the longer-term effect on Whitehall.

On 24 September 1997, a bare five months after the Labour landslide at the general election, Butler, soon to retire as head of the Home Civil Service, spoke at Church House to a seminar of academics on the Economic and Social Research Council (ESRC) about the modern Civil Service and his thirty-six-year career in it. He opened by expressing regret – relevant at that moment in his case – that there was too little free movement between Whitehall and academe. His original ambition had been to replicate the American model, in which there was continual movement between government and the Brookings Institution. The initiative never really gained momentum, as British academics were not interested; some progress had been made, however, at senior levels, thanks to open recruitment.

On the research side, the ESRC had been 'a satisfying fulfilment of what [he] had in mind in increasing the access of academics in public administration to Whitehall departments',[1] an innovation of which he was proud. This seminar at Church House was the chosen occasion for him to look back at the changes that had taken place in the thirty-six years that he had served in Whitehall. 'I am in the last few weeks of my Civil Service career', he said:

> I will spare you the nostalgia, but it is a moment for reflecting on how much the Civil Service has changed since I joined it. In the year I joined, 1961, 126 fast-stream entrants passed the Civil Service exam, of whom 118 were men and eight were women. Of 90 actually appointed, 77 were Oxbridge and 13 were non-Oxbridge. Eighty-seven had arts degrees and three had science degrees.
>
> The report of the Civil Service Commissioners was able to say: 'At all levels we have much to offer – the sense of service to the community, work of broad scope and variety, the daily comradeship of like-minded men of tried and trusted ability.' Well, at least it was true.

In 1961, the service was divided into three classes: administrative, executive and clerical. The age limit for entry into the fast stream of the administrative class was twenty-eight. The generalist was still in the ascendant and it was still possible to join by sitting a purely academic examination in the subject studied at university. To the younger members of Butler's audience, this must have sounded like an unrepealed statute from the Middle Ages.

By 1996, of the 177 people recommended that year for appointment 110 were men and 67 were women; 81 were from Oxford or Cambridge, outnumbered by the 96 from other universities; 134 had degrees in Arts subjects, against 43 with degrees in science and technology. There were fast-stream competitions for generalists, engineers, scientists, economists, accountants and statisticians. Almost 10 per cent of the successful candidates came from within the service, from levels corresponding to the old executive or clerical classes, although these classifications had long been abolished. An equally important innovation had been the admission to the fast stream of many individuals with experience in industry, commerce, academe and other parts of the public sector. No longer was it almost universal to spend one's entire working life in the service. No longer were those who did not do so known as 'mavericks'.

Between the Northcote–Trevelyan Report and the comprehensive review of the Fulton Report, 114 years elapsed. In thirty-one years, a seismic revolution had taken place. For twenty-six of those years – since his association with the CPRS in 1971 – Butler had been closely involved at the epicentre;

for the last ten years he had been principally responsible for the changes themselves.

The changes in type, gender and academic discipline of applicant, however, were only part of the story. Butler's greatest achievement lay in having broken down the barriers that separated the service from the rest of the community and, at the same time, having preserved the five principles that became known as the 'Butler Tests', which he summarised to the Treasury and Civil Service Committee of the House of Commons – the five essential elements indispensable in a Civil Service official: impartiality, integrity, objectivity, selection and promotion on merit, and accountability through ministers to Parliament.

His fear had been that 'modernisation' would be accompanied by demands for politicisation, that as the office of Prime Minister became – or was perceived to be – more 'presidential', a Prime Minister's department, along the lines of Washington's West Wing, would grow, flourish and ultimately overcome the tradition of impartiality that he believed to be the greatest asset of the service. The breaking down of barriers and the simultaneous maintenance of values posed the greatest challenge.

The process of politicisation had its genesis in the creation of Harold Wilson's Policy Unit when he returned to Downing Street in 1974; the management Rubicon crossed was that the principals of the Policy Unit had civil servants working for them. To achieve this, the Cabinet Secretary had been required to add a modification to an Order in Council to legitimise three special advisers in executive roles, a procedural nicety that Blair regarded as a 'finicky detail', but which, in Butler's view, and that of the government's legal advisers, had been necessary. Butler's goal was to make the government fireproof against the charge that they were politicising the Civil Service. Unfortunately, however many times he denied that the charge that this was happening under New Labour, the media and the government's critics continued to level the accusation against Blair and his inner circle.

On the wider role of the service, as Butler enumerated the changes that had taken place, the scale of the achievement became clear. There had been no Civil Service College in 1961 – a training in the classics had been enough. Butler, in fact, had attended what had been only the second training course in economics at the Centre for Administrative Studies, designed for fast-stream entrants, in 1964.

Contacts with the outside world had been suspect in the 1960s. The purity of Civil Service judgement and necessary impartiality might be corrupted by overly close proximity to gentlemen of commerce – or, for that matter, politicians. The variegated make-up of the Think Tank had helped to change that belief, bringing generalists and specialists, officials and entrepreneurs into contact with each other. Once again, Butler had been fortunate to be among the first group to experience such exposure.

Another cause of widespread alarm in the Civil Service when Butler had joined in 1961 was the press. It was an unwritten rule that the service operated *sub rosa*, and when Anthony Howard was appointed Whitehall correspondent of *The Times*, officers had been instructed not to speak to him. It took Peter Hennessy, a balanced and sophisticated Whitehall watcher, to break down bureaucratic barriers and persuade mandarins that a Whitehall correspondent could actually be used by the service to its advantage. By the time that Wilson took over from Butler, the press had become a necessary and tolerated evil. Wilson, when asked, several years after his tenure as head of the service, how the job had changed, responded that, while it was always changing, the only thing that had fundamentally altered his working environment was the pressure of the media. He explained:

> If you're a good bureaucrat you would like Ministers to take decisions based on the facts, the options, the arguments, costs – all considerations – and to have adequate time to reflect, discuss and take a decision. That's what your heart yearns for, but when the media are at the door, bellowing for breaking news and headlines … That pressure from the media on government for answers is now with us to stay … It's in the public interest that Ministers are able to reach decisions on an informal basis, rather than shooting from the hip.[2]

The changes that Butler had seen – and been partly responsible for – could be summed up in the word 'integration'. Instead of remaining a remote and impenetrable monolith, the service had become 'user-friendly' in a number of ways. From publishing a comprehensive telephone directory to maintaining a dialogue with 'cultures outside the service' and achieving a balance between the needs of government and those of the private sector, for example in regulations for motor vehicles, the service had become a familiar and collaborative member of the community. Medium-term to long-term attachments outside the service had not resulted in civil servants being poached by private sector companies. Instead, they had returned to Whitehall with a better understanding of 'the joint endeavour in which UK plc is involved'.

Potentially the most fundamental change was the move towards recruitment from the outside. Not only was contact to be allowed with outsiders; outsiders were to be allowed inside. The first movement in that direction had been the appointment of chief executive posts in the Next Steps agencies, but subsequently even posts of Permanent Secretaries had been advertised for outside competition. In the previous year, sixty-three senior posts – Permanent Secretaries and one rung below – had been advertised. His own job, he noted, had not been one such, as the internal field was very strong.

The procedure and results of such outside competition was bound to evolve, as the concept of a job within the service being the only one that an individual undertook in his career was less dominant. It was entirely possible that senior officials might leave the service, add to their experience and reputation outside, and then apply for an advertised senior post, bringing to the job a broader range of practical knowledge and experience than previous candidates.

It would have been immodest of Butler to claim credit for initiating such structural changes, the greater integration of the service into the community. Instead, he was grateful for the opportunities offered by the chronology. He regarded himself as fortunate to have been head of the service at the time that the Next Steps initiative was being adopted. It matched the aspiration of managers for greater autonomy of management. Most particularly, he expressed his satisfaction at having been able to hold the post for ten years – 'a rare opportunity in these restless times'.

His address paid well-deserved tribute to two of the architects of the new service, without whose efforts fundamental change might easily have been blocked for a generation. The first, Sir Peter Kemp, the first project manager of

Next Steps, had been doggedly effective in handling the delicate manoeuvres necessary to implement long-term, lasting reform. When, in 1992, John Major asked Waldegrave to set up the new Department of Public Service and Science, he was given Kemp as Permanent Secretary, whom he considered rather past his prime and unsuited to the job. He asked Kemp to take on wider responsibilities, which Kemp was reluctant to do. Waldegrave accordingly asked Butler for Richard Mottram, who was at the Ministry of Defence. Butler agreed but, having no other suitable position open, asked Kemp to take early retirement, a request that permanently soured relations between the two.* Waldegrave, however, was impressed that, despite the popular misconception, ministers could actually exercise decisive influence over Civil Service appointments.[3]

As forward thinking and as committed as Kemp to the Agency principle was Sir Terry Burns, the Permanent Secretary at the Treasury. By delegating much of the responsibility for day-to-day operations, Burns had enabled the Treasury to focus on strategic planning and allocation of resources.

Butler reminded his listeners of the scepticism that had greeted Kemp's prediction that over three-quarters of the Civil Service would be organised on Next Steps principles. At first, the number of agencies was so small that all the chief executives could have fitted in a single taxi. Four years later, there were more than 140 of them. Nor were the reforms brought about in a vacuum. To add solid purpose to the stated objectives, John Major's dedication to the Citizen's Charter had provided a measuring rod of the value of the various initiatives. The process of 'integration' of the service into the broader management of Britain had been achieved in a remarkably short time. As head, Butler had been fortunate to have such dedicated and determined lieutenants.

The alliance of Prime Minister and Cabinet Secretary in the quest for transparency in all areas of government had been the driving force behind the reform. In the early stages, while Peter Middleton was Permanent Secretary at the Treasury, there was tension between it and the Cabinet Office. Kemp felt that Middleton was determined to scotch his Next Steps ideas.

---

* The delicate question of Butler's asking Kemp to take early retirement is addressed in the *Times* obituary for Kemp (2 July 2008).

When Middleton retired in 1991 and was replaced by Terry Burns, relations improved. The basic issues that Burns addressed urgently were how to control expenditure while decentralisation and delegation were taking place, and how to rectify the disparities between the salary scale of the Civil Service and the proposed salary packages for Next Steps agencies. At the same time, Michael Heseltine joined the widening circle of the debate, urging more movement between the Civil Service and the private sector, movement that would not occur unless civil servants understood that, far from impeding their careers, it might even improve their prospects of promotion.

Considerable dexterity was required in balancing the drive for efficiency and responsiveness to public needs with the principles that Butler regarded as absolutes: his 'Tests' alongside the maintenance of morale in the service. There were anxieties about the survival of the service's traditions, the preservation of horizontal links that might be eroded in the drive for results by vertical management. It was vital that the democratic accountability of ministers not be lessened by the reforms. He was satisfied that none of the valued traditions or ethical principles of the service need be at risk.

This debate had continued through late 1993 and early 1994, culminating in the White Paper *Continuity and Change*, released in July 1994.[4] The opening paragraphs stated in blunt terms the challenge facing the service: 'For many years the British Civil Service has had a high reputation, nationally and internationally, for its standards of integrity, impartiality and loyal service to the Government of the day'.[5]

The service was being challenged to provide high-quality services at an affordable price. Greater transparency had been introduced in many ways 'within the constitutional principle that it is Ministers who are accountable to Parliament for all that their departments (including agencies) do'. Devolution would continue, specifically including:

- continued exploitation of the benefits of competition
- further delegation of responsibility for pay and grading
- allowing departments to create their own management structures
- further reduction of numbers (32,000 fewer employees than in January 1993)[6]

When Butler gave Permanent Secretaries a preview of the White Paper on 20 June, the reaffirmation of the service's traditional values was the vital element in the mix. Major and Butler had succeeded, with no little help from Waldegrave, Kemp and Kenneth Clarke, in achieving a minor revolution. The radical nature of the reforms was not lost on the media, who were amazed that the White Paper 'goes further towards shaking up the civil service than anything Lady Thatcher dared to propose'.[7]

In his 1997 address, Butler stressed that the service was dedicated to continual improvement of its services; the revolution in information technology provided new opportunities. The service could learn from other countries and still maintain that increasingly rare aspect of its tradition – its non-political nature. In recent years, the increased exposure of civil servants via the media had increased their identification with ministers and with the government in power and, consequently, there were concerns that the service could not avoid becoming politicised. This, Butler maintained, could be avoided:

> There is no doubt in my mind that a permanent and non-political Civil Service is an important guarantee of integrity, providing as it does advisers to Ministers who can afford to take a long view of the national interest, while professionally committed to serve the Government of the people's choice. That successive governments have taken the same view is a tribute to the professionalism and adaptability of the Civil Service in a fast-changing world.

The second responsibility from which he stepped away on retirement was that of Cabinet Secretary. The demands of that job had also changed significantly during his tenure – and continued to evolve under his successor, Sir Richard Wilson.[8] During the time that those two Cabinet Secretaries were in office – from 1988 to 2002 – there was the most marked movement from Cabinet government to a more presidential style of government. This, naturally, had a considerable effect on the nature of the Cabinet Secretary's role. A further contributing factor was that, whereas Butler's predecessor Robert Armstrong had served only Margaret Thatcher from 1979 to 1987, Butler served no fewer than three Prime Ministers in his term. As Armstrong pointed out, serving different Prime Ministers – he chose Heath and Wilson as examples – was akin to having different jobs. Butler agreed that the role changed with the Prime Ministers, explaining:

> Margaret Thatcher, by the time I became Cabinet Secretary, was very well established, was predominant in the Cabinet with a huge national and international reputation. She was more tired than when I had been her Principal Private Secretary … no less acute but … more abrupt in taking decisions and more dependent on people in her private office and in the end one might say that that was her undoing over Europe and the council tax. Then John Major arrived … I think he wanted to re-establish Cabinet government, to be less dominant and encourage Cabinet discussion. But by this time the Cabinet was not as self-disciplined as it should have been … Then Tony Blair arrived, which was an exciting time for the Civil Service – a change of government after 18 years and we wanted to show that we'd serve a Labour government as commitedly as we'd served Conservatives and handled the transition. It was a challenging but also exciting time.[9]

Concerning the differences between the roles of head of the Home Civil Service and Cabinet Secretary, what had impressed him most was the difference between the profiles required for each job:

> I and other Cabinet Secretaries could deal with management issues because we had easy access to the PM. One of the most difficult things is that Cab Sec is a behind-the-scenes post, whereas as head of the Home Civil Service you are much more visible. You have to stand up for the service. I didn't find combining the two posts difficult in terms of the time or the demands but publicly standing up for the Civil Service while also performing a behind-the-scenes role was much more difficult.[10]

In the past, the tradition had been that even the slightest visibility of the head of the Civil Service was to be discouraged. Certainly Edward Bridges, Norman Brook and Burke Trend had been well-concealed figures and, as Peter Hennessy comments, it took Westland and the *Spycatcher* affair to bring

Armstrong out of the shadows. With a more intrusive press corps and a very different ethic as to what was printable, scandals such as Matrix Churchill and the Aitken/Ritz affair inevitably projected the Cabinet Secretary into the limelight in a manner unknown to his predecessors.

As with his experience leading to his being head of the service, so Butler's experience prior to 1987 could not have been better tailored to fit his role as Cabinet Secretary. He had an intimate knowledge of how No. 10 worked under different Prime Ministers – first as Private Secretary, later as Principal Private Secretary – and was able to observe relations between Downing Street and the Cabinet from the perspective of the Premier. As the size of the Prime Minister's Office increased, and positions previously occupied by civil servants were filled by political sympathisers, he was better able to assess the applicability of the 'Butler Tests'.

He was also at the centre when two significant innovations came to pass: first, the creation of the Think Tank in 1971 and, three years later, Wilson's formation of the Policy Unit when Labour won the 1974 election. In the latter case, working with Bernard Donoughue and Joe Haines, neither of whom was predisposed to be tolerant of public-school-educated mandarins, he gained the respect of both and was described by Donoughue as 'the very best kind of civil servant'.[11]

Robert Armstrong had described the job of Cabinet Secretary as that of the chief engineer on the ship of state, who ensured that the machinery worked, that the Prime Minister and the ministers on the bridge could pull the levers, that these were connected up to something and that the government responded. Both Armstrong and Butler believed firmly in the responsibility of the Cabinet Secretary to the entire Cabinet. As one scholar wrote of the Cabinet Office, 'with its commitment to supporting the collective processes of British government, [it] also helped to check the pretensions of prime ministers to becoming presidential'.[12]

In this role also, Butler was confronted by trends that threatened to erode the principles on which the Civil Service function was founded. He saw those dangers very clearly but, as he had with Wilson's political appointees twenty-three years before, managed to square the circle, preserving the essential values of the Civil Service, while serving the government to the best of his ability.

When Butler spoke to the academics of the ESRC in September 1997, Sir Richard Wilson had known for two months that he was to succeed him. The dual nature of the role was relatively new (since 1981), and Butler was able to give Wilson a more detailed picture of the job that he had received from Armstrong, as Wilson recalled:

> Through the autumn I had a series of meetings with Robin Butler, during which he alerted me to questions, told me his view and said, 'It will be for you to decide'. I looked slightly paler. He was very generous in helping me. We both recognised that the roles – as it was then, Cabinet Secretary and Head of the Home Civil Service – covered a broad span and we both knew from our own experience that it was a question of following Government policy and also being there for the Government whenever anything needed attention. The position now – with the two roles separated – is quite different. It's harking back to the old régime.[13]

Wilson may be allowed a touch of nostalgic hyperbole, but the old regime has been supplanted for good. The Civil Service that Butler joined in 1961 and Wilson in 1966 would be unrecognisable in 21st-century Whitehall. Both men were aware of that in 1997. Robin Butler (Harrow and Oxford) and Richard Wilson (Radley and Cambridge) are, at the time of writing, the last Cabinet Secretaries with the educational background that was once *de rigueur* in the administrative class. The Butler legacy, continued by Wilson, has been to modernise an archaic institution and to equip it as never before to preserve traditional standards and principles while maintaining its strength to deter and prevent erosion of the system the Cabinet Office was created to serve and protect. That is a considerable achievement.

Perhaps the most remarkable aspect of the programme of reform that Butler achieved is its low-key inevitability. Everything was done with the active support of the Prime Minister and without the resistance – if not always the wholehearted support – of Permanent Secretaries. The architect of the reforms, a symbol of the establishment, achieved devolution that exceeded anything attempted even by Margaret Thatcher; he preserved the sacrosanct principles of the service and, at the same time, opened the way for even more far-reaching reform. His legacy in every aspect of his two responsibilities – as head of the Home Civil Service and as Cabinet Secretary – was pivotal. He fought hard to maintain the worthwhile traditions of the service, acting as a cohesive element among Permanent Secretaries to resist the proposals of Michael Heseltine. He maintained an enduring respect for the vital role of the Cabinet, even as that role was being eroded by New Labour. He pointed the way forward, conscious of the need for streamlining and devolution, confident that he had done as much as he could in a ten-year span.

Those achievements – and the philosophy behind them – were applauded by his colleagues. Speaking for himself and other Under-Secretaries, Sir Michael Partridge, Permanent Secretary at the Department of Social Security, wrote to Butler:

> From the start of your years as Head of the Civil Service, all of us were struck by the different approach from all of your predecessors, great though they were in their own way. You really did bring a new and modern approach to CS management, treating us as genuine colleagues and sharers in it, and encouraging a collegiate approach to our problems.

In a paragraph that must have given intense satisfaction, Partridge complimented him on 'managing so smooth a transition between Governments of very different approaches' and 'the securing of Richard [Wilson] as your successor … the beneficial effects of which will be seen for many years ahead'.[14] For his part, Wilson commented that 'it will be a hard act to follow the outstanding record of Sir Robin Butler and I look forward to working with Sir Robin over the next five months to prepare the way for succeeding him'.[15]

The last few months in the job were taken up with what the outgoing Cabinet Secretary termed 'the normal obsequies'. Farewell tours, parties, dinners, a private dinner given by Mr and Mrs Blair on 15 December in 11 Downing Street. That event, attended by, *inter alios*, Terry and Anne Burns, John and Jane Birt, and Richard and Caro Wilson, was immortalised by his daughter Nell's presentation of pairs of underpants – to Blair, embroidered 'Prime Minister' across the bottom; to Butler, the same embroidered 'Ex-Cabinet Secretary' and 'Master'.[16] Blair vowed to wear them for Prime Minister's Questions.[17]

The farewell party that Robin and Jill organised in Middle Temple Hall on 12 January 1998 was a socially challenging occasion.* Butler had served five Prime Ministers of very different stripes and thus Jill was seated between Heath and Major, with Mrs Thatcher diagonally across from her. To Butler's left was Mary Wilson and to her left Derry Irvine. To stimulate conversation with the Lord Chancellor, Mary Wilson opened with 'I'm old Labour, you know.' 'Well I'm New Labour', replied Irvine and, turning to his left, addressed not another word to the former Prime Minister's widow.

Three of the four living Prime Ministers, as well as Lady Wilson, were at the dinner, and Butler paid tribute to them all, and to friends and colleagues who had featured large in his career. From Patrick Carew, his Irish friend from Harrow, to Sir Richard Wilson, who succeeded him, he wove them into his account of his remarkable career. To cap this virtuoso performance, he asked his guests to remain seated while he and Jill drank a toast to them – their guests and friends.[18]

Once again, Nell made a characteristically irreverent and unforgettable contribution to the evening. She had conducted several interviews, many of them with guests present that evening, in which she asked her interviewees what a Cabinet Secretary actually did, and collected these into a short film. None of them could give a wholly convincing answer, which made for a satirical *leitmotif*. Simon Jenkins of *The Times* commented to Butler that only in Britain could the top civil servant's retirement be celebrated by poking fun at him.[19]

Approximately halfway through his term as Cabinet Secretary, Butler had been Sue Lawley's guest on *Desert Island Discs*. His enthusiasm for the job at that point was infectious: he had no desire to go to a desert island, no wish to leave the Cabinet Office. He would be profoundly miserable as a castaway, he maintained, as there was not a part of the job that he did not like. He had no desire to be indiscreet; he was the guardian of many, many secrets, all of which would stay firmly inside his head, even on a desert island.[20]

Four and a half years later, as he prepared to leave the Civil Service, there was no reason to suppose that he had changed his mind. There had been

* Although Butler had decided against a career at the Bar, he was invited to become an Honorary Bencher of the Middle Temple when he was Cabinet Secretary. This entitled him to use the hall for events, a privilege of which he took advantage for Nell's wedding reception.

significant and permanent changes to the scope of his job since 1993, particularly in the last few months. Yet he was able to take a historian's view of the last years of the Major government and of his short experience of New Labour. His sense of history and of optimism were perfectly illustrated by his choice of book and his favourite of the eight pieces of music chosen for the desert island. These were Paul Kennedy's *The Rise and Fall of the Great Powers, 1500–2000* and the air for soprano, 'I Know that My Redeemer Liveth' from Handel's *Messiah*. At the end of 1997, after ten years in the saddle, he left the Cabinet Office with his optimism and respect for the role of the Civil Service undimmed.*

Inevitably, despite his disdain for the press, he submitted to interviews. He saw his two major achievements as having led the service through a period of fundamental modernisation while maintaining its traditional qualities, and having overseen the successful transition to New Labour after 1 May. His best moments, he told journalists, had been setting up the central coordinating machinery during the Gulf War and the achievement of the Downing Street Declaration, leading to the ceasefire of 1994. Unsurprisingly, the Brighton bomb, the Scott Inquiry and the Aitken and Hamilton affairs stood out as his worst moments of the ten years.[21]

Nell may have lampooned the Cabinet Secretary's daily job, but it was Butler himself who wrote his own frivolous epitaph, a play on the different ways in which the Powell brothers pronounced their names (Charles Powell to rhyme with 'Hole'; Jonathan Powell to rhyme with 'Howl'):

> He accomplished his goal of surviving Charles Powell
> But Jonathan Powell made him throw in the towel.

* There was a remarkable response from listeners to the programme. Many wrote to applaud Butler's candour and approachability in the interview.

CHAPTER 18

MASTER OF UNIVERSITY COLLEGE, 1998–2008

AS CABINET SECRETARY AND head of the Home Civil Service, Butler earned an annual salary of £150,000. When he contemplated retirement, his and Jill's goal was to supplement his pension of £70,000 with a salary that would maintain his previous level of earning. There was no dearth of opportunity – he was approached by a headhunter for the vice-chairmanship of a bank – but he had certain firm criteria about the quality of life in his sixties. Being driven into the City of London at 8.00 a.m. to return, drained, late in the evening was not how he envisaged his and Jill's life after thirty-six years in his country's service.

Non-executive directorships also abounded for someone of his experience, and he was able to cherry-pick those that provided the best fit. He opted for just two – with HSBC (the HongKong and Shanghai Banking Corporation) and ICI (Imperial Chemical Industries), two blue-chip British companies with worldwide business. Each was going through a period of reorganisation in the 1990s. HSBC enjoyed a decade of expansion, acquiring banking businesses in Brazil, Argentina and New York, as well as Midland Bank in England in 1992. ICI acquired several businesses in the early part of the decade too but, heavily leveraged, was compelled to sell off a number of subsidiaries, and these sales left the company exposed to takeover bids. ICI was ultimately acquired by the Dutch conglomerate AkzoNobel in 2007.

The atmosphere in the boardrooms of the two companies was as different as their corporate fortunes at the end of the millennium. Butler felt that the formal style of HSBC's large board was used as a rubber stamp for decisions already taken by management. At ICI, by contrast, a smaller and more personal board ran the business. During the 1980s, the company had been run by John Harvey-Jones, one of the more colourful and esoteric managers of FTSE 100 companies. His heritage was a small group of directors with the power to develop and implement corporate strategy rapidly. For different reasons, each boardroom was an exciting place to be.

So far, so good. But Butler had not stumbled on anything that could reasonably be called a full-time job. As so often in his life, however, with remarkably fortuitous timing, an opportunity presented itself. Each year, around St Cuthbert's Day on 20 March, University College Oxford holds a feast to which Honorary and Foundation Fellows are invited.* Butler, an Honorary Fellow of the college since 1989, attended.[1] As he walked towards the main gate after dinner, he was approached by classics don Chris Pelling† who asked if he might be interested in applying for the Mastership of the College. John Albery, Master since 1989, would, Pelling said, be stepping down at the end of the Trinity (summer) term.[2]

Few positions could have appealed to him more and he did not hesitate to agree. He might be able to earn more money elsewhere but, as he frankly admits, 'neither Jill nor I wanted a lot of money. We wouldn't know what to do with it'. After thirty-five years of married life spent working apart, they had resolved to find a job that they could do together.[3] Since he and his son Andrew were both Univ alumni, the idea of returning as Master was most attractive. Jill, having worked with sixth-formers at Alleyn's School, was also very comfortable with the notion of working with undergraduates. In 1979, Univ had admitted female undergraduates – a radical departure at the time – and both he and Jill felt that there would be a real role for her to play. Most Masters' wives were adept at hosting an annual sherry party or two for undergraduates and graduates; few involved themselves in the running of their college.

The immediate problem, however, was that Univ needed a Master from

---

* Honorary Fellowships are awarded in recognition of achievement; Foundation Fellowships are awarded in recognition of donations to the college in excess of £1 million.

† Dr Christopher Pelling, then a classics Fellow of the college. He held the Regius Professorship in Greek at Christ Church from 2003 to 2015, and retains emeritus status for that post.

mid-June, while he would not be available until early January 1998. Furthermore, since he and Jill had promised themselves a six-month around-the-world trip, he would not be available until a year after the vacancy arose. This, he felt, was something that should be addressed before the idea went any further. The Fellows of the college agreed that, if they could reach an accord on all other particulars, the college would appoint Dr Gordon Screaton, the Vice-Master, to stand in until Butler was able to take up the post. In turn, he and Jill agreed to halve the length of their trip. This meant that he would be available in April 1998. Again, so far, so good. The next step was to go through the selection process and meet the college Fellows.

With the help of headhunters the Fellows arrived at a shortlist of four candidates. Butler began to marshal his forces and prepare for the ten-minute personal statement that he would be required to make at his interview. He contacted Pelling and Dr Leslie Mitchell, a history don at Univ, and invited them to the Cabinet Office to discuss the best way to proceed.

After the two dons had explained the procedure and outlined the nature of the Mastership, he typically summarised the job description as tripartite: presiding over the college's councils, acting as its ambassador to the university and beyond, and giving leadership to the college. An embarrassed silence followed the word 'leadership'; this clearly was not at all what the Master was meant to do. 'If you mention the word "leadership", you will be a dead duck', the two dons ventured. 'The Fellows might accept *primus inter pares*, but you would do best to avoid the whole subject.' Butler later commented that they were quite correct. 'In an Oxford college,' he said, 'the word "Master" has none of the connotations normally associated with it in the English language.'[4]

In the event, he did introduce the phrase *primus inter pares* when he spoke to the Fellows. Into a delicately crafted speech, in which he referred to Jill as 'the better half of the ticket', he carefully inserted the vague suggestion of leadership while portraying himself as the college's ambassador. His was a strong application; it was doubly so when he proposed himself as chief fundraiser at a time when university fees were a very live issue. To the surprise of no one, he was chosen as the next Master of Oxford's oldest college.

University College was founded in 1249. Originally a poor college, able to provide for four Fellows reading theology, it grew in the Middle Ages, accepted undergraduates in the sixteenth century and by the seventeenth century had acquired enough wealth to endow a number of undergraduate scholarships. The eighteenth century saw its first golden age, as Univ became one of the most intellectually active colleges in Oxford.[5] The second half of the nineteenth century saw the physical expansion of the college, and during the twentieth century Univ acquired a reputation for the diversity of background of its undergraduate body. Significantly different in make-up from many 'upper-class' colleges such as Christ Church, it continues to pride itself on the breadth and diversity of its members. As already noted, its place in the annals of twentieth-century socialism was assured by its associations with Beveridge, G. D. H. Cole, Clement Attlee and Harold Wilson. No less impressive is its list of graduates including Andrew Motion (Poet Laureate, 1999–2009), Stephen Hawking, Prince Felix Yousoupoff (Rasputin's assassin), and Roz Savage (the first woman to row alone across the three oceans). In summary, it is hard to imagine a college that Lord Butler, as he became in the 1998 New Year Honours, would be happier to run.

His ennoblement had a humorous moment, when he was asked by Garter King of Arms as to his chosen provenance. There were already several Lords Butler (one of whom had been Lord Butler of Saffron Walden, the non-rugby-playing baron of Butler's early Treasury days) so he should decide whence he derived his title. Butler replied that he and Jill rather liked the title 'Lord Butler of Brockwell', both for its alliteration and its association with the Butler family's house in Herne Hill. Pressed further, he replied that Brockwell was simply a public park. Only when Garter King of Arms had established that there was actually 'a place in Surrey' called Brockwell, did he accept the unusual title.

Lord and Lady Butler of Brockwell duly departed on their long-planned world tour to celebrate retirement. Retirement, that is, as a prelude to beginning a challenging new job, totally different from anything either had undertaken before. Now that they knew that the next decade would be spent at Univ, they tailored their itinerary to enable them to act as ambassadors for the college in various countries along the way.

As might be expected, the holiday was not an armchair vacation, but included a good measure of strenuous activity. First to South America, working their way north from Buenos Aires, to Bolivia and to the Inca sites in Peru. Despite Jill's discomfort from the altitude in Cuzco, the visit to Machu Picchu was an unforgettable experience. From South America, they crossed the Pacific to New Zealand, where they tackled three treks.

First, in the company of John Birt of the BBC, they walked the thirty-three miles of the Milford Track in the southwest corner of the South Island. Known as 'the finest walk in the world', Milford is a four-day hike, climbing to 3,740 feet above sea level on the Mackinnon Pass. Along the way, Birt encouraged Butler to talk about his career in Whitehall, using his experience in the media to probe and question. Butler later wrote that 'it was a wonderfully therapeutic and purging experience which helped me to get my Government life out of my system and clear my mind for the future'.[6]

Close by, in Fiordland National Park, is Routeburn Track, a twenty-mile walk that climbs to 4,300 feet. This was their favourite of the three great tracks, with even more stunning scenery and less regimented than Milford. After some whale watching at Kaikoura, Robin and Jill tackled their third walk, the Abel Tasman Coast Track along the north shore of the South Island. This walk, the longest of the three at thirty-seven miles, offers a combination of walking and sea kayaking in Abel Tasman National Park.

In New Zealand, the new Master took the first steps along the path for which he would become famous among old members of Univ over the next decade. In Wellington, Don and Sally Mathieson, both old members, gave a party for Robin and Jill. His message to the Univ community, one that he would repeat frequently, extolled the value of staying in touch with the college. Ultimately, as with any similar institution, the goal is to persuade old members to become donors, to help build the treasure chest that might be needed in post-Thatcher Britain. Univ's situation, moreover, was delicate, as the building of an annexe in North Oxford in the 1970s had nearly bankrupted the College.

Butler, an accomplished wordsmith after thirty-six years in the Civil Service, was not so crude as to ask old members to reach for their wallets. Instead, he stressed the value of the Univ family. Over the years, he made similar fundraising visits to different parts of the world and succeeded in bringing many Univ graduates back into the fold, helping them to revive their contacts with their Alma Mater. It became a virtuoso performance.

From New Zealand, they had originally planned to travel to South Africa, but altered their itinerary with Univ in mind to include the United States. Wherever they visited old members they were received with typical American friendliness and kindness. That kindness even extended to using influence to persuade President Bill Clinton (Univ, 1968) to receive them at the White House. An invitation had been offered, but Clinton was besieged by the Monica Lewinsky scandal, which had broken in January. Bill Bernhard, who had also been at Univ and a member of Saxophonists for Clinton, made a phone call to the White House and the path was cleared. Jill overcame her hesitation over the President's liaison with Lewinsky and, in common with the majority of people meeting Clinton for the first time, was captivated by his suave, attentive charm.

From Washington, Robin and Jill flew back to London and travelled to Edinburgh for Andrew's wedding to Catriona MacLaren. Butler who, when Andrew was born, had been overjoyed to have a son 'with whom I could share my enthusiasm for manly sports'[7] celebrated Andrew's last morning of bachelorhood by climbing Arthur's Seat with him. With a high point of 823 feet above sea level, this was a bagatelle after the Milford Track.

So, after an interval of nearly forty years, Butler returned to Univ. The elegant house on Logic Lane, the Master's Lodgings, symbol of authority to undergraduates, was now to be his residence for a decade. He and Jill were delighted with his new role. The college Fellows, with equal enthusiasm, welcomed their new Master. After a few difficult and turbulent years, the quadrangles promised to be calm once more.

Butler's predecessor as Master, Dr John Albery, was a high-spirited man with a zest for the unconventional, more often found in undergraduates than in the Master of an Oxford college. An obituary published when he died in 2013 perfectly captured the contrast between august academic leader and enthusiastic comedian:

> Respected for his scientific acumen and academic leadership, Albery was also greatly loved for his irrepressible *joie de vivre* and as the chief instigator

of – and participant in – the sort of rumbustious student high jinks, full of irreverence, laughter and alcohol, that live on joyfully – and sometimes embarrassingly – in the memory.[8]

During his last year, that irreverence had gained the upper hand, and a number of painful incidents had followed. The ostensible cause of his resignation was a speech at a 'bump-supper'* in the course of which he was alleged to have made inappropriate, 'ribald' remarks about the women's boat.[9] In an address at Albery's memorial service, Dr Leslie Mitchell addressed the former Master's conflicts, commenting that he 'always had to fight personal demons, and in the solitude of the Lodgings they overwhelmed him'. This, Mitchell believed, showed up Albery's flaws, but were also an indictment of the society in which he moved. Throughout his Mastership, the college's academic record was impeccable, a fact of which Albery 'was inordinately and justly proud'.[10]

An unofficial but widespread tradition at many Oxford colleges is that an academic is followed in the Master's Lodgings by a distinguished public servant – and vice versa – and so the arrival of a former Cabinet Secretary, a peer of the realm bringing considerable gravitas as well as a pitch-perfect wife, was welcomed. The Fellows showed their appreciative optimism by voting Jill a member of the Senior Common Room, a far from automatic honour.

Albery undertook to write briefing papers to guide his successor through the swirls of the Mastership but, in the event, ran out of time.† Instead, he wrote him a six-paragraph letter, brisk and informative, containing enough cautions to cause Butler to wonder if he was not stepping into the lion's den.[11] This feeling was compounded by another, greatly longer, letter from

---

* A bump-supper (in Cambridge known as 'bumps-supper') is a celebratory dinner held in college if the college VIII achieves a 'bump' (overhauls the boat of another college) on each day of the races in the spring or summer.

† The handover from Albery to Butler was far from smooth. At one point, the new Master was concerned that Albery would refuse to move out of the Master's Lodgings. Butler wrote to his mother that 'he seems to have gone into an alcoholic decline and to be holding on the Lodgings for as long as possible. It almost begins to look as though they will have to frog-march him out in order to get the redecoration done in time for our arrival.' Letter to Nora Butler, 19 October 1997.

his former tutor. Since Butler's time as an undergraduate at Univ, his ancient history tutor George Cawkwell had stayed at Univ, becoming Vice-Master. He had been urged by some Fellows to take on the Mastership, a suggestion he declined. After his retirement in 1987, he had maintained those links as an emeritus Fellow of the college.

Cawkwell was the ideal elder statesman, the sage to give the new Master advice on common room politics, and he excelled himself in an expert analysis of the pleasant aspects and less pleasant frustrations of the role of an Oxford head of house. Maurice Shock at Lincoln College,* Cawkwell wrote, had been criticised for conducting meetings so briskly that they were over too early; Herbert Hart at Brasenose† for letting them drag on too long. He warned:

> You will not, cannot please everyone. All new heads of houses have a honeymoon in which the lack of the predecessor's defects is warmly applauded. It lasts for between six months and two years, normally; David Keir's at Balliol lasted six weeks, for with Tommy Balogh and the like the Governing Body was uncommonly bloody.[12]

The central theme of Cawkwell's cautionary epistle was that the Master has no power, even less power than that of the monarch. He must, Cawkwell stressed, 'do it all by *auctoritas*'.‡ Butler would be used to leaks from working with politicians. 'I may be wrong', he continued, 'but you may find politicians outdone by dons for indiscretion.' He then sketched out the various 'mafias' that operated in the Senior Common Room, balancing his warnings with the reassuring comment that 'there are also some *excellent* Fellows whom you will in time discover. I hoped for you as Master because the

---

* Sir Maurice Shock, a Fellow of Univ, who was subsequently Rector of Lincoln College, Oxford from 1987 to 1994.

† Herbert Hart, known as H. L. A. Hart, legal philosopher and author of *The Concept of Law*, had been a Fellow of Univ and Professor of Jurisprudence until 1969, when he became Principal of Brasenose College.

‡ *Auctoritas* was the Roman term describing an aspect of an individual's power. It indicates authority in a practical sense – roughly equivalent to 'influence' or 'clout'.

College needs you, but I hope you will find a lot to please you. In general, the undergraduates and the graduates are very worthwhile.'

Cawkwell continued to give advice to Robin and Jill. Unsolicited but most welcome, it touched on a miscellany of issues and showed a keen understanding of both serious issues and 'trifling matters' that engaged members of the Senior Common Room in disproportionately bitter disputes. At intervals during the new Master's first year he wrote, concluding in July that 'you both need a holiday'.[13]

Butler had some experience already of the Senior Common Room, having been an Honorary Fellow of Univ since 1989. He also had intense experience of organisations containing several departmental baronies with interlocking, though not necessarily congruent, objectives. By his own admission, however, he was initially wrong-footed by Oxford's arcane *modus operandi*, which he encountered on his first day. He received a paper from the University Offices containing a proposal on which the college had to take a view. In Civil Service style, he wrote in the top right-hand corner 'Advice please' and put it in his OUT tray. Marion Hawtree, the Master's secretary* brought it back into the office and told him that only he could deal with the matter. 'Well please may I have the file on the subject?' Butler asked. 'There is no file', said Marion. 'You have to use your judgment.'[14]

There were other crossings of swords, both amusing and annoying, while he settled in and imposed his character on the Mastership. He found it a curious role, as he and Jill were at the same time guests and, despite Mitchell's and Pelling's caution, leaders of the introverted community of the college. That leadership role, however, was granted on the condition that he occupied himself exclusively with matters that the Fellows disdained – such as the abstruse university business mentioned above. On matters that Fellows, collectively or individually, judged important, he realised that his opinions were not automatically welcomed or valued.

The fountainhead of this selective superiority was, naturally enough, the academic and pedagogic aspects of the job. The body of a college's academic

* Mrs Marion Hawtree, the Master's secretary, had worked with John Albery and was able to help Butler greatly in his early days as Master. She continued to work both with the next Master, Sir Ivor Crewe, and independently for Butler after his tenure came to an end.

Fellows tends to be an exclusive group that has a clear view of the duties and responsibilities of the administrative members, including the Master. If the Master is not himself an academic, then his expertise in academic disciplines is assumed to be nugatory. Butler might boast a double first and the status of a former Cabinet Secretary, but that cut little ice in the Senior Common Room.

Typically, he took a pragmatic approach. He had contacts; many of those contacts had money; the college could always benefit from more money. Very well then; he would demonstrate to his colleagues that he had some value; he would apply himself to raising donations to the college. Targeting an old member who ran an asset management company, he set his sights on obtaining a donation of £25,000. When the old member offered to give £1.2 million to Univ to endow two junior research fellowships, Butler felt that he had proved his worth at a stroke by raising an amount greater than his total projected salary over ten years.

Fundraising, a vital component of modern educational institutions, was a continuing responsibility of the Master and usually one that Butler addressed with relish. Realistically, he recognised that donations of the magnitude of his first success would be few. Instead, he aimed to spread the net as widely as possible. He recognised that 95 per cent of donations would come from 5 per cent of the body of old members, but that by involving as many old members as possible he would increase the chances of more joining the group of 5 per cent.

At the end of his first year as Master, the development officer, responsible for fundraising, moved on. An American, Tania Jane Rawlinson, was appointed and immediately modernised Univ's approach. One innovation, about which Butler initially had concerns, was a 'telethon', in which current graduates and undergraduates volunteered to telephone old members who had read for the same degree and to talk with them about life at Univ in their respective eras. He agreed to this on the condition that old members were informed of the planned call in advance and were able to opt out if they did not want to be telephoned.

From the start, the 'telethon' was a success. Current students were impressed by the affection in which Univ was held by old members.[15] Counter to Butler's fears, many actually looked forward to receiving the phone call. Certainly, the ultimate goal was to raise money for the college, but the initiative helped to achieve his broader goal of extending the base of the active Univ community. The number of donors increased dramatically, and soon over 33 per cent of old members had become supporters of the college. Univ climbed to first place nationally in attracting the highest percentage of its graduate donors, and has remained at or close to the top of the chart ever since.

One issue that Butler identified as a potential stimulus to the majority of potential donors was an impressive new college boathouse on the south bank of the Thames to replace the original structure destroyed by arson in 1999. Unsurprisingly, building costs rose beyond the original estimate, climbing to £2.7 million, and the Estates Bursar argued that construction would have to be delayed. Butler, who had proudly announced to alumni that the boathouse would be finished on time, strongly opposed any delay in completion. This, he warned the Bursar, might well cost the college more in withheld donations than the increase in construction costs.[16] In the event, the boathouse was opened in time for Eights week in 2007; it won a RIBA prize and became an 'iconic' feature of the river.[17] There can be little doubt that Butler's view of the boathouse as an integral part of college pride was amply justified.

Butler saw fundraising as vital to the preservation of the 'brand' of the college. As late as 2003, even the wealthiest parent of an Oxford undergraduate paid only £1,100 annually towards fees. This effectively meant that every undergraduate needed a subsidy of £4,000 per year. This, Butler argued, would soon ensure that colleges would not have adequate funds to grant full bursaries to needy students. The only way that Oxford could afford to maintain its standards was to charge each student at least £5,000 in annual fees. That amount was tiny in comparison with the cost of an American university education; it might be a politically unwelcome proposal, but it was the only way that Oxford, like the better American universities, could admit the best applicants without regard for their ability to pay. The Ivy League system of 'need-blind' admissions, supported by the granting of full scholarships where needed, was central to the survival of the Oxford 'brand'. Predictably, the proposal was controversial, but this was an issue on which Butler continued to campaign.[18]

Butler's own commitment to Univ went a long way to consolidating the notion of the Univ family of which he was *paterfamilias*. Not only did he wear the college tie and carry one or two spares when he travelled on college business,* he communicated his enthusiasm to both the student body and the members of the college staff. The value of making a similar commitment was described with nostalgic objectivity by an undergraduate who had been vice-president and treasurer of the Junior Common Room:

> The Master was at once accessible but never overly familiar. He combined humour and engagement without diminishing his own gravitas. He had, I think, a very good sense of the undergraduates and took considerable time to familiarise himself with them personally. He was especially good to those he felt were good or who gave back to Univ – the Master's Travel Scholarship programme is a good example of this. As is the access he would give the students to eminent speakers who would come to the Masters Lodgings to give talks – the talks were open to all, but the Master would make an effort to introduce engaged students to eminent public figures and intellectuals. Jill was the same – always an extra step for those who went the extra distance for the college.[19]

The 'gravitas' that the Master displayed in public might have been undermined by the sight of Butler at high table for the Christmas Dinner on the last Sunday of Michaelmas term 1999. As the assembled college sang 'The Twelve Days of Christmas', Lord Butler, their Master, leapt onto the table and danced to the accompaniment of the verse 'Ten Lords a-Leaping'. After the initial shock, there was much friendly applause.[20]

Another innovation that he piloted through the Governing Body involved the position of Senior Tutor. For the first two years, Professor Helen Cooper had held the post, but found that juggling increasingly complex tutorial and teaching schedules was making impossible demands on her time. It was proposed that Univ follow the lead given by Cambridge in appointing

* When Butler was in Los Angeles on a fundraising trip in 2001, an old member commented that he had mislaid his Univ tie. 'That's terrible', exclaimed the Master, promptly producing a spare from somewhere about his person.

full-time administrators instead of relying on a teaching Fellow to take on an additional responsibility. The proposal, logical on the surface, ran counter to the traditional concept of a self-sufficient, self-administering community of scholars.

Predictably, the proposal aroused vehement conservative opposition. At a meeting of the college's Governing Body, the first five Fellows to speak rejected the principle of a non-academic handling of academic matters. Chairing the meeting, Butler was pessimistic about the outcome until, in 'one of the most dramatic moments I remember at such a meeting',[21] Helen Cooper suggested that no one should oppose the proposal who was not prepared to do the job in her place. Now holding the upper hand, but moving carefully, he suggested that any final decision be deferred until the Fellows could judge the quality of the applicants.

It was Univ's good fortune that Clare Drury, former Senior Tutor at Newnham and wife of the Dean of Christ Church, applied for the post. The availability of such a talented, personable and diligent academic ensured that the college appointed her. Univ thus became the first Oxford college to appoint a full-time Senior Tutor. Her premature death in 2004 was a grievous loss.

There were other positions – such as Dean – that were assumed by tutorial fellows, as Butler observed, often because they carried a stipend, which would increase their pension on retirement. There was, accordingly, resistance to the Master's attempts to appoint people who would do the job professionally and put their backs into it. Butler persisted and ultimately prevailed.

Not all issues were settled so effectively as that of the Senior Tutor, nor were relations with all Fellows without difficulty. His early days in the job were marred by a running battle with the Estates Bursar, who had imposed a regime of austerity after the problems caused by the North Oxford annexe.*

* The annexe, on the corner of Woodstock Road and Staverton Road, known as 'Stavertonia', had been a financial disaster and had necessitated the college making an annual profit of £500,000. The resultant austerity had continued long after the crisis had been averted. The atmosphere of financial caution caused Univ to lose the opportunity to acquire the Barclays Bank building on the High Street, which was ultimately bought by Corpus Christi College and converted into the Old Bank Hotel.

There was the issue of moving a senior Fellow from his rooms when work was needed on the floor. He dug his heels in and the issue became one of him versus the college, the latter naturally personified by Butler. There was a petty dispute when Butler suggested to the Garden Master (a Fellow of the college) that the flowerbeds in the quadrangles needed attention, causing the Garden Master to protest petulantly that 'I am not one of your staff'. Overall, however, the Master's celebrity status gave the college – and therefore the Fellows – some cachet. The trade was generally well accepted. Not least while that status translated into donations from old members.

The year of 1999 marked Univ's 750th anniversary, and Butler shrewdly determined that, if he could create an exceptional series of events to surround the date, he would consolidate his position early in his tenure. He set his sights high: a visit from the Queen,* an exceptional series of lectures, a ball, a series of events in which old members played a part. To his delight, all the planned events came to pass.

Univ is proud of its royal connections, even promoting a delightfully inaccurate story that it was founded by King Alfred in 872. The loyal toast at formal college dinners has long been 'the Queen, our visitor', and so the visit of the Queen and the Duke of Edinburgh in May 1999 was a decided coup for the Master; as Cabinet Secretary he had met the monarch on several occasions and felt that they had a good personal chemistry. Her Majesty's advisers were encouraging her to be seen speaking to 'normal' people on such occasions, and the Palace requested that she be seated next to the president of the Junior Common Room at luncheon. Ignoring the 'safe' conversational subjects that had been suggested to her, she pitched in directly with the question: 'Advise me – how can I persuade my grandsons to take their A levels seriously?' Matthew Style, the JCR president, was able to answer a concerned grandmother candidly and eloquently.

* Butler maintained excellent relations with the Queen and, as one of her favourites, was awarded the Order of the Garter. When Her Majesty visited Harrow School on 24 November 1986, Butler was present as one of the governors. At tea with the headmaster, Her Majesty spotted Butler across the room and said, 'I know that man over there', whereupon Butler was summoned to join the headmaster's table. Letter to Bernard and Nora Butler, 30 November 1986.

For the proposed series of lectures, Butler proposed the title 'Builders of the Millennium'. This was more than simply a catchy title; it flattered the lecturer – as was intended – that he or she was responsible for the history of our time. Butler used his contacts and his charm to attract Tony Blair, Luciano Violante, Hans Tietmayer, Stephen Hawking, Richard Branson, V. S. Naipaul and Rupert Murdoch to speak. The Prime Minister took as his subject 'Beveridge Revisited: A Welfare State for the 21st Century', a lecture with a definite Univ theme, delivered at Toynbee Hall, where Clement Attlee (Univ, 1901) had once worked.

The 750th anniversary was a prime opportunity to step up the fundraising campaign, and a total of £8.5 million was raised. Impressive as this total was, at a time when the government was making savage cuts in funding, it would soon be used up; the fundraising efforts should not be relaxed. Every year, Robin and Jill made a circuit of the United States, with stops in Los Angeles, San Francisco, Chicago and New York. They were well received throughout the trip and were successful in promoting the Univ community and in soliciting donations. Butler was, however, consistently confronted by one simple objection: an American old member often had a son who planned to go to an American university for his undergraduate degree – as his father had done before going up to Oxford. The father, therefore, needed to bear in mind that (for example) Harvard might also appreciate a donation. All simple facts of life, perhaps, but Butler found it galling, given that Harvard already enjoyed an endowment of over $15 billion.

Nothing could have pleased him better than to be the head of Oxford's oldest college during the year of an important anniversary – and it is hard to imagine a Master more suited to the task. The man whom John Major described as one of the most competitive men he ever knew wanted to make Univ simply the best college. Not just with the best glee club or the best gardens, but the best at sports, Head of the River, top of the Norrington table,* the most diverse, the most successful at fundraising. Indeed, fundraising was the key to that overall ambition, and so that became his principal focus.

* The Norrington Table is an annual ranking of colleges, based on the results obtained by candidates in all their final examinations.

He would arrive in an American city with the sharp-eyed determination of a regional sales director, his targets in his sights. Behind the Univ college tie and the bonhomie of a roving ambassador, there was the resolve of a Wall Street bond trader.[22] He rarely left a potential donor's presence empty-handed.*

The trans-Atlantic connection was strengthened in 2000 when President and Mrs Clinton visited Oxford with their daughter Chelsea. The President, a Rhodes scholar, had taken a post-graduate degree at Univ in 1968/69 and it was now proposed that Chelsea should read for a post-graduate degree in International Relations. Butler was placed in a similar position to that of his namesake Lord Butler of Saffron Walden, Master of Trinity Cambridge, when the Queen indicated that she would like Prince Charles to read for a degree there. Butler could not guarantee her a place, nor could the application be allowed to become public knowledge, as the decision on her admission should not be fodder for the press. Having envisaged headlines such as 'BUTLER SNUBS WHITE HOUSE', he was delighted and relieved when the Faculty of International Relations accepted Chelsea's application. The college was able to give her a room in St Helen's Court, the building in which her father had occupied a room thirty years before.[23]

Tania Rawlinson's warnings that Univ would continue to require a steady flow of contributions was emphasised when Dr John Evans, described as 'the most gifted and accomplished Canadian of his generation',† and two of his sons – all three former members of Univ – visited the Master during that year. Dr Evans, an Honorary Fellow of the college, was concerned that Oxford had for a long time occupied a sentimental place in trans-Atlantic hearts, but that the university was in a decline and no longer held the same magic. Disturbed by this analysis, Tania and the Master planned a weekend seminar at Ditchley Park, the impressive stately home between Oxford and Banbury, converted in 1958 into a conference centre.[24] This would be

* Dr Robin Darwall-Smith, an archivist of Univ, comments that 'the Development Office really took off under Butler and travel to the USA became part of what the Master did'.

† Robert Prichard, former president of the University of Toronto and CEO of Torstar Corp., so described Dr Evans. Quoted in Dr Evans's obituary in the *Globe and Mail*, 13 February 2015.

an opportunity to explain to the college's most important benefactors the challenges facing Univ in the twenty-first century and the college's proposed solutions. Twenty-three donors, eleven of them from North America, accepted the invitation and attended with their spouses.

Butler organised an impressive production. He arranged for the Permanent Secretary at the Department of Education to give an after-dinner address, explaining the government's education policy. Four Fellows of the college made presentations on their areas of research. The spring weather was perfect; the atmosphere of the splendid mansion and gardens intoxicating. The weekend was a success in every way.

One by-product of the weekend was that two of the college's donors offered on the spot to give financial support to the work of the Fellows who had made presentations. In fact, two were already adequately funded, but for the other two the support was critical. Butler recounts a bizarre sequel to the weekend's events:

> When I reported the outcome to the next College meeting, it did not receive the welcome I had expected. 'Who chose the Fellows to give the presentations, Master?' I was asked. I admitted that I had. 'Well, Master, you must never do it again. On future occasions we must have a peer review committee to make the selections.' I realised that it is not a characteristic of academics to rejoice at the good fortune of their colleagues.[25]

Butler applied himself aggressively to the business of fundraising for the simple reason that without a sizeable and constant flow of funds Univ could not hope to attract the calibre of scholars that distinguished it from lesser colleges. All flowed from that. This was not by any means his only function, however. He had a variety of responsibilities in the university – as president of the University Rugby Club, as a member of the search committee to find a new Vice-Chancellor for when Sir Colin Lucas retired in 2004.

In the appointment of a non-academic Senior Tutor in Univ, Butler had demonstrated flexibility and realism. Without underestimating the importance of the position, he was not so wedded to tradition that he saw the principle of self-governance, the running of academic institutions solely by academics, as sacrosanct. When it was proposed that the oversight of the university should be placed in the hands of a committee, of which almost half the members were to be drawn from outside, Butler was at once respectful of tradition and receptive to fundamental modernisation. On the one hand, he quoted a friend's comment that 'Oxford and Cambridge are the only internally governed universities in Europe and they are also the only European universities in the world's top ten. It is difficult to avoid the conclusion that there is some connection.' On the other hand, he concluded that 'it is now in the interests of Oxford to let in a larger element of external governance'. Change, he concluded, 'is always uncomfortable and sometimes disadvantageous, but not always'. He recounted a conversation with Sir Matthew Stevenson, a Permanent Secretary when he had been a junior civil servant: 'Someone, objecting to a change, said: "If you do what you propose, life will never be the same again." "That's true", said Sir Matthew, "but, you know, we have to accept that life does change. That's what distinguishes it from death."'[26]

Accordingly, together with Sir Derek Morris, Provost of Oriel, he actively supported Lucas's successor John Hood in his drive to implement assessment of academics as proposed by the Higher Education Funding Council. To Butler, as to Hood, it seemed reasonable that this should be a condition of the preferential financing that Oxford received. It also seemed reasonable that the University Council should have a majority of external members, otherwise there would be a clear conflict of interest. Neither of these proposals had originated with Hood, but it was he who was blamed for them in what Butler perceived as Oxford at its worst, with vested interests resisting change – particularly vehemently, he felt, because Hood had the impertinence to be a New Zealander as well as a reformer.[27]

Butler's support of Hood led to his being appointed to the donations review committee, set up by the Development Office of the university.[28] One of the committee's tasks was to conduct due diligence as to the appropriateness of accepting a donation of £75 million from Leonid ('Len') Blavatnik, a Russian oligarch with a house in Kensington. The money was to be used to found the Blavatnik School of Government, whose inaugural Dean was Ngaire Woods. Professor Woods has acted as an adviser to the International Monetary Fund, to the United Nations Development Programme's Human

Development Report, and to the Commonwealth Heads of Government. She has also served as a member of the IMF European Regional Advisory Group, as chair of a World Economic Forum's Global Agenda Council, and on several committees connected with international governance. She is the author of eight books and numerous articles on international institutions, globalisation, and governance.

She is, however, also a Fellow of University College and, as a result, there have been suggestions that Butler was motivated by his professional association and friendship with Professor Woods to overlook the source of the oligarch's contribution to facilitate a deal that gave Woods 'her' school of government. Link this with the accusation that the entire school of government is a paternalistic organisation of doubtful value, and detractors have all the elements of a first-class scandal: tainted money from a Russian oligarch, academic cronyism prompting acceptance of said money, an imperialist, racist institution in hidebound University of Oxford. These add up to a tempting story; it is no surprise that it made its appearance on the pages of *The Guardian*.

There are, it appears, four issues involved. Should the university have accepted money that flowed from a dispute between a Russian oligarch and executives of BP? Should Oxford sponsor a school of government at all? Is Professor Woods qualified to act as Dean of the school? Should Butler have recused himself from the committee to review donations? If it had indeed been decided that there was to be a school of government – a decision for the university, not the committee – Woods would seem to be eminently qualified to head it. At all events, that question, too, was beyond the remit of the committee and should not entail the recusal of a committee member. Essentially, the only question at issue that involves Butler is whether the committee should have accepted the donation of £75 million from a known Russian oligarch, allegedly with ties to Vladimir Putin – an allegation that Blavatnik denies. In that connection, a university spokesman responded that 'Oxford University has a thorough and robust scrutiny process in place with regard to philanthropic giving. The Committee to Review Donations conducts the appropriate due diligence based on publicly available information. The University is confident in this process and its outcomes.'[29]

Beyond assignments in Oxford, Butler had also agreed with the Univ Fellows that he might undertake Whitehall-related tasks, provided they could be fitted in with Univ work. He chuckles when he recalls his chairing of the Butler Review, an inquiry into the Intelligence on Weapons of Mass Destruction in Iraq:

> The Fellows, although they would never confess it, loved feeling that they had a line into national life. I made sure that I was always there for Fellows' meetings, but I also brought back to Univ stories from the big stage. That was partly why I agreed to the WMD inquiry; the Fellows loved having as Master a public figure who brought the real world into the rather restrictive atmosphere of the College.[30]

This freedom to take on outside assignments led to his serving on the Wakeham Commission on the reform of the House of Lords. In 2003, he also made a short excursion to Windsor Castle to be inducted as a Knight of the Garter. It was to University College, however, that he held his principal allegiance and, throughout his ten-year term as Master, both he and Jill contributed beyond measure to college life. This commitment to the college was illustrated in 2003 when he was approached with a suggestion that he run for the Chancellorship of the university, when Roy Jenkins, Chancellor since 1987, died in January. Butler was flattered, but did not consider the proposal seriously. There were a variety of reasons, of which the overwhelming one was that he had committed to ten years at Univ and was very happy there.[31]

One of his most important contributions, as far as the undergraduate members were concerned, was the extension of Master's scholarships designed to finance long-vacation travel to the United States, Canada or Asia. The concept, introduced by Professor Albery, might have been designed to appeal to the new Master, who substantially enlarged the programme. The college provided funds for deserving travellers; old members would be available to provide accommodation; the recipients of the awards would have the responsibility of creating their itineraries, contacting participating old members, managing their budgets and making their travel arrangements. Old members were approached, and those who were willing to offer accommodation had the benefit of meeting young Univ members and keeping a finger on the pulse of the college. It was another facet of the Univ family at work.

The college tended to make travel awards available to candidates who had contributed in some way on a voluntary basis to the running of the college. The president and secretary of the Junior Common Room, for example, the secretary of the Martlets society, captains of college sports teams – they would not automatically be awarded travel scholarships, but their voluntary contributions would count for something if they were to apply. In a typical year, about fifteen scholarships were awarded.

The programme was a success from the start. Old members offered accommodation of all kinds: from a mansion in North County, San Diego, to a mobile home in Arizona, to a studio flat in Manhattan. Venture capital barons, academics, writers, lawyers, businessmen, musicians, stage directors – all manner of former Univ folk expressed a willingness to open their homes to travelling scholars. One old member in Los Angeles who hosted scholars for several years actively looked forward to receiving them and was saddened when he moved out of the area into a city less in demand.

On 20 November 2003, two bombings in Istanbul killed twenty-seven people. Twelve were killed at the British Consulate, including the Consul-General Roger Short, an alumnus of Univ who had read 'Greats' between 1963 and 1967. Short had served two tours in Ankara, as a junior diplomat in the 1970s and as head of Chancery in the 1980s. David Sykes, a Univ contemporary and friend of Short's, proposed that a memorial fund be established in Short's name to fund travel by Univ students to Turkey and neighbouring countries. In December Sykes contacted Butler, whose reaction was immediately supportive. The Master, typically, was keen to see something positive emerge from the tragedy; after a sizeable contribution was received in 2004, in March 2005 he was able to award the first four Roger Short Travel Scholarships.[32] The 'Univ family' responded to the appeal, for the laconic Short had been an immensely popular man and, as a result, over sixty Univ students have benefited from these scholarships.

Another innovation involved soirées on Sunday evenings to which Butler would invite a well-known personality from politics, from Whitehall or from the media, to speak to open meetings of college members. Politicians, including Margaret Thatcher, John Major, Michael Heseltine and John Redwood; diplomats, such as Sir Jeremy Greenstock, ambassador to the United Nations; miscellaneous celebrities such as Boris Johnson and Richard Ingrams – a pot-pourri of individuals from Butler's varied public life were dragooned into speaking to assembled Univ people. These soirées, open to all members of college, were popular and well attended. One German student congratulated Butler, commenting that it was impossible to imagine Chancellor Schmidt sitting in the Master's drawing room, speaking to students.

One aspect of Butler's Mastership that was unusual, but quite in character, was the extent to which Jill involved herself in the daily life of the college. John Albery and Arnold Goodman had been bachelors; Kingman Brewster had suffered a stroke just before taking office as Master, so his and his wife's ability to entertain was truncated. It had therefore been twenty-two years since a Master and his wife had regularly welcomed students to the Lodgings. Robin and Jill, shocked to hear that many old members had rarely set foot in the house as undergraduates, resolved to provide a welcoming, second family to their few hundred charges. The Lodgings became 'a social centre' rather than the principal's office.[33]

The college Literary Society, the Martlets, was long established but had become increasingly supine, with few meetings held. Jill resuscitated it, arranging for graduates to make presentations explaining their work to other graduate students. Meetings were held after an informal get-together for drinks in the Master's Lodgings. The Music Society also held meetings there; when the Univ Players staged a play, the cast party was held in the Lodgings, as were dinners for the Junior and Middle Common Room committees.

There were also activities that Jill handled alone. She was careful not to project herself aggressively into projects but rather to respond to a perceived need. Like her husband, she focused on the notion of a Univ family, involving herself with those whose ties to the college had been allowed to slip. She began by taking one, then two, then several retired college staff out for lunch in a local pub. Gradually this group expanded and soon retired college staff, their widows, widowers and some retired Fellows joined in. The venture gained momentum and the costs rose until Sir John Swire (Univ 1948)* offered to fund the occasions. Jill subsequently initiated a similar scheme for widows and spouses of Univ Fellows.

Using her background as a teacher of mathematics, she instigated a course in the week before Michaelmas (autumn) term, at the beginning of the academic year. This was open to first-year undergraduates reading any course that would require some ability to grasp mathematical concepts. Unobtrusively, she became indispensable.

One other college activity in which Robin and Jill participated was 'the Chalet'. Le Chalet des Mélèzes, also known as le Chalet des Anglais, stands on a plateau at 5,500 feet above sea level in the French Alps. Originally built by the Urquhart family, of whom 'Sligger' Urquhart of Balliol was the best-known member, it is now used every summer as a base for reading parties from Univ, Balliol and New College. Every three years during Butler's tenure, he and Jill would join the party. Once again, their presence in frankly primitive conditions, albeit in a glorious location, enhanced the notion of the Univ family.

As he neared the age of seventy, the Master's retirement age, he was approached and asked if he would consider staying for a further two years – an extension within the gift of the Governing Body. Both he and Jill, however, felt that they had accomplished their task and now needed to be available for their growing number of grandchildren. Part of the ritual of departure involved a portrait of the Master to be hung in the dining hall. Butler requested that Jill appear somehow in the picture – he imagined that there might be a framed portrait of her on a wall or a photograph on his desk included in the painting. To his delight, the Fellows insisted that the picture be a portrait of the two of them and that she share equal space with the Master. It was a generous and fitting farewell gesture to 'the better half of the ticket'.

From every level of Univ came letters of thanks and appreciation, and tributes to the manner in which the Master had rebuilt the morale of his old college. One undergraduate recalled:

---

* The Swire family, particularly Sir John and his brother Sir Adrian (1952), have been substantial donors to Univ, establishing and funding scholarships for graduates and undergraduates.

> Some of my friends at other colleges had almost no interaction with their masters/provosts. I quickly gained the impression that Lord Butler was much more involved in college life and interested in the students of Univ than was perhaps required of him. His presence around college was gently supportive. He and Jill served as our benevolent guardians with whom I think without exception members of college were proud to be associated. If I passed him at a gate or in the street he would always stop to say hello and find out how I was getting on. He seemed to know everyone by name and was approachable, friendly, thoughtful and kind. I think he wanted to instil those qualities in the college as a whole and to make sure that students left Univ having had a rounded experience as well as getting the most out of their academic studies. … He had a loud laugh, which you could hear from around corners and across quadrangles that always made me smile.[34]

From the Senior Common Room came appreciation of

> your determination to get it right, to understand the currents flowing across the college, to get on top of what needed doing, and then, with great skill and precision to get on with doing what was necessary. This took a great deal of love for Univ! … You inherited a college which was in rather a sad way. You succeeded in restoring a sense of pride and purpose and collegiality and you did this with amazing speed.[35]

Another colleague commented:

> I think that Univ has benefited hugely, and in many different ways, from having had you both here. We could not have done better, and I dare not think that we deserved so well. We are all deeply indebted to you. I think that you left the College a legacy from which it will benefit for years. It became a better place in many respects.[36]

Even from members of other colleges came compliments and thanks. One Rhodes Scholar at Brasenose had met Butler at a dinner at Rhodes House.

He had wanted to take photos in Univ but found that the porters would not allow this. Accordingly, Butler wrote a note to the head porter on the back of the dinner's menu. When the young man arrived at the lodge and presented his scribbled *laissez-passer*, the porter smiled and said he could go 'wherever the Hell he liked' in college. With his letter of thanks to Butler he enclosed one of the photos he had taken, adding: 'Thank you so much for enriching my Oxford experience in this most unusual way. It will undoubtedly always be one of my most cherished memories and most oft told stories.'[37]

Assessing his own performance at Univ, Butler is most proud of leaving the college in a good state and of having created a wider and lasting Univ family. On the other side of the coin, he was disappointed by his inability to secure a permanent presence at the top of the Norrington Table. To have achieved that, however, he recognises that a certain ruthlessness would have been required:

> I always gazed admiringly at Jessica Rawson [Warden of Merton College] across the road, who always managed to put the fear of God into the Fellows. She was such a stern figure that she kept them up to the mark. In many ways I was too soft with the Univ Fellows and I let some of them get away with slackness in their teaching ... Univ, once they accepted an undergraduate, would see him or her through to the end, whereas Merton were much more ready to throw them out. I didn't want to do that, but I would have liked to create the fear of God among the Fellows to get better academic results.[38]

That was the elusive honour that Butler was unable to capture and that tends to be the basis of any criticism of his Mastership. He believed in the value to undergraduates of a broad range of activities and set a glowing example, involving himself in the intellectual, spiritual and athletic life of the college.* He believed that young Fellows took too little interest in college life;[39] this

---

* Before he was appointed Master, Butler was asked by the Revd Bill Sykes, the college Chaplain, if he would support the chapel. Butler replied that he and Jill were 'Christmas and Easter people'. Yet he attended every Holy Communion and Evensong on Sundays. Interview, Dr Robin Darwall-Smith, 2 June 2016.

brought the counter-attack that Butler, as Master, cared too little for the purely intellectual pursuits that are central to Oxford's being. He was not the first and certainly will not be the last academic administrator to incur such a criticism.

To the Mastership Butler brought the conviction that Oxford was a good thing – a good thing for professors, provosts, deans, graduates, undergraduates and everyone connected with the thirty-odd colleges that constitute the university. It is fitting that he should be remembered with affection and respect by every category of the Oxford community. That, in itself, is an achievement.

CHAPTER 19

THE BUTLER REPORT, 2004

THE MOVEMENT TO INDICT Tony Blair for war crimes, an issue reignited by the Chilcot Report published in July 2016, stems from the allegation that he took Britain into war on false pretences; specifically, that his government falsified reports on Saddam Hussein's possession of weapons of mass destruction (WMD) and appended to the false reports the claim that the WMD he allegedly possessed could be mobilised and launched within forty-five minutes. The principal document, known as the 'September Dossier', was the product of a committee that included John Scarlett, chair of the Cabinet Office Joint Intelligence Committee, and senior officers from the Secret Intelligence Service (MI6). It was chaired by Alastair Campbell.

Between 3 and 24 September 2002, the dossier was drafted and redrafted several times. By 24 September, when the document was presented by the Prime Minister to the House of Commons, the foreword stated baldly:

> In recent months, I have been increasingly alarmed by the evidence from inside Iraq that despite sanctions, despite the damage done to his capability in the past, and despite the UNSCRs expressly outlawing it, Saddam Hussein is continuing to develop WMD, and with it the ability to inflict real damage upon the region, and the stability of the world.[1]

It asserted further:

> Intelligence reports make clear that he sees the possession of WMD, and the belief overseas that he would use them, as vital to his strategic interests,

> and in particular his goal of regional domination. And the document discloses that his military planning allows for some of the WMD to be ready within 45 minutes of an order to use them. I am quite clear that he will go to extreme lengths, indeed already has done so, to avoid giving them up.[2]

On 22 May 2003, Dr David Kelly, the leading British weapons inspector, met Andrew Gilligan, a BBC reporter, at the Charing Cross Hotel to talk about Iraq. A week later, the BBC broadcast a report from Gilligan, alleging that the September Dossier had been knowingly 'sexed up' on orders from the Prime Minister's Office. The document had been rewritten; the 45-minute claim had been added; the intelligence came from a single source; and the Intelligence services had been sceptical about the contents of the document. Gilligan's report was correct in all details of its allegations, except that the 'sexing-up' of the dossier had been conscious and deliberate was fiercely contested by the government.

There was intense media speculation concerning the identity of Gilligan's source. Dr Kelly had spoken to his line manager at the Ministry of Defence about the interview and no disciplinary action had been taken against him. It is unclear how many people in Whitehall knew Kelly to be the source, but scant effort was made to protect his identity. On 8 July, sufficient clues were revealed by the Ministry of Defence for journalists to identify the source as Dr Kelly. On the evening of 17 July, Kelly died in woods close to his home in Oxfordshire.

On the following day, Lord Falconer, Secretary of State for Constitutional Affairs, appointed Lord Hutton to conduct an inquiry into the circumstances surrounding Kelly's death. On 28 January 2004, the Hutton Report was published and was received with widespread incredulity. The report 'does a great disservice to the British people', the *Daily Mail* claimed.[3] Hutton reached the conclusion that Kelly had committed suicide and severely criticised the BBC for allegedly failing to check Gilligan's story, which it termed 'unfounded'. On the broader question, the report cleared the government of exaggerating the threat posed by Saddam. The report threw the BBC into turmoil and brought about the resignations of its chairman Gavyn Davies and Director-General Greg Dyke. Several newspapers weighed in to criticise the BBC, but the overwhelming reaction from press and public was that the report was unbalanced and that its narrowness had ensured that 'the real issue – the existence of weapons of mass destruction – wasn't even touched on'.[4]

When Butler took his guide's mobile phone between Teotihuacán and Mexico City on 2 February 2004 and heard Jonathan Powell say 'Robin, your country needs you again', he had a very clear idea what lay in store. Although the Hutton Inquiry had cleared the government of deception, the decision by President Bush to appoint a commission of inquiry into American Intelligence failure, combined with the accusations of whitewash directed at the Hutton Report, had forced Blair's hand. When he discussed the matter with Jill, her strenuous advice was not to touch what was undoubtedly a poisoned chalice. True to character, impelled by 'a mixture of vanity and curiosity about why the intelligence services had been wrong', he was inclined to accept.[5]

Back in Mexico City, he was able to glean more details from Powell. Negotiations were in progress with opposition parties; more would be in place by later that evening; could Butler phone back when he arrived in Houston? At three o'clock in the morning, London time, he was able to speak to the duty officer at No. 10. He learned that the Conservatives had agreed to provide a member of the review committee, but the Liberal Democrats had refused, principally because the committee's brief was not sufficiently wide-ranging.[6]

As to the terms of reference, these were, in Butler's judgement, 'disingenuous', as they related, not simply to Iraq, but to intelligence on WMD 'in countries of concern'. This was far from being an inquiry into the legal or moral justification for the invasion of Iraq. The time frame, moreover, was demanding, allowing just five months for the inquiry to report. From the outset, therefore, he was concerned that he had been handed an unrealistic assignment. Things were not made easier by the immediate assumption by the media that Lord Butler, a pillar of the establishment, would preside over another whitewash. The report in *The Guardian*, the newspaper that had led the chase in the Jonathan Aitken affair, was typical of the media reaction:

> His record as the former head of the civil service shows that he consistently showed deference to those in power. During the height of the Conservative

> sleaze scandals of the 1990s, Sir Robin, as he then was, chose to believe the dishonest arms sales minister Jonathan Aitken and attacked journalists who were investigating him. He followed this up by defending Whitehall deceit during the Scott inquiry into covert arms sales to Iraq. During that investigation too, he went out of his way to attack the media for undermining our system of government by what he called 'grossly distorted and prejudicial allegations'.
>
> The picture of this bicycling Old Harrovian that emerged during both these scandals was of a patrician mandarin, protective of Whitehall pieties and resentful of those who sought to puncture them.[7]

Indeed, the response to the announcement that Butler would chair the inquiry was universally sceptical. Butler later recalled 'returning on the overnight plane to find my appointment treated with such derision in some morning papers that I had to hide my face on the train from Gatwick to Victoria'.[8]

He had not been the first choice to chair the inquiry. Field Marshal Lord Inge, former Chief of the General Staff and of the Defence Staff, had been offered the responsibility; he had agreed to join the committee but declined the chair. The other members were Sir John Chilcot, former Permanent Secretary at the Northern Ireland Office and a hardy perennial on review committees; Michael Mates, Conservative MP for East Hampshire and a former minister at the Northern Ireland Office; and Ann Taylor, Labour MP for Dewsbury, and chair of the Intelligence and Security Committee. The committee was to include only Privy Counsellors and, at the time, Taylor alone had that status. The other committee members were, therefore, hastily sworn in.

With one representative each from the Labour and Tory parties, two cross-benchers from the Lords and a non-party former civil servant, the committee met for the first time, issuing a statement at the end of the meeting: As Butler recalls, while the report would not hesitate to criticise any individuals who had been dishonest or negligent, its main focus would be to discover why the intelligence assessments on Iraq had reached what appeared to be false conclusions and to identify the lessons to be learned.[9]

There were similarities between post-Iraq public opinion in 2004 and post-Falklands sentiment when Lord Franks undertook his report. The differences, however, between the two were vastly greater. There had been opposition to the South Atlantic war, but that opposition had come largely from the left. For patriotic Britons, the liberation of the Falklands was a reaffirmation of British power and decency. Not so Iraq. Britain had been assigned a minor role in an American-led enterprise. Yet, unlike the Franks Report, the Butler Report had no brief to consider the rights and wrongs of the war itself. Not only the country, but New Labour itself, was radically divided over Blair's action; there was enormous political opportunity for the Tory Party to exploit. Unsurprisingly, Michael Howard, the Leader of the Opposition, was not slow to do so. In a statement at the beginning of March, he said of the committee:

> It repeats, as one of its aims, its reference to structures, systems and processes. It does not include amongst its aims an examination of the acts or omissions of individuals ... [it is a] quite unjustifiable restriction on the committee's approach ... after careful reflection, I have decided with regret to withdraw my co-operation from the Butler review.[10]

The political climate surrounding the review was fast becoming precisely the scenario that Jill had envisaged and that her husband was determined to avoid. He was greatly cheered when Michael Mates decided not to resign from the committee but to continue in a personal capacity. Having been appointed to the Privy Council specifically for this task, Mates saw it as his clear duty to continue to serve, a view not widely shared by his constituents. In this unpromising climate, increasingly fearful that he had indeed been handed a poisoned chalice, Butler began two months of acquiring all relevant documents. From the outset, he made it clear that, if the government withheld requested documents, he would resign.

By now, he had recognised the gulf between Joint Intelligence Committee (JIC) reports and the assertions made by the government in the September Dossier. It would, therefore, be vital for the committee not only to have access to all relevant JIC documents, but also to publish them alongside the government statements. The government reluctantly agreed to this stipulation, solemnly excising a few irrelevant words from each document so that there would be no precedent created for the release of JIC reports *in toto*.[11]

The hypothesised gap between JIC assessments and government statements – in the hands of a government as media-savvy as New Labour – led Butler to see the media as the third crucial element in the government's laying out of its Iraq intelligence stall. Returning to the central question of whether the government had attempted to establish a 45-minute-deployment myth in the minds of the public, he wrote to all newspaper editors and political correspondents, asking if they had been 'guided' to emphasise the myth in their reports. As he recalled, 'no one said that they had but they couldn't deny afterwards that they had been asked'.[12]

The months passed quickly – the first two devoted to assembling documents, the next two to taking verbal evidence in private sessions. There followed a visit to Iraq to meet the US-led Iraq Survey Group. This involved tense moments on arrival and, especially, on departure from Baghdad Airport. The RAF pilot informed his passengers that the aircraft would be safe from heat-seeking missiles once it reached an altitude of 18,000 feet. Never had a climb after take-off seemed so long as it did while the committee members nervously watched the altimeter. When the plane came out of its steep climb, strong gins and tonics were distributed.

After four months, at the end of May, the group was ready to reach conclusions. A weekend retreat outside Oxford gave the members an opportunity calmly to consider the mass of evidence. Butler received sound advice from his former colleague Sir Terry Burns. 'Just use the facts to tell the story', Burns advised. 'The conclusions will then fall out of the narrative and other members of the Inquiry will not be able to challenge them.'[13]

After the weekend retreat, including a seventieth birthday party for Michael Mates and a soirée in the Master's Lodgings at Univ, the chairman brought the committee together to draft its conclusions. Totally familiar now with the issues and the evidence, he found the conclusions that he drafted to be 'jejune and hardly worth the paper they were written on'. As he followed Burns's advice, however, the narrative yielded significant conclusions. It was a substantive list of criticisms that he showed to the government in a completed draft.

The initial reaction from Sir David Omand, the Permanent Secretary in the Cabinet Office, was hostile. The report was factually wrong in several areas, he maintained. Butler countered that the committee would be only too happy to amend any passages that could be shown to be incorrect. Few such errors were identified and nothing of substance was changed at the government's request.

On 14 July, the committee reported its findings.[14] There was an air of expectancy surrounding the report as the general public perception was that it would be similar to the Franks Report, specifically supporting or condemning the decision to invade Iraq. There was the added consideration that, after the Hutton Report, widely condemned as a whitewash, the Butler Report would name some guilty men. Heads, it was widely supposed and hoped, would roll.

For the many jubilantly following the tumbrel, the Butler Report was a nicely balanced, well-presented disappointment. It was what it was termed – a review of intelligence – and not a biased indictment of the Blair government. This disappointed the sizeable group that wanted no more than to see the September Dossier revealed as dishonest and a resounding rebuttal of claims by Blair or Bush that the invasion was undertaken in response to a clear and imminent threat of the use of WMD by Saddam.*

Instead, the report opened with a lengthy disclaimer concerning the reliability of intelligence, particularly where specialist knowledge is involved. Intelligence procedures were discussed, and the various agencies and their functions introduced. The limitations of intelligence were explained. It 'merely provides techniques for improving the basis of knowledge', the report warned. 'It can be a dangerous tool if its limitations are not recognised by those who seek to use it.'[15]

In addition to the potential shortcomings of the intelligence itself, there are dangers in the methodology of evaluating it. Many factors can affect evaluation: memory of past failures, overestimation, 'mirror-imaging'[16], the development of that dangerous notion, a 'prevailing wisdom'. Only then does the report turn to the activities of A. Q. Khan and Pakistan's nuclear

* Such as the bald statement that Britain had intelligence that Saddam had 'sought' uranium in Niger (President Bush, State of the Union Address, 28 January 2003). See below in this chapter for discussion of that claim.

programme, as well as those of different countries – Libya, Iran and North Korea. Not until Chapter 3 does the report address the question of terrorism.

This section is a revealing exposé of how fundamentally assessments of potential terrorist threats had changed over fifteen years. The report quoted a JIC paper of 1989, which stated:

> We believe that even the most sophisticated and well-organised terrorist group is highly unlikely to be able to steal and then detonate a nuclear weapon within the foreseeable future … At present the most feasible terrorist nuclear incident would probably be a credible hoax. A terrorist threat to detonate a nuclear device would be difficult to dismiss entirely in view of the increasing number of producers of fissile material in a variety of countries and the problems of accounting fully for all material produced. Terrorists might see a seemingly plausible and preferably well publicised warning of an imminent nuclear attack as potentially a very effective means of blackmailing governments.[17]

Five years later, in 1994, several media reports spoke of fissile material available on the black market. The JIC, however, still considered terrorist activity with nuclear weapons a remote possibility.

> Despite the possibility which now exists of obtaining fissile material, it is extremely unlikely that a terrorist group could produce even a crude nuclear device; nor is there any evidence that any group has contemplated the use of nuclear weapons. A more plausible scenario might be the dispersal of radioactive materials by conventional explosives … to achieve radiological contamination. The actual danger to the public from radioactivity would probably be small – smaller in some cases than to the terrorists. But such an attack (or its threat) could be highly effective in causing panic and public concern.[18]

By 2000/01, particularly after the attacks on the World Trade Center on 11 September 2001, the calculus of terror had significantly changed. Suicide attacks and the acceptance by terrorists that these would alienate the public (previously thought to be a constraining factor), added to Osama bin Laden's preparedness to use unconventional weapons, significantly altered the JIC's assessment.

While there was no demonstrable connection between bin Laden and Saddam Hussein, the report started from the premise that the proliferation of nuclear, chemical and biological weapons had been recognised as a threat to the interests of the United Kingdom. In July 2002, the Counter Proliferation Committee was established as the principal coordinator of strategic counter-proliferation; it was chaired by the head of the Defence and Overseas Secretariat of the Cabinet Office.

With this background forming a lengthy preamble to the presumptive main subject, the report turned to Iraq. The reader of the report must bear in mind that the committee had no brief nor any desire to determine the existence or the extent of Prime Ministerial guilt. The committee attempted to answer three broad questions, studying the period from 1990 onwards:

(i) what was the quality of intelligence about the strategic intent of Saddam's régime to pursue WMD programmes?
(ii) what was the quality of intelligence about Iraq seeking to sustain and develop a 'break-out' capability in those fields?
(iii) what was the quality of intelligence about Iraqi production or possession of WMD?

There had been something of a see-sawing of opinion in the JIC. In the early 1990s, the prevailing opinion was that it would take five years for Saddam to develop and produce nuclear weapons. In 1993, however, there was a growing belief that Saddam had concealed chemical weapons (CW), biological weapons (BW) and Scud (short-range ballistic) missiles. By 1995, JIC reports were based on the belief that Scud missiles and their components had been destroyed, a view reversed in 1996 when suspicion grew that they had merely been concealed. By 1992, there was a clear impression from JIC reports that the three criteria of strategic intent, development of capabilities and 'breakout potential', the ability to deliver weapons, were being met by the existing situation in Iraq.[19]

In an apposite phrase, the report reports a sense of what one witness called 'a creeping tide' of proliferation and growth in the WMD capabilities of 'countries of concern'. This was described by Tony Blair in a memorable linking of fear of proliferation and established fact, leading to

> a picture of, not that there were extra States necessarily coming into the proliferation and WMD business but that those States that were pushing on this were very determined, they were mainly States that you would not want to have this type of stuff because of their unstable and repressive nature and there were certainly suggestions that the potential link with terrorism, and there was also ... quite a lot of stuff about Bin Laden and his desire to acquire WMD of one sort or another and I was quite often saying ... 'what are we actually doing about this' ... there was a lot to make me concerned about this and actually at the first meeting I had with George Bush in February 2001 I raised it with him but ... after September 11th it took on a completely different aspect ... what changed for me with September 11th was that I thought then you have to change your mindset ... you have to go out and get after the different aspects of this threat ... you have to deal with this because otherwise the threat will grow ... you have to take a stand, you have to say 'Right we are not going to allow the development of WMD in breach of the will of the international community to continue'.[20]

This linking, combined with the fear ratcheted by the State of the Union speech by President Bush on 29 January 2002 – the first reference to the 'axis of evil' – led to a redefinition of policy towards Iraq. Thus, in inter-departmental advice to ministers in early March 2002, the government's objectives towards Iraq were described as: 'the least worst option ... containment of Iraq, by constraining Saddam's ability to re-arm or build WMD and to threaten his neighbours'.[21]

Officials weighed the options of containment and regime change by military means.[22] Since Saddam had various courses open to him whereby he could continue to delay through non-cooperation, officials concluded that 'despite the considerable difficulties, the use of overriding force in a ground campaign is the only option that we can be confident will remove Saddam and bring Iraq back into the international community'.[23]

The JIC continued to warn the government that 'intelligence on Iraq's WMD and ballistic missiles programmes is sporadic and patchy', at the same time pointing out that 'Iraq is also well practised at the art of deception, such as concealment and exaggeration'.[24] The JIC was confident that, for as long as sanctions were effective, Saddam could not develop a nuclear weapon without help from abroad. All JIC comments on the state of Iraq's WMD programme were, however, trumped by the meeting between Blair and Bush at Crawford, Texas, on 6–7 April and Blair's admission that 'what has changed is not the pace of Saddam Hussein's WMD programmes but our tolerance of them post 11 September'.[25]

From April to August 2002, the calculus developed to the point that the emphasis was on 'what diplomatic options Saddam has to deter, avert or limit the scope and effectiveness of a US-led attack' – in other words, to resist a course of action already decided upon. By 9 September, the JIC took the view that 'Iraq has a chemical and biological weapons capability and Saddam is prepared to use it'. But, the report added, 'intelligence remains limited and Saddam's own unpredictability complicates judgments about Iraqi use of these weapons. Much of this paper is necessarily based on judgment and assessment.'[26]

Which leads the reader into the nub of the controversy – the famous September Dossier. This has the distinction of being the first public document prepared by the government from JIC reports. This fact immediately raises the question of why the traditional secrecy surrounding all matters of intelligence was dispensed with on this occasion. That, in turn, raises the question of why the September Dossier was prepared. What was its purpose? Was it to make a case for war, its very plausibility based on the candour demonstrated by government in citing a JIC paper?[27]

The Prime Minister himself, in his foreword to the dossier, appears to be using the novelty of publicising a JIC paper by remarking that such action was unprecedented. Committee members, naturally, were sceptical about that statement 'in response to growing Parliamentary and media debate about the imminence of war and questioning of the reasons for it'.[28] The committee specifically commented on Alastair Campbell's minute of 9 September to the chairman of the JIC in which, like President Nixon after Watergate, Campbell appeared to advocate the 'limited let-it-all-hang-out' approach as a badge of total honesty. 'The first point', he wrote, 'is that this must be, and be seen to be, the work of you and your team, and that its credibility depends fundamentally on that.'[29]

Not only did the September Dossier depend for its credibility on the JIC report; it simply claimed to reproduce intelligence assessments while, at the same time, misrepresenting or simply ignoring them. The committee extrapolated three examples of the omission in the dossier of clear warnings spelled out by the JIC.

(i) The JIC assessment of 9 September 2002 stated, 'Intelligence remains limited and Saddam's own unpredictability complicates judgments about Iraqi use of these weapons. Much of this paper is necessarily based on judgment and assessment.' In the dossier this was reproduced as 'This intelligence cannot tell us about everything. However, it provides a fuller picture of Iraqi plans and capabilities.'
(ii) The JIC assessment of 21 August 2002 stated, 'we have little intelligence on Iraq's CBW doctrine, and know little about Iraq's CBW work since late 1998.' In the dossier we read 'The nature of Saddam's regime makes Iraq a difficult target for the intelligence services. Intelligence, however, has provided important insights into Iraqi programmes and Iraqi military thinking.'
(iii) The JIC assessment of 15 March 2002 included the disclaimer that, 'Intelligence on Iraq's weapons of mass destruction (WMD) and ballistic missile programmes is sporadic and patchy. Iraq is also well practised in the art of deception, such as concealment and exaggeration. A complete picture of the various programmes is therefore difficult. But it is clear that Iraq continues to pursue a policy of acquiring WMD and their delivery means.' This qualifying comment is completely ignored in the September dossier.[30]

On 24 September, the day of the publication of the dossier, the Prime Minister reported to the House of Commons on the intelligence underpinning it:

> I am aware, of course, that people will have to take elements of this on the good faith of our intelligence services, but this is what they are telling me, the British Prime Minister, and my senior colleagues. The intelligence picture that they paint is one accumulated over the last four years. It is extensive, detailed and authoritative. It concludes that Iraq has chemical and biological weapons, that Saddam has continued to produce them, that he has existing and active military plans for the use of chemical and biological weapons, which could be activated within 45 minutes, including against his own Shia population, and that he is actively trying to acquire nuclear weapons capability.[31]

Unsurprisingly, the committee concluded: 'We believe that it was a serious weakness that the JIC's warnings on the limitations of the intelligence underlying some of its judgments were not made sufficiently clear in the dossier.' This underlies the entire section headed 'The Accuracy of the Dossier'. Overall, the judgements of the JIC in its August and September reports were taken as sound, but the qualifying comments concerning the uncertainty of intelligence available were disregarded in the September Dossier.[32]

It is important to keep in mind the remit of the Butler Committee. It had not been charged to produce a report that assessed the legal justification for the invasion of Iraq, nor was it responsible, in the manner of the Franks Commission on the Falklands War, for passing any judgement on diplomacy, the build-up to invasion or the strategic issues involved. Its remit was simply:

> to investigate the intelligence coverage available in respect of WMD programmes in countries of concern and on the global trade in WMD, taking into account what is now known about these programmes; as part of this work, to investigate the accuracy of intelligence on Iraqi WMD up to March 2003, and to examine any discrepancies between the intelligence gathered, evaluated and used by the Government before the conflict, and between that intelligence and what has been discovered by the Iraq survey group since the end of the conflict; and to make recommendations to the Prime Minister for the future on the gathering, evaluation and use

of intelligence on WMD, in the light of the difficulties of operating in countries of concern.[33]

Under those circumstances, it is hardly surprising that uncertainty stalked the conclusions of the report. In 2004, commenting on the post-war looting and destruction in Iraq, speculating that this might have been, at least in part, Iraqi government policy to destroy all evidence of WMD, the committee ventured: 'We conclude that it would be a rash person who asserted at this stage that evidence of Iraqi possession of stocks of biological or chemical weapons, or even of banned missiles, does not exist or will never be found.'[34]

As to the legitimacy of invasion, without straying beyond its terms of reference, the committee judged that, as invasion and regime change could only be justified by Iraq's breach of disarmament obligations under United Security Council Resolution 687, the available intelligence 'was insufficiently robust' to support such action.[35] Moreover, 'validation of human intelligence sources after the war' had, the committee concluded, 'thrown doubt on a high proportion of those sources and of their reports'.[36] There were recommendations aplenty regarding over-reliance on dissident sources, the length of reporting chains, pushing reliable agents beyond the limits of their reliability, the need for careful handling of human intelligence sources, and the over-compartmentalisation of intelligence.[37] There was also a tendency for assessments to be coloured by over-reaction to previous errors, the committee concluded and, as a result, the risk that worst-case scenarios become treated as prevailing wisdom.[38]

Concerning the September Dossier, then, the committee made a number of strong recommendations, accompanied by unequivocal language concerning the progress of intelligence through the JIC to the dossier. The JIC, they conclude, sought to offer a dispassionate assessment of intelligence and took responsibility for the dossier, attempting to ensure that normal standards were met. Unfortunately, the Prime Minister's language gave a false impression of the reliability of sources. It was a mistake to name the JIC as the originator of the dossier, as to do so gave a false impression of authenticity. In future, those using intelligence in public debate must be sure to explain the uses and limitations of that intelligence.[39] To underscore the government's and not the JIC's responsibility for any miscommunication, the report wound up with a trenchant paragraph:

> In reaching these conclusions, we realise that our conclusions may provoke calls for the current Chairman of the JIC, Mr Scarlett, to withdraw from his appointment as the next Chief of SIS. We greatly hope that he will not do so. We have a high regard for his abilities and his record ... We have said above that it was a mistaken judgment for the dossier to be so closely associated with the JIC but it was a collective one for which the Chairman of the JIC should not bear personal responsibility.[40]

There remained one controversial issue, one 'hot potato' the warmth of which derived from the recurring semblance that there had occurred a shading of intelligence assessments in order to justify action already agreed on between Prime Minister and President. In January 2003, President Bush blandly stated that 'the British Government has learned that Saddam Hussein recently sought significant quantities of uranium from Africa'.[41]

The committee was justifiably sceptical of the truth of Bush's bald assertion. Iraqi officials, the committee conceded, had visited Niger in 1999, and British Intelligence had learned 'from several different sources'[42] that the purpose of the trip was to buy uranium. The most likely source for MI6 was the French agency DST (*Direction de la surveillance du territoire*, the equivalent of MI5), which passed the intelligence to Britain but stipulated that, while it might be shared with Washington, its source should not be disclosed. The assertion that Saddam had actually attempted to buy uranium was dismissed by the former chief of the French agency DGSE (*Direction générale de la sécurité extérieure*, the equivalent of MI6). Documents purporting to cover Iraqi purchases in Niger were proven to be forgeries in March 2003. The committee was non-committal on the matter, assessing the President's statement as 'well-founded' but, at the same time, concluding that there was no overwhelming evidence that Iraq did more than ascertain the availability of uranium.[43]

Towards the end of the report, returning to the question of the 45-minute deployment time for Saddam's ballistic armoury, the committee unequivocally stated that

> the JIC should not have included the '45 minute' report in its assessment and in the Government's dossier without stating what it was believed to refer to. The fact that the reference in the classified assessment was repeated in the dossier later led to suspicions that it had been included because of its eye-catching character.[44]

There were criticisms of government procedure, veiled barbs aimed at Blair and Campbell, strong recommendations for more responsible, unbiased chairmanship of the JIC, a post that should be 'held by someone with experience of dealing with ministers in a very senior role, and who is demonstrably beyond influence, and thus probably in his last post'.[45]

Then, with a ringing condemnation of 'sofa government', the report comes to an end:

> We do not suggest that there is or should be an ideal or unchangeable system of collective Government, still less that procedures are in aggregate any less effective now than in earlier times. However, we are concerned that the informality and circumscribed character of the Government's procedures which we saw in the context of policy-making towards Iraq risks reducing the scope for informed collective political judgment. Such risks are particularly significant in a field like the subject of our Review, where hard facts are inherently difficult to come by and the quality of judgment is accordingly all the more important.[46]

Reaction to the report, predictably, ranged from assertions that the committee had identified serious flaws in the relations between government and the Intelligence Services to incredulity that the Butler Report did not indict Blair, his Cabinet and advisers as war criminals. Accusations of 'whitewash' came from those who, after Hutton, had wanted a witch-hunt.

The most balanced attack on the report – and, not unnaturally, on Butler himself – came from Robin Cook, the former Foreign Secretary, who had resigned from the Cabinet in protest at the invasion of Iraq.* Highly critical

---

* At the time of his resignation, Robin Cook was Leader of the House of Commons and Lord President of the Council.

of the war on Iraq, which he termed 'a spectacular own goal', he was contemptuous of the Butler Report, which stopped short of allocating blame for Intelligence failures, writing with incisive irony: 'What a wonderful specimen of the British establishment is Lord Butler of Brockwell. Urbane, unflappable and understanding. He should be put on display somewhere as a prize example of our ruling classes. Possibly the Victoria and Albert Museum would provide the right grandeur and period ambiance.'[47]

The Butler Report, Cook argued, had made it 'embarrassingly clear that Parliament was misled into voting for war on the basis of unreliable sources and overheated analysis, producing between them false intelligence'. The Prime Minister, he charged, 'should have been admitting that there were serious mistakes, that lessons had been learnt and that, above all, it will never happen again'.

Instead, Blair said in a statement: 'We expected, I expected to find actual usable, chemical or biological weapons after we entered Iraq. But I have to accept, as the months have passed, it seems increasingly clear that at the time of invasion, Saddam did not have stockpiles of chemical or biological weapons ready to deploy.'[48]

By September, at the Labour Party conference, Blair had recovered his sangfroid sufficiently to sum up the issues with a positive spin. Iraq might be in internecine chaos, but Blair was able to postulate that, while the evidence for the existence of biological and chemical weapons, as opposed to the capability to develop them, had turned out to be wrong, he could not apologise for removing Saddam. 'The world', he maintained, 'was a better place with Saddam in prison not in power.'[49]

The Butler Report was neither a whitewash nor a polemic against the Blair government for misleading the Commons and the country over the justification for the invasion of Iraq. Jonathan Powell commented ruefully that, although Butler might have enjoyed the task, 'we didn't enjoy the result'.[50] The report was far from damning, however. A committee of Privy Counsellors, chaired by Lord Butler, reported to Parliament on serious errors of judgement arising between the Intelligence Services and the government. By handing John Scarlett, chair of the JIC, what journalists described as a 'get out of jail free card' Butler, implicitly at least, laid the blame for those communication failures at the Prime Minister's door. As to Blair's beliefs and convictions, however, he is surprisingly frank and understanding, writing subsequently, in a private memoir:

> Because of the protracted insurgency that followed the Iraq war and the loss of so many Iraqi, American and British lives … the decision to go to war remained controversial and, with it, the report of our Review … [Tony Blair] was widely represented as having lied about the reasons for the war.
>
> I believe, and have always said, that this is an unfair criticism. I take the view that he genuinely believed that Iraq had WMD and also wanted to develop a nuclear weapon. Most of the other intelligence services in the world shared that belief, as did Hans Blix when he went to Iraq in November 2002. In his post-arrest interrogation, Saddam Hussein admitted that he had suspended his WMD programme in order to get sanctions removed but would have resumed it when the coast was clear. With the aim of getting support for military action, Tony Blair was disingenuous about the robustness of British intelligence underlying his belief but that is a different issue.[51]

It was left to a member of the Butler Committee, the Rt Hon. John Chilcot GCB, to perform the obsequies on the Iraq war, as Lord Franks had done for the Falklands War. It was left to cynical observers to assert that Blair had 'sexed up' intelligence to feed to Bush at the Crawford ranch, that he had been 'disingenuous' in the passing on of intelligence concerning Saddam's quest for uranium. But those issues, Butler and his colleagues firmly maintain, were part of a different question.

The wider implications of that different question were raised in the House of Commons on 20 July 2004 during a debate on the Butler Report. Butler sat in the gallery through the debate, a heated affair in which Tam Dalyell, the 'Father of the House', used the report to call for Blair's resignation. Ten years of leading the Labour Party, he argued, was enough, so 'the Prime Minister should … consider making way for someone else … against the background of Butler, and set in motion the due processes of the party'.[52]

Michael Howard tried to extricate himself from his previous support of the war in order to castigate Blair for taking Britain to war. A forceful interjection came from another Tory member, Sir Patrick Cormack, MP for South Staffordshire, who asked Howard: 'Is he saying to the House that he believes that he and I, and those who voted as we did on 18 March 2003, were deliberately deceived?'[53]

It seemed for a moment that Howard might respond in the affirmative, an admission that Butler would have understood and supported. Instead, Howard equivocated, petulantly demanding that Blair answer other questions that he had posed. The opportunity was lost and the debate moved on in ponderous fashion. About half an hour before the adjournment at 7.00 p.m., Michael Meacher, Labour Member for Oldham West & Royton, raised the issue of accountability:

> The most striking characteristic of the Butler report, as many hon. Members have said, is the disjunction between analysis and judgment. It catalogues a litany of failures and then pulls all its punches by declaring that in effect no one is to blame ... It is a very British establishment charade, but as an exercise in accountability, which is the crux of what is needed, it is completely unacceptable.[54]

The Butler Committee had, as charged, investigated the accuracy of intelligence reports, examined discrepancies between those reports and government documents, and made recommendations for the future on the gathering, evaluation and use of intelligence on WMD. It pulled no punches. Sir Patrick Cormack raised the question that flowed from the report's conclusions; the Leader of the Opposition let it fall. The Prime Minister emerged from the debate not only unscathed, but even exultant. The media was almost unanimous in hailing Blair's 'triumph', a notable dissenting voice being that of Matthew Parris in *The Times*:

> Well if 'yah, booh, sucks, see if I care' counts as a debating triumph; if cheap, point-scoring quotation from Michael Howard's local newspaper counts as an answer to Lord Butler's troubling report; and if two fingers cocked in the face of all the evidence counts as a moral victory, then, yes, Mr Blair has

> won. He might as well have mooned at the populace from the back of his prime ministerial limousine as he left London. That too would have been described by the quality press as a 'characteristically confident performance' and 'another tour de force', and by the tabloids as 'Cheeky Tony!'[55]

After the publication of the report, Butler discreetly withdrew from centre stage; he spoke, after some hesitation, in the House of Lords debate on 7 September, but not until December did he speak to the media.[56] When he did speak out, in an interview with Boris Johnson, then editor of *The Spectator*, he managed to avoid answering the obvious questions. Try as he might, Johnson was unable to inveigle Butler into apportioning blame for Intelligence failures. Beyond the comment that John Scarlett would have been 'toast' had the report not specifically exonerated him, there was no lifting of the veils of the British secret world.[57]

Instead, in what Anthony Howard described as 'the views of the former Cabinet Secretary [lapping] gently enough on the shores of the citadel of Government', Butler elaborated on his criticisms of New Labour's *modus operandi*.[58] Johnson recorded:

> I realise, as the evening starts to rub its back against the window panes of Doughty Street, that Robin doesn't want to talk about the detail of his report, not any more. He wants to make some general and far more important points – but with implications for the WMD fiasco – about the way Labour governs the country.

For all the detachment of Johnson's account of the interview, Butler produced an alarmingly comprehensive list of criticisms. 'Politically appointed people carry great weight in the government', he admitted, 'and there is nothing necessarily wrong with that, but if it's done to the exclusion of advice from civil servants, you tend to get into error, you make mistakes.' New Labour, he maintained, gave too much emphasis to selling, exercised too much central control and engaged too little in 'reasoned deliberation' at Cabinet level.

The country, he believed, suffered 'very badly from Parliament not having sufficient control over the executive … a very grave flaw'. As a result,

> The executive is much too free to bring in a huge number of extremely bad Bills, a huge amount of regulation and to do whatever it likes – and whatever it likes is what will get the best headlines tomorrow. All that is part of what is bad government in this country.

The *Daily Mail* described Butler's criticisms as 'a savage attack, possibly the most excoriating ever from such an authoritative source', and the response from Downing Street was immediate. Jack Cunningham, known as the Labour Cabinet 'enforcer', was entrusted the task of refuting the criticisms on BBC's *Today* programme. How dare Butler, clearly a dyed-in-the-wool Conservative 'stooge', who had served Tory governments for a decade, presume to speak out after just eight months of working with New Labour?

As Anthony Howard pointed out, 'no government ever started with a greater fund of good will from the Whitehall machine' than did Tony Blair's. It was 'a significant development' if that goodwill had evaporated. Amid the shrill demands that those responsible for failures of intelligence be named, that heads should roll, the far more pervasive threat to democracy was widely ignored.

Almost twelve years on, as the publication of the Chilcot Report was eagerly awaited, the linking of inadequate intelligence and inadequate reasoned deliberation was again remarked on in the media:

> We have known for almost as long that the intelligence justified nothing at all. In his 2004 review … Butler said as much. Unfortunately he said it in a Whitehall dialect so opaque that few understood the meaning of 'the British Government put a weight on available intelligence that it could not bear'. My Mandarin-English translation software renders this as: 'Blair and his gang of sofa-hogging gangsters flamed up gossip into hard fact to pull a fast one on the public'.[59]

CHAPTER 20

BARON BUTLER OF BROCKWELL, CROSS-BENCHER

THERE ARE PERIODS IN life that are defined by an event, by where one lives, by a task or series of tasks undertaken. In retrospect, those periods seem to have flown by more quickly than others, differently punctuated, more radically segmented. For the Butlers, the 'Half Moon Lane Period' was a span of eighteen years in which events piled on top of each other to create, in retrospect, a breathtaking narrative. The importance for Butler of that period is proven by the title that he chose for his barony. Brockwell Park, across the road from Half Moon Lane, may not be a household name, but it defined the Butler household for two decades.

Between 1979, when they moved into their first true family home, until 1998, when they decamped to the Master's Lodgings of University College, Half Moon Lane was a family home, a discreet office where Prime Ministers met with Butler for off-the-record talks, a solid base from which Butler commuted to Whitehall. The children, who were fifteen, twelve and eleven when they bought the house, were thirty-four, thirty-one and thirty when they moved out. A decade later, when they moved back to London from Oxford, Robin and Jill had seven grandchildren. They had not been inattentive parents or grandparents, but they might be forgiven for feeling that those three decades had hurtled by rather more quickly than they had expected.

When Robin and Jill moved to Oxford in 1998, they took the decision to sell the house in Half Moon Lane. Sophie and Nick Trend had two children; Nell and Justin Rushbrooke also had two. Andrew was called to the bar in 1993 and married in May 1998. With all three children married and established, the house that had been the family home in the children's teenage years was surplus to requirements. Over eighteen years, the house had appreciated to a sale price eight times as much as they had paid in 1979. Looking beyond their time at Univ, Robin and Jill bought a flat in Westminster and a cottage at Wighton, between Fakenham and Wells-next-the-Sea in Norfolk. Somehow the three-way move of furniture and packing cases worked and, by the end of 1997, they were prepared for the future when the Mastership came to an end.

During their time at Univ, Nora Butler, having survived her husband by twelve years, died in February 2000 at the age of ninety-two. A proud and independent woman, she had resisted all suggestions that she move from her house to a home, even as her mobility failed. When she fell and cracked a hip, her son and daughter-in-law conspired with her doctor to persuade her to spend two weeks of convalescence in a retirement home. To her surprise, she found the home acceptable and moved in permanently. Her death ended Butler's ties to the north-west; his life was now spent in the triangle of Oxford, London and Norfolk.

Leaving Univ was an easy decision. Their time there had been a decade that they had greatly enjoyed in an environment that had important associations for both of them. Marion Hawtree, the Master's secretary at Univ, who continued to work for him after, observed that Butler never did anything without a clear agenda. He would have come to Univ with a fixed term in mind and, much as he had done as head of the Home Civil Service, would have paced himself to achieve all his targets in the decade that he allotted. After ten years, she judged, 'he felt he had achieved many of his original aims for the College, and … no doubt had a stint of 10 years pretty firmly in his mind from the outset.'[1]

Jill also felt that it was time to move on. During their years at Univ, three grandchildren had arrived, bringing the total to seven. Mrs Hawtree sensed that Jill in particular yearned to return to London to be closer to them and to help with childminding when required. As an Honorary Fellow, Butler would remain in contact with the college – without becoming mired in the endless debates among the Governing Body over all matters, even the most trivial. Both the college and the university had brought their share of frustrations to a pragmatic man of action. Moreover, as an experienced amateur thespian, he probably sensed that it was time to leave the stage.

At the same time as the ten-year appointment at Univ came to an end, Butler left the board of HSBC after a decade as a non-executive director. In his memoir, he wrote that the company went 'from strength to strength, although encountering some problems at the end of my ten years on the Board'. That sentence involves a considerable understatement, although the extent of the problems that beset HSBC was not revealed until three years after Butler's departure.

On 17 July 2012, the US Senate Permanent Subcommittee of Investigations released a report entitled 'U.S. Vulnerability to Money Laundering, Drugs and Terrorist Financing: HSBC Case History'. The 333-page report, issued after a year-long investigation, revealed that HSBC had been a conduit for drug money, had disguised the sources of funds to evade sanctions against Iran, and had handled accounts for clients with alleged ties to terrorism. Carl Levin, a Michigan senator involved in the investigation, concluded that HSBC's internal culture had been 'pervasively polluted for a long time'.[2]

Since at least 2005, the report alleged, there had been repeated failures by HSBC to control money laundering, a notable example of which had occurred in 2007 when a Mexican businessman, a long-time client of HSBC, had been raided by the Mexican authorities, who found a stockpile of $205 million hidden in a locked room.[3] Additionally, the Mexican division of HSBC had sent $7 billion to HSBC (US) in 2007 and 2008, a sum that could only have been generated from illegal activities. A former head of the financial crimes unit at the FBI commented: 'Frankly, they're lucky somebody is not getting prosecuted here.' In the event, HSBC paid a $1.9 billion penalty in the US in 2012, prompting one weekly newsletter to comment that 'the HSBC's [*sic*] of this world are dirty participants in the real drug triangle; namely, drug traffickers, crooked government elements and complicit moneychangers'.[4]

There can be little doubt that money laundering took place at HSBC during Butler's time on the board. There is, however, no evidence to suggest that he was aware of the activities of the Mexican division of the bank, nor anything to suggest that he was derelict in his duties as a non-executive director. According to the UK Corporate Governance Code, the duties of a non-executive director are:

- constructive challenge and help in developing proposals on strategy;
- scrutiny of management's performance in meeting agreed goals and objectives and the monitoring of performance reports;
- satisfying themselves on the integrity of financial information and that controls and risk management systems are robust and defensible;
- determining appropriate levels of remuneration for executive directors;
- appointing and removing executive directors, and succession planning.[5]

The third of these duties, arguably, was inadequately performed by the non-executive directors. It must be said, however, that in a corporation with 4,400 offices in seventy-one countries it would not be impossible for the executive team to conceal the activities of a handful of its subsidiary companies. By the time that he retired from the board in 2008, money laundering activities were undoubtedly more difficult to hide, as the interest of the authorities was becoming intense. The current board of HSBC Holdings plc is made up of twenty individuals, fifteen of whom hold non-executive roles; if the ratio was the same in 2007, then the executive directors would appear to have been adroit at concealing unwelcome facts from their non-executive colleagues.

Throughout Butler's career, major moves have been preceded by a longish holiday, time away to think and take stock. No surprise, then, that at the end of the 2007/08 academic year he and Jill had already signed up for two months away from England. By then aged seventy, however, he managed to suppress the habit of a lifetime to tackle some challenging trail or mountain. Instead, they decided to realise a dream that they had often mentioned.

As part of her university degree course in 1984/85 Sophie had spent a term in Florence. She had so much enjoyed the experience of studying Renaissance art in such a perfect setting that her parents had promised themselves that they would follow their daughter's example. Butler had heard of excellent courses offered by the British Institute in Florence, and in 2008 he accordingly signed them up for two of these – 'The Birth of the Renaissance' in September and 'The Early Renaissance' in October. Again, in the tradition of Butler holidays, they persuaded friends to join them for each of the four-week sessions.

The main pedestrian highway for tourists in Florence runs south from San Marco and the Accademia di Belle Arti to the cathedral and baptistery, Giotto's *Campanile* and on to the Piazza della Signoria and the Uffizi Galleries. Tucked away to the east of the cathedral, in a relatively quiet and elegant street, is 25 Via dell'Oriuolo. It is hard to imagine a better base from which to explore the city; here Robin and Jill set themselves up in a comfortable two-bedroomed flat.

Lectures were held in the afternoons, leaving mornings free to visit churches and galleries. Additionally, the British Institute offered a full programme of films and lectures. They were welcomed hospitably and felt quite at home; Butler relearned the carefree skills of carrying no keys and strolling at a leisurely pace. At weekends, they travelled by train to other Italian towns; for a septuagenarian couple it was the closest thing possible to a student life with no responsibilities.

There was no obligation to take end-of-term exams, although Butler's competitive nature yearned to enter the lists. Eighteen months later, after returning for the third module, 'The High Renaissance', they took a voluntary test. To their surprise, the younger students decided not to show up; Jill and Robin were the only candidates. The exam involved identifying buildings, paintings and sculptures, their artists and dates. Jill distinguished herself by scoring 100 per cent; her husband misidentified a Brunelleschi chapel. Typically, he comments that the Butlers achieved both first and last places in the examination.

Doubtless, Butler used his time in Florence to take stock and plan for his life after Univ. There were opportunities, responsibilities, interests – but perhaps the one certain aspect of his future that attracted him was his role as a peer of the realm. He had a very clear idea of the role that the House of Lords could play in British democracy, and ten years earlier had been involved in an attempt to institute long-overdue reform. This, the latest initiative in a century-long debate, involved a Royal Commission, chaired by Lord Wakeham.*

---

* Lord Wakeham had been staying at the Grand Hotel for the 1994 Conservative Party conference. His wife was killed in the explosion.

Early in Butler's Mastership at Univ, he had invited Tony Blair, David Frost and their families to lunch at the Lodgings. In true Butler fashion, the meal could not be taken without competitive sport, and the Blair family plus Butler took on the Frost family at garden football in the Master's garden. News of the event quickly spread through the college, and undergraduates packed the upper-floor rooms to watch the celebrity show.

After lunch, there was more serious fare when the future of the House of Lords came up in conversation. In their 1997 election manifesto, New Labour had undertaken to create 'a modern House of Lords':

> The House of Lords must be reformed. As an initial, self-contained reform, not dependent on further reform in the future, the right of hereditary peers to sit and vote in the House of Lords will be ended by statute ... The system of appointment of life peers to the House of Lords will be reviewed. Our objective will be to ensure that over time party appointees as life peers more accurately reflect the proportion of votes cast at the previous general election. We are committed to maintaining an independent cross-bench presence of life peers. No one political party should seek a majority in the House of Lords.[6]

Aware that the government proposed to appoint a Royal Commission, Butler spoke out in his maiden speech in the Lords, making it clear that he, too, felt that reform was necessary, though not perhaps for the same reasons as New Labour. Comparing twentieth-century Britain with Augustan Rome, he stated the maxim that it was 'of the highest importance, in the absence of hereditary Peers, for the Royal Commission to find a way in which to select Members of your Lordships' House which does not depend solely on the patronage of the Executive'.[7] The speech was duly interpreted by the media as a signal to the government that he was available to serve on the commission.[8]

The House of Lords, in Butler's view, should not be, or be perceived as, a rival to the Commons, which must inevitably retain primacy. However, in order to ensure that the Lords represent the gender, ethnic and cultural make-up of Britain, the majority of members would have to be appointed, rather than elected.

Butler believes that this view was totally congruent with government policy, as he was approached soon after by Richard Wilson and asked if he would chair the commission. Having only recently taken on the Mastership of Univ, he felt that the chairmanship would be too time-consuming, but was happy to be a member.[9] An impressive group was assembled,* and over the following fifteen months it embarked on another attempt to square the circle of having a House of unelected, appointed notables within a democratic system.

The methodology was logical. The starting point was to address the question of whether there was any need for a second House, particularly if it was not, like the United States Senate, to be made up of elected members. The primacy of the House of Commons was an established, immutable fact; the purpose of the Lords, in Butler's view, was to provide checks and balances, like those envisaged by the American Founding Fathers, to curb executive power. The Lords, he felt, should exist to bring a number of different perspectives to bear on legislation proposed by government. Unless the House of Lords – in which the government should not have an overall majority – was able to function in that capacity, there would be no legislative restraint on a government with a workable majority. For that function to be fulfilled, the Lords would have to be largely composed of appointed members.

While the commission members agreed that there must be some elected and some appointed members, they had difficulty in agreeing on the number of each in a reformed House. That uncertainty assisted the commission's critics in their dismissal of any kind of 'hybrid' House. At all events, critics argued, it would create two classes of member and, if appointed members were to constitute the majority, it would not do away with cronyism or the use of peerages to repay favours or raise campaign cash. When the report was presented in March 2000, it was unenthusiastically received. Most memorable was the description of it as 'a dog's breakfast'. Butler stated the dilemma – or, as he pointed out, the trilemma – by setting out the choices:

* The other members were John Wakeham, Douglas Hurd, Gerald Kaufman, Professors Dawn Oliver and Anthony King, trade union leaders Brenda Dean and Bill Morris, Kenneth Munro and Ann Beynon (protecting Scottish and Welsh interests), Sir Michael Wheeler-Booth, former Senior Clerk of the House of Lords, and Richard Harries, Bishop of Oxford.

> Indeed, there are logically only three bases for composing your Lordships' House – or perhaps three-and-a-half if one includes lottery, which I beg leave to exclude today. The three are a fully elected House, a fully appointed House, or some mixture of the two. Just as some reject *a priori* an elected House, and others reject *a priori* an appointed House, yet others reject a mixture of the two on the grounds that it is, to use the fashionable phrase, a dog's breakfast.[10]

The dismissive epithet, naturally, stuck, and three months later continued to be derisively used, on one occasion by Patrick Nicholls, MP for Teignbridge: 'the more I read of it, the more troubled I became. I expected that, in the way of these things, it would turn out to be, at best, a curate's egg, but it is a complete dog's breakfast.'[11]

In short, everyone found some basis for rejecting the Bill. Yet Butler remained very clear in his mind concerning the role that he, as a member of the House of Lords, should attempt to perform. During his tenure at Univ, he attended the Lords as time allowed. It was after his return from Florence in the autumn of 2008 that it became what he describes as 'my staple occupation'.[12]

The separation of powers, the horror of absolute power wielded by a king that impelled Thomas Jefferson, James Madison and their colleagues at the Constitutional Convention of 1787 to restrict the power of the American President,[13] had been uppermost in his mind in his dealings with Prime Ministers as Cabinet Secretary. He had no wish to put the clock back in the manner of American conservatives, but he viewed with considerable concern the creeping acquisition of power by the executive. Successive special advisers in Downing Street had exacerbated that concern.

He was realistic enough to recognise that the House of Lords, reformed or unreformed, would not be the grand stage that a politician needed to check the assumption of power by 10 Downing Street. He did, however, continue to have a voice that commanded attention and, as he expressed it: 'I had felt frustration at the Executive's dominance over Parliament and their consequent irresponsibility in bringing forward excessive and ill-prepared legislation. The Lords gave me a small platform from which to try to do something about it.'[14]

This frustration, shared by several of his former colleagues, led him to be part of the Better Government Initiative, an organisation that describes its formation as 'a response to widespread concerns about the practical difficulties that government today faces as it seeks to run the country against a background of rapid change'.[15] Butler is one of the four members of the board of governors who are concerned with the broad strategy of the group. The second tier, the executive committee, prepares the group's reports and provides advice to parliamentary committees. The executive committee is made up principally of former Civil Service mandarins and was until recently chaired by Sir Christopher Foster, the group's founder, formerly an executive member of the board of Coopers & Lybrand, a professor of economics at the LSE and senior adviser to successive governments. It is in 2017 chaired by Sir Richard Mottram.*

The group came to the public's notice in January 2010 when it released an outspoken report entitled *Good Government: Reforming Parliament and the Executive*. In a section bluntly titled 'What Has Gone Wrong', the report argues:

> Over the last 20 years, the public and the media have come to regard several events as notorious examples of bad government: the Community Charge (now remembered as the Poll Tax) in 1990, the Dangerous Dogs Act 1991, the failure of the Child Support Agency, the Hunting Act 2004, the story of the Millennium Dome. More complicated failures have resulted from the constant changes of policy and legislation and the constant stream of new, centrally-directed initiatives which have affected areas such as education, health, social care and criminal justice over a period of 20 years. Policy failures have often been cumulative as one new initiative and one Act of Parliament has followed another on the same subject.[16]

This theme is central to the paper. 'There has been too much government in recent years', the report charges. 'Some of it has been unnecessary and too

---

* Sir Richard Mottram has one of the most varied résumés of any mandarin, having been Permanent Secretary at several ministries. He came to the public's attention for his remarkably plain speaking at a meeting in the Department for the Environment, Transport and the Regions in 2002.

much of it has been badly prepared.' Much of the blame can be attributed to the media, but it is precisely the unholy alliance between Downing Street and the media that, Butler felt, made for the 'dumbing down' of media and public relations in the Blair government. 'Sofa government', the increase and extension of influence of special advisers to the point that the centre directs the actions of accountable ministers, had resulted in the sloppily prepared legislation mentioned above.

Departments should focus on developing policy with less interference from central government. Parliament should insist that Bills are prepared and presented in accordance with formalised standards and procedures that allow time for thorough scrutiny. The role of the Civil Service as an impartial advisory service should be recognised and formalised; at the same time, 'there should be greater transparency over the roles, knowledge and experience of those appointed as special advisers, and constraints over the number of or budget for special advisers'.[17]

At the launch of the report, Butler pulled no punches in his predictions. The Personal Care at Home Bill, a measure going through Parliament at that time and guaranteeing free personal care for 280,000 people with 'the highest needs' could, he believed, in time be regretted as much as the Community Charge.[18] These were strong words – although it was far from clear how much impact the report was likely to have. Butler had been resisting the deformalisation of executive decision-making since Haines and Donoughue were at No. 10 with Wilson in the 1970s. The movement in the intervening thirty-five years had been entirely in one direction.

The fact remains that, for the former Cabinet Secretary, these were fundamental questions as to how Britain should be governed. The relations between the centre, the Civil Service, departmental ministers and the Cabinet was, in his view, vital to the smooth functioning of British democracy. The House of Lords provided both a modest check to the power of the executive and a platform, albeit a narrow one, for Butler to reverse the one-way flow of power.

Lord Butler enjoys a position as an elder statesman perhaps without equal. He was first seconded as a Private Secretary to Downing Street in 1972, and he has a perspective with a wide sweep over politics at the top over the past five decades. This lengthy personal experience, combined with bipartisan exposure, gives him an almost unique pulpit from which to speak on issues of the day. As an example, during the build-up to the 2016 referendum on Britain's continued membership of the European Union, he was able to draw comparisons between the original referendum, instigated by Harold Wilson in 1975, and the 2016 version.

That in turn led to a comparison of the political skills of Wilson and David Cameron. The latter, he argued, would be placed in an intolerable position if the referendum favoured a British departure. This, indeed, turned out to be an accurate prediction, as Cameron, despite his confidence that he could continue as Prime Minister, promptly stepped down. Wilson, by contrast, had kept his cards close to his chest and only at the very last moment shown his hand. By that time, he had outmanoeuvred Michael Foot, Tony Benn and Peter Shore – while persuading them that he had acceded to their conditions – and declared the terms on which he would favour entry; he had also ensured that those conditions would be favoured by Helmut Schmidt. It was a consummate piece of political artistry that impressed the young Butler with its virtuoso simplicity.[19]

The position of David Cameron, by contrast, would be very different, he argued, if the referendum were to go against his wishes. 'Having committed himself so very strongly to the Remain campaign, his authority as PM would have been shattered … I think he would go and fairly quickly.' The referendum, he pointed out, was only advisory in law; Parliament could push for a second one if there was a narrow vote for Leave on a low turnout.[20] As rhetoric from both sides became increasingly shrill in the days immediately preceding the referendum, it was refreshing to hear a balanced opinion that put it in historical and political perspective. His predictions, moreover, turned out to be cannily accurate.

The House of Lords also provides an institution to which he feels a genuine affiliation. A contemporary at Harrow remarked that, while he was highly ambitious, he was also a 'team player'. He may have sought the best parts in a play, but he was always a loyal member of the cast.[21] He enjoyed the conviviality of rugby as a young man. He belongs to several dining clubs: The Club, The Other Club and Grillions; he is a member of Brooks's, the

Athenaeum, the Oxford and Cambridge Club and the Beefsteak. And, perhaps inevitably, he is an honorary member of one of the great City livery companies, the Salters' Company.

The Salters' Company, one of the oldest of the many livery companies in the City of London, is ninth in the order of precedence. In common with other livery companies, it is an actively philanthropic entity. Its particular interest is in supporting science education at secondary and university level. In addition, it maintains almshouses in Maidenhead and Watford.

With some trepidation, principally at the thought of eating endless starchy dinners all year, Butler became second warden of the Company in 2009, with a view to becoming Master in 2011. His year as Master turned out to be a very enjoyable year, during which, predictably, he 'tried to inject some novelty into the Company's entertainments'.[22] Just as he had brought speakers of all persuasions to the Univ Master's Lodgings and created a musical soirée during the final stages of the Butler Report, he sought out political speakers, invited the Harrow School XII to sing and persuaded Michael Mates to attend and offer after-dinner entertainment.

In small things as in large, he has a practical and direct approach to institutions and customs. Far from being a root-and-branch revolutionary, he approaches every challenge with the attitude that, if a custom has survived for a long time, it is probably not all bad, but it probably also could benefit from a new approach in certain aspects. Whether he is dealing with the Civil Service, the Cabinet Office, an Oxford college, a City livery company or a college literary society, his approach has been fundamentally the same.

First, consult as many knowledgeable people as possible to discover current opinions. Next, take time to analyse what is worth preserving, what needs to be modified, what needs to be abandoned. Finally, discuss what can be done to maximise the value of that which is to be preserved – and act. Time and again, he employs the same approach; time and again, when he moves on to a new challenge, he leaves the institution in better shape than it was when he arrived.

This ability to discuss and understand different people's attitudes to a question is one of his greatest strengths. It is the stronger for his being quite unbiased as to sources. He is as likely to be persuaded by a young person as by a contemporary, principally because young people recognise that he takes them seriously. They return the compliment. That is the case with his grandchildren, who adore him; with undergraduates, who remember his Mastership as a collaborative adventure with Junior Common Room and Senior Common Room pulling together; by Civil Service colleagues, impressed by the lengths to which he would go in order to be sure that they had all the information they needed.

Marion Hawtree describes his thoroughness in an initial foray into reform during the early years of his Mastership at Univ:

> Knowing how well Robin always researches things, I suspect he was fully aware that things at Univ were likely to be done very differently from that in the Civil Service, and he would have been prepared for that. However, there must have been many occasions when he became frustrated by the Oxford experience, both at college level and within the university as a whole. Many of the minor problems which arose in College often simply required someone with a common sense approach to take immediate action and move the situation forward to conclusion. Such an approach would have been second nature to Robin in his Civil Service days. In college though, every decision great or small, invariably required consideration via a series of committee meetings before finally arriving at the Governing Body committee … fifty plus Fellows, all of whom run the college. Many of them relish the idea of a good debate with their peers at the Governing Body meetings and consequently, it can take an age to reach a committee decision for action and conclusion, even over fairly minor agenda items.[23]

Within a very short time, he had learned to guide this disparate, querulous body; he had resuscitated the Shakespeare Club, Oxford's oldest dining club, in a form that was more faithful than before to its august name; Jill had revived the Martlets for graduate students to speak to their peers about their research work. Both innovations used traditional groups to meet a need that he and Jill identified; both were successful. When he prepared to leave after ten years, the Fellows met to discuss his successor, informing Butler that he was entitled neither to contribute, nor even to know the identity of the candidates. Instead of taking offence, he reckoned simply that there was little to be gained by eroding the precious rights of the Fellows. What possible good would it serve for him to protest? The Fellows made an excellent choice, following tradition and electing an academic, Sir Ivor Crewe, Vice-Chancellor of the University of Essex. Univ was a better place than it had been in 1997. The Fellows knew that. They needed no urgings from the outgoing Master to ensure that it stayed that way.

To achieve similar results with the government of Britain is a tougher challenge. Moreover, so great has been the erosion of the bedrock of government by Cabinet that it would be impossible to reverse the creeping assimilation of power at the centre. The world of 'sofa government', where the media, not the Cabinet, is the arbiter of action, has now become the accepted reality in Britain. The observer can be sure, however, that for as long as Lord Butler of Brockwell has voice, he will be an active and outspoken goad, urging the executive to pay due respect to Parliament, to avail itself of the Civil Service and to maintain a system that allows proper scrutiny of properly prepared legislation.

That, after all, is what he has been doing, in different fields, for almost sixty years.

CHAPTER 21

OUT OF THE LIMELIGHT

IT WAS SAID OF Lord Redcliffe-Maud, civil servant and an earlier Master of Univ, that 'with John Maud you have to take the smooth with the smooth'.* With Robin Butler one has a similar experience: one has no choice but to accept the authorised version of events, smoothly delivered. It will not be inaccurate; it will not be self-serving; but it will be the authorised version, and it will be the only one ever heard from his lips.

John Redwood, MP for Wokingham and a minister in Major's government, said that Butler's minutes of Cabinet meetings would 'tell historians very little about the Major years'. Cabinet minutes are traditionally somewhat selective, carefully including only conclusions and omitting inter-personal tensions. Even by those standards, Butler's are sparse, pragmatic statements of items for action.† They would read well in Latin, Butler's second language. Not in flowing Ciceronian prose, but in the elliptic Tacitean style that is his official narrative manner. Events are events. They happened only in one way. Here, his record states, is how they happened.

It is a curious experience to transcribe the results of an interview and then to encounter the same words, the same cadence in the record of events in the memoir that Butler has written for his family. It is even more curious to encounter word-for-word the same description taken from an interview with, for example, Charles Moore, the biographer of Margaret Thatcher. Butler has, in fact, done what he believed Harold Wilson did – created what he

---

* Sir John Maud, later Lord Redcliffe-Maud, was Master of Univ from 1963 to 1976.

† Discussions of nuclear defence, for example, are systematically omitted from Cabinet minutes.

called 'tapes', the authorised version of events. Robin Butler is an historian; he is not seduced by contrafactual hypotheses or unfulfilled conditionals. Just as he prepared forty-minute answers to philosophical questions for his Oxford philosophy finals, so he retains versions of events that are, from then on, the record of the facts.

He is far from being unimaginative; he has a vivid imagination and a mind that ranges in different directions over myriad questions. Like Robert Kennedy, he looks at what could be and asks 'Why not?' Generally traditionalist in outlook, once he embraces change, he pursues it without reservation, as his personal commitment to the Citizen's Charter demonstrated. He surprised Harold Wilson and members of his Policy Unit with the flexibility of his outlook. It is a mistake to pigeonhole Butler according to any of the stereotypes that he appears to fit.

The most commonly repeated fact, the label most automatically applied, is that he was head of school at Harrow. Peter Hennessy describes him as the sort of schoolboy that we were all jealous of, as he accumulated honours in sports, won academic prizes, swam effortlessly to the top. Granted, he was always like that and, equally, as a boy he was judged 'too fond of Robin' at prep school and somewhat undiplomatically intolerant of his inferiors at Harrow. As a teenager, he bestrode the earth; yet he absorbed words of caution from his housemaster; from having a sister born with various disabilities, he was always sensitive to the problems of others. He saw what it was, as a parent, to give hostages to fortune; he cares deeply about levelling the playing field. Parity of opportunity; parity of esteem.

Asked by Sir Anthony Seldon to name the most interesting people whom he had met over the course of his career, Butler chose three individuals: Nelson Mandela, Oleg Gordiewsky and Deng Xiaoping.[1] Mandela had spent seventeen years as a prisoner on Robben Island but was able to take a statesmanlike and charitable stance when he came to power. Gordiewsky, a former colonel in the KGB, rejected the Soviet system after the invasion of Czechoslovakia in 1968 and spied for the British Secret Intelligence Service (MI6), living in acute danger of detection until he was able escape from the USSR in 1985. Deng Xiaoping, the twice purged Chinese leader, survived the Cultural Revolution and, on Mao's death, outwitted his opponents, finally rising to power at the age of seventy-three.

These three individuals, in Butler's estimation, were men whom one could not meet without being fascinated by them, by their ability to survive continued oppression and repeated setbacks. All three, he said, had experienced things that he could hardly imagine. All three had overcome unthinkable adversity – lives totally different from the unchallenged succession of promotions that Butler himself had enjoyed. Like a form of 'survivor's guilt', Butler's experience of a privileged life enhanced his admiration for individuals whose success had been less assured than his own.

He is decidedly not a man who seeks only the company of people like him. He enjoys the challenge of new ideas and has always been comfortable among young people; his teenage daughters brought friends to Half Moon Lane and their father did not embarrass them. Even as Cabinet Secretary, he made himself accessible to students and he gave interviews to them whenever he was approached. One annual event was always on his calendar: Peter Hennessy used to bring students on his 'Politics and Government' course to the Cabinet Office, where they would ask questions, rather sophisticated questions, that Butler strongly suspected were framed by Hennessy. Approached by a student writing a thesis on government, he always made himself available and tried to help.

Hennessy has been able to observe Butler at close quarters for over thirty years and, with a journalist's objectivity, reflects on their association since they met through Bernard Donoughue in 1976:

> He was like an elder brother to me. Later he sponsored me for membership of the House of Lords and helped me to get Top Secret clearance … He is unique in having so many of the requirements for the job, not all of them expected. He writes superbly, making complex issues understandable. He has the necessary stamina, which is most important. He is not indispensable, but he is confidence-inspiring. He has great ambition, tempered by great charm.[2]

Butler's progress up Britain's *cursus honorum* has left no scarred bodies in his wake. He is, even eighteen years after leaving the job, very much the mandarin. And yes, he is still, unmistakably, the head boy. Cerebral, practical, decidedly not an intellectual seeker, but someone who takes a problem away, unwraps it, studies it intently, finds a solution and applies himself to implementing it. The clarity and breadth of vision with which he addressed the question of ownership of council houses astounded Joe Haines. If he needed to appoint a committee to process his preferred solution, he displayed a particular genius in choosing members of that committee, individuals who ostensibly reflected all shades of opinion. Then, as Professor Pelling found over the question of a professional Senior Tutor at Univ, somehow time and again the committee that he appointed approved the Butler-preferred solution.

It is a special and rare combination of talents that coalesced to facilitate his ascent in the Civil Service. John Major referred to his gentler side, describing him as 'easy-going, helpful and efficient'. Underneath the polished veneer, however, as the former Prime Minister observed, was one of the most competitive men he had ever met.[3] And Major made that observation after Butler had already reached the top. Much as a compulsive gambler will bet on anything, Butler fastens on to the competitive aspect of every situation. Every week, he and Jill join battle over the Polygon puzzle in *The Times*. In the weekday editions, from Monday to Friday, they compete; on the Saturday Polygon they cooperate. It would be quite wrong to have rules that allow the result to be a draw, so the best of five with one friendly day is the solution. Their children have made a trophy that goes to the winner each Friday. By and large, the honours are equally divided.

Spoofs and April Fools have also featured throughout his life. Spoof telegrams in the Think Tank, April Fool's menus listing unspeakable dishes to trick his mother – all are part of Butler's rollicking attitude to life. Jill, moreover, is a match for him and once drove him to apoplexy before she admitted the hoax. When Andrew's Harrow School bill arrived, she doctored it by adding to the outfitters' account a sizeable sum for sweets, chocolate and ice cream. In a fury, Butler was on the point of writing to Andrew's housemaster to protest against such indiscipline before Jill confessed.

In June 2011, Butler was about to become Master of the Salters' Company, one of whose charitable activities is to produce GCSE and A level syllabuses, used by about 20 per cent of British schoolchildren. Feeling that he should know something about this activity, and since his Harrow education had not included a single science lesson, he decided to take the GCSE. Jill offered to take it with him and arranged sponsorship for them both through St Paul's Girls' School, where she had taught mathematics. After lining up with the girls to take the papers in the school sports hall, they awaited the results with some anxiety. On 25 August, their wedding anniversary, the results came through:

> We opened them in acute anxiety. It turned out that we both got A* and over the four papers I got two more marks than Jill. The reason for this was we turned up to do Paper 3 when they had put Paper 4 on the schedule and I had prepared for both whereas Jill had concentrated on Paper 3. Anyhow the A*s were a great relief because no St Paul's girl gets anything less and we didn't want to spoil their record.[4]

Most people, I hear the reader say, are competitive. What is surprising about Butler's desire to win – and to do better than Jill? In response, one can point out that he lists 'competitive sports' first among his interests in *Who's Who*. He has many interests, ranging from opera to rock-climbing, from archaeology to theatre to wine-tasting, but competitive sports top the list. His preferred sport is rugby football, which he played and studied until, having climbed into Twickenham at midnight, he was able recreate the most famous tries scored there for the benefit of Jill, then his fiancée. His position of wing-forward requires a certain bloodlust in those who occupy it and among his papers are photographs of him doing bloodcurdling things to members of the opposing three-quarter line.

All of which leads us to say that it was scarcely surprising that he became Cabinet Secretary. Hennessy said as much when he was appointed, that he had, by chance or design, occupied the most suitable positions along the way. It was, in fact, more by official design than by chance. At the time, it was Civil Service practice to groom high-fliers and to shape their careers on their way to the top. With the opening up of applications for senior positions and amid accusations of elitism and paternalism, that practice has been discontinued.

The job, as it was in Butler's early career and is once again now, is, in truth, two jobs: Cabinet Secretary and head of the Home Civil Service. There is a permanent, lively difference of opinion as to whether the roles should be linked or separated. David Cameron separated the roles and subsequently combined them again. Most former Cabinet Secretaries believe that they should be combined; Gus O'Donnell, Cabinet Secretary from 2005 to 2011, using considerable diplomacy, said that, while the roles were separated, it might make sense to combine them again one day.[5] Richard Wilson said that separating the roles was 'harking back to the old regime'.[6] And so the debate continues. To understand the question, one should be clear exactly what the Cabinet Secretary's job consists of in order to form any opinions.

For the Chilcot Inquiry, all extant Cabinet Secretaries were asked to put their heads together and produce a job description. The consensus was that the job had four principal features:

- supporting proper and effective government decision-making, including the administration and provision of advice to Cabinet and its sub-committees; administering the Ministerial Code; and advising the Prime Minister on policy, process and propriety;
- the organisation and recording of Cabinet meetings;
- as head of the Civil Service, maintaining an impartial UK Civil Service that can command the confidence of ministers from all political parties;
- overall responsibility for security and intelligence systems and structures.

On these matters, the Cabinet Secretary's responsibility is to the Prime Minister as Chair of the Cabinet and Head of Government. The Prime Minister determines the Cabinet Secretary's priorities and objectives.[7]

While this is undoubtedly accurate, it is far from illuminating as a description of how the Cabinet Secretary passes the day. Less formally, we have the description penned by Sir Maurice Hankey, the first Cabinet Secretary, and quoted by Robert Armstrong in a lecture:

> When the great ones go off to their drinks and their dinner
> The Secretary stays, getting thinner and thinner,
> Wracking his brains to record and report
> What he thinks that they think that they ought to have thought.[8]

In that same address, Armstrong gave his own description of the job, likening the Cabinet Office to

> the engine room of the ship of state. The Prime Minister is up there on the bridge with his Ministerial colleagues, steering the ship and sending orders down to the engine room. The Secretary of the Cabinet is responsible for the smooth running of the engines; for the smooth working of the machinery of collective decision-taking, and – as the Head of the Home Civil Service – for the civil service which mans the machine and the various departments.[9]

From the first definition and from Armstrong's picture of the relations between Cabinet Secretary and Prime Minister, it is clear that the nature of the job is to a great extent dependent on the Prime Minister's perception of it. Butler was Cabinet Secretary to three Prime Ministers and he would be the first to agree that it involved three very different relationships. Under Thatcher, he was occasionally made to feel like something of a turncoat because he was no longer the Principal Private Secretary that he had once been; under John Major, the Cabinet regained its stature and Butler was approvingly supportive, able to advise the PM on Cabinet decisions and, most importantly, to channel all information from the Iraq war to Cabinet ministers in timely fashion. Under Blair, the Cabinet was treated as largely irrelevant and, with it, the Cabinet Secretary, unless he was prepared to operate in lockstep with the joined-up government as the Prime Minister's agent.

Butler's successor Richard Wilson proved to be much more accommodating in that capacity, pursuing the matter of Geoffrey Robinson's loan to Peter Mandelson in a manner that Butler had not adopted in dealing with Aitken, Hamilton or Tim Smith. In that matter, as in others, Butler can be seen as the last of a certain kind of Cabinet Secretary, the last, arguably, of the traditionalists who believed in the sacrosanctity of Cabinet government. The Cabinet Secretary in David Cameron's Downing Street, Jeremy Heywood, described his responsibilities as twofold: first, as chief policy adviser to the Prime Minister, and second, as 'custodian of the Cabinet system'.[10] That encapsulates a charming phrase, one which Butler also merited, but his description seems to place more importance on advising the Premier on policy.

Central to Butler's view of the job was the concept of teamwork between the Civil Service and politicians. The Civil Service might be junior partners, but the cooperation is a partnership nonetheless. If the Cabinet Secretary becomes the Prime Minister's creature, then the partnership loses its force. Richard Wilson believes that the drive to create a Prime Minister's department arose from Butler's being distant from the office of No. 10.[11] Butler would argue that it was essential to maintain a distance, that too much propinquity was dangerous.

At all events, No. 10 has changed immeasurably since Butler first worked there in the 1970s. His frequent protest that 'Number Ten is not an office; it's a house' is not persuasive any more than would be the claim that the White House is simply the residence of the American President.

Within the many constraints and, surrounded by a changing landscape, was Robin Butler an effective Cabinet Secretary? For as long as the Cabinet had a valid role to play, without doubt he was. He was prepared for the job by the Civil Service establishment; he was appointed despite not being the most senior man available; he worked effectively with Thatcher, asserting the importance of the Civil Service when it was threatened and being prepared to resign if the PM insisted on a certain course of action in the argument over Charles Powell. Under Major, he set up efficient procedures for running the Gulf War. In the transition from Tory to New Labour government in 1997 the work of the Civil Service, in Blair's view, was 'quite superlative'. Those are significant achievements to be proud of.

In spite of his years at Univ, his double first and his rugby Blue, he was arguably less prepared to be an Oxford Head of House than he had been to be Cabinet Secretary. In typical manner, he studied the job objectively, identified the potential minefields, then proposed solutions without imposing them on his colleagues. He provided leadership to a group of independent fiefdoms who often did not quite realise that they were being led. It would have been impossible to satisfy that group of fiefs all the time, but he made a noble effort, while putting the interests of the college first.

If there were criticisms, they were predictable and, curiously, they resonated with his days in Whitehall. Ultimately, they concerned the concepts of accountability and responsibility, the distinction that he had drawn as Cabinet Secretary. In the face of media that were increasingly aggressive towards ministers, demanding that heads roll as soon as something went awry, the Butler doctrine postulated that ministers were certainly accountable for everything in their departments, but were not necessarily responsible. This, predictably, was ill-received by the media, who wanted a straight line from action to blame to retribution.

As described in Chapter 18, as Master of Univ, Butler's secretary Marion Hawtree observed him pass papers to his OUT tray with a note that he would like more details or advice on the issues raised by the paper. For the majority of these questions, there was no one responsible for settling matters, and Marion later commented that he 'found it rather unusual not to have had a larger team of administrative staff working alongside him, thus enabling him to draw on their advice and expertise, and to be able to delegate work to others'.[12] With no one accountable and no one responsible, like President Harry Truman, he must not infrequently have felt that 'the buck stops here'.

Civil Service training proved invaluable for his time as Master. Not for nothing had he rallied the Permanent Secretaries on the issue of the Sunningdale Training College. Obtaining near unanimity from the assorted fiefs of Whitehall should have been, he thought, vastly more complex than guiding twoscore academics to the desired decision. That invaluable Whitehall weapon, the committee, was employed in the Senior Common Room. Choosing the battles to fight and ignoring incendiary issues that were best avoided, he left his mark on the college and is generally reckoned to have been a very good Master. If he failed to achieve all his goals – for example, in the Norrington Table of colleges' academic results – the Butler doctrine was relevant. He was not a tutorial Fellow; he took no part in teaching, and so could not be held responsible. As Master, on the other hand, he readily accepted a measure of accountability.

If there were Fellows of Univ who were less than enthusiastic about his tenure, they were those academics who would never have been satisfied with anyone other than a fellow academic in the Master's Lodgings. It would have been easy to predict such criticisms as he did, in fact, incur: that he allowed college activities and sport to play too large a part in an overall assessment of an undergraduate; that by hiring administrative Fellows such as a professional Senior Tutor, he was diluting the pure wine of the academic, almost monastic, community of the college. He would not deny the charges; he would simply respond that he left the college a happier place – and one greatly more in tune with the twenty-first century – than the institution he had come to in 1998.

While he was Master of Univ, he held his most public appointment – as chair of the Butler Inquiry. Here, too, the bloodlust and disappointment of the media, who had hoped to see heads roll from the guillotine, prompted the popular press to cry that the report was a whitewash. It was decidedly nothing of the kind; the report clearly illustrated where intelligence had been unreliable or had been dressed up; it reached conclusions critical of the Blair government, although it failed to satisfy the media by hanging any particular minister out to dry. While it must have made the Prime Minister distinctly uncomfortable, its patent fairness and balanced conclusions did not alienate him.

In 2008, still in sound physical and mental health, he stepped down not simply from Univ, but from any measurable and direct, lasting influence on government. He is realistic about the modicum of influence that he wields in the House of Lords and about the power of the Better Government Initiative to reverse the trends in government. He and his former colleagues are most unlikely to reduce the executive's dominance over Parliament. While he recognises that fact, he would argue that not to put his experience to work to achieve better-prepared legislation would be to waste the small stage allowed him to press for better government. But this low-key activity is not an attempt to reclaim centre stage. Those days are decidedly past.

In the fifty-five years since he joined the Civil Service, many aspects of Britain and the country's politics have changed beyond recognition. Sir Jeremy Heywood, the Cabinet Secretary appointed in 2012, was born a few months after Butler first went to the Treasury. If Butler represents the old guard with a degree in 'Greats', Heywood is decidedly more up-to-date with an Oxford degree in History and Economics, an MSc from the London School of Economics and an MBA from Harvard to his credit. It seems part of a curious time warp that Butler's retirement took place less than two decades ago; since then, the pace of change has been breathtaking.

The personal qualifications for the Cabinet Secretary's job remain largely the same, involving a considerable presence, great charm and outstanding communication skills. A great part of Butler's charm lies in his lack of remoteness, his approachability. For a man who was once among the three most powerful in Britain, he is remarkably accessible. He also has the quality, shared by Bill Clinton, that when he listens to you, you are able to believe that you are the only person that matters to him at that moment, that your opinion on the topic under discussion was the very one he had been waiting to hear. It is a powerful asset.

Most people can be imagined in other jobs. They intended, perhaps, to take one particular course until something came up and changed their direction. Robin Butler does not belong to that group; the path he followed is, in all details, precisely the path that one most easily imagines for him. Yet until his early twenties, he had no idea what he wanted to do with his life; he knew what he did not want to do but, beyond an unspecific notion of public service, had no positive ambitions.

If we accept that he chose a career in the Civil Service in the belief that he could make a difference to life in Britain, it is tempting to ask why he did not take the more direct approach offered by politics. It is worth considering what he might have achieved if he had chosen that course. It is not impossible to imagine him opting for an academic career from which he could have pursued political ambitions, perhaps as a centrist, even a progressive Tory, winning a seat in the 1966 election, becoming a junior minister in Heath's 1970 government.

Allowing rein to that contrafactual notion, and assuming his success, we can imagine a British version of Woodrow Wilson, the 28th President of the United States. Wilson, a devotee of Walter Bagehot, saw the primacy of the Cabinet as 'perfected party government'.[13] His analysis of the American separation of powers, the first scholarly attempt to examine the American system from a purely pragmatic point of view, is very similar to what Butler might have written about British government. Both Wilson, in 1884, and Butler, a century later, were witnessing the assumption of increased power of the executive and erosion of the power of the legislative.

Like Wilson, Butler has a tendency to believe that his actions are stimulated by the best motives and, as a politician, he might have aroused the same kind of resistance that Wilson ignited both at Versailles and, after returning to the United States, from Congress.* Like Wilson, Butler might have been too much the head boy once his competitive political instincts were aroused. A colleague at the Treasury comments that, while Butler had strong convictions, he did not have them in 'a political way', adding:

> I once asked him which department he would like to have been in, if he had not been sent to the Treasury. He said the Department of Transport. That is the answer of a manager rather than a politician, I think. The other thing is that you have to enjoy being ruthless from time to time … I'm not sure Robin would have found this quite to his taste. He made his way to the top by being very good at all his jobs and not, I think, by stabbing people in the back. The other thing about politics is that a certain amount depends on luck; you can be rewarded (or punished) by the roll of the dice. Robin might have been happy as a politician in an ancient Greek city, where you were elected by the choice of a relatively small number of your (known) peers. Indeed advancement in the Civil Service operated just a bit like that. But his meritocratic instincts would have been rather against the element of luck of modern politics.[14]

Sarah Hogg was blunter in her assessment. 'He did not have the emotional antennae that a politician needs', she said. Contrafactual speculation is not history. Butler never became a politician – and, when we allow that speculation rein, we should be delighted with his choice. His career as a 'modern mandarin' was more suited to his talents than that of a party politician.

Long before he became Cabinet Secretary, he had a clear idea of how he would reform the Civil Service. At the end of his first year as head of the service, he persuaded Mrs Thatcher to allow him to present his vision for a modernised Civil Service on television. In a thirty-minute televised interview with Sue Cameron on BBC2, he addressed questions concerning the service's

---

* At Versailles, Wilson's idealism infuriated French president Georges Clemenceau. When Wilson enumerated his sacrosanct 'Fourteen Points', Clemenceau exclaimed: 'Fourteen! The Good Lord had only ten.'

impartiality and accountability.[15] Perhaps the most graphic statement of his personal hopes was expressed on the name badge that he wore to the launch of the Citizen's Charter at No. 10 – 'I'm Robin. Can I help you?'

That anecdote of the name badge reflects a quality that he has possessed from boyhood: he relishes life, its challenge, triumphs and reversals. They are all tremendous fun. Jeremy Lemmon recalled that at Harrow he could join the party wholeheartedly, but that there was always 'much more to him'. He was never sanctimonious, never what Tom Bower described as 'the star schoolboy who led Harrow's Bible society'.[16] Dr Robin Darwall-Smith of University College believes that he really enjoyed being Master. The current Master, Sir Ivor Crewe, is excellent at the job, adds Darwall-Smith, 'but he doesn't take the same pleasure in it as Robin did'.[17]

Perhaps the most telling comment comes from Butler himself, when he describes the excitement of his 'black boxes' each evening as Cabinet Secretary:

> One of the things that excited me most about the job was the joy of opening my black boxes in the evening. Ministers had red; I had black. I used to say that it was like dipping into a bran tub, as the variety of its contents was so huge, and any problems that the Prime Minister had, he would ask the Cabinet Secretary to handle ... In that sense I was the Prime Minister's right-hand person.[18]

A further clue as to how Butler viewed his job is given by a short article that he wrote for the National Gallery's monthly magazine. Each month, dignitaries were asked to write about their favourite picture; Butler chose *The Ambassadors* by Holbein.

His three reasons for this choice were, first, that he and Jill had been introduced to the picture soon after they met and it therefore had tender associations. Second, it was the first picture that he had been taught to analyse. Third, and most revealingly, he identified with the two ambassadors: 'I recognise the look on the faces of the ambassadors', he wrote:

> They are representing their country in a very difficult matter – the divorce of Henry VIII from Catherine of Aragon. One can imagine that this was

> also quite a dangerous mission – there was a practical reason for the *memento mori* in the picture. But I take it that the real reason … is to remind these men and spectators, that despite their dignity and the finery of their office, they are only men and that what really matters is not the trappings of office but the lasting things represented by science, music, literature and art. I like to think the two ambassadors recognise that.[19]

In a world where only 13 per cent of people enjoy going to work,[20] it is a pleasure to encounter someone who tackles enormous challenges with the enthusiasm of a teenager. Youthfulness is a quality that his daughter Nell described lovingly in her father's seventy-eighth year:

> My earliest memories are of him lying on a toboggan and me sitting on his back while he shot down the hill near where we lived. He was always full of the most harum-scarum schemes, whether it be climbing trees and jumping off garages, or go-karting down the street. He's still like that, only now he does it with our children.[21]

There is certainly much of the 'head boy' about Robin Butler. But the most remarkable characteristic of The Right Honourable Baron Butler of Brockwell, KG GCB CVO PC is that there is a part of him that perversely remains simply, unmistakably, a boy. Armchair psychologists will perhaps speculate that he is compensating for some aspect of boyhood of which he was deprived. To the contrary, he greatly enjoyed his childhood, his adolescence, and his adulthood too. He is one of the fortunate few who have nothing to complain about. If he were writing a *Contio Latina* of his life he might be tempted to echo Horace: 'That man will live a happy life and be master of himself who can say at the end of each day "I have lived".'[22]

APPENDIX

LORD BUTLER'S CIVIL SERVICE CAREER

1961 Joins the Treasury after coming first in the Civil Service admissions examination.
1964 Appointed Private Secretary to the Financial Secretary at the Treasury.
1965 Promoted Principal.
1968 Posted to the Bank of England on a six-month exchange.
1971 Recruited by Lord Rothschild to the Central Policy Review Staff ('Think Tank').
1972 Posted to 10 Downing Street as Private Secretary to PM, Edward Heath.
1974 Remains at Downing Street as Private Secretary to Harold Wilson.
1975 Promoted Assistant Secretary. Returns to the Treasury.
1977 Promoted Under-Secretary for general expenditure policies.
1980 Becomes Principal Establishment Officer in the Treasury.
1982 Appointed Principal Private Secretary to PM, Margaret Thatcher.
1983 Promoted Deputy Secretary.
1985 Returns to the Treasury. Appointed Second Permanent Secretary in charge of public spending.
1987 Appointed Cabinet Secretary and head of the Home Civil Service.
1988 Knighted in New Year's Honours List.
1997 Retires on 31 December, three days before his sixtieth birthday.
1998 Created life peer as Lord Butler of Brockwell in New Year's Honours List.

BIBLIOGRAPHY

A NOTE ON THE [illegible]

[illegible] source to [illegible] ... [illegible]

PRIMARY SOURCES

[illegible]

BIBLIOGRAPHY

A NOTE ON THE SOURCES

The principal source to determine the shape of this narrative has been Lord Butler of Brockwell himself. Between January 2015 and October 2016 he has been outstandingly generous with his time for interviews, often lengthy, in which he has been as frank and open as security considerations permitted. He also allowed access to his personal papers and letters, notably the memoir *Dear Descendants*, that he wrote because he 'realised that knowledge of [his parents'] lives and [his] family history had died with them'. This has proved an invaluable document, not because it offers a collection of unchallengeable verities on important events, but because it is an aid to understanding Lord Butler's priorities in dealing with them. In common with all personal memoirs, its content must be treated with some caution, but that in no way diminishes its importance.

PRIMARY SOURCES

Butler, Lord, *Dear Descendants: A Legacy of Personal Memories* (2014), unpublished family memoir.

Lord Butler Archive of personal papers and memorabilia, 1946–2015.

Margaret Thatcher Foundation: Thatcher Archive ('THCR') at Churchill College, Cambridge, prefaced in references with 'CCC'.

The National Archives: FO, CAB and PREM files, prefaced in references with 'TNA'.

SECONDARY SOURCES

Aitken, Jonathan, *Porridge and Passion* (2005), London: Continuum.

———, *Pride and Perjury* (2000), London: HarperCollins.

Baker, James A. and Lee Hamilton (co-chairs), *The Iraq Group Study Report* (2006), New York: Vintage Books.

Baker, Norman, *The Strange Death of David Kelly* (2007), London: Methuen.

Balogh, Thomas, Roger Opie, Dudley Seers, Hugh Thomas (eds), *Crisis in the Civil Service* (1968), London: Anthony Blond.

Beesley, Ian, *The Official History of the Cabinet Secretaries* (2016), London: Routledge.

Benn, Tony, *Office Without Power: Diaries, 1968–1972* (1988), London: Hutchinson.

Billière, Sir Peter de la, *Storm Command: A Personal Account of the Gulf War* (1992), London: HarperCollins.

Bishop, Patrick and Eamonn Mallie, *The Provisional IRA* (1987), London: Heinemann.

Blackstone, Tessa and William Plowden, *Inside the Think Tank: Advising the Cabinet 1971–1983* (1988), London: Heinemann.

Blair, Tony, *A Journey: My Political Life* (2010), New York: Random House.

Blix, Hans, *Disarming Iraq: The Search for Weapons of Mass Destruction* (2004), London: Bloomsbury.

Bower, Tom, *Broken Vows: Tony Blair, The Tragedy of Power* (2016), London: Faber & Faber.

Brandreth, Gyles, *Breaking the Code, Westminster Diaries* (2014), London: Biteback Publishing.

Brown, George, *In My Way* (1971), London: Victor Gollancz.

Bush, George, *Public Papers of the Presidents, 1990* (1991), Washington: US Government Printing Office.

——— and Brent Scowcroft, *A World Transformed* (1998), New York: Vintage.

Butler, David and Anthony King, *The British General Election of 1964* (1965), London: Macmillan.

——— and Dennis Kavanagh, *The British General Election of October 1974* (1975), London: Macmillan.

Campbell, John, *Edward Heath: A Biography* (1993), London: Jonathan Cape.

———, *Margaret Thatcher*, vols 1–2 (2000, 2003), London: Jonathan Cape.

———, *Roy Jenkins: A Biography* (1983), London: Weidenfeld & Nicolson.

Castle, Barbara, *The Castle Diaries, 1964–1970* (1984), London: Weidenfeld & Nicolson.

———, *The Castle Diaries 1974–1976* (1980), London: Weidenfeld & Nicolson.

Cavendish, Anthony, *Inside Intelligence* (1990), London: Collins.

Clark, Alan, *Diaries* (1993), London: Weidenfeld & Nicolson.

———, ed. Ion Trewin, *Alan Clark: The Last Diaries* (2002), London: Weidenfeld & Nicolson.

Clarke, Peter, *A Question of Leadership: From Gladstone to Thatcher* (1991), London: Hamish Hamilton.

Coates, Tim (ed.), *The Hutton Inquiry, 2003* (2004), London: Tim Coates.

———, *Lord Butler's Report: Espionage and the Iraq War* (2004), London: Tim Coates.

Cohen, Nick, *What's Left: How Liberals Lost Their Way* (2007), London: Fourth Estate.

Cradock, Percy, *In Pursuit of British Interests: Reflections on Foreign Policy under Margaret Thatcher and John Major* (1997), London: John Murray.

Crick, Michael, *Michael Heseltine: A Biography* (1997), London: Hamish Hamilton.

Critchley, Julian, *Heseltine: The Unauthorised Biography* (1987), London: André Deutsch.

Daalder, Hans, *Cabinet Reform in Britain, 1914–1963* (1964), Oxford: OUP.

Danchev, Alex, *Establishing the Anglo-American Alliance: The Second World War Diaries of Brigadier Vivian Dykes* (1990), London: Brassey's.

Darwall-Smith, Robin, *A History of University College, Oxford* (2008), Oxford: OUP.

Davis, Jon, *Prime Ministers and Whitehall 1960–1974* (2007), London: Hambledon Continuum.

Dell, Edmund, *The Chancellors: A History of the Chancellors of the Exchequer, 1945–1950* (1997), London: HarperCollins.

Donoughue, Bernard, *Downing Street Diary* (2005), London: Jonathan Cape.

———, *The Heat of the Kitchen* (2004), London: Politico's.

———, *Prime Minister: The Conduct of Policy under Harold Wilson and James Callaghan* (1987), London: Jonathan Cape.

———, *Westminster Diary: A Reluctant Minister under Tony Blair* (2016), London: I. B. Tauris.

Eddy, Paul and Magnus Linklater with Peter Gilman, *War in the Falklands* (1982), London: Times Newspapers Ltd.

Faulkner, Brian, *Memoirs of a Statesman* (1978), London: Weidenfeld & Nicolson.

Foley, Michael, *John Major, Tony Blair and a Conflict of Leadership: Collision Course* (2002), Manchester: Manchester University Press.

Fowler, Norman, *Ministers Decide* (1991), London: Chapmans.

Hailsham of St Marylebone, Baron (Quintin Hogg), *The Dilemma of Democracy: Diagnosis and Prescription* (1978), London: William Collins.

Haines, Joe, *The Politics of Power* (1977), London: Jonathan Cape.

Harris, Kenneth, *David Owen, Personally Speaking* (1987), London: Weidenfeld & Nicolson.

———, *Thatcher* (1998), Boston: Little, Brown.

Harrison, Brian, *The Transformation of British Politics 1860–1995* (1996), Oxford: OUP.

Healey, Denis, *The Time of My Life* (1989), London: Norton.

Heath, Sir Edward, *The Course of My Life* (1998), London: Hodder & Stoughton.

———, *My Style of Government* (1972), London: Evening Standard Publications.

Hennessy, Peter, *The Prime Minister: The Office and Its Holders since 1945* (2000), London: Allen Lane.

———, *Whitehall* (1989), London: Secker & Warburg.

Heseltine, Michael, *Life in the Jungle* (2000), London: Hodder & Stoughton.

Hogg, Sarah and Jonathan Hill, *Too Close to Call* (1995), London: Little, Brown.

Holmes, Martin, *Thatcherism: Scope and Limits, 1983–1987* (1989), Basingstoke: Palgrave Macmillan.

Howe, Geoffrey, *Conflict of Loyalty* (1994), London: Macmillan.

Hurd, Douglas, *An End to Promises: Sketch of a Government 1970–1974* (1979), London: Collins.

Ingham, Bernard, *Kill the Messenger* (1991), London: HarperCollins.

James, Simon, *British Cabinet Government* (1992), London: Routledge.

Jenkins, Kate, Karen Caines and Andrew Jackson, *Improving Management in Government: The Next Steps* (1988), London: HMSO.

Jenkins, Simon, *Thatcher and Sons: A Revolution in Three Acts* (2006), London: Allen Lane.

Jenkinson, Neil, *Richard Daft: On a Pedestal* (2008), Cardiff: Association of Cricket Statisticians and Historians.

Jephson, Patrick, *Shadows of a Princess* (2000), London: HarperCollins.

Kavanagh, Dennis and Anthony Seldon, *The Major Effect* (1994), London: Macmillan.

Kemp, Sir Peter, *Beyond Next Steps: A Civil Service for the 21st Century* (1993), London: The Social Market Foundation.

Lawson, Nigel, *The View from No. 11* (1992), London: Transworld.

Lee, Joseph J., *Ireland, 1912–1985: Politics and Society* (1990), Cambridge: CUP.

Leigh, David and Ed Vulliamy, *Sleaze: The Corruption of Parliament* (1997), London: Fourth Estate.

Link, Arthur S., *Wilson*, 5 vols (1947–1965), Princeton: Princeton University Press.

Major, John, *The Autobiography* (1999), London: HarperCollins.

Mallie, Eamonn and David McKittrick, *The Fight for Peace: The Secret Story Behind the Irish Peace Process* (1996), London: Heinemann.

Margach, James, *Abuse of Power: The War between Downing Street and the Media from Lloyd George to Callaghan* (1978), London: W. H. Allen.

Maudling, Reginald, *Memoirs* (1978), London: Sidgwick & Jackson.

Mayer, Allan, *Madam Prime Minister: Margaret Thatcher and Her Rise to Power* (1979), New York: Newsweek Books.

Money, Ernle, *Margaret Thatcher: First Lady of the House* (1975), London: Leslie Frewin.

Moore, Charles, *Margaret Thatcher: The Authorized Biography*, vols 1–2, (2013, 2015), London: Allen Lane.

Morrison, Susan, Richard Townsend and Peter Hennessy, *Routine Punctuated by Orgies: The Central Policy Review Staff, 1970–1983* (1985), Glasgow: University of Strathclyde.

Mount, Ferdinand, *Cold Cream: My Early Life and Other Mistakes* (2008), London: Bloomsbury.

Norton-Taylor, Richard, Mark Lloyd and Stephen Cook, *Knee Deep in Dishonour: The Scott Report and Its Aftermath* (1996), London: Victor Gollancz.

Pallister, David, Luke Harding and David Leigh, *The Liar: The Fall of Jonathan Aitken* (1999), London: Fourth Estate.

Peatling, G. K., *The Failure of the Northern Ireland Peace Process* (2004), Dublin: Irish Academic Press.

Pimlott, Ben, *Harold Wilson* (1992), London: HarperCollins.

Plowden, William (ed.), *Advising the Rulers* (1987), Oxford: Basil Blackwell.

Powell, Jonathan, *The New Machiavelli: How to Wield Power in the Modern World* (2010), London: The Bodley Head.

Private Eye, *The Secret Diary of John Major, Aged 47 ¾* (1992), London: Corgi.

———, *The 2nd Secret Diary of John Major* (1993), London: Corgi.

Proudfoot, Mary, *British Politics and Government 1951–1970* (1974), London: Faber & Faber.

Ramsden, John, *The Winds of Change: Macmillan to Heath, 1957–1975* (1996), London: Longman.

Rentoul, John, *Tony Blair: Prime Minister* (2001), London: Little, Brown.

Rothschild, Lord (Victor), *Meditations of a Broomstick* (1977), London: Collins.

———, *Random Variables* (1984), London: Collins.

Sampson, Anthony, *Anatomy of Britain Today* (1965), London: Hodder & Stoughton.

Sandbrook, Dominic, *State of Emergency: The Way We Were, Britain 1970–1974* (2010), London: Allen Lane.

Schultz, George, *Turmoil and Triumph* (1993), New York: Charles Scribner's.

Seldon, Anthony, *The Blair Effect* (2001), London: Little, Brown.

———, *Major: A Political Life* (1998), London: Phoenix.

——— and Jonathan Meakin, *The Cabinet Office 1916–2016* (2016), London: Biteback Publishing.

Smith, Leslie, *Harold Wilson: The Authentic Portrait* (1964), London: Hodder & Stoughton.

Stuart, Gisela (ed.), *The House Parliament's Magazine Guide to 10 Downing Street* (2015), London: Dods.

Taylor, Peter, *Brits: The War Against the IRA* (2001), London: Bloomsbury.

———, *Provos: The IRA and Sinn Féin* (1997), London: Bloomsbury.

Thatcher, Margaret, *The Downing Street Years* (1993), London: HarperCollins.

Thomas, James, *Popular Newspapers, the Labour Party and British Politics* (2015), Abingdon: Taylor and Francis.

Thompson, Brian and F. F. Ridley (eds), *Under the Scott-light: British Government Seen through the Scott Report* (1997), Oxford: OUP.

Trewin, Ion, *Alan Clark: The Biography* (2009), London: Weidenfeld & Nicolson.

Tyerman, Christopher, *A History of Harrow School* (2000), Oxford: OUP.

Waldegrave, William, *A Different Kind of Weather* (2015), London: Constable.

Wells, A. F. et al., *More Oxford Compositions* (1964), Oxford: OUP.

Whitelaw, William, *The Whitelaw Memoirs* (1989), London: Aurum Press.

Williams, Marcia, *Inside Number 10* (1972), London: Weidenfeld & Nicolson.

Wilson, Colin and Damon Wilson, *Scandal!* (2007), London: Virgin Books.

Wilson, Harold, *The Governance of Britain* (1976), London: Weidenfeld & Nicolson.

———, *A Personal Record: The Labour Government 1964–1970* (1971), London: Weidenfeld & Nicolson.

Wilson, Woodrow, *Congressional Government* (1885), Boston: Houghton Mifflin.

———, *The State* (1889), Boston: D. C. Heath.

Woodward, Robert, *Bush at War* (2002), New York: Simon & Schuster.

———, *Plan of Attack* (2004), New York: Simon & Schuster.

———, *State of Denial: Bush at War, Part III* (2006), New York: Simon & Schuster.

Wright, Peter, *Spycatcher* (1987), New York: Viking Penguin.

Young, Hugo, *One of Us* (1993), London: Pan Books.

ENDNOTES

PREFACE AND INTRODUCTION

1 Lord Armstrong, interview, 20 December 2016.
2 Lord Butler, speech at Washington and Lee University, Lexington, Virginia, 26 January 2010. A light-hearted version of the events is given by Ann Treneman in 'Please don't spoil the plot, just when your country needs you', *The Times*, 22 October 2004.
3 Lord Butler, speech at Washington and Lee University, Lexington, Virginia, 26 January 2010.
4 Robin Cook, 'Britain's worst intelligence failure, and Lord Butler says no one is to blame', *The Independent*, 15 July 2004. Cook, former Foreign Secretary, had resigned from the Cabinet over the invasion of Iraq.
5 John Major, *The Autobiography* (1999), London: HarperCollins, p. 100.
6 For a description of the changes to the *Literae Humaniores* ('Greats') course in the late twentieth century, see Peter Brown, 'Tempora Mutantur', *Oxford Today*, vol. 15.2 (Hilary 2003).
7 Gordon Clough, interview to discuss the new Cabinet Secretary, *The World at One*, BBC Radio 4, 9 July 1987.
8 Headmaster's report from Orley Farm Preparatory School, 1952.
9 Housemaster's report by Mr K. S. Snell, summer 1956.
10 Tom Bower, *Broken Vows* (2016), London: Faber & Faber, p. 402.
11 Bernard Donoughue, *Prime Minister: The Conduct of Policy under Harold Wilson and James Callaghan* (1987), London: Jonathan Cape, p. 19.
12 Donoughue, *Downing Street Diary* (2005), London: Jonathan Cape, pp. 292–3, 400.
13 Baroness Hogg, interview, 14 December 2016.
14 Lord Butler, interview, 6 January 2015.

CHAPTER 1: CHILDHOOD AND SCHOOL, 1938–1956

1 *Western Gazette*, 15 July 1932. Bernard's solicitor, Conrad Oldham, submitted that the defence had no case to answer as Bernard had control over the vehicle and, ingeniously, pointed out that there was no law against a one-armed man driving a car.
2 Neil Jenkinson, *Richard Daft: On a Pedestal* (2008), Cardiff: Association of Cricket Statisticians and Historians, pp. 7–8.
3 This was record number 1 when Butler was Sue Lawley's guest on *Desert Island Discs* BBC Radio 4, 21 February 1993.

4 *The Harrovian*, vol. 65, no. 24, 21 May 1952.
5 *Ibid.*, no. 26, 4 June 1952; no. 27, 11 June 1952; no. 28, 18 June 1952; no. 33, 23 July 1952.
6 Conversation with M. G. Balme, August 1985.
7 Butler, letter to Peter Hennessy, 11 July 1987. Cited in Hennessy, *Whitehall* (1989), London: Secker & Warburg, p. 672.
8 J. P. Lemmon, interview, 5 March 2015. All comments from Mr Lemmon in this chapter come from this interview.
9 *The Times*, 9 June 1954.
10 *The Harrovian*, vol. 69, no. 27, 7 June 1956.
11 Lord Butler, interview, 6 October 2015.
12 *Ibid.*
13 Bernard Butler, letter to Robin, 4 August 1956.

CHAPTER 2: ST DUNSTAN'S AND OXFORD, 1956–1961

1 Lord Butler, *Dear Descendants: A Legacy of Personal Memories*.
2 Robin Butler, letter sent from St Dunstan's, 2 December 1956. The factual detail of the year spent there is gleaned from these letters to his parents.
3 *Burnham and Highbridge Gazette*, 27 January 1988.
4 Lord Butler, *Dear Descendants: A Legacy of Personal Memories*.
5 Comment on *Desert Island Discs*, BBC Radio 4, 21 February 1993.
6 Freddie Wells was a Fellow and tutor in Classics at Univ from 1935 until his death in 1966. Some of his writing in Latin appears in *More Oxford Compositions* (1964), Oxford: Clarendon Press.
7 Lord Butler Papers, A. F. Wells, Dean of University College, letter to F. E. R. Butler, 18 April 1959.
8 Plato, *Republic*, books VI–VII.
9 *Daily Telegraph*, 8 November 1959.
10 *The Guardian*, 7 December 1960.
11 Lord Butler Papers, 'The Hell Fire Club', a paper given to University College Literary Society, Hilary Term 1961.
12 Butler remained friendly with the Carew family. When Lord Carew died in 1994, he sent a wreath to the funeral. By coincidence, he attended a memorial service for Edmund Compton in the same week. Letter to Nora Butler, 17 July 1994.
13 After-dinner speech by Lord Butler on the occasion of his retirement from the Civil Service. Middle Temple Hall, 12 January 1998.

CHAPTER 3: THE TREASURY AND THE LABOUR GOVERNMENT, 1961–1970

1 Robin to Bernard and Nora Butler, letters of August–September 1961.
2 'Soul of Discretion', *The House*, 17 May 2010.
3 Letter to Diana ('Dids') Butler, 26 November 1961.
4 *Daily Telegraph*, 25 March 1962.
5 Letter to Bernard and Nora Butler, 25 February 1962.
6 Letter to Bernard and Nora Butler, 3 September 1962.
7 Iain Macleod, 'The Tory leadership', *The Spectator*, 17 January 1964, p. 5.
8 Hennessy, *Whitehall*, p. 219. The comment was made in July 1976 when Heath was no longer leader of the Tory Party and Roy Jenkins had moved from the Treasury to the Home Office in the Labour government.

9 Harold Wilson, *A Personal Record: The Labour Government 1964–1970* (1971), London: Weidenfeld & Nicolson, p. 2.
10 Letter to Bernard and Nora, 10 February 1963. Of one dinner party he attended he wrote: 'They are a lively lot as you can imagine, but very nice and friendly with it ... David Frost was just about to go out and do cabaret at "The Blue Angel" – a night club – as we departed for bed. That's the way they live.'
11 Thomas Balogh, 'The apotheosis of the dilettante', in Balogh et al. (eds), *Crisis in the Civil Service* (1968), London: Anthony Blond, pp. 11–51.
12 Dudley Seers, 'The Structure of Power', in *Ibid.*, pp. 83–109.
13 *Financial Times*, 9 July 1987.
14 Much later, when both Butler and the Mandarins were established and Butler captained the team, his colleagues joked that if you ran the captain out, your career in the service was finished. Retold in, 'Lord Butler: the man who will investigate', *The Guardian*, 4 February 2004.
15 Conversation with Professor Robert Neild, Trinity College Cambridge, 19 January 2016.
16 Wilson, *A Personal Record*, pp. 249–50.
17 *Ibid.*, pp. 251–2.
18 Hansard, HC Deb, 16 November 1967, vol. 754, col. 635. Much later, when Butler was giving evidence to a parliamentary committee, he cited this occasion as one on which it was justifiable to be less than totally honest with Parliament. This comment aroused Callaghan's anger and prompted a 'haughty' letter from the former Chancellor and Prime Minister to Butler.
19 Callaghan, letter to Butler, 29 November 1967.
20 Lord Butler, *Dear Descendants: A Legacy of Personal Memories*.
21 Lord Butler, interview, 1 June 2016.
22 Lord Butler, *Dear Descendants: A Legacy of Personal Memories*.
23 Ben Pimlott, *Harold Wilson* (1992), London: HarperCollins, p. 558.
24 Tony Benn, *Office Without Power: Diaries, 1968–1972* (1988), London: Hutchinson, entry for 18 June 1970, p. 293.
25 Barbara Castle, *The Castle Diaries, 1964–1970* (1984), London: Weidenfeld & Nicolson, p. 805.
26 Wilson, *A Personal Record*, pp. 789–90.
27 Peter Jenkins, 'Roy muffed it', *The Guardian*, 25 June 1970.
28 *The Guardian*, 10 June 1976. Cited in Pimlott, *Harold Wilson*, p. 559.
29 Lord Butler, interview, 1 June 2016.
30 John Ramsden, *The Winds of Change: Macmillan to Heath, 1957–1975* (1996), London: Longman, p. 317. Cited in Hennessy, *The Prime Minister: The Office and Its Holders since 1945* (2000), London: Allen Lane, p. 327.

CHAPTER 4: THE QUIET REVOLUTION AND THE THINK TANK, 1970–1972

1 Conservative Party manifesto, *A Better Tomorrow*, pp. 1–2.
2 John Campbell, *Edward Heath: A Biography* (1993), London: Jonathan Cape, p. 299.
3 Lord Butler, interview, 1 June 2016.
4 *Conservative Party Conference Report* (1970), pp. 128–32.
5 *Evening Standard*, 12 October 1970.
6 Douglas Hurd, *An End to Promises: Sketch of a Government 1970–1974* (1979), London: Collins, p. 138.

7 Lord Butler, interview, 1 June 2016.
8 Hennessy, *Whitehall*, pp. 235–6.
9 Jon Davis, *Prime Ministers and Whitehall 1960–1974* (2007), London: Hambledon Continuum, p. 106.
10 Edward Heath, *The Course of My Life* (1998), London: Hodder & Stoughton, p. 314.
11 *Ibid.*, p. 315.
12 *Ibid.*
13 Hans Daalder, *Cabinet Reform in Britain, 1914–1963*. Cited in Tessa Blackstone and William Plowden, *Inside the Think Tank: Advising the Cabinet 1971–1983* (1988), London: Heinemann, p. 3.
14 Baroness Sharp, letter to William Plowden, 3 September 1982, cited in Blackstone and Plowden, *Inside the Think Tank*, p. 7.
15 Edward Heath, *My Style of Government* (1972), London: Evening Standard Publications, p. 3. Cited in Hennessy, *Whitehall*, p. 209.
16 Hennessy, *Whitehall*, pp. 220–21.
17 TNA, PREM 15/406, Jellicoe to Prime Minister, 3 September 1970.
18 *Ibid.*, Minutes of a meeting at 10 Downing Street, 4 September 1970, distributed by Robert Armstrong.
19 *Ibid.*, Memorandum for the record by Robert Armstrong, 16 September 1970. Also PREM 15/406, Memorandum from Sir William Armstrong, 17 September 1970. Kit McMahon rose to be Deputy Governor and might have taken the top job had he not offended Margaret Thatcher in 1983.
20 *Ibid.*, Memorandum from Robert Armstrong, 'Note for the Record', 18 September 1970. See also Jon Davis, *Prime Ministers and Whitehall 1960–1974*, p. 108.
21 Lord Butler, interview, 1 June 2016.
22 *Ibid.*, Memorandum from Robert Armstrong, 'Note for the Record', 29 September 1970. Also *Ibid.*, Armstrong to Trend, 29 September 1970.
23 Professor Ford accepted the offer on 5 October 1970 (*Ibid.*, Minutes of a meeting held on 5 October) and, after reconsidering his commitments, refused it in a letter to the Prime Minister (*Ibid.*, Ford to PM, 12 October 1970).
24 Lord Rothschild, *Random Variables* (1984), London: Collins, p. 75.
25 TNA, PREM 15/406, 10 Downing Street press notice, 29 October 1970.
26 Lord Rothschild, *Random Variables*, pp. 81–2.
27 Lord Rothschild, *Meditations of a Broomstick* (1977), London: Collins, pp. 112–13.
28 *Ibid.*, p. 114.
29 Lord Butler, interview, 1 June 2016.
30 TNA, CAB 139/748, A2054, Rothschild to Moser, 11 February 1971.
31 Robert Wade-Gery, born in April 1929, attended Winchester and New College, Oxford, where he took a double first in Mods and Greats, and was elected to a fellowship at All Souls. William Plowden, born in February 1935, was educated at Eton and King's College, Cambridge, and was a Commonwealth Fund fellow at Berkeley. William Waldegrave, eight years younger than Butler, was the youngest of the group, aged twenty-four, an alumnus of Eton and Corpus Christi, Oxford, and fresh from a Kennedy Scholarship at Harvard. He too was a Prize Fellow at All Souls.
32 Butler, letter to Bernard and Nora, 9 January 1971.
33 William Waldegrave, *A Different Kind of Weather* (2015), London: Constable, pp. 107–8.
34 Lord Butler, *Dear Descendants: A Legacy of Personal Memories*.

35 TNA, PREM 15/406, Mark Schreiber to Hurd, 17 March 1971.
36 *Ibid.*, Sir Burke Trend to Prime Minister, MCA(71)1, 2 March 1971.
37 Blackstone and Plowden, *Inside the Think Tank*, p. 33.
38 Lord Rothschild, *Meditations of a Broomstick*, p. 115.
39 *Ibid.*, p. 112.
40 Blackstone and Plowden, *Inside the Think Tank*, pp. 33–4.
41 Waldegrave, *A Different Kind of Weather*, p. 108.
42 *Ibid.*, pp. 109–10.
43 *Ibid.*, p. 16.
44 Lord Rothschild, *Random Variables*, p. 82.
45 Lord Rothschild, *Meditations of a Broomstick*, p. 114.
46 Heath, *The Course of My Life*, p. 347.
47 Lord Rothschild, *Meditations of a Broomstick*, p. 115.
48 Possibly even the Think Tank underestimated the scale of the Concorde deficit. Ten years later, the annual cost of keeping the plane airborne was estimated at more than £40 million (see *Private Eye*, no. 511, 17 July 1981).
49 Hennessy, *Whitehall*, pp. 229–30.
50 Heath, *The Course of My Life*, p. 340.
51 Davis, *Prime Ministers and Whitehall 1960–1974*, p. 113.
52 Susan Morrison, Richard Townsend and Peter Hennessy, *Routine Punctuated by Orgies* (1985), Glasgow: University of Strathclyde, p. 10. The title comes from a comment of Aldous Huxley.
53 Hennessy, *Whitehall*, p. 209.
54 *The Levin Interviews*, BBC2, 12 August 1984; cited in Hennessy, *Whitehall*, p. 230.
55 Lord Butler, *Dear Descendants: A Legacy of Personal Memories.*

CHAPTER 5: 10 DOWNING STREET: FIRST TOUR, 1972–1974

1 Heath, *The Course of My Life*, pp. 308–9.
2 Lord Butler, *Dear Descendants: A Legacy of Personal Memories.*
3 *Ibid.*
4 J. J. Lee, *Ireland, 1912–1985: Politics and Society* (1990), Cambridge: CUP, p. 434.
5 *Ibid.*
6 Hansard, HC Deb, 31 January 1972, vol. 830, cols 32–43.
7 Reginald Maudling, *Memoirs* (1978), London: Sidgwick & Jackson, p. 186.
8 Brian Faulkner, *Memoirs of a Statesman* (1978), London: Weidenfeld & Nicolson, p. 235.
9 *Ibid.*, p. 236.
10 Peter Taylor, *Brits: The War Against the IRA* (2001), London: Bloomsbury, p. 160.
11 Faulkner, *Memoirs of a Statesman*, p. 226.
12 Hansard, HC Deb, 17 February 1972, vol. 832, cols 752–3.
13 Kenneth Harris, *David Owen, Personally Speaking* (1987), London: Weidenfeld & Nicolson, p. 102.
14 *The Economist*, 4 April 1972.
15 *The Times*, 28 February 1972.
16 For Barber's optimistic, if unrealistic, Budget speech, see Hansard, HC Deb, 21 March 1972, vol. 833, cols 1343–4.
17 Joe Haines, *The Politics of Power* (1977), London: Jonathan Cape, p. 38.
18 Hurd, *An End to Promises: Sketch of a Government 1970–1974*, pp. 92–3.

19 Dominic Sandbrook, *State of Emergency: The Way We Were, Britain 1970–1974* (2010), London: Allen Lane.
20 *The Spectator*, 9 March 1974. Cited in Campbell, *Edward Heath*, p. 618.
21 James Margach, *The Abuse of Power: The War Between Downing Street and the Media from Lloyd George to Callaghan* (1978), London: W. H. Allen, p. 160.
22 Lord Armstrong, interview, 20 December 2016.
23 Letter to Heath, 10 March 1974.

CHAPTER 6: INTERMEZZO: BETWEEN TORY GOVERNMENTS, 1974–1979

1 Lord Butler, *Dear Descendants: A Legacy of Personal Memories.*
2 Marcia Williams, *Inside Number 10* (1972), London: Weidenfeld & Nicolson, p. 12.
3 Haines, *The Politics of Power*, p. 32. See also Bernard Donoughue, *The Heat of the Kitchen* (2004), London: Politico's, p. 137.
4 Haines, *The Politics of Power*, p. 16.
5 Lord Donoughue, interview, 11 December 2016.
6 TNA, PREM 16/135, 'Note for the Record: Settlement of the Coal Miners' Dispute', 7 March 1974.
7 *Ibid.*, 'NCB Deficit', Eric Varley to Joel Barnett, 7 March 1974.
8 Donoughue, *Downing Street Diary*, p. 58.
9 Lord Donoughue, interview, 11 December 2016.
10 *Ibid.*
11 Donoughue, *The Heat of the Kitchen*, p. 146.
12 Donoughue, *Downing Street Diary*, entry for 16 April 1975, p. 355.
13 Donoughue, *The Heat of the Kitchen*, p. 152.
14 *Daily Mail*, 18 March 1974. Butler and Kavanagh, *The British General Election of October 1974* (1975), London: Macmillan, p. 24.
15 Interview with Lord Donoughue, 11 December 2016.
16 Haines, *The Politics of Power*, p. 33.
17 *Ibid.*, pp. 100–101.
18 Donoughue, *Prime Minister: The Conduct of Policy under Harold Wilson and James Callaghan*, p. 106.
19 Donoughue, *Downing Street Diary*, entry for 16 January 1975, p. 283.
20 *Ibid.*, entry for 21 January 1975, pp. 292–3.
21 *Ibid.*, entry for 5 June 1975, p. 400.
22 Donoughue, *The Heat of the Kitchen*, pp. 185–90.
23 *Ibid.*, pp. 192–3.
24 Donoughue, *Downing Street Diary*, entry for 28 November 1975, p. 587.
25 Lord Donoughue, interview, 11 December 2016. Donoughue added that he had spent thirty-two years in the House of Lords with Lady Falkender (Marcia Williams) and not exchanged a word with her.
26 Donoughue, *Downing Street Diary*, entry for 23 October 1975, p. 537. Donoughue, too, had a running feud with Williams, and recorded in his diary, referring to No. 10 as 'the zoo', that he was determined to resign and to make his reasons for doing so very clear. 'I went back and saw Robert Armstrong. We went into the Cabinet Room and sat at the Cabinet table and talked for half an hour. I told him that I was not going to put up with this nonsense much longer and that I proposed to resign' (*Downing Street Diary*, pp. 228–9).

Donoughue records that Armstrong viewed Williams as 'utterly contemptible' (*The Heat of the Kitchen*, p. 168).

27 Donoughue, *Downing Street Diary*, entry for 3 September 1974, p. 175.

28 Balogh, 'The apotheosis of the dilettante', reprinted in *Crisis in the Civil Service*, p. 12.

29 John Fulton, 'The Civil Service today' (Chapter 1) in *The Civil Service* (1968), London: HMSO, paras 15–20.

30 Donoughue, *Downing Street Diary*, entry for 22 October 1975, p. 537.

31 *Ibid.*, entry for 30 October 1975, p. 548.

32 *Ibid.*, entry for 29 October 1975, p. 545.

33 Peter Wright gives the background to MI5 concerns in *Spycatcher* (1987), New York: Viking Penguin at pp. 362–5, and describes the plan to release information to damage Wilson at pp. 368–72.

34 A detailed record of the smears and dirty tricks used to discredit the Prime Minister is given in Pimlott, *Harold Wilson*, pp. 707–23.

35 *Ibid.*, p. 722.

36 Donoughue, *The Heat of the Kitchen*, pp. 136, 146.

37 This is the crux of the conspiracy theory. Anthony Cavendish stated categorically that there was such a 'something' and that Sir Maurice Oldfield, the head of MI6, had shown that 'something' to Jim Callaghan. Cavendish, *Inside Intelligence* (1990), London: Collins, pp. 164–5.

38 Lord Butler, *Dear Descendants: A Legacy of Personal Memories*.

39 In his Budget speech of 17 April 1956, Macmillan said of economic prospects for the forthcoming year: 'Then I am told that some of our statistics are too late to be as useful as they ought to be. We are always, as it were, looking up a train in last year's Bradshaw.' Hansard, HC Deb, 17 April 1956, vol. 551, col. 867.

40 Lord Butler, interview, 1 June 2016.

41 Denis Healey, *The Time of My Life* (1989), London: Norton, pp. 432–3.

42 *Civil Service World*, 13 April 1977.

CHAPTER 7: MIDPOINT, 1979

1 *The Harrovian*, vol. 77, no. 21, 15 May 1964.

2 *Daily Telegraph*, 25 March 1963. Rab Butler, even in his youth, had not been an athlete. He was a popular subject with the press and the leaked story, published in several newspapers, first introduced Robin Butler to the public.

3 He did, however, continue to return to Harrow to play for Old Harrovian football teams until he was one of the oldest men on the field. *The Harrovian*, vol. 79, nos. 13 and 17, 25 February and 19 March 1966.

4 Lady Butler, interview, 13 December 2016.

5 Harrow Governing Board minutes of 7 November 1970, cited in Christopher Tyerman, *A History of Harrow School 1324–1991* (2000), Oxford: OUP, p. 546.

6 *Ibid.*, p. 492.

7 J. P. Lemmon, interview, 5 March 2015.

CHAPTER 8: FOUR BUSY YEARS, 1979–1983

1 Geoffrey Howe, *Conflict of Loyalty* (1994), London: Macmillan, pp. 128–9.

2 Peter Riddell, 'Reshuffle among Treasury staff to take place', *Financial Times*, 31 January 1980.

3 *The Guardian*, 12 June 1981.
4 Sir Douglas Wass, letter to F. E. R. Butler, 20 August 1982.
5 Letter to Bernard and Nora Butler, 1 February 1981.
6 *The Times*, 23 July 1982. Mrs Thatcher is said to have demanded of her Foreign Minister Francis Pym: 'Will you make up your mind or will Clive and I have to make it up for you?' Hugo Young, *One of Us* (1993), London: Pan Books, p. 165.
7 *The Economist*, 24 July 1982.
8 Lord Butler Papers: letter to Bernard and Nora Butler, 11 July 1982.
9 Charles Moore, *Margaret Thatcher, vol. 1: Not for Turning* (2013), London: Allen Lane, p. 237.
10 References (in the order of subjects listed): CCC, THCR 6/2/2/50f4; TNA, PREM 19/697f167; PREM 19/816f91; PREM 19/714f192; PREM 19/6812f108; CCC, THCR 6/2/2/51f29; TNA, PREM 19/1602f3; PREM 19/655f87; PREM 19/721f206; CCC, THCR 1/10/37A part2f67; TNA, PREM 19/697f128; CCC, THCR 6/2/2/51f22; CCC, THCR 2/6/2/85 part2f79; TNA, PREM 19/962f182; CCC, THCR 6/2/2/51f18.
11 Ferdinand Mount, *Cold Cream: My Early Life and Other Mistakes* (2008), London: Bloomsbury, p. 296.
12 *Ibid.*, p. 298.
13 Obituary of Lord Laing of Dunphail, *Daily Telegraph*, 27 June 2010.
14 Letter to Bernard and Nora Butler, 12 September 1982.
15 Lord Butler, *Dear Descendants: A Legacy of Personal Memories*.
16 Mount, *Cold Cream*, p. 323.
17 In 2014, Nissan's Sunderland plant manufactured 500,000 cars, the greatest output of any UK car manufacturing plant. According to Professor David Bailey of Aston Business School, Sunderland makes more cars than the entire Italian car industry. 'Nissan invests £100m in Sunderland plant', *BBC News* [online] (3 September 2015) <http://www.bbc.co.uk/news/business-34136541>, accessed 4 February 2017.
18 TNA, PREM 19/962f69.
19 TNA, PREM 19/962f38.
20 Lord Armstrong, interview, 20 December 2016.
21 Major, *The Autobiography*, p. 85.
22 For some time, Mrs Thatcher had wanted to have 'one or two more people in to help' with No. 10's dealings with the FCO. Romola Christopherson's memo to Butler of 18 October 1982 (CCC, THCR 5/2/98f7) reports on an interview that Mrs Thatcher gave to Tony Shrimsley, in which she had floated the idea.
23 CCC, WTRS 3/1/2, Alan Walters, diary entry for 22 October 1982.
24 TNA, PREM 19/677f6, Butler to PM and her response, 26 November 1982.
25 TNA, PREM 19/677f8, Ingham to Butler, 26 November 1982.
26 TNA, PREM 19/677f2, Butler to Sir Douglas Wass, 29 November 1982.
27 CCC, THCR 1/3/9f8, Butler to PM, 28 December 1982.
28 Hansard, HC Deb, 6 July 1982, vol. 27, col. 145.
29 'Margaret Thatcher vetoed William Hague Treasury job', *BBC News* [online] (1 August 2013) <http://www.bbc.com/news/uk-politics-23518593>, accessed 4 February 2017.
30 The incident was widely reported in the press, for example, retrospectively, in 'Mandarin who got on his bike', *The Times*, 9 July 1987.
31 Lord Butler, interview, 7 October 2015.
32 Lord Butler, *Dear Descendants: A Legacy of Personal Memories*. Moore, *Margaret Thatcher*, vol. 2, pp. 88–9.

33 George Schultz, *Turmoil and Triumph* (1993), New York: Charles Scribner's, pp. 332–4.
34 *Ibid.*, p. 335.
35 Lord Butler, *Dear Descendants: A Legacy of Personal Memories*. Moore, *Margaret Thatcher*, vol. 2, p. 127.
36 Comments made by the Prime Minister in a phone-in programme on BBC World Service, Sunday 30 October 1983.
37 Letter to Bernard and Nora Butler, 19 February 1984. Also Lord Butler, *Dear Descendants: A Legacy of Personal Memories*. For the Moscow visit, Mrs Thatcher wore fur-lined boots rather than high heels, as Butler had persuaded her that this would be more sensible for standing for hours in Moscow in February. She was pleased to have listened and commented that, after she had taken a look at Chernenko, 'the thought crossed my mind that they would probably come in useful again soon' (Thatcher, *The Downing Street Years*, p. 458).

CHAPTER 9: VISIBILITY, 1984–1985

1 Hennessy, *Whitehall*, p. 213.
2 *Desert Island Discs*, BBC Radio 4, 21 February 1993.
3 *The Times*, 7 June 1983.
4 Bernard Ingham, *Kill the Messenger* (1991), London: HarperCollins, pp. 174–6.
5 Letter to Bernard and Nora Butler, 22 January 1984.
6 See Mary Kenny, 'No wonder that Mitterand said that Margaret Thatcher had the eyes of Caligula and the mouth of Marilyn Monroe', *The Independent*, 28 March 2009.
7 *The Observer*, 15 January 1984.
8 Letter to Bernard and Nora Butler, 5 February 1984.
9 Lord Butler, interview, 4 June 2016.
10 Lord Butler, *Dear Descendants: A Legacy of Personal Memories*.
11 On 5 November 1984, Armstrong informed Butler that 'steps are being taken to prompt journalistic enquiries' about the NUM's connections with the USSR and the Eastern Bloc. TNA, PREM 19/1335, f.165.
12 Moore, *Margaret Thatcher*, vol. 2, pp. 141–2.
13 Martin Holmes, *Thatcherism: Scope and Limits, 1983–1987* (1989), New York: St Martin's, p. 45.
14 CCC, THCR 2/6/3/160f22, Sherbourne to PM, 13 January 1984.
15 CCC, THCR 2/6/3/160f50, Sherbourne to David Wolfson, 18 January 1984; Williams to Butler, 12 January 1984.
16 As an example of this, see Butler's memorandum to Armstrong of 10 February 1984, TNA, PREM 19/1206f35. In May of that year, Alan Walters submitted the manuscript of his book on monetary policy to Butler for approval. Normally, this was the responsibility of the Cabinet Secretary, but in this instance Butler read it and replied with his suggestions for editing the text. He did so with decisive and impressive authority. TNA, PREM 19/1199f268.
17 TNA, PREM 19/1331f30, Butler to PM, 17 July 1984.
18 E.g. TNA, PREM 19/1332f303, Butler to Peter Grayson, Cabinet Office, 20 July 1984.
19 TNA, PREM 19/1332f302, Butler to Armstrong, 20 July 1984.
20 CCC, THCR 1/12/23f12, Arthur Cockfield to Butler, 27 July 1984.
21 General Ismay to Kingsley Dykes, 9 February 1943. Danchev, *Establishing the Anglo-American Alliance: The Second World War Diaries of Brigadier Vivian Dykes* (1990), London: Brassey's, p. 2.
22 See in particular TNA, PREM 19/1334f307, Butler to PM, 25 September 1984; PREM 19/1334f295, Butler to PM, 26 September 1984; PREM 19/1334f257, Butler to PM, 2 October 1984.

23 Letter to Bernard and Nora Butler, 16 September 1984.
24 Letter to Bernard and Nora Butler, 23 September 1984.
25 Interviewed by Anthony Seldon in 'Men of Secrets: The Cabinet Secretaries', *Mile End Group* [online resource] (undated) <http://www.cabinetsecretaries.com/>, accessed 4 February 2017. All quotations relating to the explosion in the Grand Hotel are from this interview.
26 *Daily Telegraph* and *Daily Express*, 13 October 1984.
27 Taylor, *Brits: The War Against the IRA*, p. 265.
28 Lord Butler, *Dear Descendants: A Legacy of Personal Memories*.
29 St Christopher's was founded by Dame Cicely Saunders and opened in 1967. The website of the hospice describes its mission as embracing 'a holistic approach, caring for a patient's physical, spiritual and psychological wellbeing, [which] marked a new beginning, not only for the care of the dying but for the practice of medicine as a whole.' 'History and Dame Cicely Saunders', *St Christopher's* [website] (undated) <http://www.stchristophers.org.uk/about/history>, accessed 4 February 2017.
30 *The Guardian*, 13 April 1981.
31 *Private Eye*, no. 750, 14 September 1990, p. 8
32 Lord Butler, *Dear Descendants: A Legacy of Personal Memories*. Also recorded by Charles Moore, *Margaret Thatcher*, vol. 2, pp. 669–70.
33 CCC, THCR 1/14/14, Butler to PM, 22 May 1985 See also Charles Moore, *Margaret Thatcher*, vol. 2, p. 425.
34 Charles Moore, *Margaret Thatcher*, vol. 2, p. 385. The meeting took place on 29 November 1984.
35 *Private Eye*, no. 569, 10 October 1983, p. 8.
36 Lord Butler, interview, 1 June 2016.
37 Lord Butler, *Dear Descendants: A Legacy of Personal Memories*.
38 Bernard Ingham, 'My life with the lioness, Margaret Thatcher', *Daily Telegraph*, 9 April 2013.
39 'Downing Street forges closer links with Treasury', *The Times*, 31 July 1985.
40 'Number 10's Butler sets dovecotes fluttering', *The Times*, 31 July 1985.
41 'Prime Minister's head boy', *Palatinate*, 31 January 1985. Interviewer and author Richard Calland read Law at Durham University, was called to the Bar in 1987, and spent seven years in Lincoln's Inn, before emigrating to South Africa. He is now Associate Professor in Public Law at the University of Cape Town.
42 'Men and matters', *Financial Times*, 31 July 1985.
43 'Thatcher's advisers gain posts at Treasury', *Financial Times*, 31 July 1985.
44 Hennessy, 'Head boy of Downing Street', *The Times*, 7 June 1983.

CHAPTER 10: CONSOLIDATION, 1985–1987

1 Lord Butler, interview, 3 June 2016.
2 Lord Butler, interview, 4 June 2016.
3 *The Dulwich Society Newsletter*, Spring 2016.
4 *Private Eye*, 4 April 1986.
5 Lord Butler, interview, 4 June 2016.
6 *Sunday Times*, 11 January 1987.
7 *Ibid.*, 18 January 1987.
8 Lord Butler, interview, 4 June 2016.
9 *Ibid.*

10 Moore, *Margaret Thatcher*, vol. 2, caption to photograph facing p. 470.
11 Lord Butler, interview, 4 June 2016.
12 *Ibid.*
13 Hennessy, *Whitehall*, p. 673.
14 *Ibid.*, p. 630.
15 Lord Butler, *Dear Descendants: A Legacy of Personal Memories.*
16 Lord Butler, interview, 4 June 2016.
17 Michael Crick, *Michael Heseltine: A Biography* (1997), London: Hamish Hamilton, p. 288.
18 Lord Armstrong, interview, 20 December 2016.
19 Lord Donoughue, interview, 11 December 2016.
20 Lord Butler, interview, 4 June 2016.
21 *Ibid.*
22 Lord Butler, *Dear Descendants: A Legacy of Personal Memories.*

CHAPTER 11: CABINET SECRETARY: THE FIRST YEARS, 1987–1990

1 10 Downing Street press notice, 8 July 1987.
2 Memorandum from G. T. Morgan to Sir Robert Armstrong, 8 July 1987. Research conducted by Miss Dickinson.
3 Lord Butler Papers, Q&A brief on the appointment of Secretary to the Cabinet and head of the Civil Service (undated).
4 Widely reported in several national and local newspapers (*The Scotsman*, *Birmingham Post*, *Glasgow Herald*, *Yorkshire Post* etc.), 9 July 1987.
5 *Newsnight*, BBC2, 9 July 1987.
6 *Financial Times*, 9 July 1987.
7 The *Glasgow Herald*, on 14 July 1987, wrote that 'the harshest thing ever said of him appears to be that he is too perfect a civil servant, too protective of his political masters'.
8 Cited in Peter Hennessy, 'Whitehall watch', *The Times*, 20 October 1988.
9 Hailsham, *The Dilemma of Democracy: Diagnosis and Prescription* (1978), London: William Collins, pp. 203–7.
10 Hennessy, *Whitehall*, p. 595.
11 *Ibid.*, p. 618.
12 Hennessy, 'Whitehall watch: Civil Service revolution that fell short', *The Independent*, 22 February 1988.
13 Sir Robin Butler, evidence to the Treasury and Civil Service Committee, 9 March 1988.
14 The alleged offence concerned a 'breach of confidence in relation to information on matters of state security given to authors' and was raised in the House of Commons by Tam Dalyell, MP for Linlithgow. Hansard, HC Deb, 6 February 1987, vol. 109, cols 1291–8.
15 Speeches were banned at Think Tank reunions, but spoofs in the form of minutes, memoranda and telegrams were read out by all present.
16 'Butler's cabinet pudding', *Sunday Telegraph*, 12 July 1987.
17 Lord Rothschild to Butler, 7 July 1987.
18 Hennessy, *Whitehall*, p. 671.
19 *The Times*, 7 June 1983. See Chapter 9.
20 Lord Armstrong, interview, 20 December 2016.
21 Evidence to the Commons Treasury and Civil Service Committee, 9 March 1988. Cited in Hennessy, *Whitehall*, p. 675.

22 Lord O'Donnell, interview, 14 December 2016.
23 Speech to the Institute of Personnel Management, 20 September 1988. For a summary of the issues see 'Chief mandarin urges caution over Whitehall', *Daily Telegraph*, 21 September 1988.
24 Whitelaw, *The Whitelaw Memoirs* (1989), London: Aurum Press, p. 250.
25 Lord Butler, *Dear Descendants: A Legacy of Personal Memories*.
26 Percy Cradock, *In Pursuit of British Interests: Reflections on Foreign Policy Under Margaret Thatcher and John Major* (1997), London: John Murray, p. 15.
27 Anthony Seldon and Jonathan Meakin, *The Cabinet Office 1916–2016* (2016), London: Biteback Publishing.
28 Lord Butler, interview, 4 June 2016.
29 *The Guardian*, 7 February 2010.
30 Smithers, who owned a villa on Lake Lugano close to the Thyssen villa, was a passionate gardener and was frivolously referred to by friends as 'the spy who loved magnolias'. *Daily Mail*, 25 June 2011.
31 For an indication of the general optimism that the collection would come to Britain, see *The Times*, 13 June 1988, p. 1.
32 Obituary of Baron 'Heini' Thyssen Bornemisza, *Daily Telegraph*, 29 April 2002.
33 Thatcher, *The Downing Street Years*, pp. 633–4.
34 *Ibid.*, p. 633.
35 Lord Butler, *Dear Descendants: A Legacy of Personal Memories*.
36 *Ibid.*
37 Hennessy, *The Prime Minister: The Office and Its Holders since 1945*, pp. 441–2.
38 Hansard, HC Deb, 30 October 1990, vol. 178, col. 872.
39 *Ibid.*, col. 873.
40 *The Times*, 5 November 1990. Cited in Heseltine, *Life in the Jungle* (2000), London: Hodder & Stoughton, p. 356.
41 Lord Butler, interview, 1 June 2016.
42 Hansard, HC Deb, 13 November 1990, vol. 180, col. 461.
43 *Ibid.*, col. 464.
44 Thatcher, *The Downing Street Years*, p. 839.
45 Hansard, HC Deb, 13 November 1990, vol. 180, col. 465.
46 Thatcher, *The Downing Street Years*, p. 839.
47 Lord Butler, *Dear Descendants: A Legacy of Personal Memories*.
48 Patrick Kidd, 'Boris's job is selling books', *The Times*, 2 December 2016.
49 Lord Butler, interview, 1 June 2016.
50 Robert Armstrong says much the same, recalling his experience with Mrs Thatcher: 'Working with Margaret Thatcher was an experience that one never forgets. She was an elemental force. One had an instinctive desire to befriend her, even when she was at her most maddening. She could be wayward at times, but one took that in one's stride.' Interview, 20 December 2016.

CHAPTER 12: CIVIS BRITANNICUS SUM, 1990–1991

1 Baroness Hogg, interview, 14 December 2016.
2 *Ibid.*
3 Hennessy, *The Prime Minister*, p. 447.
4 Jenkinson, *Richard Daft: On a Pedestal*, pp. 7–8.

5 The phrase that might more accurately be used is 'a society with class mobility'. *Daily Telegraph*, 24 November 1990. Cited in Foley, *John Major, Tony Blair and a Conflict of Leadership: Collision Course* (2002), Manchester: Manchester University Press, p. 26.
6 Interviewed by Anthony Seldon, 'Men of Secrets: The Cabinet Secretaries'.
7 Peter de la Billière, *Storm Command: A Personal Account of the Gulf War* (1992), London: HarperCollins, pp. 185–91.
8 *The Guardian*, 19 January 1991. Cited in Seldon, *Major: A Political Life* (1998), London: Phoenix, p. 157.
9 Interviewed by Anthony Seldon, 'Men of Secrets: The Cabinet Secretaries'.
10 Peter Taylor, *Provos: The IRA and Sinn Féin* (1997), London: Bloomsbury, pp. 321–2.
11 For example, Joe Rogaly in the *Financial Times*, 22 January 1991.
12 Sarah Hogg and Jonathan Hill, *Too Close to Call* (1995), London: Little, Brown, p. 10.
13 Seldon, *Major: A Political Life*, pp. 143–4.
14 Hogg and Hill, *Too Close to Call*, p. 94.
15 Patrick Wintour in *The Guardian*, 26 March 1991.
16 'Civil Servants' move troubles Sir Robin', *The Times*, 22 April 1993, pp. 8–9.
17 Hogg and Hill, *Too Close to Call*, p. 95.
18 Baroness Hogg, interview, 14 December 2016.
19 Lecture on 'Cabinet Government', the Attlee Foundation Lecture, given at the Mansion House, London, on 18 March 1999.
20 Seldon, *Major: A Political Life*, pp. 190–91.
21 Lord Butler, interview, 2 June 2016.
22 Hogg and Hill, *Too Close to Call*, p. 98.
23 Letter to Nora Butler, 18 November 1989.
24 The White Paper was published as *The Citizen's Charter – Raising the Standard*, Cm 1599, HMSO, July 1991. The verbal play of 'raising the standard', an image associated with a battle charge, was quite intentional.
25 Conservative Party election manifesto (1992), para. 15.
26 Major, *The Autobiography*, p. 246.
27 Hansard, HC Deb, 20 November 1991, vol. 199, cols 269–70.
28 Hansard, HC Deb, 21 November 1991, vol. 199, col. 518.
29 Lord Butler, interview, 1 June 2016.
30 *Financial Times*, 24 December 1992.
31 Lord Butler, interview, 31 May 2016.
32 Lord Butler, *Dear Descendants: A Legacy of Personal Memories*.
33 For an objective analysis of Butler's preparations in case of a Labour victory, see 'Win who may, he will be waiting', *The Independent*, 7 March 1992.
34 Lord Butler, *Dear Descendants: A Legacy of Personal Memories*.
35 Gyles Brandreth, *Breaking the Code: Westminster Diaries* (2014), London: Biteback Publishing, entry for 28 September 1992.

CHAPTER 13: ANNUS HORRIBILIS, 1992

1 See Chapter 8.
2 Lord Butler, *Dear Descendants: A Legacy of Personal Memories*.
3 Major, *The Autobiography*, p. 288.
4 Lord Butler, interview, 1 June 2016.
5 While Butler admired Major's ability as a negotiator, he was less impressed, according to

Jill, by his tendency to be 'a bit indecisive'. Bernard Donoughue believes that Jill was using 'diplomatic understatement'. Donoughue, *Westminster Diary: A Reluctant Minister Under Tony Blair* (2016), London: I. B. Tauris, p. 62.

6 Major, *The Autobiography*, p. 291.
7 E.g. *The Independent*, 15 September 1992.
8 Major, *The Autobiography*, p. 553.
9 *The Guardian*, 9 February 2005.
10 Lord Butler, *Dear Descendants: A Legacy of Personal Memories.*
11 Attlee Foundation Lecture, 18 March 1999. Hennessy, *The Prime Minister*, p. 445.
12 P. D. Jephson, *Shadows of a Princess* (2000), London: HarperCollins, p. 258.
13 *Ibid.*, p. 288.
14 Hansard, HC Deb, 9 December 1992, vol. 215, col. 845.
15 Lord Butler, interview, 1 June 2016.
16 Lord Butler, *Dear Descendants: A Legacy of Personal Memories.*
17 Sir Geoffrey Howe, Hansard, HC Written Answers, 29 October 1985, vol. 84, col. 450W.
18 William Waldegrave, *A Different Kind of Weather*, p. 234.
19 *Ibid.*, p. 234.
20 *Ibid.*, p. 239.
21 'Cabinet chief's attack over twisted stories', *The Times*, 10 February 1994.
22 Lord Butler Papers: Sir Christopher France to Sir Robin Butler, 9 February 1994.
23 *The Sun*, 9 March 1996.
24 'Whitehall's costliest farce', *The Times*, 11 December 1993.
25 *The Spectator*, 27 January 1996.
26 Lord Butler, *Dear Descendants: A Legacy of Personal Memories*. Also letter to Nora Butler, 18 February 1996.
27 A useful summary of the content and implications of the Scott Report can be found in 'The Scott Report: the essential guide', *The Independent*, 15 February 1996.
28 Hansard, HC Deb, 26 February 1996, vol. 272, cols 603–4.
29 Lord Butler, *Dear Descendants: A Legacy of Personal Memories.*
30 Alan Clark, *Diaries* (1993), London: Weidenfeld & Nicolson, pp. 333, 396.
31 Lord Butler, *Dear Descendants: A Legacy of Personal Memories.*
32 Waldegrave, *A Different Kind of Weather*, p. 265.
33 Paul Foot, 'Armed and dangerous', *Socialist Review*, March 1996.
34 Sue Cameron addressed the question of Civil Service incompetence and its relations with Cabinet Ministers in 'Mr Waldegrave and Sir Robin Butler', *The Spectator*, 2 March 1996. The close association of minister and mandarin was also questioned in 'The view from inside', *The Economist*, 30 April 1994.
35 *The Guardian*, 25 February 2002.

CHAPTER 14: IRELAND: TENTATIVE STEPS, 1993

1 *Irish Independent*, 26 January 2002.
2 *The Guardian*, 7 February 1992.
3 Speech to Ard Fheis (annual conference) of Sinn Féin, 20 February 1993, quoted in 'Setting the record straight', *Sinn Féin* [party website] (5 January 1994) <http://www.sinnfein.ie/contents/15216>, accessed 4 February 2017.
4 The wording of this note is recorded by Butler but the existence of any accompanying note is denied in 'Setting the record straight' (*ibid.*).

5 *Ibid.*
6 *Ibid.*
7 *Sunday Tribune*, 11 April 1993.
8 *The Times*, 16 November 1993.
9 Major to Reynolds, 25 November 1993. Cited in Eamonn Mallie and David McKittrick, *The Fight for Peace: Secret Story Behind the Irish Peace Process* (1996), London: William Heinemann, pp. 228–9.
10 Lord Butler, *Dear Descendants: A Legacy of Personal Memories.*
11 Sean Duignan, diary entry for 26 November 1993. Quoted by Mallie and McKittrick, *The Fight for Peace*, p. 230.
12 Hansard, HC Deb, 29 November 1993, vol. 233, col. 786.
13 *Ibid.*, col. 787.
14 *Ibid.*, col. 789.
15 Reynolds further confirmed this, pithily describing a one-on-one with Major: 'It went all right – I chewed his bollocks off and he took a few lumps outa me.' Mallie and McKittrick, *The Fight for Peace*, p. 259.
16 Lord Butler, *Dear Descendants: A Legacy of Personal Memories.*
17 Joint Declaration on Peace: The Downing Street Declaration, para. 2. <https://web.archive.org/web/20130404221626/http://dfa.ie/home/index.aspx?id=8734>, accessed 13 February 2017.
18 *Ibid.*, para. 7.
19 Major, *The Autobiography*, p. 454.
20 Joint Declaration of the Prime Minister and the Taoiseach, 15 December 1993, para. 12.
21 *Ibid.*, para. 4.
22 *Irish Times*, 2 January 2010.
23 John Major, in a speech at the London School of Economics, 24 April 2007.
24 Lord Butler, *Dear Descendants: A Legacy of Personal Memories.*

CHAPTER 15: THE MOST DIFFICULT MOMENTS, 1994–1995

1 Interviewed by Anthony Seldon, 'Men of Secrets: The Cabinet Secretaries'.
2 Gyles Brandreth recorded his own disgust with the Tory's public image at this time, writing of the Labour Party: 'They've discovered the will to win while we don't seem to be able to get our sticky fingers off the button marked "self-destruct".' Diary entry for 1 October 1993, *Breaking the Code: Westminster Diaries*, p. 183.
3 Lord Butler, interview, 5 June 2016.
4 David Pallister subsequently chronicled the Aitken affair with Luke Harding and David Leigh in *The Liar: The Fall of Jonathan Aitken* (1999), London: Fourth Estate.
5 Lord Butler, interview, 5 June 2016.
6 Hansard, HC Deb, 27 October 1994, vol. 248, cols 992–3.
7 Lord Butler, *Dear Descendants: A Legacy of Personal Memories.*
8 Lord Butler, interview, 5 June 2016.
9 *The Guardian*, 11 April 1995.
10 Major, *The Autobiography*, p. 571; Lord Butler, interview, 5 June 2016.
11 *The Economist*, 26 November 1994.
12 *Sunday Times*, 10 July 1994.
13 *The Times*, 12 July 1994.

14 *The Guardian*, 20 October 1994.
15 Hansard, HC Written Answers, 25 October 1994, vol. 248, cols. 523–4W.
16 Lord Butler, *Dear Descendants: A Legacy of Personal Memories.*
17 Heseltine, *Life In the Jungle*, pp. 465–6.
18 Hansard, HC Deb, 25 October 1994, vol. 248, col. 758.
19 Lord Armstrong, interview, 20 December 2016.
20 Lord O'Donnell, interview, 14 December 2016.
21 Report of the Nolan Committee (1995), para. 2.104.
22 Lord Butler, interview, 5 June 2016.
23 *Ibid.*
24 *Ibid.*
25 'Mr Major's resignation speech', *The Rt Hon Sir John Major KG CH* [website] (undated) <http://www.johnmajor.co.uk/page724.html>, accessed 4 February 2017.
26 'PM assails "malcontent" Redwood', *The Independent*, 26 June 1995.
27 Heseltine, *Life in the Jungle*, p. 488.
28 *Ibid.*, p. 492.
29 In his memoirs, Heseltine suggests that Butler prompted the Permanent Secretaries with suitable responses to Heseltine's proposals (*ibid.*, p. 492). Butler roundly denies the suggestion.
30 Lord Butler, *Dear Descendants: A Legacy of Personal Memories.*
31 Heseltine, *Life in the Jungle*, p. 484

CHAPTER 16: NEW LABOUR, 1997–1998

1 Lord Butler, interview, 5 June 2016.
2 Lord Donoughue, interview, 11 December 2016.
3 The efficiency of the Labour operation in contrast to the Tory campaign is highlighted by Gyles Brandreth in his diary entry for 12 April 1997. He refers to 'the Stalinist nature of Labour's high command'. *Breaking the Code*, p. 448.
4 Jonathan Powell, *The New Machiavelli: How to Wield Power in the Modern World* (2010), London: The Bodley Head, pp. 19–20.
5 Peter Riddell, 'How to take power', *The Times*, 2 October 2009.
6 Lord Butler, interview, 7 June 2016.
7 Foley, *John Major, Tony Blair and a Conflict of Leadership*, p. 7.
8 *The Times*, 7 May 1993.
9 Tony Blair, *A Journey: My Political Life* (2010), New York: Random House, pp. 4–5.
10 John Rentoul, *Tony Blair: Prime Minister* (2001), London: Little, Brown, p. 333.
11 Tony Blair's recollections of his first moments in 10 Downing Street are recorded in *A Journey*, pp. 18–19. Butler saw it as vitally important that the transition be handled as smoothly as possible. He wrote to his mother, 'I knew that seeing in a new government was going to be my last big job in the Civil and I am determined to give it my best shot'. Letter to Nora Butler, 3 May 1997.
12 Hennessy, *The Prime Minister*, p. 479.
13 Powell, *The New Machiavelli*, p. 18.
14 Lord Butler, interview, 7 June 2016.
15 Personal minute, Prime Minister to Sir Robin Butler, 12 May 1997. See also Anthony Seldon, *The Blair Effect* (2001), London: Little, Brown, p. 102.
16 Powell, *The New Machiavelli*, pp. 19–20.

17 The number of political advisers rose from thirty-eight under Major to seventy-four under Blair. The No. 10 Policy Unit had twenty-five advisers. Anthony Seldon, *The Blair Effect*, p. 103.
18 Powell, *The New Machiavelli*, p. 20.
19 *Ibid.*, p. 21.
20 Rentoul, *Tony Blair, Prime Minister*, pp. 535–6.
21 Seldon, *The Blair Effect*, p. 10.
22 Lord Butler, interview, 14 June 2016.
23 Powell, *The New Machiavelli*, p. 60.
24 *Ibid.*, p. 59.
25 Lord Butler, interview, 14 June 2016.
26 Blair, *A Journey: My Political Life*, p. 19.
27 *The Times*, 29 October 1997.
28 Powell, *The New Machiavelli*, pp. 213–15.
29 Seldon, *The Blair Effect*, p. 12.
30 Lord Butler, interview, 14 June 2016.
31 Blair, *A Journey: My Political Life*, pp. 18–19.
32 Lord Butler, interview, 7 October 2015.
33 Lord Butler, *Dear Descendants: A Legacy of Personal Memories.*
34 Bower, *Broken Vows*, p. 31.
35 Powell, *The New Machiavelli*, pp. 79–81.
36 *Ibid.*, pp. 79–81.
37 Birt, described as one of the best-connected men in Britain, was accused by Geoffrey Robinson of being part of a cabal that included Fellowes and Butler. 'Focus: Birt's Web', *The Times*, 8 February 2004.
38 Lord Butler, *Dear Descendants: A Legacy of Personal Memories.*
39 *The Times*, 6 September 1997.
40 Lord Butler, *Dear Descendants: A Legacy of Personal Memories.*
41 Rentoul, *Tony Blair*, p. 538.
42 *The House*, June 2015, p. 12.
43 *The Times*, 14 April 2010.
44 Lord Butler, *Dear Descendants: A Legacy of Personal Memories.*
45 Hennessy, *The Prime Minister*, p. 490.
46 Lord Butler, interview, 14 June 2016.
47 *The Times*, 3 May 2005. The other candidates were John Gieve (Home Office), Nigel Crisp (Department of Health) and David Normington (Education).
48 Lord O'Donnell, interview, 14 December 2016.
49 *Ibid.*
50 Lord Butler, interview, 14 June 2016.
51 Interviewed by Anthony Seldon, 'Men of Secrets: The Cabinet Secretaries'.
52 Lord Butler, interview, 14 June 2016.

CHAPTER 17: PASSING THE TORCH, 1997

1 Lord Butler Papers: speech at Church House, 24 September 1997.
2 Interviewed by Anthony Seldon, 'Men of Secrets: The Cabinet Secretaries'.
3 Waldegrave, *A Different Kind of Weather*, p. 172.
4 Cmnd 2627. White Paper, *Continuity and Change.*

5 *Continuity and Change*, para. 1.1
6 *Ibid.*, paras 1.4 and 1.5.
7 *Evening Standard*, 13 July 1004.
8 Interviewed by Anthony Seldon, 'Men of Secrets: The Cabinet Secretaries'.
9 *Ibid.*
10 *Ibid.*
11 Donoughue, *Downing Street Diary*, p. 655.
12 G. W. Jones, 'The United Kingdom' in William Plowden, *Advising the Rulers* (1987), Oxford: Basil Blackwell, p. 43.
13 Interviewed by Anthony Seldon, 'Men of Secrets: The Cabinet Secretaries'.
14 Lord Butler Papers: Sir Michael Partridge KCB to Butler, 6 September 1997.
15 Press release from 10 Downing Street, 1 August 1997.
16 Letter to Nora Butler, 21 December 1997.
17 Lord Butler, *Dear Descendants: A Legacy of Personal Memories.*
18 Lord Butler, after-dinner speech on the occasion of his retirement from the Civil Service, Middle Temple Hall, 12 January 1998.
19 Lord Butler, *Dear Descendants: A Legacy of Personal Memories.*
20 Butler did, however, worry that he had been too open with Sue Lawley. Letter to Nora Butler, 31 January 1993.
21 Lord Butler Papers: 'Media Briefing on My Retirement'.

CHAPTER 18: MASTER OF UNIVERSITY COLLEGE, 1998–2008

1 Butler had been elected an Honorary Fellow on 16 March 1989. Lord Butler Papers: letter of that date from Professor W. J. Albery to Butler.
2 In fact, this was not the first time that Butler had been considered for the Mastership. A decade before, at a Univ garden party, Lady (Mary) Wilson had said to Butler that he was 'on the list for a future Master of Univ'. Letter to Bernard and Nora Butler, 28 June 1987.
3 Lord Butler, interview, 3 June 2016.
4 Lord Butler, *Dear Descendants: A Legacy of Personal Memories.* Butler commented that when he was ennobled and elected Master of Univ at about the same time, he had suddenly become 'Lord and Master'.
5 These brief historical notes are taken from 'History', *University College Oxford* [college website] (undated) <www.univ.ox.ac.uk/content/history-0>, accessed 4 February 2017. For the best history of the college, see Robin Darwall-Smith, *A History of University College, Oxford* (2008), Oxford: OUP.
6 Lord Butler, *Dear Descendants: A Legacy of Personal Memories.*
7 Lord Butler, *Dear Descendants: A Legacy of Personal Memories.*
8 *Daily Telegraph*, 13 December 2013.
9 *Ibid.*
10 Address by Dr Leslie Mitchell at Professor Albery's memorial service, the University Church of St Mary the Virgin, 5 April 2014.
11 Professor W. J. Albery, letter to Lord Butler, 2 January 1998.
12 This and subsequent quotations are from G. L. Cawkwell's letter to Sir Robin Butler, 30 December 1997.
13 G. L. Cawkwell, letter to Lord Butler, 5 July 1998.
14 Lord Butler, *Dear Descendants: A Legacy of Personal Memories.*

15 Conversations with 'telethon' participants, 2000–10.
16 Lord Butler Papers: Butler, letter to Dr G. Screaton (undated).
17 Isabelle Lomholt, 'University College Oxford Boathouse', *e-architect* [online architecture resource] (6 March 2014) <http://www.e-architect.co.uk/oxford/oxford-boathouse>, accessed 4 February 2017.
18 See, for example, 'Top-up fee heroes face a modern day public flogging', *The Times*, 17 October 2003. Butler wrote to *The Times*, defending the controversial 'top-up fees', on 20 November 2002.
19 Interview with Can Yeginsu, English scholar, now a barrister, 15 June 2016
20 Recalled by Dr Raymond Davis, interview, 9 August 2016. Dr Davis was present at the dinner.
21 Lord Butler, *Dear Descendants: A Legacy of Personal Memories*.
22 Comments of the Los Angeles organiser for the Master's visits, 2002–06.
23 Chelsea Clinton later earned a Doctorate of Philosophy (DPhil) with a thesis entitled 'The Global Fund: An Experiment in Global Governance' (2014, under the supervision of Ngaire Woods).
24 'The Ditchley Foundation was established by Sir David Wills in 1958 to advance international learning and to bring transatlantic and other experts together to discuss international issues. Sir David's original objective was to promote Anglo-American understanding. American and Canadian sister Foundations, set up in 1964 and 1981 respectively, remain our most active partners. Since then Ditchley conferences have broadened to include the concerns and participation of nations all over the globe.' 'The Ditchley Foundation', *The Ditchley Foundation* [website] (undated) <www.ditchley.co.uk>, accessed 4 February 2017.
25 Lord Butler, *Dear Descendants: A Legacy of Personal Memories*.
26 'Oxford cannot carry on like this', *The Times*, 31 October 2005. The story of Sir Matthew Stevenson is also mentioned by Butler in his foreword to Michel Khoury and Rabih Abouchakra, *Government for a New Age: The Transformation Agenda* (2014), Oxford: Infinite Ideas.
27 For a brief but informative summary of the issues involved, see Alexandra Blair, 'Oxford dons ready for final battle over who controls their university', *The Times*, 13 November 2006.
28 *The Guardian*, 3 November 2015.
29 This response to a *Guardian* journalist was reported in *The Guardian*, 3 November 2015.
30 Lord Butler, interview, 3 June 2016.
31 Dr Robin Darwall-Smith, interview, 2 June 2016.
32 Details of the fund and its operation can be viewed at 'The Roger Short Memorial Fund', *University College Oxford* [college website] (undated) <http://www.univ.ox.ac.uk/content/roger-short-memorial-fund>, accessed 4 February 2017.
33 Dr Robin Darwall-Smith, interview, 2 June 2016.
34 Liv Anderman, English scholar, interview, 15 March 2016.
35 Professor Ngaire Woods, letter to Lord and Lady Butler, 30 July 2008.
36 Professor J. N. P. Rawlins, letter to Lord Butler, 18 August 2008.
37 Willem van der Colff, letter to Lord Butler.
38 Lord Butler, interview, 3 June 2016.
39 Dr Robin Darwall-Smith, interview, 2 June 2016.

CHAPTER 19: THE BUTLER REPORT, 2004

1 TNA, CAB 11/0074, 'Iraq's Weapons of Mass Destruction – The Assessment of the British Government'.

2 TNA, CAB 11/0075, *ibid.*
3 *Daily Mail*, 29 January 2004.
4 *Daily Mirror*, 29 January 2004.
5 Lord Butler, *Dear Descendants: A Legacy of Personal Memories.*
6 Nick Assinder, 'How Bad for Blair?', *BBC News* [online] (14 July 2004) <http://news.bbc.co.uk/2/hi/uk_news/politics/3893857.stm>, accessed 5 February 2017.
7 *The Guardian*, 4 February 2004.
8 'My week', *The House*, 14 February 2005.
9 Lord Butler, *Dear Descendants: A Legacy of Personal Memories.*
10 *Daily Telegraph*, 2 March 2004.
11 Lord Butler, *Dear Descendants: A Legacy of Personal Memories.*
12 *Ibid.*
13 *Ibid.*
14 *Review of Intelligence on Weapons of Mass Destruction*, HC 898, 14 July 2004, HMSO. Hereinafter referred to as the Butler Report.
15 Butler Report, para. 47.
16 Mirror-imaging is a term used in the intelligence community to describe the dangerous practice of viewing and processing information through the filter of personal experience.
17 JIC paper, 3 July 1989. Quoted in Butler Report, para. 111.
18 JIC paper, 13–19 October 1994. Quoted in Butler Report, para. 114.
19 Butler Report, para. 255.
20 Evidence of the Prime Minister to the Butler Committee. Cited in *ibid.*, para. 257.
21 *Ibid.*, para. 260.
22 *Ibid.*, para. 263.
23 *Ibid.*, para. 268.
24 JIC paper of 15 March 2002. Quoted in Butler Report, para. 270.
25 Butler Report, para. 284.
26 JIC paper, 9 September 2002. Quoted in Butler Report, para. 295.
27 The Butler Committee asked the question of the dossier's purpose in paras 315–19.
28 Butler Report, para. 308.
29 Alastair Campbell to John Scarlett, 9 September 2002. Cited in *ibid.*, para. 323.
30 Butler Report, para. 330.
31 Hansard, HC Deb, 24 September 2002, vol. 390, col. 3.
32 Butler Report, paras 334–41.
33 *Ibid.*, para. 1.
34 *Ibid.*, para. 392.
35 *Ibid.*, para. 429.
36 *Ibid.*, para. 436.
37 *Ibid.*, paras 438–52.
38 *Ibid.*, para. 458.
39 *Ibid.*, paras 463–8.
40 *Ibid.*, para. 469.
41 President George W. Bush, State of the Union Address, 28 January 2003. Cited in *ibid.*, para. 499.
42 *Ibid.*, para. 503.
43 There were several criticisms of the report's dealing with the intelligence that Saddam attempted to buy uranium from Niger. For example 'Clutching at straws', *Private Eye*, no. 1113, 20 August–3 September 2004. For clarification of the origin of the intelligence

concerning Niger and French reports, I am indebted to Michael Smith, *Anatomy of a Traitor* (forthcoming, 2017), London: Aurum Press.

44 Butler Report, para. 511.

45 *Ibid.*, para. 597.

46 *Ibid.*, para. 611.

47 This passage and subsequent quotations are from Robin Cook, 'Britain's worst intelligence failure, and Lord Butler says no one is to blame', *The Independent*, 15 July 2004.

48 Tony Blair, statement on the Butler Report, 14 July 2014.

49 Tony Blair, keynote speech at the Labour Party conference, 28 September 2004.

50 Jonathan Powell, *The New Machiavelli*, pp. 223–4.

51 Lord Butler, *Dear Descendants: A Legacy of Personal Memories*.

52 Hansard, HC Deb, 20 July 2004, vol. 424, col. 237.

53 *Ibid.*, col. 214.

54 *Ibid.*, col. 260.

55 Matthew Parris, 'Blair has won – in his playground cheat way', *The Times*, 24 July 2004.

56 Hansard, HL Deb, 7 September 2004, vol. 664, cols 462–4. His speech was followed by expressions of approval from several peers, including Butler's predecessor as Cabinet Secretary, Lord Armstrong, who complimented Butler on 'a very impressive report'.

57 'How not to run a country', *The Spectator*, 11 December 2004.

58 'Sofa, so bad: that's why Sir Humphrey put the boot in', Anthony Howard, *The Times*, 14 December 2004.

59 Matthew Norman, 'The Chilcot Report won't tell us anything new, but there is one lesson we can take from it', *The Independent*, 22 May 2016.

CHAPTER 20: BARON BUTLER OF BROCKWELL, CROSS-BENCHER

1 Marion Hawtree, interview, 23 May 2016.

2 *The Globe and Mail*, 17 July 2012.

3 US Senate Permanent Subcommittee of Investigations report, 17 July 2012, p. 58. <https://www.documentcloud.org/documents/537231-psi-report-hsbc-case-history-9-6-2.html>, accessed 13 February 2017.

4 James Hall, 'Long History of HSBC Money Laundering', *Breaking All the Rules* [website] (19 December 2012) <http://www.batr.org/negotium/121912.html>, accessed 4 February 2017.

5 'The role of the board, chairman and non-executive directors – the UK Corporate Governance Code', *Out-Law.com* [website] (undated) <http://www.out-law.com/page-8215>, accessed 4 February 2017.

6 Labour Party election manifesto (1997), 'We Will Clean Up Politics', section 1.

7 Hansard, HL Deb, 25 November 1998, vol. 595, cols 41–2.

8 'Lord faces test of his peers', *The Times*, 16 January 1999.

9 Lord Butler Papers: Lord Butler, letter to Sir Richard Wilson, 20 January 1999.

10 Hansard, HL Deb, 7 March 2000, vol. 610, cols 947–8.

11 Hansard, HC Deb, 19 June 2000, vol. 352, col. 94.

12 Lord Butler, *Dear Descendants: A Legacy of Personal Memories*.

13 United States Constitution, Article II, Section 2.

14 Lord Butler, *Dear Descendants: A Legacy of Personal Memories*.

15 'Welcome to the Better Government Initiative', *Better Government Initiative* [website] (undated) <bettergovernmentinitiative.co.uk>, accessed 4 February 2017.

16 'Good Government: Reforming Parliament and the Executive', *Better Government Initiative* (24 January 2010) <http://www.bettergovernmentinitiative.co.uk/reports-and-papers/good-government-2/>, p. 8, accessed 4 February 2017.
17 *Ibid.*, pp. 53–6.
18 'Ministers passing too many "bad" laws, say ex mandarins', *BBC News* [online] (27 January 2010) <http://news.bbc.co.uk/2/hi/uk_news/politics/8481943.stm>, accessed 4 February 2017.
19 *Civil Service World*, February 2016, pp. 38–9.
20 Michael Savage, 'Brexit would shatter Cameron's authority', *The Times*, 14 June 2016.
21 Jeremy Lemmon, interview, February 2015.
22 Lord Butler, *Dear Descendants: A Legacy of Personal Memories.*
23 Marion Hawtree, interview, 23 May 2016.

CHAPTER 21: OUT OF THE LIMELIGHT

1 Interviewed by Anthony Seldon, 'Men of Secrets: The Cabinet Secretaries'.
2 Lord Hennessy, interview, 13 December 2016.
3 Major, *The Autobiography*, p. 101.
4 Lord Butler, email to the author, 22 July 2016. Lord Butler believes that he is the only male student ever to have been sponsored by St Paul's Girls' School.
5 Interviewed by Anthony Seldon, 'Men of Secrets: The Cabinet Secretaries'.
6 *Ibid.*
7 Lord Butler, interview, 3 June 2016.
8 'The Ship of State', a lecture by Lord Armstrong of Ilminster, November 1992.
9 *Ibid.*
10 Interviewed by Anthony Seldon, 'Men of Secrets: The Cabinet Secretaries'.
11 *Ibid.*
12 Marion Hawtree, interview, 31 May 2016.
13 Woodrow Wilson, *Congressional Government* (1885), Boston: Houghton Mifflin, p. 52.
14 Robin Martin, interview, 16 August 2016.
15 Broadcast on 20 December 1988, 8.30 p.m.
16 Bower, *Broken Vows*, p. 402.
17 Dr Robin Darwall-Smith, interview, 3 June 2016.
18 Lord Butler, interview, 2 June 2016.
19 *National Gallery News*, August 1991.
20 *Washington Post*, 10 October 2013.
21 Ria Higgins, 'Lord Butler of Brockwell, and his daughter Nell', *Sunday Times* [online] (1 November 2015) <http://www.thesundaytimes.co.uk/sto/Magazine/article1624657.ece>, accessed 5 February 2017.
22 Ode to Maecenas, *Odes*, III.xxix.41–3: '*ille potens sui laetusque deget, cui licet in diem dixisse "vixi".*'

INDEX

Acland, Sir Anthony 195
Adams, Gerry 234–238
Aitken, Jonathan xiv, 245–250, 253, 292, 296, 325–326, 365
Aitken, Lolicia 249
Aitken, Victoria 246
AkzoNobel 297
Albery, Professor John 298, 302–303, 305, 316, 318
Al-Fayed, Mohammed 245, 246, 250–252
Allan, Sir Alexander 116*n*, 211, 264, 268
Andrew, H. R. H. Prince 219
Andropov, Yuri 135, 147
Anne, H. R. H. Princess 219,
Appleyard, Sir Leonard 228
Armstrong, Robert; Baron Armstrong of Ilminster viii, xiii, xiv, 50, 54, 68, 83, 86, 87, 89, 90, 92, 93, 94, 98, 99, 102, 111, 112*n*, 119 and *n*, 120, 121, 126, 127, 128, 137, 141, 142, 157 and *n*, 162, 163 and *n*, 164, 165, 166, 170, 171, 174, 176, 177, 178, 212, 224, 232, 249, 253, 262*n*, 279, 283, 290, 292, 293, 364, 365
Armstrong, William; Baron Armstrong of Sanderstead 37, 40 and *n*, 43, 44–45, 51, 54, 55, 78 and *n*, 79, 82, 86, 137,
Arthur Andersen 101
Armstrong-Jones, Anthony; Earl of Snowdon 28, 219,
Attlee, Clement; Earl Attlee 45, 47, 172, 202, 300, 311
Ayas, Said 246–249

Babylon (Project) 221
Ball, Jonathan 236
Balls, Ed 281
Balme, Maurice viii, 8
Balogh, Thomas; Baron Balogh of Hampstead 38, 96, 97, 304,
Bandar bin Sultan, Prince 195
Barber, Anthony; Baron Barber of Wentbridge 79, 80
Barlow Clowes 181
Barnett, Joel 87
Barratt Homes 148, 158, 159
Barratt, Sir Lawrie 158, 159
Bashir, Martin 218
Bauwens, Mona 214
Baxendale QC, Presiley 223, 225
Bedford, Tommy 106
Begley, Thomas 238
Beith, Alan 170, 172
Benn, Tony 46, 61, 355,
Bernhard, Bill 302
Bethell, Nicholas 90
Better Government Initiative xvii, 353, 368
Beveridge, William; Baron Beveridge of Tuggal 46, 202, 300, 311
Beyond the Fringe 36
Bichard, Michael 279
Billière, General Sir Peter de196
Bin-Fahd, Prince Mohammed 246, 248
Birt, John; Baron Birt of Liverpool 150, 218, 276, 294, 301
Bishop, Prime Minister Maurice 133
Black Wednesday 215, 261
Blackstone, Tessa; Baroness Blackstone of Stoke Newington 175
Blair, Cherie xviii, 263, 294,
Blair, Tony vii, viii, xi and *n*, xiv, 147*n*, 262, 263, 262–282, 285, 291, 294, 311, 323, 324, 327, 329, 332, 333, 338, 339, 340–341, 343, 350, 354, 365, 366, 368,
Blavatnik, Leonid ('Len') 314–315
Boissier, Roger 108
Booker, Christopher 38
Bower, Tom xvi, 273*n*, 371
Bradman, Sir Donald 12, 14
Bramall, Field Marshall Sir Edwin 121
Branson, Sir Richard 311
Brewster, Kingman 318
Brezhnev, Leonid 37

Bridger, John 14
Bridges, Edward; Baron Bridges of Headley 52, 87, 291
Bridges, Thomas 75, 99
Brixton riots 148–149
Brockwell Park 110 and *n*, 118, 300, 345
Brook, Norman; Lord Normanbrook 169, 291,
Brookes, Peter 281 and *n*
Brown, George; Lord George Brown 42,
Brown, Gordon 247, 263, 265, 269, 271, 275, 276, 281
Burns, Sir Terry 212, 288, 289, 294, 328
Bush, President George H. W. xvi and *n*, 194–195, 196,
Bush, President George W. 325, 329, 332, 333, 337, 340
Butler, Andrew 44, 106, 109*n*, 155, 156, 162, 298, 302, 345, 362
Butler, Bernard 1–8, 10, 12–15, 19, 35, 118, 162, 168
Butler, Catriona 302, 345
Butler, Diana 5, 12, 34, 118,
Butler, F. E. R. (Robin)
  Baron Butler of Brockwell, birth 1
  family origins 1–4
  at Orley Farm and wins Harrow scholarship 6
  all-round ability 7*ff*
  Head of the School 9–10
  character as a young man 10–12
  choosing a career 12–13
  at VPS camps 14–15
  rejected for National Service 17
  at St Dunstan's School 17–20
  plays rugby for Bridgwater 19
  at University College 21*ff*
  gains First in Moderations 23
  approach to Philosophy 24–26
  wins rugby Blue 26–27
  meets Jill Galley 28–29
  gains First in 'Greats' 30–31
  engaged to Jill 31
  joins Treasury 33*ff*
  buys first house and marries Jill 35
  political views in 1960s 35–37
  fast-streamed' at Treasury 38–39
  Private Secretary to Financial Secretary 39–40
  and 1966 election 40–41
  and devaluation 42–43
  birth of three children 40, 42, 44
  at Bank of England 44–45
  and 1970 election 46–47
  working with the CPRS 57–64
  impresses Edward Heath 64
  first posting to Downing Street 68
  tour of USA 68–69
  working with Heath 69*ff*
  and miners' strike 72
  and Sunningdale agreement 72–77
  and the fall of the Heath Government 77–84
  working with Wilson's team 85*ff*, 91–92, 93–95
  relations with Wilson 86, 88, 91
  relations with Marcia Williams 90, 95, 98–99
  status at No. 10 89–90
  and changes in Civil Service 96–98
  and FIS1 99–101
  promotion in 1977 102–103
  and amateur dramatics 105
  playing club rugby 105–106
  family holidays 106–107
  becomes governor of Harrow School 107–109
  moves to Half Moon Lane 110–111
  and Royal Opera House 111
  and 1979 election 111–112
  achieves massive expenditure cuts 113–114
  seeks further savings in expenditure 114–116
  and abolition of Civil Service department 116–117
  and family 1981–82 118
  appointed PPS to Thatcher 119–120
  nature of work with Thatcher 120–122, 126–129, 132–133, 150–151
  visit to Balmoral 122–123
  Asian tour 124–126
  visit to Falkland Islands 130
  and 1983 election 131–132
  handles Parkinson affair 133
  visit to Moscow 135
  cleans Treasury windows 137–138
  assessment by observers 138–139
  and NUM 140*ff*
  and GCHQ 141
  and SPADs 141–142
  grows in self-confidence 142–143
  and IRA attack in Brighton 143–145
  at European summit in Dublin 145–146
  round-the-world trip with Thatcher 146–147
  introduces Thatchers to Dulwich 147–150, 158–159
  promoted to rank of Permanent Secretary 151–152
  return to Treasury 152–153
  trips with Jill to Israel and Egypt, Jordan and Syria 155–156
  working at Treasury 156*ff*
  relations with Thatcher 161–162
  and 8 Aquinas Street 162
  appointed Cabinet Secretary and Head of Home Civil Service 163–166
  and Tory Party leadership 167–168
  and death of his father 168
  reaction to his new appointment 169–172
  view of Cabinet government 172–173
  and Next Steps initiative 173–175
  support for Rothschild 175
  as a moderniser 176–178

Butler, F. E. R. (Robin) *cont.*
as Cabinet Secretary 178–179
concern at Thatcher's style and Charles Powell 179–180, 183, 187
and Barlow Clowes affair 181–182
ambassador to Baron Thyssen 182–183
and troubles with Lawson and Walters 183–185
and decline of party support for Thatcher 185–186
stage-managing Cabinet 190
and Harrow Songs 190–191
relations with Major as PM 193–194
visits Camp David with Major 194–196
streamlines Whitehall in time of war 196
in mortar attack on Downing Street 197–198
works with Brent Scowcroft after Gulf War 198
advises Major 199
supports Citizen's Charter 200*ff*
and Maastricht treaty 206–207
briefings of Kinnock, Labour leader 208–210
uses friendship to move levers of power 211–213
confidence in Major 213
concern at Major's closure of coal mines 215–216
and relations between the Waleses 216–219
and prosecution of Matrix Churchill directors 219–222
and Scott inquiry 222–226
on William Waldegrave's position 226
deals with Alan Clark's diaries 226–229
friendship with Ian Gow 232
and *n*; meets Charles Haughey 232
flies to Dublin to meet Dermot Nally 236–237
flies to Dublin again 238–239
sceptical about reaching Irish agreement 240
satisfaction at signing of Downing Street Declaration 242–243
involved in Aitken affair 245–249
criticised for lack of judgement 249–251
interviews Tim Smith and Neil Hamilton re corruption 251–253
and Nolan Committee 253–255
assessment of John Major 256
and leadership challenge 256
relations with Heseltine 257–259
and the 1997 election 261–262
arranges smooth transfer of power 263–264, 266
and Powell as Chief of Staff 266–267
on SPADs in Blair's Downing St 267–268
on Blair and Civil Service 268–269
on Irvine and devolution 270
relations with Campbell and Powell 270–271, 275, 281
on New Labour and the media 274, 280
handles matters after death of Princess of Wales 276–277
on split of Cabinet Secretary's responsibilities 278–279
recommends Wilson as successor 279
assesses tradition and modernity 279–280
on PMs he served 281–282
speaks to ESRC about changes during his career 283*ff*
on politicisation of Civil Service 285
on the Service's relations with the media 286
tribute to Kemp for Next Steps initiative 287–288
on balancing efficiency and traditions 289–290
on visibility in the Service 291–292
his retirement party 294–295
on *Desert Island Discs* 295–296
accepts non-executive directorships with HSBC and ICI 297–298
learns of Univ Mastership 298–299
applies for Mastership 299
creates title of his barony 300
travels to New Zealand and USA as Master elect 300–302
climbs Arthur's Seat with Andrew 302
learns that academe is different from Civil Service 305–306
becomes successful fundraiser for College 306–307
extends Univ 'family' 306*ff*
appoints non-academic Senior Tutor 308–309
encounters petty resentment from Fellows 310
plans 750th anniversary programme 310–311
agrees to accept Chelsea Clinton 312
arranges fundraising seminar at Ditchley 312–313
supports Vice-Chancellor 314
sits on donations review committee 314–315
and Butler Review in Oxford context 316
serves on Wakeham Commission on House of Lords 316
is inducted as a Knight of the Garter 316
does not stand for election as University Chancellor 316
extends Master's Travel Scholarship programme 316–317
handles Mastership in collaboration with Jill 318–319
compliments on his retirement from Mastership 319–321
assesses his performance 321–322
agrees to Butler Review 325–326
visits Iraq 328; finalises Butler Report 328*ff*
is equivocal about presence of WMD in Iraq 332–336
absolves Scarlett from blame 337

Butler, F. E. R. (Robin) *cont.*
criticises 'informality' of Blair Government 338
denies that Blair lied about WMD 339–340
gives interview to Boris Johnson 342–343
sells house in Half Moon Lane, buys flat in Westminster and house in Norfolk 345–346
resigns from HSBC board 347
he and Jill attend Renaissance Art course in Florence 348–349
sits on Wakeham Commission for reform of Lords 349–352
takes part in Better Government Initiative 353–354
speaks out on several current issues, including Brexit 355, 358
Master of Salters' Company 356
skill in communicating with young as well as old 356–357
names most interesting people 360–361
helpful to others 361
has succeeded without leaving victims in his wake 361–362
takes Science GCSE 362–363
believes in government as partnership between politicians and Civil Service 366
Butler doctrine of accountability / responsibility 367
potential as a politician 369–370
enjoyed his youth, his maturity, his career 371
Nell's memory of his harum-scarum schemes 372.
Butler, Gillian (Jill) Lady Butler
Meets Robin and coxes boat 29
goes to Greece with Robin and friends 30–31
becomes engaged on the Acropolis 31
teaches at St Paul's Girls School 33
lives in Central London but buys house in Dulwich 34–36
marriage and honeymoon 36
birth of Sophie 40
moves to Sydenham 105
birth of Nell and Andrew 42, 44
spends 12 years away from teaching 106
teaches at Alleyn's 107
love of travel 106
yields to Tess' pleas for a dog 118
has Thatchers to dinner 148
trip to Middle East 155
trip to Jordan and Syria 156
buys house for children 162
commissions cartoon from Peter Brookes 281
at Robin's retirement party 295
plans to work together with Robin 298
seeks challenge more than wealth 297, 298
plans round-the-world trip 298–299
'the better half of the ticket' at Univ 299
discomfort at high altitude 301
travels to New Zealand 301
hesitates to meet President Clinton because of Lewinsky affair 302
enjoys role at Univ 302
elected member of Senior Common Room 303
visits USA with the Master each year 311
involves herself in college life 316, 318–319
is pictured with the Master in college portrait 319
seen as a 'benevolent guardian' by undergraduates 320
advises Butler not to undertake inquiry 325
and grandchildren 319, 345
sells house in Half Moon Lane
buys flat in Westminster and house in Norfolk 345–346
ready to move on from Univ in 2008 346
spends two months in Florence 348–349
scores better than her husband in examination 349
revives Martlets society in Univ 318, 357
competes daily with her husband on Polygon word puzzle 362.
Butler, Sir J. R. M.; ('Jim') 10 and *n*
Butler, Nell: see Rushbrooke, Justin & Nell
Butler, Nora (née Jones) 1–6, 12, 35, 112*n*, 118, 346
Butler, R. A. ('Rab') 10, 37*n*, 43, 50, 105, 106, 312
Butler, Sophie: see Trend, Nick and Sophie

Callaghan, James; Baron Callaghan of Cardiff 30, 40, 41, 42–43, 92*n*, 100, 103, 110, 116, 119, 129, 205
Calland, Richard 152
Cameron, Prime Minister David 23, 278, 355, 364, 365,
Campbell, Alastair viii, xvii, 268, 269, 270, 271, 272, 273, 274, 275, 277, 281, 323, 334
Campbell, Jean 50
Campbell, John 79
Canner, Steve 68
Carew, 6th Lord 13, 30
Carey, Sir Peter 57, 175
Carington, Peter; 6th Baron Carrington 111, 129,
Carter, President Jimmy 103
Castle, Barbara; Baroness Castle of Blackburn 46
Central Policy Review Staff ('CPRS') 52, 53, 56, 58–65, 88, 120, 121, 284
Cawkwell, George 24, 304, 305
Cervera, Carmen ('Tita') 183 and *n*
Chalet des Mélèzes 319
Charles, HRH Prince of Wales 211, 216–220, 276, 312,
Chernenko, Konstantin 135, 147
Chilcot, Sir John 323, 326, 340, 343, 364
Christopherson, Romola 139
Churchill, Sir Winston 47, 52, 60*n*, 81*n*, 190,

Citizen's Charter 200–205, 210, 212, 288, 360, 371
Civil Service Training College 74–76, 258, 272
Clark, Alan 221–223, 226–228 and 228*n*
Clarke, Charles 208–209 and *n*
Clarke, Sir Richard ('Otto') 208, 209*n*
Clinton, Chelsea 312
Clinton, President W. J. 262, 276, 302, 312, 369
Clowes, Peter 181
COBRA 197 and *n*
Cole, G. D. H. 202, 300
Coles, Sir John 130
Compton, Sir Edmund 13, 30, 156
Concorde (aircraft) 55, 60, 62
Connolly-Carew, Diana 13
Connolly-Carew, Patrick, 7th Lord Carew 13 and *n*, 295
Continuity and Change, White Paper 289
Cook, Robin xii, xiv, 226, 269, 271, 338 and *n*, 339
Cooper, Sir Frank 119
Cooper, Professor Helen 308–309
Cormack, Sir Patrick 341
Cortazzi, Sir Hugh 124, 126
Cosgrave, Liam 74, 76
Crewe, Sir Ivor 305*n*, 358, 371
Crosland, Anthony ('Tony') 81
Cunningham, Jack 262, 343

Daft, Richard 1–3, 193,
Darwall-Smith, Dr Robin 312*n*, 321*n*, 371
Dashwood, Sir Francis 28
Davies, Gavyn 88, 89, 324
Davies, John 61
Davies, Robin 22
Delors, Jacques 186, 206
Democratic Unionist Party 241
Deng Xiao Peng 126, 146, 360
Desert Storm 196
Devlin, Bernadette 73
Diana, HRH. Princess of Wales 123, 211, 216–219, 276–277
Donoughue, Bernard; Baron Donoughue of Ashton viii, xvi, xviii, 86, 87, 88, 89–91, 92–95, 98–99, 100, 166, 176, 262, 275, 292, 354, 361
Downing Street Declaration 237, 241, 242, 243, 296
Drury, Clare 309
Duignan, Sean 239
Dyke, Greg 324
Dykes, Brigadier Vivian 142–143

Eames, Robin; Archbishop of Armagh 237, 240
Ecclestone, Bernie 271, 272
Eddington, Paul 139
Eden, Sir Anthony; Earl of Avon 81, 85,
Edwards, Huw 202
Eisenhower, President Dwight D. 142*n*, 229
Elizabeth, HM The Queen 41, 122, 123, 131, 158, 169, 198, 209, 216 and *n*, 218, 276, 277, 310, 312
European Economic Community ('EEC') 42, 78, 83, 194, 213
Evans, Dr John 312 and *n*
Evans, Roger 201–202

Falconer, Charles; Baron Falconer of Thoroton 324
Faulkner, Brian; Baron Faulkner of Downpatrick 73–77
Fellgett, Robin 204
Fellowes, Lady Jane 211, 276
Fellowes, Robert; Baron Fellowes of Shottesham 211 and *n*, 217, 218, 219, 276, 277
Field, Tony 90
Firth, Tony 28
FitzGerald, Garret 231
Foley, Michael 265
Foot, Michael 132, 355
Foot, Paul 228
Ford, Professor Hugh 54
Forrester, Mark 87
Foster, Sir Christopher 353
Fox, Sir Marcus 151
Fox, Robert 29
Fox, Robin 20
Franks Report 121, 129–130, 326–327, 329, 335, 340
Frost, Sir David 38, 350
Fulton Report 97, 116, 284

Gadaffi, Colonel Muammar 141
Gaitskell, Hugh 36, 37*n*, 38, 43, 99 and *n*
Galley, Gillian see Butler, Jill
Garter King of Arms 110*n*, 300
George, Edward; Baron George of St Tudy 45
Gilbey, James 217
Gilligan, Andrew 324
Gilmour, Ian; Baron Gilmour of Craigmillar 185
Good Friday Agreement 243
Goodman, Arnold; Baron Goodman of the City of Westminster 318
Gorbachev, Mikhail 135, 146, 147
Gould, Philip 265
Government Communications Headquarters ('GCHQ') 140, 141, 171
Gow, Ian 232 and *n*
Gowrie, 2nd Earl of ('Grey') 141
Grace, William Gilbert ('WG') 1
Graham, Andrew 88, 89, 93
Graham, Richard 98
Greenstock, Sir Jeremy 318
Greer, Ian 251,252
Grenada, invasion of 133–134

Hague, William 130, 131, 274

Haines, Joe xvi, xviii, 79, 86, 87, 89, 90, 91–92, 94, 95, 138, 176, 274, 275, 292, 354, 362
Haldeman, H. R. 270
Hamilton, Neil 246, 251, 252, 296, 365
Hankes-Drielsma, Sir Claude 182
Hankey, Maurice; Baron Hankey of The Chart 52, 169, 364
Hart, Professor H. L. A. 322 and *n*
Harvey-Jones, John 298
Hassan al-Majid, Ali 194
Haughey, Charles 231, 232, 233
Hawking, Professor Stephen 300, 311
Hawthorne, Nigel 139
Hawtree, Marion 305, 346, 357, 367
Hayes, Sir Brian 181
Healey, Denis; Baron Healey of Riddlesdon 81, 94, 101
Heath, Sir Edward 37, 53–54, 68, 72, 91, 94, 141, 209, 261;
replaces Douglas-Home as Tory leader 38, 40
is stiff and uncharismatic 46
confident he could lead Tories to victory 47
and Selsdon Park conference 49
his general strategy 50
his 'quiet revolution' 51
his use of businessmen 51
creates CPRS 52
meets Lord Rothschild 54–55, 56
and Upper Clyde Shipbuilders 61
wants to reduce power of Treasury 63
approves of Butler's work with CPRS 64
projects different image from Wilson 67
is difficult socially 69
rejects Butler's draft of a speech 70
refuses to accept Thatcher as his successor 71
efforts in Northern Ireland 73–74
at the Sunningdale peace talks 75–77, 232
attitude to joining the EEC 78
battles with the NUM and the three-day week 79–81
loses majority and tries to form coalition with Liberals 81–82
is seen by Butler as a traditionalist 83–84, 95
relations break down with Thatcher 112
good relations with Butler 112, 171
brought Sir Denis Rayner to improve Civil Service performance 173–174
features in Brookes' cartoon 281
at Butler's retirement party 295.
Hell Fire Club 28
Hennessy, Peter; Baron Hennessy of Nympsfield viii, xiii-xiv, 10, 37, 51, 62, 138, 153, 164, 165, 173, 174, 175, 176, 266, 267, 279, 286, 291, 360, 361, 363
Her Majesty's Stationery Office ('HMSO') 258
Heseltine, Michael; Baron Heseltine of Thenford 165, 167, 169, 187, 189, 190, 252, 256–259
Heywood, Sir Jeremy xv, 271, 278, 368
Hezbollah 156
Hogg, Quintin; Baron Hailsham of St Marylebone 132, 173,
Hogg, Sarah; Baroness Hogg of Kettlethorpe viii, xvi, 152, 193, 199, 201, 202, 204, 209, 256, 370
Holt, R. A. A. ('Bimby') 109 and *n*
Home, Earl of; Sir Alec Douglas-Home 36, 37, 38, 85,
Hong Kong and Shanghai Banking Corporation ('HSBC') x, 297, 347–348
Hood, Sir John 314
House of Lords reform xvii, 316, 349–352, 354, 355
Howard, Anthony 286, 342, 343
Howard, Michael; Baron Howard of Lympne 141*n*, 207, 327, 340–341,
Howe, Sir Geoffrey; Baron Howe of Aberavon
Hume, John 75, 237, 238
Hunt, John; Baron Hunt of Tanworth 64, 95, 169, 178,
Hunter, Anji 273 and *n*
Hurd, Douglas; Baron Hurd of Westwell 51, 58, 67, 70, 79, 82, 167, 217, 236, 351*n*
Hussey, Lady Susan 59
Hutton Report xii, 89, 324, 325, 329, 338

Ibbs, Sir Robin 174 and *n*, 176
Imperial Chemical Industries ('ICI') 297–298
Inge, Field Marshall Lord 326
Ingham, Sir Bernard 128, 130, 131, 138, 139, 145, 150, 151, 168, 178, 179, 182, 187, 199, 200, 205, 274
Ingrams, Richard 36, 38, 90, 176, 318
Irish Republican Army ('IRA') 141, 144, 145, 162*n*, 197–198, 234*n*, 235–240
Irvine, Derry; Baron Irvine of Lairg 270, 271, 278, 295
Ishihara, Takashi 125
Ismay, General Hastings ('Pug') 142
Isserlis, David ('Sandy') 68

James, Dr R. L. ('Jimmy') 9, 17, 108
Jay, The Hon. Peter 30 and *n*
Jefferson, Thomas 352
Jellicoe, George; 2nd Earl Jellicoe 53
Jenkins, The Right Revd David 143
Jenkins, Roy; Baron Jenkins of Hillhead 37, 43, 316
Jenkins, Simon 225, 295
Johnson, Boris 23, 318, 342
Joint Intelligence Committee ('JIC') 327–328, 330–331, 333–339
Jones, Fred 3

Kaldor, Nicholas 40
Keays, Sarah 133, 151
Keir, David 304
Kelly, Dr David 342

Kemp, Sir Peter 177, 287–288 and *n*, 290
Kennedy, President John F. 35, 50, 70, 96
Khrushchev, Nikita 37–38
Kinnock, Neil 161, 186, 209 and *n*
Kissinger, Henry 55
Kitson, Sir Timothy ('Tim') 82, 84
Kohl, Helmut 207, 213
Korean Airlines flight 135

Laborde, Charles 9–10
Laing, Hector; Baron Laing of Dunphail 122 and *n*
Lamont, Norman; Baron Lamont of Lerwick 206, 215
Lankester, Sir Tim 122
Lawley, Sue 295
Lawson, Nigel; Baron Lawson of Blaby 167, 173*n*, 178, 183, 184
Lee, J. J. 72–73
Lemmon, Jeremy 10, 11, 12, 108*n*, 111, 371
Letwin, Oliver 278
Lewinsky, Monica 302
Loudon, Annabella 31
Lubbers, Ruud 207, 213
Lucas, Sir Colin 313, 314
Lyalin, Oleg 99

Maastricht Treaty 206–207, 213, 214
MacDermot, Niall 39 and *n*
McFarlane, Robert ('Bud') 146
MacGregor, John; Baron MacGregor of Pulham Market 158, 160
McGuinness, Martin 234
Mackay, Baron of Clashfern 190
MacLaren, Catriona: See Butler, Catriona
Macleod, Iain 36–37, 72
McMahon, Christopher ('Kit') 54
Macmillan, Harold; Earl of Stockton xiii, 36, 37, 47, 53, 85, 95, 100, 189
Madison, James 352
Maitland, Sir Donald 50, 67
Major, Sir John vii, xii
  on Thatcher's pugnaciousness 127
  follows MacGregor as Chief Secretary 159–160
  as Minister of State for Social Security 160
  his rapid promotion 160–161
  becomes Foreign Secretary 184
  becomes Chancellor of the Exchequer and Thatcher's chosen successor 185
  and leadership election 187
  is loyal to Thatcher but ambitious 189
  becomes Prime Minister 193
  his love of cricket is a bond with Butler 2, 193–194
  meets President Bush at Camp David 194–196
  and Gulf War 196–197*ff*
  and bomb attack on Downing St 197–198
  chooses David Waddington to succeed Whitelaw 199
  appoints Gus O'Donnell Press Secretary 199
  early agenda as PM 200
  and Citizen's Charter 200–203, 205–206
  EEC and Maastricht Treaty 206–207, 213
  his continued optimism 207
  build-up to 1992 election 208–209
  gains confidence after election 210, 211
  body blows to Government in 1992 and Black Wednesday 213–216
  Butler's impressions of him 216
  and divorce of Charles and Diana 217
  Matrix Churchill and Scott Inquiry 222–223
  survives vote in Commons 226
  works for peace in Ireland 231*ff*
  meets Haughey 232–233
  his approach to North and South 233
  refusal to deal with terrorists 235
  and the nine-paragraph letter 235
  avoids meeting Reynolds but sends Butler 236–237
  meets Reynolds in London 237
  clears final obstacles before Downing Street meeting with Reynolds 239–240
  'sleaze' in last years of his Government 245*ff*
  and Aitken affair 247, 250*f*
  appoints Lord Nolan to chair committee 253
  growing dissatisfaction within party 255
  Butler's assessment of his thin skin 256
  resigns and stands for re-election 256–257
  adjudicates between Butler and Heseltine 259
  build-up to 1997 election 261–262
  loses 1997 election 262
  Blair's distance from him 264–265, 273
  and Civil Service reform 290
  his use of Cabinet 291, 365
  at Butler's farewell party 295
  speaks at University College 318
  his view of Butler 362.
Mallon, Seamus 240
Mandarins, The (cricket team) 39, 176,
Mandelson, Peter 265, 269, 271, 272, 274, 275, 279, 365
Margaret, HRH Princess 28*n*, 219
Marshall, Robert 53
Martin, Robin 12, 18, 370
Mates, Michael 171, 172, 326, 327, 328, 356
Mathieson, Don and Sally 301
Matrix Churchill 219, 221, 222, 225, 229, 292
Maud, Sir John, Lord Redcliffe-Maud 359 and *n*
Maude, Francis; Baron Maude of Horsham 204
Maudling, Reginald ('Reggie') 47, 72, 73
Mayhew, Patrick; Baron Mayhew of Twysden 236, 238, 239, 240
Mayne, John 63
Meacher, Michael 341

Meegeren, Hans van91
Mellor, David 214
Meyer, Sir Anthony 185
Middleton, Sir Peter 164, 165, 166, 212, 288, 289
Miers, Sir David 20, 31 and *n*
Miliband, David 264, 281
Millar, Ronald ('Ronnie') 132, 133
Mitchell, Dr Leslie 299, 303, 305
Mittérand, François 139, 150
Molyneaux, Jim; Baron Molyneaux of Killead 131, 237, 238, 240, 241, 243
Moore, Charles 141, 161, 359
Moore, Sir Philip; Baron Moore of Wolvercote 123, 131
Morris, Sir Derek 314
Morriss, Hugo 23
Morton, Andrew 216–217
Moser, Professor Claus 56
Moses, Alan QC 225
Motion, Sir Andrew 300
Mottram, Sir Richard 229, 288, 353
Mount, Sir Ferdinand ('Ferdie') 121, 124,
Murdoch, Rupert 311
Murray, Albert; Baron Murray of Gravesend 87
Muttukumaru, Christopher 225

Naipaul, Sir V. S. 311
Nairne, Patrick ('Pat') 89
Nally, Dermot 222, 223, 237, 239, 242, 243
National Union of Miners ('NUM') 40*n*, 72, 77, 79, 80, 81, 84, 87, 88, 140, 141, 142
Neild, Professor Robert 40
Neill, Patrick; Baron Neill of Bladen 271
Next Steps initiative 166, 174, 175, 177, 178, 212, 287, 288, 289
Nicholls, Patrick 352
Nield, Sir William 79
Nissan 125
Nixon, President Richard 63, 138, 270, 334
Nolan Committee 253–255
Norman, Sir Montagu; Baron Norman of St Clere 44
Northcote Trevelyan Report 97, 284

O'Brien, Leslie; Baron O'Brien of Lothbury 44
O'Donnell, Gus; Baron O'Donnell of Clapham viii, xv, 177, 199, 213, 253, 279, 280, 364
Omand, Sir David 328
Osmond, Andrew 36, 90
Owen, Dr David; Baron Owen of the City of Plymouth 64, 78

Paisley, The Revd Ian 76, 231, 233, 240, 241
Pallister, David 246, 248,
Parker-Bowles, Camilla 217, 218
Parkinson, Cecil 133, 151, 167
Parr, Butler 2
Parris, Matthew 341
Parry, Tim 236
Parsons, Sir Anthony 127, 128
Pelling, Professor Christopher 298, 299, 305, 362
Perle, Richard 146
Philip, HRH The Duke of Edinburgh 123, 310,
Phillips, Mark 219
Pimlott, Ben 100
Pliatzky, Sir Leo 88
Plowden, William 63, 88
Plumptre, E. V. C. ('Plum') 10, 11
Pompidou, President Georges 42
Powell, Charles 147, 163, 168, 178–179, 180, 183, 198, 199, 296
Powell, Enoch 49, 64, 72
Powell, Jonathan viii, xi, xvii, 262, 264, 266, 267, 268, 269, 270–271, 272, 273, 275–276, 279, 281, 296, 325, 339, 366
Prescott, John 259, 265, 269
Preston, Peter 246–247, 248
Priestley, Clive 174
Primrose, Andrew 23
Prior, James; Baron Prior of Brampton 111,
Private Eye 36, 72, 90, 99, 149, 151, 158, 159, 176
Pym, Francis; Baron Pym of Sandy 67, 121

Quinlan, Sir Michael 137, 221, 229

Rawlinson, Peter; Baron Rawlinson of Ewell 76
Rawlinson, Tania Jane 306, 312
Rawson, Professor Dame Jessica 321
Rayner, Derek; Baron Rayner of Crowborough 174
Reagan, President Ronald 133, 134 and *n*, 135, 146, 179, 195
Redwood, John 256, 257, 318, 359
Reynolds, Albert 231, 233, 236, 237, 239, 240, 241, 242
Richard, Ivor 262
Riddick, Graham 250
Ridley, Sir Adam 175
Ridley, Nicholas; Baron Ridley of Liddesdale 121
Robb-Silverman Commission xi, 343
Robbins, Peter 22
Roberts, Christopher 73
Robinson, Geoffrey 272, 365
Rolls Royce 61, 62–63
Ross, Dick 53, 54, 55, 63
Rothschild, Evelyn de 108
Rothschild, Lord ('Victor') 54–55, 56–57, 58, 59, 62, 63, 64, 65, 98, 137, 162, 175, 212
Rumor, Mariano 74, 75, 76
Rusbridger, Alan 248
Rushbrooke, Justin and Nell 42, 106, 107, 118, 155, 162, 294, 295 and *n*, 296, 345, 372
Rushdie, Salman 220
Ryder, Richard 252

Saddam, Hussein xii, 185, 194, 197, 198, 199, 221, 323, 324, 329, 331–333, 334, 335, 337, 339, 340
Salters' Company 356, 362–363
Sancha, Antonia de 214
Saunders, Dame Cicely 148
Savage, Roz 300
Scargill, Arthur 140, 143
Scarlett, Sir John 323, 337, 339, 342
Schmidt, Chancellor Helmut 318, 355
Scholar, Sir Michael 122
Schreiber, Mark; Baron Schreiber of Marlesford 53, 58 and *n*
Schultz, George 133, 146
Scott Report xii, 222, 223–226, 228–229, 255, 261, 296, 326
Scowcroft, General Brent KBE 198, 199
Screaton, Dr Gordon 299
Seldon, Sir Anthony 200, 203, 211, 245, 268, 360
Selsdon Man 49
September Dossier 323, 324, 327, 329, 333, 334, 335, 336, 337, 338
Sharp, Evelyn; Baroness Sharp of Hornsey 53
Sheppard, The Right Revd David 14, 15
Sherbourne, Stephen; Baron Sherbourne of Didsbury 141 and *n*
Shock, Sir Maurice 322 and *n*
Shore, Peter 355
Short, Roger 317
Sinn Féin 233 and *n*, 234, 235, 236, 238, 239, 240,
Smith, General Bedell 160 and *n*
Smith, Steve 27
Smith, Tim 246, 251, 252, 365
Smithers, Sir Peter 182
Snell, Kenneth 7
Sorensen, Theodore ('Ted') 70
Soros, George 214–215
Spycatcher 175, 222, 224, 291
Stowe, Sir Kenneth 92 and *n*, 94, 99, 119, 151–152, 164, 170
Strang, Gavin 263
Strawson, Sir Peter xvii, 24
Stuart, Nicholas ('Nick') 87
Style, Matthew 310
Sunningdale Agreement 74–81, 232
Swire, Sir John 319
Sykes, The Revd Bill 321*n*
Sykes, David 317

Taylor, Ann 262, 326
That Was the Week that Was 36, 38
Thatcher, Sir Denis 123, 127, 129, 133, 139, 144, 145, 148, 149, 151, 164, 189, 190, 191
Thatcher, Margaret vii, xii, xiii, xvi, xvii, 111
  at Dept of Education and Science 63
  poisonous relations with Heath 71, 112
  and 1979 election campaign 103
  demands £800 million and £400 million reductions in spending 113–115
  makes cuts in Civil Service staffing 117, 173–175
  has Stowe then Whitmore as PPS 119
  reminds Butler of his acceptance of inflation in 1971 120
  Butler's view of the 'Iron Lady' 122
  visits Royal Family at Balmoral 123
  1982 trip to Japan, China, Hong Kong 124–126
  robust exchange with Major 127
  abolishes CPRS 127
  and Foreign Policy Unit at No. 10 127–128
  and Douglas Wass 128–129
  and Franks committee 129–130
  and William Hague 130–131
  and 1983 election 131–132
  method of composing speeches 132–133
  and Parkinson affair 133
  disagreement with Reagan over invasion of Grenada 133–135
  and Kremlin succession 135
  her inner circle 138–139
  battles with Scargill 140–141
  Mitterand's description of her 139
  and SPADs 141–142
  assassination attempt in Brighton 143–145
  visit to Beijing 146
  and Camp David 147
  viewing and purchase of house in Dulwich 147–150
  relations with Butler 150–151, 153–154, 161, 366
  views on Channel Tunnel 150
  hosts farewell dinner for Butler 151
  continues to seek advice from Butler 161
  appoints Butler Cabinet Secretary 163–166
  discontent with her leadership 167, 170
  opposed to Heseltine as possible leader 167
  holds fewer Cabinet meetings 167–168, 172
  retains Charles Powell as foreign affairs private secretary 178–180
  and the Thyssen art collection 183
  certainty in her own methods 183–184
  supports Walters over Lawson 184
  challenged by Sir A. Meyer 185–186
  rejects federal Europe 186–187, 194
  is attacked by Howe in Commons statement 187–189
  is challenged again for the leadership and resigns 189–191
  differences between her and John Major 193–194, 196–197
  good relations with Reagan 195
  retirement followed by Tory gains in polls 199
  dependence on Whitelaw and Charles Powell 199
  retirement welcomed in Civil Service 200
  accuses Major of being 'a deviant' 206

Thatcher, Margaret *cont.*
election timetable 208
and Scott Report 229
signs unpopular agreement with Fitzgerald 231
commends both Major and Redwood 257
as a model for New Labour 262, 264, 273
features in Brookes' cartoon 281
at Butler's retirement party 295
speaks at University College 318.
Thatcher, Mark 139–140, 246
The Thick of It 274
Think Tank, see Central Policy Review Staff
Thorpe, Jeremy 81, 82, 103
Thyssen, Baron Hans Heinrich 182–183
Tietmayer, Hans 311
Toxteth riots 148
Tredinnick, David 250
Trend, Burke; Baron Trend of Greenwich xiii, xiv, 53, 54–55, 56, 58, 59, 137, 169, 178, 291
Trend, Nick and Sophie 40, 105, 106, 118, 155, 162, 345, 348
Turnbull, Andrew; Baron Turnbull of Enfield viii, 180, 204, 278, 280
Turvey, Ralph 53

Ulster Unionist Party 75, 235, 237 and *n*, 241
Unwin, Sir Brian 221
Upper Clyde Shipbuilders ('UCS') 61, 79
Urquhart, Francis ('Sligger') 319

Violante, Luciano 311

Waddell, Gordon 27
Waddington, David; Baron Waddington of Read 199
Wade-Gery, Sir Robert 55, 57, 175
Wakeham, John; Baron Wakeham of Maldon 144*n*, 349 and *n*, 351*n*
Waldegrave, William; Baron Waldegrave of North Hill 57, 59, 60, 61, 63, 64, 175, 212, 220, 223, 225, 226, 228
Walker, David 33, 45*n*
Walters, Professor Sir Alan 127, 183, 184
Warman, Mark 11
Wass, Sir Douglas 98, 113, 117, 118, 128, 153, 164
Watergate 138, 270*n*, 334
Waugh, Auberon 99
Weinberger, Caspar 146
Wells, A. F. ('Freddie') 21, 22, 23
Westland Helicopters 161, 165, 171, 291
Whetnall, Andrew 203, 204
Whitelaw, William; Viscount Whitelaw 67, 68, 73, 76, 111, 150, 157–158, 178, 199
Whitmore, Sir Clive 119, 120, 140, 151*n*, 156, 157*n*, 163 and *n*, 164, 165, 166, 169, 176
Wicks, Sir Nigel 99, 152, 177
William, HRH Prince 218, 219, 277
Williams, Marcia; Baroness Falkender of West Haddon 51, 72, 85*n*, 86, 87, 90, 95, 98, 99*n*
Wilson, Harold; Lord Wilson of Rievaulx vii, xvi
becomes leader of Labour Party 36
and 1964 election 37–38
holds another election to increase Labour's majority 40–41
resists devaluation 42–43
as part of University College's socialist tradition 46, 300
is favourite at 1970 election, but loses 46–47
mocks 'Selsdon Man' 49
and Marcia Williams 50–51, 82, 85–86, 95
is criticised by Heath over UCS 61
differences between him and Heath 67–68, 69
sent troops to Northern Ireland 74
wins 1974 election 82
inherits Butler as Private Secretary 86–88
relations with Butler 88–89, 95
creates policy unit 87–88, 292
tactics when making speeches 91
suddenness of his retirement and allegations that he was a Soviet agent 99–100
struggle with far Left of Labour Party 103
creates Civil Service Department 116
hires Kenneth Stowe as PPS 119
his use of SPADs and expansion of No. 10 staff 273
politicisation of civil servants in Policy Unit 285
attitude to the EEC and the 1975 referendum 355.
Wilson, Lady (Mary Wilson) vii, xviii, 151
Wilson, Richard; Baron Wilson of Dinton viii, 167, 204*n*, 272, 276, 279, 280, 281, 286, 290, 293, 294, 351, 364, 365, 366,
Wilson, President Woodrow 369–370
Woods, Professor Ngaire 314–315
World Trade Center attacks 330
Wright, Sir Patrick 99, 186, 262*n*
Wright, Peter 100

Yeltsin, Boris 222
Youssoupoff, Prince Felix 300

Zuckerman, Solly; Baron Zuckerman of Burnham Thorpe 121